Dimensions of Oral Communication Instruction

Dimensions of Oral Communication Instruction

Readings in Speech Education

KEITH ERICKSON
University of Houston

WM. C. BROWN COMPANY PUBLISHERS
Dubuque, Iowa

Printed in the United States of America

Contents

CHAPTER 2   TEACHING, TEACHING STRATEGIES, AND THE TEACHER OF SPEECH

CHAPTER 3   PRINCIPLES OF CRITICISM AND EVALUATION

CHAPTER 4   THE RETICENT, THE FEARFUL, AND DEFECTIVE SPEECH AND HEARING STUDENT

Preface

While the physical ability to produce utterances is possessed by all men, the ability to effectively communicate orally is not. This skill must be learned. In the opinion of the editor, the development of this faculty is of primary importance, for man is little more than the thoughts he holds, and his facility at communicating them.

Training in speech, however, has often been neglected or omitted from the curriculum of the public school. The myth persists in some quarters that anyone capable of speaking has little need of speech instruction. Many school administrators equate speech instruction with the stereotypical master having his charges repeat ad nauseam, "the rain in Spain falls mainly on the plain." These administrators more than likely fell victim to "speech" courses offering such gems as how to answer the telephone, deep chest breathing, gesture exercises, or the excessive shaping of delivery patterns. Not all adminstrators, however, are unaware of the importance of effective speech training. More and more educators are recognizing the correlation between success in personal and professional life and competence as an oral communicator. As a result, speech education may soon become a reality for all American youth, perhaps reflected in an upsurge in course offerings in both secondary and higher institutions of learning.

The contemporary teacher of speech should perceive training in speech not as an artistic artifact, but rather as a vital and indispensable ingredient of preparation for later life. Today, speech is less likely to be taught as an art form and more as a social force in human relations. Performance for its own sake has given way to the systematic examination and analysis of communication processes with attention to how the learner may improve his communication skills in light of this body of knowledge. Such instruction has relevance to the real world. The learner is equipped with more than mere public speaking skills. Acquiring a cognitive grasp of communication (as interpreted by rhetoricians, psychologists, sociologists, anthropologists, mathematicians, etc.) will aid the learner-communicator in all fields.

Facilitating the acquisition of this knowledge is the responsibility of the teacher. By any standard this is a demanding occupation, at once both rewarding and frustrating. Yet, each year thousands of new teachers are graduated from our colleges and universities. Optimistically, these individuals realize that the great reward and challenge of teaching is the possibility it affords for real service to learners. This, after all, is the primary goal of teaching.

How one becomes an effective facilitator of learning is a question asked by all conscientious teachers. There is no simple answer to their query. For some, teaching comes "naturally." Others may work years before becoming effective teachers. The teacher-in-training can perhaps hedge on those years by insuring that his training is thorough and his understanding of the discipline, subject matter, students, and so forth, is clear and complete. A careful analysis of the readings to be found in this book ought to assist the reader in reaching that goal.

The purpose of this book is to provide teachers-in-training and experienced teachers of speech with materials relevant to the development of a philosophy of education, and rationales for instructional strategies grounded on sound pedagogical principles. This book does not subscribe to a "what to teach" format. Rather it focuses upon the facilitation of learning in respect to the discipline, teacher, and student of speech. Thus it should assist the alert, creative facilitator of learning in structuring a conceptual framework of these factors into a gestalt of the teacher-student encounter. Hopefully, the resultant will be a teacher conducive to fostering the learning process.

The term "philosophy of education" is a nebulous concept. To some it signifies mystic philosophical idealizations having little bearing upon reality, while to others it connotes a pragmatic, empirically based description of what one does to facilitate the learning process. The former description more adequately serves our purpose.

All teachers of speech must be capable of defining clearly and adequately a philosophy of education. Many teachers, however, respond with non-salient opinions and worn out generlizations having little relevance to their classroom behavior. "I advocate a sturdy disciplinarian approach which piles on the work . . ." or "Well, taken in a global sense, I suspect a phenomenological approach would . . . uh . . . uh . . . ," often illustrates the ability of teachers to verbalize their teaching behavior. Think of the student's plight. He is "taught" by an instructor unable to verbalize his behaviors or to offer justification for their use. Clearly, such teachers are unlikely to enhance the learning process.

Instructional strategies, simply defined, are any methods, resources or materials employed by an instructor in the teaching process. All conscious behaviors, in fact, of the facilitator of learning constitute instructional strategies.

The collected essays and studies, in the opinion of the editor, constitute essential reading for the teacher of speech in that their collective magnitude demonstrates and amplifies the unique implications of speech and its instruction. Each selection was ultimately chosen for its originality, clarity, relevance, and scholarship.

It goes without saying that numerous individuals have influenced the eventual outcome of this volume. An editor of a book of readings cannot help but feel, as I do, an overwhelming sense of gratitude to all those authors who granted permission to reprint their copyrighted works. I wish to thank as well my colleagues at The Pennsylvania State University who gave so freely of their time to advise and counsel me in the progress of this book.

Keith V. Erickson

Chapter 1

The Discipline: Function and Scope of Speech

The discipline of speech has developed from a body of loosely conceived and formulated generalizations into focused and defined clarity, only to be disjointedly reapportioned to other academic disciplines, and finally to emerge once again redefined, this time to take on an almost interdisciplinary posture. The study of these transformations is a study of cultural influences. From the Golden Age of Greece to the Medieval and Renaissance periods, and into the twentieth century one may perceive the effects of "the times" upon the practice and study of speech. The discipline of speech has always been influenced by the period in which it has been studied and practiced. Unlike the sciences where man has little control or function in the determination of fact (since the "laws" of nature supercede the suspicions of man) the study of speech is tempered by those who investigate it. The discipline of speech is flexible, for there are no natural laws nor rules governing the observation or usage of speech. It has been defined in as many different ways as one could think were rational descriptions of the nature and scope of the discipline. Nevertheless, the study of speech persists, perhaps to adapt and change to the needs of future teachers and practitioners.

The purpose of this chapter is to outline the history of the discipline and its instruction—the domain, provinces, and courses of action that ought to be taken in a speech education program.

Loren Reid, "The Discipline of Speech," conceptualizes the field of speech as an academic discipline. In qualifying his thesis he chooses to define speech in the generic sense to include oral interpretation, debate, voice and diction, phonetics, drama, public speaking, discussion and speech pathology. Reid suggests that for a subject area to qualify as an academic discipline it must adequately reflect certain criteria. "A

1

discipline may be viewed metaphorically as a community of scholars sharing a domain of intellectual inquiry. The members of such a community inherit a common tradition and participate in common dialog." In demonstrating how speech meets such criteria, Reid examines (1) speech as a community of persons, (2) the history of speech, (3) the modes of scholarly inquiry, (4) the domain of speech.

A discipline must first be a community of persons, sharing, relating, recording and advancing a common intellectual inquiry. Participants in this community must necessarily be active, thus engaging in common dialog, but nevertheless maintaining the intellectual honesty and curiosity necessary for advancing knowledge and disproving the untrue. The largest and most active learned society (or community) of the discipline of speech is the Speech Association of America. The S. A. A. provides unity, strength and a sense of centrality to its 10,000 plus members. The S. A. A. publishes three professional journals. *Speech Monographs* serves as an outlet for significant research monographs. The *Quarterly Journal of Speech* is also a scholarly research journal, but of a more general nature, while the *Speech Teacher* is designed to meet, describe and suggest pedagogical information related and pertinent to the teaching of speech. In addition the Eastern, Central, Pacific, Southern, and Western speech associations serve the needs of their respective members geographically. Also, many state speech associations publish journals and meet periodically in convention.

Reid, in the second part of his analysis, describes the history of speech as a colorful and dramatic panorama, graced by many thinkers and teachers. Rhetoric is the oldest discipline in all academe. The Precepts of Kagemni and Ptah-Hotep, approximately 5,000 years old, offered advice and counsel on rhetorical discourse. It was the Greeks, however, who attempted to formalize and systematize rhetoric to make it a relevant and pragmatic study in the affairs of state. Greek history is replete with rhetoricians the likes of Corax, Protagoraus, Prodicus, Lysias, Isocrates, Plato, Socrates, and perhaps the most notable and erudite of them all, Aristotle. Likewise, Roman influence (primarily Quintilian and Cicero) upon the development of rhetoric added much to the discipline in both a scholarly and pedagogical sense.

In the third step, Reid examines modes of inquiry available to speech scholars. He suggests that three principal forms of intellectual inquiry are most likely to be employed: (1) historical and/or rhetorical analysis (2) description, and (3) experimentation. Reid demonstrates how each of these modes differ and are commonly related. Historical and/or rhetorical analysis leans extensively on recorded evidence in the form of texts, witnesses, documents, and so forth, in order that accuracy (truth) may be extracted and evaluated. Descriptive research investigates the nature of an event, speaker, institution, or idea. It employs such research tools as questionnaires, surveys, polls, samples, and case histories. Experimental research in speech tests a variety of hypotheses with primary emphasis focusing upon why phenomena occur, the presence and influence of certain factors, and under what circumstances the manipulation of certain variables produces predictable outcomes or events.

Reid concludes his paper by examining the discipline's domain, which is essentially the study of oral communication. By oral communication is meant all those factors and variables which contribute to a complete communication act. With an emphasis upon oral communication, the transmission, reception, channel, noise, feedback and message components of communication, as well as operant psycho-sociological influences, are investigated by the student of communication.

A curricular program must be conducive to the attainment of individual behaviors thought necessary for social adaptability, asserts Harry G. Barnes, "Basic Concepts of Speech Education." Speech, as one member of a school's curricular program, has as its major function the responsibility of acquainting learners with those concepts, ideas, and indispensable habits essential in meeting the public speaking encounter. In order to do so a program of speech education must be readily available to all students.

Barnes outlines what a speech education program must accomplish in terms of effecting for the learner adequate cognitive, affective and psycho-motor behavioral goals. He expresses these goals in terms of informal and formal speaking situations, and two basic kinds of speaking—original and interpretative. Accepting this premise, suggests Barnes, it follows that the process of speech development is not complete if the learner has not adequately mastered these concepts. To insure that a speech education program will not be at variance with the factors and conditions related to the learners acquisition of these concepts certain considerations must be understood and reckoned with by the teacher of speech.

First among these considerations: basic habits of language and speech are fixed by the time the child is exposed to his first teacher. A child's speech pattern and configuration is his "trade mark" distinguishing him, in part, from other individuals. Thus, even at an early age speech is an integral part of a child's personality, requiring of a teacher careful observation and expertise at handling any "defects" or sub-normal speech behavior, for a change in that pattern is as well a change in that child's personality.

Second, few children are poised and purposive when facing a speaking situation, whether that situation be before his class or other peer groups. The child, obviously, has had few models to emulate and in all likelihood will not have been guided systematically and purposively by any individual, save his parents, to express himself more accurately or to articulate his words more clearly. Virtually all children, then, are in need of speech instruction in one form or another.

Third, maturation is not an antidote or cure for speech inadequacies or defects. Time will not heal the wounds of established habits. Teachers of speech must not assume that merely providing a child with an opportunity to speak will counteract bad habits. Rather, defective or sub-normal speech behavior may be eliminated or reduced only when systematic, specific, time-consuming instruction is aimed directly at the discrepant speech behaviors.

Fourth, teachers must clearly understand that each learner exhibits speaking behaviors exquisitely unique from any other learner. A child's speech personality is an expression of all those factors influencing his environmental rearing, heredity, and maturation as a socially and psychologically well-balanced individual.

Barnes concludes by emphasizing that all those functions and factors bringing the reality of the world closer and more relevant to the learner influences his perceptions and therefore his need for and ability to speak effectively. Thus, a speech education program must be viewed as an on-going process. "The great need in the field of speech is for a speech education program, which begins in the pre-school and which systematically and progressively affords instruction as a coordinate part of the school program throughout the elementary grades, through the junior and senior high schools and into the colleges and universities."

Franklin H. Knower, "A Philosophy of Speech for the Secondary School," clarifies the necessity for speech training and the relationship of speech education to the curriculum of the public school. Knower's article can assist teachers-in-training in formulating and developing a philosophy of speech education. In the article are explored such questions as "What is speech?", "Does speech contribute to the curriculum of a school?", "What is a teacher of speech?", and "Who needs speech instruction?" While there may be no one clear and correct answer for any of these questions, they must, nevertheless, be answered by the teacher of speech if he is to possess an adequate philosophy of speech education. A philosophy of education is the most important educational statement by which a teacher lives. "It is an intellectual core which provides us with the facts, the principles, and the educational creed to sustain our programs. It provides a rationale for our program which may help us evaluate and improve it."

Knower examines how speech varies with specific activity patterns, speaking as activity, the necessity for purpose in speaking, and the functions of speech, which he classifies as expression, representation, projection and social behavior. Also covered are pedagogical principles of the speech discipline. He attacks vigorously old pedagogical adages unjustly assumed educationally sound by many teachers. The efficacy of practice, for example, is resoundingly denounced as a half-truth. The old bromide that "practice makes perfect" is nonsense since practice not only does not insure perfection, but does not necessarily make learning permanent. Secondly, many teachers assume speaking assignments or exercises required of the learner will guarantee that speaking skills will be transferable to later life. It goes without saying, however, that no training or specific exercises will assure such long range effects. Knower also indicates that training in speech must be adapted to all levels of achievement and instruction. There should not exist an arbitrary demarcation line indicating where or when speech instruction ought to begin or leave off. Finally, extra or co-curricular activities must not be substituted for the curricular program, for while forensic and dramatic events are extremely valuable when properly employed, they traditionally serve a limited few and are not readily equated with systematic instruction.

Elwood Murray, "Speech In The Total School Curriculum," warns that the discipline of speech must alter its posture if it is to remain an indispensable agent in the education of America's youth. This need seems to be most evident at the high school level where frequently instruction is at best tenuous. Speech courses, unfortunately, are often blatant examples of a discipline whose behavioral goals and objectives are viewed by learners to be of marginal value. It appears that as long as some teachers of speech persist in forsaking (or overlooking for one reason or another) content in preference for the "mechanical" aspects of delivery, the discipline will be little more than an educational pacifier. This is particularly evident in programs extensively oriented toward extra-curricular speech activities. While winning debate teams and/or a class play which receives a standing ovation are credits to the teacher, these accomplishments, taken by themselves, are insufficient goals of an effective and essential speech education program in the public school. For the great work of this world will not be accomplished by debaters blindly pontificating past their opponents, nor by individuals continually engaged in portraying the role of some dramatic personage. Extra-curricular activities must not supplant curricular learning. But how can this be avoided?

Speech educators are cautioned not to sell themselves or the discipline short. Many teachers unwisely and artificially limit the behavioral goals sought in oral communication training. Often the majority of cognitive materials explicating communication theory are passed over as "too difficult for young minds to comprehend." Perhaps an inadequate preparation for teaching content or a low estimate of the province of speech accounts for the withholding of many valuable principles and concepts associated with the communication process. Whatever the reason it is necessary for this group to refocus their emphasis to include as well the reception process. Hopefully, such an orientation will effectuate in learners a more adequate perspective of communication factors and variables. In essence, instruction in delivery must cease as a teacher's "specialty of the house." The teacher of speech must avoid stressing the gross, outward factors of communication and focus more upon the underlying principles and concepts.

What is needed, suggests Murray, is a speech education program focusing upon the goals of intercommunication. "Effective interpersonal relations must be paralled by effective human intercommunication; in fact, communication wherein mind meets mind is both an aspect and a function of relations, particularly interpersonal relations." Facilitating student understanding and employment of intercommunication principles will lead to what Murray contends are the essential demands the speech profession must meet: (1) instruction in democratic processes and institutions, (2) contribution to the personal-social adjustment, personality development, and effective human relationships (3) speech instruction having relevance to and implications for the development of the learners vocational and professional abilities.

Donald K. Smith, "Teaching Speech to Facilitate Understanding," charges that the improvement of interpersonal and intergroup understanding ought to be the important goal of speech education. While not disputing the worthiness of this goal, the pragmatic engineering of our pedagogical energies to efficiently execute such an order is another matter. To determine those instructional paradigms or designs which will best improve the possibility of human understanding is a sobering task. Initially, the facilitator of understanding must discover those issues, ideas, concepts and perceptions germaine to common understanding. There does not exist, however, a standard or signpost capable of detecting for the teacher mutual referents. A phenomonologist might assert there never will be: Yet the nature of man and his propensity for catastrophe demands that mutual understanding be fostered. What are the alternatives? Many exist by which man might more nearly come to perceive accurately the beliefs, attitudes, and feelings of his fellow man—among them education. Education, though, cannot be equated with salvation, for as a singular agency via the instructional group the fruition of the goal of mutual understanding is nearly unobtainable. "And most certainly speech instruction in and of itself has neither the power nor the sanction greatly to change the shape of our culture. We can hope at best to design our own instruction so that it increases the possibility of understanding."

Smith suggests that the key to the facilitation of human understanding in the oral communications classroom is to teach *understanding* of speech. Teaching speech understanding implies that instruction is not simply skill oriented. It is necessary that teachers of speech add cognitive dimensions to their curriculum. The learner must be acquainted with an understanding of the nature of communication. A speaker must, for example, understand a communication barrier for what it is when its occurrence is felt and known by the learner. The learner, then, must be capable of recognizing and diagnosing the problems inhibiting a particular communication. "The implicit point is this: that the person who is not just skillful in speaking, but also understands speech, is in a much better position to use speech to develop genuine understanding when he encounters situations in which communication seems to have broken down."

The reader is advised to analyze carefully Smith's article. His philosophy of education is a worthy one. The pedagogical structures that must be constructed in order to facilitate speech understanding, however, will be complex and perhaps initially cumbersome. The reader's willingness to structure the behavioral goals of speech instruction to elicit affective and cognitive learning, in addition to psycho-motor skills, however, will be the only true test of whether speech will play a vital role in sensitizing man to understand his fellow man. Let us hope that we as teachers are adept and concerned enough to facilitate human understanding.

Ruth Monroe, "Renewal of a Public Philosophy: Role of Teachers of Speech," encourages teachers of speech to assist learners in formulating and adopting a public philosophy. Philosophy, in this sense, may be thought an attempt to clarify reality. For, suggests Monroe, "every person by virtue of his presence in the universe must develop a sense of reality which is valid for him. Out of this sense of reality come the principles and purposes which may be called his personal philosophy." This is a most challenging proposition. It is a clear challenge to teachers of speech to assist learners in developing for themselves a personal frame of reference—a public philosophy extendable to real life. Without such a philosophy learners on becoming adults may talk past and around each other in inarticulate and meaningless dialogue. Therefore, Monroe claims that the overriding question "is how modern man can rediscover and espouse that truth upon which all men by virtue of their humanity will tend to agree." This is, obviously, no small task. How may teachers of speech aid the learner in developing a public philosophy?

First, dialogue between individuals and groups of men possessing different views ought to be reopened. Vagueness must not suffice as an end of tolerance. Indefinable and unclear positions leave in their wake only chaos from which individuals are expected to make sense. The learner faced with an existence in a milieu of conflicting issues and polarized idealizations must be given the opportunity to think out, talk out, and discover what to him is a viable personal philosophy. For only by doing this shall our youth be given an opportunity to arrive at some defined position on significant ideas, issues and concepts. The teacher of speech may speed this process by "(1) emphasizing the articulation and thinking through of significant issues (2) recreating a 'questing curiosity' (3) requiring students to put cognitive information into practical social contexts (4) developing the learner's communication tools (5) looking for a universal language and (6) demonstrating to learners the receptive as well as the transmittive functions of the communication process."

To the teacher of speech, Monroe posits, the key words to remember are information, dialogue and articulation. This should be clear, for without information the process of communication would be hypocritical; without dialogue pointless; and with the exclusion of articulation frustrating and fruitless.

The Discipline of Speech

LOREN REID

The term *speech* is more than fifty years old. Originally it was proposed as a generic term to include public speaking, discussion and debate, oral interpretation, phonetics, voice science, speech pathology, drama, and related subjects. Almost from the outset, however, it did not entirely suit teachers of drama, so that some of the earliest departments were entitled "Department of Speech *and* Dramatic Art." Teachers of speech pathology and of radio-TV likewise have tended to drift away from *speech* as an all-inclusive term.

No other term, however, serves so well to describe the broad area just indicated. *Speech* associations include teachers of all these subjects, and *speech* journals publish their research studies. Hence this paper will use *speech* in the original, generic sense. Despite different interests. and emphases, practitioners of this discipline start with a common base —voice, action, thought, language—in short, with some variety of oral communication. At times, however, this paper will make specific references to various of the individual subjects.

Although the development of the discipline the last half century has been especially striking, its heritage of theory and practice stretches back to ancient times.

I. SPEECH AS A COMMUNITY OF PERSONS

A discipline may be viewed metaphorically as a community of scholars sharing a domain of intellectual inquiry.[1] The members of such a community inherit a common tradition and participate in a common dialog.

The speech community can be described in part by scanning its learned societies. The Speech Association of America is one of the oldest and is the most inclusive. It has a current membership of more than 6,000. More than 2,500 libraries subscribe to its publications. Its annual conventions attract from 1500 to 2000 people, who listen to papers cov-

From *The Speech Teacher*, Vol. XVI, No. 1 (January, 1967), pp. 1-10.

Loren Reid (Ph.D., University of Iowa) is Professor of Speech and Chairman of the Department of Speech at the University of Missouri. He has served as Executive Secretary of the Speech Association of America from 1945 to 1951 and as President in 1957. The present article was adapted from a paper prepared for the Hawaii Curriculum Conference, Honolulu, June 6-17, 1966.

[1]Part of the discussion in this paper based upon points of view expressed in Arthur R. King, Jr. and John A. Brownell, *The Curriculum and the Disciplines of Knowledge* (New York, Wiley, 1966).

ering every conceivable aspect of the discipline. It promotes research, sets standards, maintains a teacher-placement arm, and advances in various ways the professional concerns of the discipline.

Membership in the Association is drawn largely from the United States, but since the contributions of American scholars have attracted attention the world over, its membership roll and library roll include currently twenty-two foreign countries. Many predict that the Association will eventually incorporate the word "International" in its official title. Its range of activity is shown in that it is a constituent member of the American Council on Education and an institutional member of the National Education Association.

Closely related are the American Educational Theatre Association, the American Speech and Hearing Association, the National Society for the Study of Communication, the National University Extension Association, the American Forensic Association, and others. Each of these in years past has met concurrently with the Speech Association of America, and some still do. Each is, however, a separate and independent organization.

Regional associations abound, serving Eastern, Central, Southern, Western, and Pacific groups. Most of these have memberships in the neighborhood of 1,000. The newest, the Pacific Speech Association, last year had a membership of 165, a doubling over the previous figure. These regional associations are each the national organization in miniature; in addition they serve regional cultures and regional needs of accreditation, standards, and research. Forty-five states have state associations.

Another category of organization, serving special interests, includes Delta Sigma Rho-Tau Kappa Alpha, Pi Kappa Delta, National Forensic League National Thespian League, and half a dozen others.

Most of these associations, including the state groups, publish journals. The Speech Association of America publishes three principal journals: *Quarterly Journal of Speech, Speech Teacher, Speech Monographs.* These have a combined circulation in excess of 10,000.

In addition to the annual conferences sponsored by these associations, dozens of city, sectional, and regional organizations hold meetings to discuss special problems. Each winter, for example, directors of the beginning speech courses in ten universities from the central part of the country meet to discuss pedagogy and to plan research. Contests and festivals in debate, dramatics, oral interpretation, discussion, and individual speaking, at both high school and college level, are held by the hundreds. Teachers and students alike have opportunity to see what is going on in other schools and to listen to the observations of critic specialists. Students exchange ideas and bring recognition to their institutions by their participation in these nation-wide events.

In these and other ways the growth of the speech community since the founding of the Speech Association of America in 1914 has been phenomenal. I know of no intellectual movement in education that approaches it. At the turn of the century our forebears had been plac-ing excessive and outmoded emphasis on matters of voice, gesture, and other sorts of forms and conventions instead of upon the meaning of the idea or emotion being communicated. The spirit of inquiry and research had too long lain dormant. I still occasionally meet someone who had a speech course long ago, who possibly was exposed to the older system of teaching, and who still thinks of speech as being en-tirely concerned with refinements of gesture or niceties of voice. But the founding of the new association, however, provided new leadership. Old concepts were reexamined; many were kept, some were swept away. Scholars became concerned with the history and rhetoric of the dis-cipline, with its relation to science, with its possibilities for creativity as one of the arts. Over the country by the scores and later by the hundreds new departments were organized. Graduate study at the doc-toral level got under way. Especially after 1930 was the pace accelerated. In 1932 a grand total of 30 Ph.D.'s had been awarded by 5 institutions. By 1966 the number was in excess of 3,000 awarded by 47 institutions. Another 159 institutions now regularly offer master's degrees, the total of which has now exceeded 22,000.[2]

So far the community described has been the academic one. Many practitioners of the discipline are attached to hospitals (speech path-ology and audiology), to theatres (drama), to broadcasting companies (radio-TV-film). Tangential also, is a vast group of others who com-municate: statesmen, preachers, diplomats, attorneys, journalists, sales-men, physicians, and scores of other categories. It is not necessary to argue the usefulness of speech in the pursuit of a vocation.

Actually the community also has a remote past and a beckoning future. Primitive man could improve his lot not only because he had (a) a forebrain, (b) fingers and opposed thumb, and (c) a superior heart design; but also because he had (d) the faculty of speech. Quite possibly some elemental ability to communicate was the prime factor in bringing man's unicellular ancestor out of the primeval ooze. At any rate, with his communicative faculty and his anatomical advantages man was able to dispose of or manage creatures that were bigger,

---

[2]Each year the August issue of *Speech Monographs* provides complete statistics.

tougher, and faster than he. Leaving behind this prehistoric speculation and turning to the speech community of the foreseeable future,
we can see that as population increases, as nations become more numerous, as domestic and foreign problems become more complex, as
business and professional life becomes more competitive, the need for
oral communication—largely through face-to-face discussion—becomes
imperative.

II. HISTORY

Originally the name of the discipline of speech was *rhetoric*. Early
statements in the field of rhetorical theory were informal, but eventually
systematic treatises appeared. Many of these latter contained observations about the management of the voice, so in a way they fore-
shadowed present-day speech correction and pathology. Some of them
also offered comments about drama and the theatre, but this area independently brought forth treatises in *poetic*. The discussion that follows, however, is limited in the main to the development of the rhetorical
aspects of the field of speech.

Rhetoric has been defined today as the rationale of discourse. The
discourse may be entertaining, expository, persuasive. It may be spoken
or written, though for the most of the way this paper will deal with
spoken discourse.

In one form or another the discipline goes back, so far as there are
records, 5,000 years. Egyptian papyri roughly dated 2900 B.C. contain
bits and pieces of rhetorical advice.[3] The *Precepts* identified with Kagemni and Ptah-Hotep clearly show that the Egyptians were concerned
about principles of speech. "If you carry a message from one noble to
another, be exact in the repetition . . . give his message even as he
hath said it." This statement foreshadows the current interest in listening. "If you are in the council chamber, follow the procedures." This
statement foreshadows parliamentary orderliness. "Avoid speaking of
that of which you know nothing. . . . If you know what you are talking
about, speak with authority, and avoid false modesty." This statement
is good medicine in all times and places.

The Greeks undertook the problem of systematizing rhetoric, as they
systematized politics and a good many other theories. Wisely has it
been observed that if a modern thinker starts down a long, dusty road
of reflection, he will not have gone far before he meets an old Greek
trudging back. Corax in 466 B.C. was the first to make clear that rhetoric

---

[3]See the article by Giles Wilkeson Gray, "The Precepts of Kagemni and Ptah-
Hotep," *Quarterly Journal of Speech*, XXXII (December, 1946), 446-454.

involved principles—that it was not merely a knack or skill or gift sent from heaven—and that these principles were teachable and learnable. He demonstrated further that rhetoric had a structure, an organization, an architecture, a design—and that a message set in a frame would be more clear, more persuasive, than one lacking pattern or contour. The human race never learned a wiser or more enduring lesson. From his slender quiver he drew another powerful bolt: since human problems are wrapped in contingencies, alternatives, choices, rhetoric must involve itself with what is likely and believable as well as with what is certain and provable.

Corax's rhetoric was a vast improvement over the timid Egyptian cautions and admonitions. Greeks who followed him fleshed the bones, each with his own contribution. You meet their names in any history of education. Protagoras reminded his students that there were two sides to any rhetorical act. Prodicus was interested in the correct use of words. He sought exactness and in so doing probed into the study of synonyms. Lysias was the first ghostwriter. So good was he that of 233 speeches he wrote, only two failed to achieve their purpose. He opened the secret of ghost-writing: strive not for a universal style but select a style that somehow fits the person for whom the speech is being ghosted. Gorgias demonstrated the uses of artistry in oral composition. Isocrates deserves more than these sentences, being memorable because he scrutinized the character of the speaker. "Words carry greater conviction when spoken by men who live under a cloud."

Contemporaries can be proud to practice the same intellectual discipline that these towering Greeks helped to develop. But mightier rhetoricians were still to come. Plato, like Corax, saw the virtues of form. The message should have a head, a body, and a tail, like a living creature. But Plato did more. As he looked around him, he observed the varying mood and temper of listeners—the nature of the human soul, as he called it—and noted that the message must be adapted to the different kinds of soul: the calm, the angry, and so on. Plato, who spoke through Socrates as through a mask, uttered much in criticism of rhetoric, but these comment are passed over in favor of the powerful support he gave it. Without rhetoric, even one who knows the truth—this is Plato speaking—is unable to persuade. The naked truth itself is valueless—but the combination of truth and rhetoric forms a lever that can move the earth.

When Aristotle moved onto the Athenian scene, he could draw upon this substantial body of rhetorical theory, plus the contributions of dozens not mentioned. Moreover, he could hear effective oratory in the courts and in the public places. Following his natural bent, he constructed a system of criticism. Its framework in a nutshell: the speaker, the speech, the person addressed. Here are a slender five of the leading Aristotelian ideas:

1. A listener can be persuaded in any or all of three ways: through the character of the speaker, through the logic of the argument, through his own feelings and emotions. Any other way of persuading a listener—i.e. with the help of a shotgun—would have to be called non-rhetorical.
2. The character of the speaker is of paramount importance. This statement has grown in significance through the years. Today, knowledge being increasingly complex, we must depend upon one another—we must take one another's word—more than ever.
3. A speech has four parts. You must state your case and then prove it —these are the two most essential parts. But, audiences being what they are, you are advised to open with some kind of introduction and finish with some kind of summarizing, interpreting, or action-seeking conclusion.

   This notion has proved extremely helpful over the years. Think again of the pupil in the classroom, reporting on a school project. He is so full of his subject that he forgets his classmates are still empty. So he plunges into the middle of his exposition. Places, events, people, are named but not identified. The listeners are puzzled like playgoers who arrive late. Somewhere in his education this pupil overlooked the Greeks. Better remind him to start at the beginning (Plato); listeners being what they are he should open with some kind of orienting introduction (Aristotle).
4. The end and object of the speech is the audience—the listener—the judge. Aristotle elaborates on and systematizes Plato's notions about the audience. Listeners can be viewed according to their age, their wealth and position, their mood and temper.
5. Language is a matter for careful attention. First of all, it must be clear. Not to be clear is to fail at the outset. Second, however, it must have another quality: interest. Here come the aspects of vividnes, color, strikingness, force. Here are metaphor, inversion, parallel structure. Each of these qualities must be used as appropriate to listener and occasion. English and speech teachers, playwrights and sermonizers, presidents and ad-writers, all spend countless hours on this ancient formula.

Aristotle applied the same kind of intellectual vigor to the answering of basic questions about drama and the theatre. In his *Poetics* he talked about plot, character, diction, thought, melody, and staging. He discussed the requirements for a tragic hero, the formula for developing a plot, the catharsis that must be wrought in the spectator. He saw the close relationship between rhetoric and poetic (for example, the speaker could learn about delivery by observing the actor, and the playwright could enhance the thought, the message, of his play through applying principles of rhetoric). The two arts, however, were beginning to develop their own rationales. More could be introduced at this point about the historical development of poetic, with appropriate reference to Horace, Longinus, and others.

Nor need the history of rhetoric be discussed lengthily, other than to call a few illustrious names. Marcus Tullius Cicero—the "sweet Tully" of succeeding centuries—acquired the unique distinction of being the only celebrated orator to set down a systematic treatise on the theory of oratory. Cicero gathered his rhetorical notions under five headings: (a) idea, (b) organization, (c) delivery, (d) style, and (e) memory. Quintilian, well known to historians of education as well as to teachers of speech, evolved a theory of teaching the young speaker that covered his entire career, starting with the selection of a proper nurse (she should not have a faulty dialect) and concluding with advice about the proper time to retire (well before being completely done in).

In the pages of the Greek and Roman rhetorics are written the early beginnings of speech pathology. The classical writers and those who followed distinguished differences in loudness and quality. They observed weak voices and thin, hoarse, rasping voices. They wrote advice about the speed of utterance. They noticed that breathiness obscured resonance and carrying power. They were aware of mannerisms like excessive heaving and panting. They noted that a few pupils hoisted phlegm from their lungs and sprayed their listeners. They commented on vocalized pauses like *uh, uh, uh*. They advised against visual intrusions like excessive movements of the tongue or lips. They did not, however, set down much in the way of therapy: singing, proper diet, and exercise appeared to them to be generally efficacious.

Much of what the early rhetoricians said can also be applied to the teaching of English. Aristotle had much to say about grammar and syntax, though it happens to be Greek that he was concerned with and not English. Cicero's contributions to style are well known. High school students can today venture only a little way into Latin before they confront Cicero. He shook Latin style, loosened it up, replaced its formal correctness with colloquial vigor, introduced all sorts of stylistic adornment.

In the Middle Ages the spokesmen of the Catholic church needed to develop and defend their doctrines, both from schism within and from heresy without. This defense called for close reasoning, a need that sent priests like Saint Augustine back to their logics and rhetorics. Eighteenth century England, busy with the devolpment of a parliamentary society, concerned also with the need of communication in the law court, the pulpit, and the university, provided a fruitful climate for intense rhetorical output. The fulsome nineteenth century busied itself particularly with matters of language and style. On the list of distinguished theorists are English names, Scottish names, Irish names, American names—one from this last group being John Quincy Adams, scholar, diplomat, president, congressman, and lecturer on rhetoric at Harvard.

The steadily mounting interest in science of the twentieth century stimulated the need for a system of communication that combined clarity with persuasiveness. In turn rhetorical principles themselves have been supported or modified by experimental investigation. Researchers in speech and also researchers in sociology, psychology, and social psychology have launched inquiries concerning the credibility of the speaker, the organization of the message, the behavior of the listener. "Speaking behavior" is a relatively new term that has come to the discipline. The line of thought, however, is continuous; the old questions are being cast in more specific language and are being approached through new techniques.

III. MODES OF INQUIRY

Broadly, three modes of inquiry are available to the practitioners of this discipline: (1) historical or rhetorical analysis and synthesis, (2) description, (3) experimentation.

1. The method of analysis and synthesis leans heavily on documents, witnesses, texts, and inferences therefrom. It employs many of the procedures of the historian as it inquires into the authenticity of documents, the problems of selection, arrangement, and interpretation. It explores and compares different drafts and versions of a speech (or of a play), searches journals and diaries, pores over contemporary correspondence, reads newspaper accounts, and looks for other evidences of preparation or presentation. It may utilize personal interview. Principles of criticism are examined, applied, and compared as the investigator moves into matters of language structure, and the other sorts of appraisal that he makes of the speech, the debate, the literary interpretation, the play.
2. Descriptive research utilizes surveys, questionnaires, samples, case studies, rating scales, statistical procedures.

3. Experimental research involves a hypothesis, a design, control of variables, statistical or other methods of analysis and comparison, interpretation of findings.

With these modes of inquiry at his command the researcher is able to seek answers to a variety of questions. He may want to know why Sir Winston Churchill was an effective speaker—or why, for that matter, a certain teacher gives an exceptionally clear lecture or a certain pupil makes an excellent recitation. He may want to know how to rate or rank good speaking, or good reading aloud, or good acting, in his classroom. He may want to know the optimum size of a class in a given subject—and to that end may construct a questionnaire. He may want to know which of two speeches, experimentally contrived to focus on a rhetorical principle, was more effective with listeners—and so he invites listeners to state their opinions on the subject before the experiment and after. He may want to identify a group of the best speakers, or the best teachers of public speaking or acting, and, having located this group, study it to learn more about education, experience, methods of teaching.

Although this paper has suggested three modes of inquiry, the discussion that follows is limited only to the first—the method of analysis and synthesis. Each is highly specialized: this writer deals with the method he knows best.

a. What does a practitioner *do* when he makes or gets new knowledge? He starts by asking a question, generally dealing with the effectiveness of a speaker, or of a group of speakers. From this question flow scores of lesser questions: sources of ideas, preparation of speeches, characteristics of presentation and delivery, the occasion with any special significance or meaning attached, organization, language, evidence, style, the audience, the effect or influence. Note that these questions are distinctive to this discipline and are not likely to be systematically pursued by practitioners of another discipline. After having asked his questions, he proceeds by observing, or interviewing, or by reading correspondence, journals, and newspapers. He goes from general materials (like biographies) to specific treatises (like articles, monographs). Since, however, most of the data in which he is interested are not likely to have been utilized by other kinds of researchers, he soon finds himself plunging into original documents. Since the spoken word is elusive, he is particularly interested in eye-and ear-witnesses, if the passage of time has not been too great. His search is illuminated by the theory of the discipline, though he is as alert for variations and exceptions as for exemplars.

b. What evidence is he willing to consider? He is willing to consider all kinds of evidence, the biassed as well as the impartial. Any one may or may not like any speech. Like the historian, however, he tries to be aware of possible bias, distortion, special or vested interest, that might debase the testimony. Along the way he may have to restate or modify his original question or hypothesis. He is guided by reports of the way the speech was received by the contemporary listeners. Churchill's speech was or was not effective with the 1940 House of Commons. It may also have qualities of universality that make it appealing to later generations of readers. The researcher seeks a preponderance of evidence on one side or the other. If he is seeking various opinions about Truman's speaking, he might note that Democrats tend to approve, Republicans to disapprove. If to Democratic approval he can add evidence of Republican approval, plus approval of neutrals like London editorial writers, French political commentators, etc., plus the subsequent indorsement of events, he emerges with a favorable verdict of Truman's speech-making and is correspondingly more certain that the verdict is an accurate one.

c. What is the end point of his inquiry? He does, or should, end with a synthesis: he illuminates the special nature of the virtues of the speech; if he identifies short-comings, he relates those to the whole picture; he compares or contrasts the speaker with others; he estimates his effectiveness, both for his own day and for the foreseeable future. The end point is thus an appraisal, a judgment, an interpretation. It is not a formula for success, but it may have ingredients that warrent emulation; it may reemphasize old principles that are teachable once again to others.

d. Have newer modes of inquiry been added to the discipline recently? Recently criticism has been launched against Aristotelian or neo-Aristotelian standards of criticism in favor of standards that are more flexible and adaptable. Modern researchers try not only to answer the standard questions more or less applicable to any rhetorical event, but also to probe into the special conditions of time, place, or circumstance that might lead to more helpful analysis and synthesis.

Here is considered only one type of investigation. Those familiar with surveys, rating scales, questionnaires, experimental design, and other techniques could supply a parallel set of answers to questions (a) through (d).

IV. DOMAIN

The domain of the discipline is the act or process of communication. No institution, system, or process can exist without it. Take as an example the scientist working in his laboratory. This task would appear to be a lonely and isolated one. First of all, however, he needs to ask himself: Has this problem been solved already? Are others now working on it? Second, while he is working on it, he needs to communicate with others: to gain financial support, to seek technical assistance with details. Third, when it is finished, he needs to tell two groups of people about it: other scientists, to whom he will talk in a technical language; laymen, to whom he will talk in everyday idiom. Actually the lonely scientist is becoming more and more scarce. The big problems call for teams of scientists. If one of the team cannot communicate effectively, he is by that much not only less of a communicator but less of a scientist.

When the teacher of speech talks about communication, however, he means more than the crude, barren, minimal transmission of an idea. He holds steadily in mind the communicator, the message, the medium, the receiver. He wants the idea to go from communicator to receiver in its greatest effectiveness. The teacher of oral interpretation guides students of a poem, an essay, a speech, or other literary work into a careful study of what the words on the page mean. This study should lead to a penetrating inquiry into author, setting, circumstances, and other factors as relevant. Mind, voice, and body must then be set to work, in a disciplined manner, at the task of putting the meaning of the words into visible and audible symbols. If what is done is sincere, honest, intelligent, the listener will have a fuller appreciation of the work than he would have had otherwise. The teacher of acting sets about much the same task, using different conventions and a different medium. The speech clinician may appear at times to be working entirely with the vocal problems of the communicator, but he, too, is well aware of voice and articulation simply as parts of the total communicative act. Enough has already been said about rhetoric and public speaking to show again the interactions of speaker, message, and listeners to understand, to change or modify a belief, or to take action.

Speech is based on principles that are teachable and usable. Its practitioners are aware that there are exceptions to these principles, and so it is not a science, *per se,* though certain aspects of it, like phonetics, pathology, and audiology, have solid scientific underpinnings. It is not merely a technique, a knack, a skill. None of these words says enough; *principle, method, system, rationale* are more descriptive. As students master the principles, they improve, and the fact of their improvement is noticeable both to themselves and to their classmates. Although there has invariably been a backward glance at native talent and genius—the claim that speakers are born and not made—there has been a positive insistence that nearly everyone can improve. This belief finds strong support in the study of the careers of eminent speakers—those who might be thought to have the greatest natural gifts. Here it is found that Clay, Webster, Calhoun, Bryan, Roosevelt, and others had ample instruction in speech while young men. All of them gained public speaking experience in the classroom, in the debating society, or in both. Each of them served an arduous apprenticeship. Webster, for example, was so gripped and seized with stagefright at Exeter Academy that he could not speak at all. From this tender beginning he rose to the heights.

The discipline of communication has close ties with nearly every other discipline that might be mentioned, perhaps excluding botany. Graduate students in speech regularly find that their assignments carry them to the general classics, physics, psychology, education, language, mathematics, chemistry, physiology, and law collections. They customarily seek out supporting courses in other disciplines. One writing a dissertation, for example, on a nineteenth century orator would find it advisable to have courses in history, literature, and political science. If he had an experimental problem, he would find himself in various psychometric and statistical studies. If he operated in speech pathology, he would study anatomy, neurology, psychology, physiology, and related fields; and as a practitioner would consult and confer with orthodontists, pediatricians, orthopedic surgeons, clinical psychologists, and others, as well as with parents and teachers. The graduate student in drama draws upon theory and practice of other arts, and from history, psychology, or sociology. National speech conventions often invite to their programs professors of these related disciplines to share in both general and special discussions. Speech journals likewise invite scholarly articles from practitioners in these adjunct fields.

As the Committee on the Nature of the Field of Speech has worded it, speech, like other contemporary academic disciplines, has moved from its original center into expanding segments of specialized study. The report of the Committee continues:

> Today the specialist in speech may find his interests akin to those of the linguist who analyzes the structure of spoken language, the psychologist who studies verbal behavior, the sociologist who relates social structure to symbolic interaction, the anthropologist who studies the structure of speech and language as reflecting the structure of culture,

the philosopher who investigates the problem of meaning in everyday language, and so on.[4]

Says Gilbert Highet in his *Art of Teaching*: "Communication, the transmission of thought from one mind to others, is one of the basic activities of the human race; it is . . . an art without which genius is dumb, power brutal and aimless, mankind a planet load of squabbling tribes. Communication is an essential function of civilization. Teaching is only one of the many occupations that depend upon it, and depend upon it absolutely."[5] Statements that set forth the qualifications of an educated person, or that define the place of a discipline in the curriculum, include the requisite that the ability to express oneself orally is an essential attribute. The nature of the discipline of speech as described in the foregoing pages suggests its relevance to society, its concern with intelligent inquiry on the part of both teacher and student, and its utility to the individual as he goes about his business of making a living.

---

[4]Donald K. Smith, Andrew T. Weaver, and Karl R. Wallace, in *Quarterly Journal of Speech*, L (February, 1964), 67.
[5]New York, Alfred A. Knopf, p. 97.

A Philosophy of Speech
for the Secondary School

FRANKLIN H. KNOWER

What do you mean by *Speech?* Is it something new? Isn't it just oral English? Or voice and diction? Or gestures? Are you a teacher of Oratory? Or Elocution? Or Expression? Is the objective of your program a bag of tricks? A little courtesy? A form of flattery? Can it make a substantial contribution to the curriculum of a school? How can you hope to do anything worthwhile in a short course with the habits a person has been developing all his life? Shouldn't every teacher be a teacher of Speech? Isn't it true that all the speech education an average person needs is a little practice? Why these interscholastic competitions anyway? Can't we do a better job by sticking to the classroom?

Do you have an answer for such questions? If you do, you have a philosophy of speech education. If not, perhaps you will find this discussion helpful next time someone asks you one of these questions. You may not agree with these answers. But some philosophy you cannot escape. It is an intellectual core which provides us with the facts, the principles, and the educational creed to sustain our programs. It provides a rationale for our program which may help us evaluate and improve it.

THE ACADEMIC TRADITION OF SPEECH

Speech education appears to be as old as socially organized efforts to instruct the young. It played an important part in the schools of classical Greece, Renaissance England, Colonial America, our early academies, and our first public grammar schools. During the latter part of the nineteenth and early twentieth centuries it was temporarily clouded by the influence of Teutonic authoritarianism on our schools. But during the last twenty-five years progressive schools of the Mid-West have lead the way in according it an important place in education. *Speech* now ranks with the most widely studied subjects in America's colleges and universities. Many high schools are finding a place for it in their programs. Its future rests with our ability to demonstrate that it has a substantial contribution to make to the world in which we live.

From *The Speech Teacher*, Volume I, No. 2 (March, 1952), pp. 79-85.

Mr. Knower (Ph.D., Minnesota, 1933) is Professor of Speech in Ohio State University where he is in charge of the work in Speech Education. He is also the present Editor of Speech Monographs.

SPEECH IS SYMBOLIC BEHAVIOR

Our first point leads to the recognition of the intellectual nature of speech. Speech is an intellectual activity for it is a symbolic activity. In fact, speech involves several symbolic systems and processes. Whether we call them fundamental processes is not important. It is important that we so analyze the subject that our categories provide the best possible organization of units for teaching. Woolbert said, "A man speaking is four things: thought, language, voice, and action." This definition refers to three symbol systems, and a process (thinking) by which symbol systems are used. It so emphasizes the idea of *a man speaking* that we recognize in it something more than its parts: thinking, language, etc. In other words, speaking is a complex multi-symbolic form of social behavior. The study of speech is not thorough unless we concern ourselves with the integration of the speaker's behavior as a whole as well as with its several processes. Some writers refer to these aspects of speech as its elements. There may be a particular value in designating them as processes because such a term focuses attention on the active nature of speech phenomena. There are other analyses of speech processes but the one used here may be defended as simple, systematic, and meaningful. The use of other categories in analysis would not violate the basic point we have tried to make here.

SPEECH VARIES WITH SPECIFIC ACTIVITY PATTERNS

Students of speech find it convenient to classify speech as to its forms and types of activity. These forms of activity reveal something of total patterns and adaptations to speech situations which are not implied by a process analysis. Informal speech is by definition speech free from form, yet this very freedom identifies it. Conversation is different from debate, a sermon has a different pattern from an employment interview, an actor has a speech job which differs from that of a labor management arbitrator. The number of variations in these and other speech activities is legion. They have a strong component in them of the culture in which speech occurs. They are adaptations to situations. Some have a greater amount of originality than others, but all require some conformity to expectations.

Fortunately there are a great many common elements in speech activities. But it would be a mistake to assume that education in one activity, or that attention to fundamental processes alone, would produce skill in all. Since it is impossible to educate a student in all possible types of speech activity, it behooves us to emphasize in education those activities which have the greatest number of elements common to various activities, to encourage students to look for the application of principles in various speech situations, and to include a reasonable diversity of experience in activity patterns studied. The recognized need for teaching the function activities should not blind us to the value of special exercises for the study of the processes of speech. While we may well start and end our program with the emphasis on functional activities, it can be shown that as needs become apparent skill in the activities improved by drill on the processes.

It may be useful at this point to refer to two other concepts of the word *activity* as it is used by speech teachers. To some a speech activity means simply that speech is studied in an extra, or co-curricular program. Acting in school play, debating on a school debating team, participating in community discussion programs are said to be speech activities. The use of the word in this sense should not be confused with its use to describe our focus or a type of learning experience which goes beyond fundamental processes.

SPEAKING IS ACTIVITY

The other concept of activity to which I want to call special attention is that the study of speech is the study of an active form of behavior, which is the product of learning, and subject to change. Speech is a dynamic social process. A manuscript is not speech. A recording is not speech. They are evidence that a speech has been prepared or that speaking has occurred but they are not speech. The speech, or any speaking, is an on-going form of social behavior, an event which occurs in a situation. The study of speech, like the study of history, is a study of unique events in time. They can never be recalled, or repeated. The full understanding of the implications of this fact might do much to help us focus our educational efforts on crucial aspects of the phenomenon.

SPEECH MUST HAVE PURPOSE

Speaking always has a purpose; sometimes it is not well defined, sometimes it is carefully and skillfully hidden, but there is a purpose never-the-less. The child's first speech purposes are simple, purely personal, and operate subconsciously. The process of developing social maturity, among other things, includes the process of learning what speech purposes are socially approved, what purposes are acceptable only in certain situations, and what purposes are generally not approved by society.

We teach certain commonly accepted general ends of speech, and the specific purposes which associates the general ends with the subject matter discussed. It may be well to explore these general purposes more thoroughly than we have. If we do we shall probably find other general speech purposes to which we may give more attention in our teaching. The main point we seek to make here is that speech is multi-purposed. It is not enough to say that the purpose of speech is to get a response. We must ask "what response?"

SPEECH SERVES MANY FUNCTIONS

Speech courses are sometimes called courses in expression. The word is an inadequate designation for speech because: first, there are other ways in which this human function may be served, and second, speech also serves other functions. In fact, speech must serve five functions of personal-social behavior. Unless all five are served at the same time we do not have a typical and profitable speech act. The first of these functions is expression. To express means to press out; when a thing is pressed out it usually retains something of the mold used as the press. Perhaps this is just another way of saying that speech as well as style reflects the man. Speech always tells us something about the speaker. In fact, we often evaluate what is said in light of what his speech tells us about him. It is important, then, that we acquire skill in so speaking that others will judge us as we want to be judged. Even character and good will may not be enough; they are not always self-evident. We must teach our students to so speak that their character and good will are not in doubt. This point brings us again to the idea that the student of speech must be a student of man and his personality.

Speech is also representative. Speech is always about something. It requires a subject to talk about. Most arguments as to whether content or form is more important create a false issue. They are both important. In fact, what we say depends on how we say it. Therefore, speech of high standard cannot exist in an idealological vacuum. The student must learn that improvement of his knowledge contributes to his speech, and improvement of his speech contributes to his knowledge. Growth in speech, as in knowledge and all education, is a process of learning to make finer, sharper, and more useful discriminations. A key problem of speech is the selection of the ideas to stand for the subject we talk about. Skill in accumulation and development of ideas as well as analysis and discrimination of the important from related ideas we talk about must be a persistent objective of the student of speech. Knowledge may not be power unless the speaker possesses the skill to use it in social interaction.

The third function of speech is that it is projective. Typical speech sense organs are distance ceptors. Whether speech travels the necessary distance is the speaker's responsibility. He must talk loudly and clearly enough to be heard and understood. He must so control all his behavior that it not only is free from contradictions but that it focuses and supplements the voice. Speech teachers often spend a considerable part of their energies in the teaching of this speech function. In fact, this function is sometimes considered synonymous with speech. Important though it is, it should not dominate our program.

Since speech is a form of social behavior it must be adapted to those who are its intended receivers. Effective speech cannot be a shot in the dark. It is not just a process of getting an idea off our tongues. Indeed some discussions of "delivery" seem to suggest that a speech is just a process of unloading a cargo we have taken in store. It is not more realistic to consider speech a series of adaptive acts, a process of more or less continuous ordering and reordering the resources at our command in adjustment to our social environment. Just as the actor may suggest the roles of life in reciting Jacques' "Seven Ages of Man" speech in a few brief moments so in all talking the effective speaker is prepared to take the roles which situations and people demand. Unless he can do this his preparation is wanting.

There is a final function often overlooked which is an inherent and vital factor in any concept of speech as a form of social behavior. This function is *adaptive listening* by the audience in a speech situation. Unless it operates no amount of skill in the speaker may bring success. Of course the speaker determines whether or not his speech is easy to listen to. But easy or difficult listeners also have a responsibility. Therefore proper education of the listener is an important part of a speech program.

OBJECTIVES OF SPEECH EDUCATION

We study speech for many purposes. Perhaps the basic purposes are to increase our usefulness to, and satisfaction from, the society in which we live. The fact that speech is one of the oldest subjects of study in organized instruction suggests that its problems have long aroused man's intellectual curiosity, and perhaps that men throughout the ages have recognized need for such instruction. Differences in the development of speech skill among intellectual equals no doubt reflect differences in social insight, motivation, environment, and opportunity to learn.

The purposes for the study of speech are brought into focus by the question who needs speech education? The answer to this question is colored by our concepts of both speech and society. If we are primarily disturbed by what we call defective speech, or think of speech education as a process of speech correction, we may well excuse all but the defectives from our consideration. Or we may specialize in work with the talented and see in our work with them the need for developing leaders of men. Some administrators have deplored the time and expense of work with the few at either end of the distribution of skills and seem to have reached the conclusion that the greatest need is for giving some instruction to all. Is it not true that any program based on a limited concept of need is deficient? Who is to say whose needs are greatest? I submit that it is impossible to make a valid choice. Is not the answer that all need speech education, each to receive it at the level from which he and all the rest of us may most benefit?

SPEECH STANDARDS

The question of speech needs leads logically to the concept of speech standards. By what values in our culture are we to evaluate this form of social behavior? Much confusion no doubt prevails because of unverbalized and unanalyzed concepts of the standards by which speech is judged. The very concept of standards needs clarification. They certainly do not mean the elements, processes, or criteria into which we analyze a concept such as speech. They are not language, voice, articulation, organization of ideas, etc. These are the parts which make up or stand for the whole. They are the criteria evaluated, not the standards by which the evaluating is done.

Some common speech values or standards are intelligibility, correctness, consistency, logic, acceptability or taste, aesthetics, effectiveness, effort, social responsibility, classical rhetoric, comparison, and change (we may call it improvement). There are situations in which each if not all these and other standards are applicable. Each at some time may have been invoked when it was not the standard actually used or meaningful in the situation. The speech critic should learn to analyze his standards, to apply them with care, and to make known the value premises with which he operates. This practice may serve to clarify and improve the processes of speech instruction.

PEDAGOGICAL PRINCIPLES

Practice: No discussion of the philosophy of speech education would be complete without consideration of the pedagogical principles and procedures under which we operate. The first of these principles is that speech programs should be directed to the understanding as well as to behavior. The old adage that "We learn to speak by speaking," has been mouthed so frequently that some apparently do not recognize it for the mere half-truth which it is. Practice not only does not make perfect, it may not even make its learning permanent. One of the main distinctions between an educational institution and a training center is that the former is organized to appeal to the intellect, the latter is satisfied with teaching procedures which condition the organism to respond reflectively and subconsciously. A speech program that is just a bag of tricks has little justification in an educational institution. Neither is speech education a mere verbal achievement. It must also educate the emotions and overt behavior. Since the whole person speaks, speech education must be directed to the development of the whole person.

Goals and Understanding: Most of our instruction is terminal course teaching. Although real progress can be made in improving speech habits even in a short course, a more significant achievement may lie in clarification of the understanding of problems and principles involved. When this is achieved the student may go forth in a self-directed program of speech improvement which he may continue to follow all his life. No set of specific practice exercises can achieve such far reaching results.

Individual Differences: The curriculum should be adapted to all levels of instruction and to all leves of achievement in each grade. If the program includes adequate provision for the study of speech behavior many speech defects and harmful habits of communication can be prevented. The potentially talented are given an early start on the development of their talents. Continuous exercise of effective speech habits is vital to their preservation and development. There should be no question of where is the best place for speech instruction. It should start early and be a continuous process from the lowest to the highest grades of instruction.

Extra-Curricular Program: A useful although not essential part of the program of speech education is the extra-curricular program. It is most successful when it is based upon and closely correlated with the curriculum. There is some feeling among administrators that the extra-curricular program does not operate upon the basis of functional learning situations. It can be perverted as can many good things. But speech teachers commonly find in it a very stimulating learning situation. It takes the student actively into the world in which he lives. It challenges him to achieve his highest learning potential!

Perhaps we err most in not making its functional value clear for those who doubt. Most speech teachers who work with such activities as declamation, debate, dramatics, or radio do so not to develop professional skill in such activities. They emphasize general education and fundamental skills in speaking. They focus attention on intellectual and democratic values. This point apparently needs clarification for administrators.

Speech teachers also err in permitting the substitution of the extra-curricular program for a curricular program. This activity program can ordinarily serve only a few and those it serves cannot readily be given a systematic speech education by this process alone.

The Curriculum: A curricular program in speech education is a substantial program. It is directed toward the whole child. It seeks to develop his mind, to broaden and control his emotional sensitivities, and to facilitate his adjustments to his fellows. It recognizes in speech a tool to educate the student through active experience with literature, logic, and life. The traditions and the goals of democracy are its foundations and its goals. It gives meaning and function to the concept of freedom of speech. Through it we hope our students may achieve a clearer understanding of their duties and responsibilities as communicators. In Speech education the future citizen of democracy should gain a richer understanding of his place among his fellows, a higher goal of loyalty and service to mankind.

The speech program can be fitted to the framework of any curriculum. If all instruction is integrated, speech can be taught in such a pattern. If most instruction is specialized then speech should also be taught as a specialized subject. Even when taught as a departmental subject speech should be related to other subjects in the curriculum. The student should be directed in the practice of speech in varied functional life activities. It is a mistake to assume that specialists are needed to teach other subjects but that any teacher can do the speech teaching. What is everybody's business in education as in other social affairs is nobody's business. School administrators who see this have found a place for speech in the curriculum. Those who do not see it have found excuses.

Research: Let us conclude with one additional point. While speech is one of the oldest subjects of curriculums, much of the modern program is based on research carried on within the last twenty-five years. There is still much research to be undertaken for the improvement of our field. Every teacher should prepare himself for and carry on some research. The philosophy of speech education, though less tangible than some other research topics, may be one of our most far reaching problems for research. Here is an aspect of the philosophy of speech worthy of our best efforts.

Basic Concepts of Speech Education

HARRY G. BARNES

Modern educational philosophy emphasizes the development of a curriculum conducive to the acquisition of indispensable habits of behavior which make for greater social adaptability on the part of the individual. The modern educator conceives of a school that adjusts its program to the needs and abilities of its students in terms of the solution of problematic situations with which they are, or may be, confronted.

The term speech education is used to describe a program of speech training for *all* students, consistent with this modern educational philosophy. Speech education has as its major function the development of those indispensable habits and techniques of speaking essential to normal behavior by the individual when meeting speaking situations.

In discussing the basic concepts of speech education, it is necessary, first, to present premises upon which the speech education program is based.

Speech is an acquired process in which the speaker learns to produce patterns of physical stimuli designed to affect a listener or listeners. Though speech occurs under varied types of conditions, there are two basic types of situations, *informal* and *formal*, and two basic kinds of speaking, *original* and *interpretative*.

The informal speaking situation is characterized by conversation about, or discussion of, a subject by two or more persons to which each contributes as and when he desires. The *formal speaking* situation is characterized by the speaker-audience relationship, in which the speaker at a given time, place, and occasion communicates his thought, or the thoughts of another, relative to a particular subject, to a group of listeners for their benefit, or for the benefit of himself, or for the benefit of a cause.

In *original speaking*, exemplified by conversation, group discussion, and public speaking in its many forms, the speaker creates, formulates, and expresses his own ideas. In *Interpretative speaking*, exemplified by simple reading aloud, interpretation, impersonation, and acting, the speaker expresses the thoughts, feelings, and moods of another. In either case, the manner in which the speaker expresses the thoughts and

From *The Speech Teacher,* Vol. 1, No. 1 (January, 1952) pp. 14-19.

Mr. Barnes (Ph.D., Iowa) was formerly in charge of the speech fundamentals course at the State University of Iowa and the teaching of speech at the same institution.

feelings involved is determined by the nature of the response he desires from the listener.

Regardless of the type of speaking situation, *informal* or *formal*, and regardless of the kind of speaking, *original* or *interpretative*, the speaker must in general assume four fundamental burdens. *First*, he must gain the attention of the listener, or listeners, and interest him, or them, in his subject or material. *Second*, he must hold that attention and interest in spite of factors that may cause it to fluctuate. *Third*, he must be clear in order that his thoughts may be understood and comprehended exactly. *Fourth*, he must cause his thoughts and their relation to his subject, thesis or theme to be remembered.

For speech to be normal in the *informal* speaking situation, the speaker must as a single, unified total bodily response exercise adequately four fundamental processes which involve basic and specific habits. These fundamental processes are: (1) adjustment to the speaking situation, (2) symbolic formulation and expression (thought and language), (3) phonation, and (4) articulation. They all occur coordinately as a unified whole during normal speech. For purposes of diagnosis, re-training, and training they are separated.

To speak effectively in the *formal* speaking situation requires the development and exercise of the four fundamental processes as well as the adequate development and exercise of special techniques. These special techniques of *original* speaking are: (1) *choice of subject*, (2) *choice of thought*, (3) *choice of material*, (4) *organization of thought and material*, (5) *use of language*, (6) *projection to the audience*, (7) *control of bodily activity*, (8) *rhythm*, (9) *pronunciation*, (10) *voice control*, and (11) *response*.[1]

By eliminating from this list, (2) *choice of thought*, (3) *choice of material*, and (5) *use of language*, and changing the term, (1) *choice of subject* to *choice of material*, and the term (4) *organization of thought and material* to *arrangement of material*, the basic techniques of *interpretative speaking* are also included and without introducing other basic principles.

In learning to speak, the individual acquires first, an ability to exercise the fundamental processes. The normally developed but untrained speaker is for the most part adequate in these processes according to his level of maturation. If he is not, he presents a speech deficiency or defect, necessitating correction, through a re-educative process. The normally developed but untrained speaker does not necessarily possess the special techniques of effective speaking. If he does not, he presents,

---

[1]Harry G. Barnes, *Speech Handbook* (New York, 1941).

rather than a deficiency or defect, a lack of skill which he has not been stimulated to acquire. The process of speech development is not complete, and the individual is not equipped to meet speaking situations as they arise in the immediate as well as the remote environment without the ability to exercise at least adequately, the fundamental processes of speech and the special techniques of effective speaking.

An adequate development of the four fundamental processes and the habits entailed equips the individual to meet the informal speaking situation. Acquisition of the special techniques essential to effective speaking in the formal speaking situation, together with skills in the fundamental processes, equips the speaker to meet at least adequately any type or kind of speaking situation.

I have listed these processes and techniques of speaking in order to make clear what the speech education program must accomplish. The classification lends itself readily to the development of a graded program of instruction for all students leading progressively from necessary basic habits to techniques needed only occasionally. The elementary school should concern itself primarily with a systematic development of adequacy in the fundamental processes; it should provide for the fixation of good habits already acquired, the acquisition of other good habits characteristic of the normal speaker at that level of maturation, and prevention of new and undesirable habits which may be directly or indirectly acquired as maturation continues. At the junior and senior high school and college levels, the speech education program should concern itself primarily with the special techniques of effective speaking.

It is clear that these fundamental processes and special techniques of effective speaking must be learned. Analysis of factors and conditions inherent in, or incident to, the learning thereof reveals the following important considerations that must be reckoned with by those who are concerned with the speech education program:

1. By the time the child has reached school age he has developed some proficiency in the four fundamental processes. Basic habits of speech, adequate and inadequate, have been fixed for some time.

2. Though at any grade level most children have some form of speech pattern, adequate or inadequate, it must be emphasized that these habits have been acquired under diverse, uncontrolled, and unsystematic conditions. Because the child speaks at school age and thereafter, it cannot be assumed that he does, or should, speak adequately. In fact, it can be shown that at any grade level, extending

into the college and the graduate school, large numbers have speech defects and deficiencies and that few are adequate in all the fundamental processes. Large numbers of pupils make sounds incorrectly. Larger numbers make many of the sounds inaccurately in connected discourse. Many voices are unpleasant; still more are monotonous; few are pleasant and flexible. Language is generalized, inaccurate, inexpensive. Many pupils are ill at ease, inhibited, uncertain; few are poised and purposive when facing the simplest of speaking situations.

3. Though speech in its more common forms is an integrated, vital, and necessary part of school life, it can be shown that instruction in speech is indirect, diverse, unsystematic. It is a deplorable fact that many teachers, even some teachers of speech, do not present adequate speech habits. Even more deplorable is the fact that teachers in general, even some teachers of speech, are uninformed concerning the most elemental facts concerning the growth and functioning of the organism in the production of speech. They have no conception of normal speech. Moreover, they do nothing for any inadequacies they may recognize, but hope that maturation will undo what it has already brought about. It cannot be assumed that by merely providing opportunities for the pupil to speak that proper habits will develop when bad ones exist. As in other functions, bad habits are eliminated and new ones acquired through specific and systematic instruction.

4. Speech habits are personal, intimate, and individual. They are an expression and summation of heredity, the influences of environment, and the maturation of the individual in terms of social growth. It must be emphasized, that at any grade level, though group tendencies exist, individual differences are wide and varied. *Group tendencies* in speech performance at any grade level, as a basis for the building of units of instructions with specific aims and objectives, *can* be determined. The range and peculiar nature of *individual differences* within the group can be ascertained. *Both must be determined* if teaching is to be efficient, economical, and progressive. A serviceable, reliable, and valid diagnostic technique is the first and most important requirement of those who should improve the speech habits of their pupils.

5. As the child matures, his environment continues to change and grows more complicated. Speech is ever present; the demands upon the speech process are ever greater. Environment exercises a vital influence on the child's behavior. Physiological changes must be reckoned with. Though the child speaks early and forms certain basic

habits, it must be emphasized that the development of the speech functions is a continuous one. Good habits must be maintained; bad ones eliminated; the acquisition of new and necessary habits must be made possible. Instruction in speech must be continuous and persistent, following the growth of the child and the changes in his environment.

The great need in the field of speech is for a speech education program, which begins in the pre-school and which systematically and progressively afford instruction as a coordinate part of the school program throughout the elementary and intermediate grades, through the junior and senior high schools, and into the colleges and universities.

The general aims of such programs, as I visualize them, are as follows:

1. To make the student aware of acceptable standards of good speech as related to personal culture and individual achievement in speaking performance.
2. To give him an understanding of, and a correct attitude toward, the speaking situation.
3. To give him insight into his own speech habits to the extent that he is aware and critical of them.
4. To develop in him a general facility for meeting speaking situations.
5. To develop at least adequacy in his exercise of the indispensable fundamental processes of speech.
6. To acquaint him with the nature and use of the basic and indispensable attributes and techniques of effective speaking.
7. To stimulate him to achieve creatively and artistically as far as his talent will permit.

These aims of a speech program bespeak a philosophy of approach on the part of the teacher, based on the following premises:

I. Since the pupil is a product of heredity and environment, he posesses characteristics and exhibits behavior which are peculiar to him. Because he has been speaking for some years, he does not, therefore, speak adequately, nor can it be assumed that he should speak adequately. His immediate behavior, his level of achievement, his needs and abilities as evidenced in performance, are the initial foundations upon which the teacher must build.
II. The pupil moves in an environment which selects him and which he selects. Speech is a vital factor to him in this environment. As he matures normally, the environment widens and becomes more complicated. He must be trained to meet the environment of the future through the environment of the present. No one can tell

specifically what special types of speaking situations are going to confront him eventually. Not all situations stimulate the same patterns of response; hence, the acquisition by the pupil of basic indispensable habits and techniques of speaking, and an ability to interpret and apply them from situation to situation, is the real goal of instruction.

III. Speaking is both a tool and an art. As a tool for the many, adequacy in the exercise of the fundamental processes and basic techniques may be sufficient. As an art, adequacy in the exercise of these processes and techniques is the base from which the skill and technique of the professional speaker and the artistic performer evolve.

By adequacy, I mean a degree of proficiency which may be described as satisfactory, acceptable, normal; deficienices are absent minimum essentials are present. Adequacy is thus a *stage of development* in the maturation and learning process which when attained satisfies the minimum requirements of speech as a tool and equips the individual to behave normally in a complex society which demands such behavior. This statement must not be interpreted to mean that the goal of the speech program is adequacy. Through continuation of the learning process at advanced levels, perfection may be approached or achieved dependent upon the capacity of the individual to respond at these higher levels. As the exercise of the basic processes and attributes is refined and perfected the individual matures into an artist. The standards of speech as a tool, therefore, must be recognized as minimum essentials but the standards of speech must be maintained as maximum essentials. To serve the needs of the many and the talents of the few, should be the objective of the modern educational program as a whole, and the goal of the speech program as a part of that whole.

IV. Though teaching methods may vary from teacher to teacher, class to class, and student to student, the following principles[2] should be basic to all methods:

1. Effective speech is more than a combination of separate attributes, qualities, or skills.
2. Speech and the speaker develop as a whole.
3. Any reaction of the speech mechanism is a unified response to a total situation of some kind. Any response of a part of the

---

[2]Adapted from Raymond Holder Wheeler, *Readings in Psychology* (New York, 1930), in "The Individual and The Group: An Application of Eight Organismic Laws," pp. 3-22.

mechanism is made in relation to every other part and in terms of the whole.

4. The parts of the speech mechanism respond in accordance with the nature, the structure, and the characteristics of the entire bodily mechanism.

5. Existing physical and feeling states in the bodily mechanism influence the functioning of the parts.

6. Learning begins with the acquisition of gross or general skills. Refined and specific skills evolve from gross or general skills through a process of individuation.

7. Speech habits once established cannot be easily or quickly supplanted. New and desirable habits are not acquired by suggestion alone. Each student must be sufficiently motivated to exert the maximum energy necessary to acquire them. When existent, this motivation occurs in the form of tensions toward specific goals. These tensions are aroused by a knowledge of a specific inadequacy and a strong desire to eliminate it in favor of a known and acceptable habit. The potential energy thus in readiness must be directed and controlled for learning to take place.

8. Learning occurs through *insight* in terms of immediate and remote, but specific goals. Insight develops through *maturation*. Immediate goals are stages in the maturation process which progressively lead to the remote and more complex goals. The optimum condition for learning exists when desirable tensions in terms of a specific and *attainable* goal in a speaking situation are set up within the student, accompanied by a clearly defined method for achieving the desired goal. Insight is the key to resolution of tension and approach to the goal, and should occur immediately if the goal is related to the level of maturation of the learner, if it is specific, if it is clearly understood, and if the method of reaching it is definite and known to the learner. If these conditions are met, a skill may be exercised adequately with the first response of the learner. A new immediate goal in the series should then be presented which incorporates and reinforces the old in a similar or different problematic situation. By development of assignments in such a progressive series, integration becomes a part of the process. Complete skills are thus developed systematically in the shortest possible time with a minimum of energy.

In general, therefore, and in respect to the broader aspects of the program as applied to large numbers of unselected students, the teacher should endeavor to develop in each student: (1) a general facility in meeting the speaking situations, (2) at least adequacy in the fundamental processes of speech, and (3) as much skill as possible in the exercise of the basic techniques of effective speaking. It must be emphasized that the ultimate test of the development of a habit or a technique is whether the individual has absorbed it and made it his own. The teacher should endeavor to develop in each individual a style of speaking which is as natural and effective for *him* as possible. Otherwise, much harm may be done, many students may not improve at all, and many may acquire artificialities which are a hindrance rather than a help. The teacher must realize that the student is being trained to speak outside the classroom as well as in it, that speech has social utility as well as beauty, and that the average man in the average audience, untrained in appreciating the extreme niceties of speech, is the eventual critic.

In brief, then, the speech education program, because of the peculiar nature of speech, the conditions under which it occurs, and the factors inherent in and the principles governing its development, begins with the individual—his needs, abilities, and his immediate environment. Through systematic and progressive instruction it acquaints him with standards and gives him insight and knowledge as a basis for developing natural, normal habits of speaking. Thereby it aids him to develop a general facility in meeting speaking situations and stimulates him to acquire as much skill as his talent will permit in order that when speaking situations confront him in the future he may meet them normally and well.

Speech in the Total School Curriculum

ELWOOD MURRAY

Probably no field of teaching has a more interesting and useful future than the field of speech education. Whether the potentialities will be realized depends upon the extent to which we are able to prepare ourselves to make changes in our programs to meet the opportunities in education in general and in the communication arts and sciences in particular. Our place in the educational picture and our place in the total school curriculum is determined by educational policy makers. In the making of policies our part is necessarily minor and our members are usually only occasionally represented. We must work closely within the directives implied by the policies made by others. Our contribution can be vastly extended as we adapt and develop our programs to enhance these policies and hence bring about a greater demand for our work.

Fortunately we have a subject which may contribute directly both to enhance the policies of our educational leaders and meet the needs of our students in the rapid changes, difficult problems, and vast demands in the world of today. We may expect to strengthen our programs to meet the following three continuing demands: first, we must, along with the rest of the curriculum, help students sustain and build that heritage of democracy, order, and freedom which has contributed to our greatness as a people; second, we have a unique opportunity and a corresponding responsibility to contribute to the personal-social adjustment, personality development, and human relations effectiveness of our students; third, we must contribute to our students' vocational and professional fitness and help them perform better in their major fields.[1] To make appropriate contribution to meeting these requirements we find that we should develop and activate work in the whole gamut of education from the mother of the pre-school and the kindergarten child to the graduate student and the adult extension class.[2]

Perhaps our overall objective may best be described in terms of communication behavior wherein we look at the person in his whole situation. We should do all that is feasible to develop individuals who are serene and friendly, persons with infinite curiosity, stability, and char-

From *The Southern Speech Journal* (May, 1952), pp. 234-240.

Elwood Murray is Director, School of Speech, University of Denver.

[1]See bulletins on *Speech in the Elementary School* and *Speech in the Secondary School* published by The Speech Association of America.

[2]Joseph H. Smith, D. Mack Easton, and Elwood Murray, "The Integrated Speech Program," special monograph published by The Western Speech Association (1937).

acter. Central in this maturity of personality is a general scientific attitude which the student becomes able to apply, not only to the behavior of others, but also to himself. These characteristics appear to be a part of that basic competency in human relations and human intercommunication whereby the student will become able to deal with a world made rather dangerous by immature persons and groups who, too frequently, operate our modern technologies. Much more of this competency also seems to be necessary if our students are to transmit their share of the heritage and contribute to the furthering of human welfare and human evolution.

The contribution we make to these large objectives will be restricted by the view we take of our subject, the extent to which we teach the functions of our subject, and our own efforts and abilities. Sometimes our problem is with our administrative superiors who do not define speech in the same broad respects; other times we are not prepared to achieve the broader and more functionally vital ends which many of our profound and more forward-looking administrators expect of our subject and us. If our chief end is so-called speech skill we will confine our understandings and methods accordingly; if our end, in addition to skill, includes personal-social effectiveness, our understanding and methodologies must be vastly expanded. If our end is to put on a play that will "bring down the house" or a debate which will "bring honors to the school"—that is laudible, perhaps; but if our aim is to teach better human inter-communication, we will need to do much more.[3]

If we desire to extend our usefulness and at the same time give our work its most solid academic basis in the total educational program we will either teach our subject in relation to the whole communication process or incorporate that process as a part of our field. At present we are teaching only a part of the basic communication processes. Those processes of reception, seeing—listening—reading, we scarcely teach at all; the assimilation, evaluation, and invention processes we teach very inadequately; we teach the organization, supporting, and verbal formulation processes too isolated from their whole social situations; we teach the vocal forms of transmission fairly well; but we fail to teach our students to check upon the reception of their messages. We specialize upon certain aspects of what are primarily the transmission process—such things as delivery in public speaking and oral interpretation, in acting and in radio performance. Radio and television fundamentally serve as media for transmission of speech. In debate and discussion we teach the elements of reasoning and a logic which

---

[3]Elwood Murray, "The Evaluating and Integrating Functions of Speech," *Teachers College Journal*, XIII (January, 1942).

are primarily Aristotelian, but we neglect the more complex psychological, semantic, and sociological aspects and the necessary two-way
reception and transmission behavior of our communicators. We spend
great effort in training persons in "persuasion" with too little attempt
to gear this ability into a basis of sound evaluation. We are weak in,
or we omit entirely, training whereby our students may avoid in themselves and deal with in others, those very subtle reactions which resist,
distort, confuse, or block communication at many of these points. In
the main we tend to neglect the underlying fundamentals of communication while we continue to stress the isolated and outward mechanical
factors. While we must not neglect matters of mechanics and delivery,
we might better deal with them from a basis of the whole communication process and whole communication situation.[4]

Effective interpersonal relations must be paralleled by effective human intercommunication; in fact, communication wherein mind meets
mind is both an aspect and a function of relations, particularly interpersonal relations. Because we do not ground our work sufficiently
deep in the fundamentals of human intercommunication there is confusion and uncertainty concerning the place and scope of our work
in the total school program; there is confusion concerning our relations
to other programs in the school. There is developing in particular a
fantastic situation of confusion, overlapping, and educational ineffi-
ciency with regard to what belongs in our field, such as professional
theatre, radio, and television as well as with regard to other subjects
which involve the teaching of communications such as journalism, writing, and visual-audio aids. Failure to provide a sufficiently wide and
unifying basis is contributing to splitting of radio, television, and motion
picture production training into separate and distinct departments and
programs. Into all of these programs there must be incorporated a
great proportion of our traditional materials from phonetics, voice training, and speech correction; from rhetoric, public speaking, discussion,
and oral interpretation. In multiplying these programs of communication
all of us become less capable of doing a respectable job in our own
specialties. Worst of all, our students are cheated; they graduate as
narrow and inflexible practitioners and not very good ones at that.
Certainly they are not the adequate citizens we have described in the
foregoing part of this paper as the objective of our efforts.

Neither are the so-called "Basic Communications" courses thus far
living up to their earlier and enthusiastic promises. In some cases the
originators of these programs merely put together a mixture of work

---

[4]Elwood Murray, "Personality, Communication, and Interpersonal Relations,"
Southern Speech Journal, XIII (January, 1948).

pertaining to reading, writing, speaking, and listening "skills." The result is frequently a multiplication of problems in the classroom for an instructor who is unprepared to meet them. In other cases there is a gesture toward a wider and more vital program. In these, the objectives include statements concerning "improvement in personality and the relations of the student" through these new courses. These objectives are not implemented and the work has never risen above what is largely a sort of streamlined English course with some greater emphasis in our direction upon "oral communication." With two or three exceptions there is no serious attempt in any comprehensive in-service training and reorientation of the teachers which is necessary if we are to have education for genuine human intercommunication and improved interpersonal relations.[5]

Then there are the so-called "Communication Centers" in which radio, television, journalism, theatre, and sometimes speech are being "brought together" with courses in public opinion, public opinion measurement, and sociology. The functional integration in these programs seems to be only in the bringing together of the writing aspects of communication. As yet they include neither the essential aspects of the personality development of the communicator or the cultural dynamics of the communication situation. All of this, I think, should be taught if we are to make the contribution of which our subject is capable; if we are to teach the fundamentals of human intercommunication. Furthermore, thus far, these programs in their emphasis upon mass communication seem not to have applied the available methodologies whereby the different communications will in themselves be interrelated. With an unnatural and false emphasis upon writing, these programs are set up outside of their speech bases. This is to the grave detriment of sound communication training in the future as well as to the speech profession.

There are scientific bases whereby the entire area of communication may be unified and which will enable all of this work to find its proper and efficient place in the total school curriculum. These bases are found in the organismal biologies, psychologies, and sociologies,[6] the same bases out of which have come the philosophies of human dynamics and integration in education in general. The speech mechanism in its personality and semantic involvements is the fundamental mechanism of all language communication. It is as fundamental for listening and

---

[5]Wilson B. Paul, Frederick W. Sorenson, and Elwood Murray, "A Functional Core for the Basic Communications Course," *Quarterly Journal of Speech*, XXXII (April, 1946), 232-244.

[6]See the works of John Dewey, Raymond Holder Wheeler, George H. Mead, William H. Kilpatrick, and L. Thomas Hopkins.

writing as it is for speech. This was first apparent in studies of the different aphasias as well as in work with the deaf. All persons who wish to communicate effectively should be trained in overcoming those things which cause this delicate mechanism to block, to be confused, to distort in its reception, assimilation, or transmission of messages. This is as important as the study of grammar or delivery. Although many of our speech teachers have been in contact with these matters through their work in speech correction, perhaps few have seen their significance for the normal student as a basis for the understanding and improvement of all the human aspects of communication. Parallel with this new information concerning the nature of the communication process and behavior in individuals are the new methodologies which have evolved from group dynamics and group work;[7] namely, the case method whereby communicating may be studied within groups: sociometry, sociodrama, and psychodrama. General semantics brings a general scientific method whereby specific communication reactions both in the human receiver and the human transmitter may be studied and improved in very definite ways.[8] Language as a manifestation of human behavior and adjustment thus may be improved for the larger ends of human welfare. These are in reality all fundamental methodologies of communication. For the development and application of these methodologies no group of educators have a better basic preparation and hence potential responsibility. It is, in fact, highly improbable that the potentialities of this work as suggested here will ever be utilized unless a sufficient number of leading speech scientists and scholars enlist their abilities for the larger ends.

The extent to which we develop our subject as the fundamental and central medium of communication is especially important for our future relations with television. In the near future, television will become the greatest and most influential of the mass media. The field will become vastly important as a vocational outlet for our students and as an extension of the educational activities of our programs and institutions. While proper training in television has its bases in speech functioning, our contribution will not be adequate unless our work incorporates into speech training the whole psycho-communication process. Although some of this broader training may be picked up piece-meal in other departments, the results will scarcely be adequate unless presented

---

[7]See publication lists and bibliography for Research Center on Group Dynamics, Ann Arbor, Michigan; also for Psychodramatic Institute, 101 Park Ave., N. Y.

[8]See publication list and bibliography for Institute on General Semantics, Lakeville, Connecticut.

systematically as a corpus or unified body of communication methods and philosophy.

If all of this appears to be getting beyond the bounds of what we have been doing traditionally, perhaps the development of sound programs of the teaching of communication as well as the maintenance of the integrity of our profession requires that we extend the title of our programs from "speech" to "speech and communication" or "communication." We may be certain that our friends in English will not be able to make the drastic reorientation of their subject which is required if genuine human intercommunication training is to be developed. In fact, it is the dominance of the traditional "English" point of view in most of the so-called "communication" programs which seems to be apparent in the "retrogression" of most of these programs which is underway. In this regard we should not forget that "speech" and "communication" are multi-lingual in their scope, which can never be possible with the necessarily mono-lingual point-of-view to which "English" is confined.

The behavioral objectives we have outlined for the mature communicator are in many respects similar to the objectives which some of the leaders of so-called general education have for all students. They are particularly similar to the objectives for the newer training of elementary school teachers and to a less extent teachers of all high school and junior college subjects. Perhaps the speech-communication trainers of these teachers would take their greatest satisfaction if they could thus multiply the effectiveness of their work.

It may be said that we are making all of this very complicated, very difficult, very impractical. It may be said that all we need to communicate is plain simple English, spoken clearly and to the point. I would point out that whatever becomes important to us immediately becomes complicated. While the communicator must above all be clear, he must not over simplify; he must "tell the truth." Those things, such as our subject, which deal with human nature and human behavior are the most complicated and paradoxical of all. In these matters often the most practical starts out as the most theoretical and impractical. We know that wherever there is great skill and great art, with its seemingly effortless simplicity, there is also the most thorough and the most profound information, preparation, and practice. As others have said, our subject enables all of us to benefit from the experiences and abilities of each other in carrying human advancement forward to the coming generations. In a matter so important as this we must not skimp, we must take the long way.

Teaching Speech to Facilitate Understanding

DONALD K. SMITH

I

Classical thought about language tended to glorify speech, treating it as a gift, and the highest of man's capabilities. Contemporary students of language find in this behavior a source of much sickness. "Man first learned to speak when he learned to lie," comments one linguist, and his comment is more than a cynical reference to human nature; it is directed to the heart of the paradoxical power of the gift of speech. For the power to tell the truth about events remote in time or space—a power available only to language using humans—is also the power to spin an illusion, to create a lie about these same events. Similarly, the power of speech to enable each of us to escape the prison of our own skins and enter into community with our neighbors, even at moments to feel ourselves of one substance with all mankind,—this gift of language too has its paradoxical corollary. Speech, the instrument of community, can destroy community. Speech, the instrument that makes it possible for us to conceive of interpersonal and intergroup understanding, is also the instrument of abuse, suspicion, ill will, and all the corrosive phenomena of human misunderstanding.

II

The term "understanding" looms large in the consciousness of contemporary speech teachers. We are aware of the thread running through history which defines our study as one devoted to the techniques of making the "worse seem the better case." As an instrumental action, speaking skill seems to serve the knave as well as the honest man, and there is only cold comfort in the thought that in a world in which knaves speak effectively, honest men ought to learn to do so. It is possible to teach the art of speech making with the same level of moral indifference that scientists exploring the power producing potential of the atom once brought to their work.

But in a world in which men hunger for understanding as they hunger for food and sleep—in which nations toy with the possibility that the fruits of group and national misunderstanding could be pre-

From *The Speech Teacher*, Vol. XI, No. 2 (March, 1962), pp. 90-100.

Donald K. Smith is Professor of Speech and Chairman of the Department of Speech at the University of Minnesota.

liminary to world's end—in such a world indifference to the moral possibilities in our study seems no longer an available choice. In his address
to the 1960 convention of the Speech Association of America, Professor
Andrew Weaver put the issue forcefully before us:

> "Contributing to fuller understanding among men is no minor mis-
> sion in education. It is the vital core of our obligation as teachers of
> speech. . . . As teachers of speech, our supreme task is to open satis-
> factory communication channels among men. It is our special mission
> to see to it that our fellow human beings, with all their getting, get
> understanding. May we ever keep our eyes lifted to that great goal."[1]

I assume that few speech teachers who hear or read Professor Weaver's words would reject the charge he laid on our profession. That
charge, as I see it, is that in the decades just ahead we should take as
the central goal of our instruction the improvement of man's capability for interpersonal and intergroup understanding. The merit of the
goal seems to me beyond dispute. However, the strategy by which the
teaching of speech may be successfully and realistically linked to this
goal is a matter needing the closest attention. How can we design our
classroom instruction in speech to improve the possibility of human
understanding?

The question needs to be treated cautiously: "Understanding" is
itself an abstract concept involving a variety of possible referents. To
know another's meaning, or to perceive the way in which he interprets
his world, is only a first though necessary step to that ultimate form
of understanding which heals tension, mistrust and abuse. If we seek
a world in which people find it possible to participate with trust and
candor in each other's experience, we seek no inconsiderable goal. We
should remind ourselves that it is a goal not likely to yield easily, nor
all at once, nor even altogether. Nor is it a goal attainable simply
through the agencies of formal classroom instruction. And most certainly speech instruction in and of itself has neither the power nor the
sanction greatly to change the shape of our culture. We can at best
hope to design our own instruction so that it increases the possibility
of understanding. And we must acknowledge to ourselves, and teach
to our students, the formidable nature of the commitment that both
people and nations have to the processes that breed misunderstanding.
Specifically, we should acknowledge and instruct concerning three limitations, built into our culture, which impede the use of language to
develop understanding.

---

[1] Andrew Thomas Weaver, "Toward Understanding Through Speech." *Vital
Speeches*, 27: Feb. 1, 1961. pp. 245, 247.

The first of these rests in the fact that both individuals and nations often learn that the deliberate production of misunderstanding serves their ends. Men and nations alike exploit the ambiguities of certain symbols and of certain speech forms in the service of personal and national self-interest.

From the vantage point of this nation, we easily observe the extent to which the Russian nation exploits such words as democracy, freedom, and peace in the conduct of foreign policy. To people who seek self-government, Russia proclaims the slogan of a "people's democracy," based on *freedom* for the working masses, and dedicated to *peace* for mankind. In true Orwellian *1984* fashion, however, these words do not always mean what they seem to mean, and in all likelihood their users are content with the potential usefulness of transient misunderstanding. A people's democracy turns out to be not government of the people, but government which *causes* people to do what certain rulers think ought to be done. But the word democracy has been used: it can do its *Alice in Wonderland* work, and it is not difficult for us to see it as a counter of misunderstanding used in the game of international power politics.

It is perhaps less easy for us to see the uses of misunderstanding in our own national rhetoric, but it is there. Our national intentions toward Cuba seem to have been widely misunderstood not only abroad, but even within our own boundaries—and there is no reason to believe that this misunderstanding was not to some extent intended. In both the Eisenhower and Kennedy administrations, verbal commitment to a national policy of non-intervention seems to have been a cloak for an intention to intervene. And there are many who would defend the "realism" of such deception. "Baffling, bewildering, and confounding" one's foes is an old habit in human affairs, and from at least the time of the Trojan horse the use of symbols to create deliberate misunderstanding has not only been widely practiced, it has often been applauded. Politcians understand this. When some years ago a candidate for the United States Senate accused his election opponent, a bachelor, of being a "celibate who practiced misogyny on the banks of the Potomac," he knew that he would be misunderstood by some voters. He doubtless also knew that he would be applauded as a man of wit by those who understood him. He couldn't lose.

We are a people only half-civilized in our use of language. The extent to which we have substituted combat by words for combat by force of arms is a measure of our advance; but the extent to which we use words simply to clothe naked self-interest is a measure of the distance we yet have to travel.

Our students come to us children of a culture in which the strategic uses of the language of misunderstanding abounds. They would be ill equipped to live in this world if they didn't understand this fact; and they must be forgiven if they practice language habits the culture has taught them. They come also with personal needs, some of which are served by the cloak of misunderstanding. They may have learned that to be misunderstood is one way of getting attention. Indeed, some of them, at a tender age, have already assumed that their lot in life is to be misunderstood, and they assiduously practice this role of martyrdom. Some of them may have learned that to be fully understood in an environment in which one's own views are unpopular may be somewhat punishing. I once told a group of business executives that I thought that many of the communication problems in their organization would be alleviated if each of them would set about to maximize the practice of candor in his own communications with others. I had been impressed at that time by David Reisman's concept of "collective ignorance" in our national life. Reisman says that so many of us advocate our beliefs for what we think will be popular reasons, rather than for the reasons which are really ours, that we all live in the shadow of ignorance as to the real thoughts of one another. Thus we fumble for our agreements like half blind men in a blackened room. Now the audience to which I revealed these Truths was less than impressed with my good advice. One member told me after the speech that he thought I was advocating professional suicide. "Saying what you really believe is one way to lose a good job," he told me.

So I would say that one formidable limitation to our work is the fact that misunderstanding has its uses. It is a general tendency that men like one another better as they understand one another better— but it is not a tendency that pertains in each particular case. It is the case that the better we understand some people's ideas the less we care to talk with them.

A second limitation rests in the fact that language is a cultural institution, and that people who are reared in different cultures have different sets of values and different reference norms for the same verbal category. This fact is admirably illustrated by the problem of misunderstanding which seems all but inherent as Americans attempt to communicate with representatives of other nations, even friendly nations. To be "on time" for a meeting means one thing for an American —or at least most Americans. It is likely to mean a quite different thing to a Laotian or Egyptian—and the intercultural conference which starts three hours or three days after a set time can easily get off under con-

ditions of considerable tension.[2] "Time talks" to Americans one way,
says the anthropologist E. T. Hall; it talks a different way to other
cultures. An American diplomat kept waiting for 50 minutes for an
appointment thought himself the object of insult or incompetence. The
foreign diplomat who kept him waiting thought the fifty minute in-
terval just right—a shorter delay would be obsequious, a longer delay
insulting.[3]

We teachers all have had innumerable experience with the extent to
which the reference norm for the word *promptness* can vary sharply
among our own students. One of the relentless problems of education
seems to be that of getting students to accept the notion that a speech
ought to be given on the day it is scheduled. I have always admired
the simple analogy used by Dr. Ewbank at the University of Wisconsin
some years ago as a method of clarifying the meaning of a time schedule
set up for classroom reports. "Your reports," he told us students, "are
scheduled with the same assumptions used in setting up the football
schedule. If Wisconsin or the other team didn't show up on the Saturday scheduled, it would be considered a scandal, and the absent
team would forfeit the game. I take the same attitude toward the
speaking schedule." I have used the same analogy with my classes,
but it has never worked as well for me as it did for Dr. Ewbank.
Possibly my own reference norm for "promptness" is so loose that students see the visible cues that make my strong words ambiguous.
Possibly their own reference norms for "promptness" are too culturally
scattered to permit other than a scattered interpretation of my meaning.
Misunderstandings based on the differing reference norms we use for
the same concepts are difficult to sort out from misunderstandings
stemming from other causes. But there is no doubt that they exist.
And their existence is a serious limitation to the level of understanding
people can achieve through speech.

A third limitation to our effort is one which may mark a sort of
absolute limit to the work we can do toward perfecting human understanding. In one sense the idea of misunderstanding is linked to the
search for personal freedom. We have all known the double nature
of our own lives. We experience, at one and the same time, a profound
sense of individuality—of being set apart, an entity unto ourselves,
different from all others—and yet at the same time an equally deep
sense of our membership in all mankind—of our need for, and identification with others. "No man is an island unto himself," says the one
poet with truth; and with equal truth his fellow artist echoes, "be

---

[2]A good discussion of the problem of communication across social systems appears
in David K. Berlo: *The Process of Communication* (New York, 1960), pp. 160-164.
[3]Edward T. Hall, *The Silent Language* (New York, 1959).

faithful to that which exists only in yourself." At a trivial level we observe that no moment is more frightening than that in which we believe for a moment that someone understands us completely. In that moment we may perform some act of unreason, some ambiguous or equivocal gesture to restore the sense of being set apart. Dostoevsky understood well this perverse link between our search for freedom and our sometimes capricious actions. Man is such a creature, his narrator observes in *Notes From Underground,* that . . . "shower upon him every earthly blessing, drown him in bliss . . . and even then man would play you some loathsome trick. He would risk his cakes . . . simply to prove to you that men are men and not piano keys." To Dostoevsky the yearning for individuality is so strong that it can, for some men, turn a law of nature into an insult, and a statement such as "two times two equals four," into sheer insolence. "Two times two equals five is sometimes also a very charming little thing,"[4] he writes.

I mean what I mean, says each of us to himself on one day, and if others do not understand me, so much the worse for them. We teachers, with all our good works, will not heal all the alienations which rest within man himself, and were we to do so we should not like our work for we should have reduced all men to one language, and all thought to one mold. No one would be 'out of step' because there would be no different drummer to be heard.

Now I have taken some time to talk of the limitations to the pursuit of human understanding—limitations resting in the social uses of misunderstanding, in the culture bound nature of language, and in the existential tension of individual man and social man. I have done so not because I doubt either the significance or the possibility of the search for understanding, but only that we should know the resourcefulness of the quarry called "misunderstanding" before we undertake his pursuit. We undertake a goal that will not be approached simply by adding some new unit of instruction in the eleventh grade, or by articulating some series of homilies on how it is more blessed to be understood than to be rich. We undertake a goal that must impinge upon the form we give to all our instruction in speech, from the first grade through the University.

III

The key to "teaching speech skills to facilitate human understanding" seems to me simply this: that we should teach understanding of speech.

---

[4]Fyodor Dostoevsky, *Notes From Underground and The Grand Inquisitor,* Trans. by Ralph Matlow. (New York, 1960), pp. 27-30.

The statement may seem an inconsequential juggling of word order, but it is not so intended. We should teach *understanding* of speech— not simply skill in speech—but *understanding* of speech.

It seems to me that the teaching of speech *skill simply as skill,* and the teaching of speech *skill as both a product of understanding and an avenue to understanding* require somewhat different strategies of instruction. This difference is crucial to the task of increasing the possibility of human understanding. Perhaps I can illustrate the difference in these two approaches to the study of speech, as they might apply to the study of bodily action, or the physical-gestural code used in speech. If we ask simply, do our students use bodily action skillfully in their speech, we will discover that a certain percentage of them are skillful, at least in the contexts in which we observe them. They are skillful even though they may have little or no conscious understanding of the nature, source, or significance of their skill. These students seem possessed of reasonable spontaneity or physical expressiveness, a certain minimum of physical coordination or grace, and to have acquired, as unconscious and habitual responses, the ability to support their talking with the kinds of physical behavior deemed meaningful and appropriate by their culture. They have a type of skill—and a useful skill it is—and it exists almost entirely outside the context of understanding. Others among our students seem not to have developed this skill, and not to have developed it for a number of reasons, some of which are readily remediable through purposeful classroom speaking exercises, and some of which are less amenable to change. We may work with these students to help them acquire increased skill in the use of bodily action without very much reference to the question of understanding physical symbolism. For example, we may suggest certain behaviors to these students, and when the behaviors are successful in improving the effectiveness of the student's speech, we may seek to reinforce the successful behavior through our own approval, and through the approval of their fellow students. This is all standard speech instruction. It is useful; it sometimes works. Speech teachers have always done it and they ought to go on doing it. But speech instruction at this level still exists outside the context of understanding.

Now if we raise with ourselves and our students the question of what it means to understand physical symbolism, we add a genuine cognitive dimension to our study—a dimension as unlikely to have been tapped by those who seem to have good habits of bodily action as by those who need assistance. This dimension of knowledge about speech becomes organized as a set of observations, or information related to some generalization which presumably gives us insight into the way physical symbolism functions. Professor Gladys Borchers has illustrated for a number of years at the University of Wisconsin how the teaching of bodily action may be approached at the level of understanding leading to skill, rather than simply at the level of skill. As I have observed her teaching and interpreted her writing, she approaches the study of physical symbolism through the concept of empathy rather than through prescriptions about posture or gesture. A student may bring an onion before the class and slice it, while others in the class watch and react, and still others watch the class to report what they observe. Another student tries to cut a grapefruit with a dull knife. Another tries to wrap a package using sticky cellophane tape. Observers discover the extent to which observers mirror the overt attitudes and actions of those whom they watch, and the class is on its way toward the discovery of the concept of how one "feels into" the experience of another through empathic response. From the concept, reinforced by discussion, students better understand the importance of their own physical behavior as a means of getting others to participate in a speaker's experience.

There are other concepts about bodily action or physical symbolism that can be taught. High school students can observe, for example, the lack of ambiguity of a communicative action in which language, vocal behavior and physical behavior all reinforce one another—all "say the same thing." They can observe that congruous use of symbols makes for maximum immediate clarity. But they can go further to observe that ambiguous action—the incongruous use of physical and language symbols—can also achieve certain ends. Such usage is a rich source of humor, as any comic actor knows.

High school students can also learn that "space talks," to use another of Hall's metaphors. The location of the speaker *vis a vis* his listeners has significance. He can learn that cultural preferences influence the choice of certain space relationships. Americans, for example, seem generally to believe that a distance of two or three feet is a good distance for warm, personal conversation, and we consider the person who gets closer as "pushy," or unaccountably secretive. If the scene and gender relationships are right we may believe or even hope that sexual overtones have entered the conversation. Latin Americans, as Hall observes, feel comfortable in conversation only at closer distances than those we prefer. They may consider an American, who thinks his position exceedingly friendly, as cold, unfriendly, censorious. One sees the possibility of the tragic-comic misunderstanding in a situation in which the Latin American approaches the North American in all good will—the American retreats—and both parties wind up irritated with one another. Neither would need to misunderstand if he knew enough about physical symbolism as a cultural convention.

One could go further in illustrating the notion that the study of bodily action, or physical symbolism is one which can be approached not simply as the learning of skill—but as the development of understanding as a part of skill. But I think I may have clarified this point sufficiently to go on to underline a related point that has been implicit in my discussion. The implicit point is this: that the person who is not just skillful in speaking, but who also understands speech, is in a much better position to use speech to develop genuine understanding when he encounters situations in which communication seems to have broken down.

The able, skillful, confident speaker, filled with a backlog of successful speaking ventures—but who does not understand the nature of speech—this person may live in a state of illusion which will cloud with misunderstanding many speaking situations he may encounter. The illusion of the skillful speaker who knows little about speech is this: confronted with a break down of communication, he is likely to assign the failure either to the ignorance or malice of his listener. He *knows* he is doing the right thing. People have always commented on his skill as a speaker. He got the only "A" grade in advanced public speaking. If things are going badly in some act of communication, the fault can't possibly be his. The perversity of such an illusion—its power for mischief—is made clear I believe in the hypothetical example I have already given of the North American and the Latin American conversing with one another.

Thus far I have illustrated the concept of teaching understanding of speech with examples drawn from the study of physical symbolism, or bodily action. I should next like to indicate at least two rather important understandings about the nature of speech which I think we can achieve with many of our students, and which I think have rather important implications for the nourishment of interpersonal, and intergroup understanding.

The first of these understandings is that of a fully realistic knowledge of the difficulty inherent in any act of communication. For a variety of reasons, the act of communication is always a partial failure, and only one who understands the full range of perils which surround the effort of people to talk with one another is in good position either to regulate his own interpersonal behavior, or to understand and accommodate to partial failure rather than rail against it. In this regard I have always thought it remarkable that so many speech teachers, who ought to know most about the fragile nature of communication, seem to fail to comprehend how it is that judges at speech contests don't always agree with one another very well in their evaluations of particular acts of speaking. It is understandable that high school students should have difficulty in this circumstance, but it is not understandable that we should nourish their misunderstanding of the nature of speech, rather than seeking to build their understanding.

I am indebted to one of my colleagues at Minnesota for a type of classroom exercise which I have found a fruitful approach to the discovery of the problem of communication. We assign an expository speech, and after the first minute of speaking permit members of the audience to ask three kinds of questions of the speaker. The first question must be a variant of "What do you mean?" The second question a variant of "How do you know?" And the third question a variant of "What difference does it make?" Audience members are asked to use the questions honestly—seeking clarification from the speaker only if something has been said which raises a genuine question of the kind listed. For the most part listeners seem to play the game honorably. Now as you might suspect, few student speakers can complete a planned four minute speech in the presence of such questions—at least on the first try. The questions uncover a nest of problems in almost every speech. Abstract and technical words are tossed out by the speaker, without clarification, and proceedings grind to a halt as definitions are sought. Assertions of the "it is well known that many states lack the means to support adequate schools," often produce the "how do you know question?" and the dialogue that ensues may reveal that the speaker is not so certain that he really knows what he has just said. I have found that many speakers give somewhat different speeches the second time they are confronted with the threat of an active, concerned audience, and that most of them succeed somewhat better from the point of view of clarity on the second trial.

Of course some speakers always reach the conclusion that permitting interruptions leads to chaos in speech. "Life," they seem to say, "is easier if we don't really have to worry about the clarity of understanding while we are enjoying the sound of our own voice." Well it is easier—that is, it's easier if you are willing to live with the level of misunderstanding which now clouds much of our public communication. But do we really want to live with such misunderstanding? I can see those students who prefer good order to good understanding in some future managerial role—issuing directives, calling employees together to "get the word," cursing the shortage of intelligent employees this day and age, and in general making life miserable for themselves and those with whom they live. Students who really accept the implications of the difficulty of interpersonal understanding are sometimes ready to play the "Rogers game."[5] Professor Carl Rogers of the University of Wisconsin suggests that each of us might improve his speech habits if, when we hear a statement that we consider obviously false or mistaken, we would relinquish the pleasure of saying, "I disagree," or, "You are quite mistaken." Instead, Rogers contends, we ought to force ourselves to restate as accurately as we can the statement we have just heard. "Let me see," we say if we play the game of understanding. "I understood you to say that the moon is indubitably made of green cheese. Is that right?" More often than not, of course, the person to whom we feed back our understanding will say, "No that's not what I said." Or, "No, that's not exactly what I meant." Sometimes he says this because our "filters" have garbled his utterance. Sometimes we get the words right, but the speaker in re-listening to these words clothed in the attitude we have interpolated is not satisfied that he has been properly interpreted. Not all students who play the "Rogers game" will be pleased with its results. A student told me that the game takes the fun out of life by cutting down on the number of "good" arguments one gets into.

Now such exercises as the "interrupted speech," and the Roger's dialogue are only ways of getting at a real concept of the fragile nature of interpersonal meaning. Students need to know that meaning rises, if at all, like a flame between people. If they possess this idea, and its importance, they may be ready to comprehend the power of persistent dialogue to find meaning. But if they don't possess this idea, they will remain impatient and unskillful in the conduct of the kind of interpersonal communication which alone builds genuine understanding.

I think we can help our students to a real comprehension of the fragile nature of human communication, and of its need for nourishment. As a second major goal we can also encourage our students to take a more experimental attitude toward the forms of speaking they use in the pursuit of certain objectives. All of us learn our speech as a traditional system, and as long as we lack understanding of the system—as long as we play the game without realizing that its rules are simply social conventions—we are likely to think that there is something sinful about experimenting with forms in an effort better to adjust them to our purposes. I always have some students who will stand before an audience, just in front of a blackboard, and attempt some involved verbal description of a simple mechanical structure that could be made twice as clear in half the time with a simple blackboard diagram. "Why

---

[5]See Carl Rogers, "Communication: Its Blocking and Facilitation." In *Mind, Meaning and Naturity*. Edited by S. T. Hayakawa (New York, 1954), pp. 53-60.

didn't you put a diagram on the blackboard," I ask. Explanations are various, but the one I find most notable is the statement, "I didn't know we were allowed to." Students making this explanation, assuming it to be an honest one, have an interesting formal attitude toward speech. "Blackboards," they say, "are for teachers, and mere speakers should not touch them." Students aren't the only ones who have trouble perceiving that they have some freedom of choice in restructuring a speaking situation to make it better suit their purpose. A colleague of mine reported to me that he had attended a conference of college professors at which the chairman had asked that the group list all possible solutions to a given problem before commenting on the merits of any one solution. This is a way of structuring a discussion of a certain type which has some theoretical merit. The interesting thing was that the members of this learned group agreed to the procedure, and then were utterly unable to follow it. I would suspect these teachers of being victims of the traditional form by which professors relate to ideas: Hear an idea, dissect it, but don't give it a moment of peace.

IV

Teaching students to understand speech comprehends and includes instruction in speaking skills, but the teaching of skills can be approached with little or no attention to an orderly acquisition of information and concepts. I think it is chargeable that speech teachers over the years have too often erred in the direction of justifying the complaint that we teach "merely skill." And if the charge against us is true, it ought to be taken seriously. I would not discount the central importance of skill in language instruction. But the merely skillful man dealing with a behavior as complex as speech may stand as a threat both to his own best purposes, and the highest aspirations of his society. Men possessing power without wisdom, or skill stripped of understanding, have always been their own worst enemies. And men who simply speak effectively, but who know little of the complexities of this most significant of all behaviors represent an important instance of power without wisdom.

We speech teachers cannot reform human nature. But we can do a better job of teaching genuine understanding of speech. To the extent that we are right in assuming that most men and most nations hunger for interpersonal and intergroup understanding, our instruction can free these men and nations to pursue this goal. I would not want history, assuming that it can be written to say this of speech teachers in our century: That in an era torn by dissention, crying out for ways of healing the estrangements of man with man and the animosities of group toward group—that in such an age we taught speech only as a skill, only as an instrument for power, influence, or personal success.

Renewal of a Public Philosophy: Role of Teachers of Speech

RUTH MONROE

I.

Public philosophy in a liberal democracy. The Scottish philosopher John Macmurray said of philosophy that "it is the attempt to express reality. For reality is essentially the concrete wholeness which characterizes immediate experience."[1] Every person by virtue of his presence in the universe must develop a sense of reality which is valid for him. Out of this sense of reality come the principles and purposes which may be called his personal philosophy.

If a person is to live creatively, he should integrate his life with principles which are compatible with the real nature of humanity. A man with false principles or no defined principles may maintain existence. But existence is threatened ultimately when a person tries to live with one philosophy dictating his beliefs while a conflicting one governs his actions.

Like individuals, so groups of people if they are to be a creative community must espouse a common body of principles which transcend individual differences. As Hutchins said:

> A community implies that people are working together, and people cannot work together unless they have common principles and purposes. If half a crew of men are tearing down a house as the other half are building it, we do not say they are working together. . . .[2]

Neither can we say that men are working together when they have no basic plan of action and each has a different idea of how to proceed.

Having stated that the life of both individuals and communities is dependent upon the espousal of some basic philosophy, we may look briefly at the public philosophy upon which the liberal democratic community is based. The basic tenet of this philosophy is that human personality is inviolate. Lippmann wrote:

> In the dominion of men over men, be it the master over his slave, the despot over his subjects, the patriarch over his wives and children,

From *The Speech Teacher* Vol. XVI, No. 1 (January, 1967) pp. 38-46.

Ruth Monroe (M.A., Temple University, 1966) is an Instructor in Speech and Drama at Westmar College, LeMars, Iowa.

[1]*Interpreting the Universe*, 2nd ed. (London: Faber and Faber, 1936) pp:33-34.
[2]Robert M. Hutchins, "What shall we defend? We are losing our moral principles," *Vital Speeches of the Day* (July 1, 1940) pp. 548.

the nexus is personal and those who are underneath are in effect the property of those above them. But as their relationships are progressively defined by law and custom in terms of specific rights and duties this personal and possessive nexus dissolves. By the reduction of general supremacy to particular obligations, something is left over—a residual essence in each man which is not at anyone's disposal. That essence becomes autonomous. And so out of the slave who was a living person treated as a thing, there emerges a person who is no longer a thing.

It is just here . . . that the ultimate issue is joined on the question whether men shall be treated as inviolate persons or as things to be disposed of. . . . The self-evident truth which makes men invincible is that inalienably they are inviolate persons.[3]

Upon this truth rest the familiar phrases which articulate the ethical principles upon which the liberal democracies were founded, *e.g.*, "these inalienable rights . . . life, liberty and the pursuit of happiness" and "liberty, equality, and fraternity." Man's inviolability is not provable through the experience of the senses, but throughout the generations of man's personal experience with man it has repeatedly emerged.

Given the truth that human personality is inviolate, it follows that certain rights belong to man by virtue of his humanity. But as soon as these rights are stated, the problems of their attainment in the face of conflicting individual interest become apparent:

If I claim a liberty as a right or privilege, I imply that someone has the duty of respecting this claim. One man's liberty is another man's duty. Freedom and obligation develop together. Once a liberty is conceived as a right it is moralized, that is, it is conceived as publicly recognized, an obligation among members of a community. . . . Any right is both a liberty and a duty and either taken out of the context of public community becomes a mystery.[4]

To achieve these "inalienable rights," a man must prove his humanity by accepting the responsibilities of an autonomous member of the community.

Having defined liberty within the social context, we turn to equality. Men are not created equal when it comes to their mental, emotional, and physical capacities. Neither is there nor has there ever been equality of economic and social position. In fact, the desirability of any of these types of equality is debatable. That equality which is part of the public philosophy might best be stated as equity or equal justice. By virtue of his inviolate nature, every man is entitled to the same justice accorded to every other man. This justice is broader than the justice of the law court.

[3]Walter Lippmann, *The Good Society* (New York: Grosset's Library, Grosset and Dunlap, 1943), pp. 374-375.
[4]Herbert W. Schneider, *Three Dimensions of Public Morality* (Bloomington: Indiana University Press, 1950), pp. 58-59.

It is, first of all, that justice which must be in effect to allow any human being to lay claim on the rights and obligations which are his because he is a member of the community of man. Secondly, this justice involves meeting the needs of members of the community by the responsible use of public and private resources.

The principle of fraternity or brotherly love is an integral part of the public philosophy. Fraternity implies family or mutual interest and concern. There needs to be "a lively communication between the present generation and those of the past and the future. . . ."[5]

The maintenance of justice and hence of liberty and equality as defined in the public philosophy is dependent upon law. Law in a liberal democracy must be based upon the inviolability of man and developed by rational discussion. The truth of man's dignity is above all law. Law based upon this truth is the standard by which the validity of the opinion of the people and their elected officials may be judged.

Thus, for our purposes the public philosophy may be further defined as liberty and equality, tempered by justice, interpreted by laws based upon the truth of man's inviolability.

II.

Departure from the public philosophy. The dilemma in which the modern descendents of those who established the public philosophy find themselves has its roots in the philosophies which flowered with the dawn of science and technology in the nineteenth century. Scientific knowledge brought man to a new awareness of his capacities. At the same time, science pointed out the superstitions and fallacies of medieval religious belief. On the tide of this new knowledge rode a reaffirmation of man's misconception of his Godlike capacities.

The great progress being made in the physical world gave the impetus for the assumption that similar strides in the realm of the intangible were inevitable. This outlook provided fertile soil in which the Jacobin gospel that had arisen late in the eighteenth century could flourish:

> Like Saint Paul the Jacobins promised a new creature who would be "led by the spirit" and would not be "under the law." But . . . this transformation was to be achieved by the revolutionary act of emancipation from authority. There was to be no dark night of the soul for each person in the labor of his own regeneration.[6]

---

[5]Schneider, pp. 142-143.
[6]Walter Lippmann, *The Public Philosophy* (New York: Mentor Books, 1955), pp. 60-61.

This doctrine was brought to bear on education by Jean Jacques Rousseau and his followers. They asserted that education should provide a channel through which nature could work in the growth and development of the child. The best developed person, said they, is the natural person. Perversion was considered to be the result of yielding to forces contrary to nature.

The effect of this philosophy on mass education was a gradual deletion from the curriculum of those disciplines related to morals and faith. The primary thrust of education became the preparation of the individual for a successful career. The natural goodness which was to be the result of this natural education would take care of everything else.

The men who were responsible for the great reaction which came at the end of the nineteenth century had little regard for traditional thought. They intended to attack bigotry and superstition, but in the process they "threw out the baby with the bath." Following the lead of Nietzsche, the secular existentialists of the twentieth century with Jean Paul Sartre as their principal spokesman have done away with God and have placed upon man the burden of giving meaning to life. By so doing, they have "done away not only with God the Father but with the recognition that beyond our private worlds there is a public world to which we all belong."[7]

As a result of the shift in man's view of himself and the relinquishing of his belief in what had previously been self-evident truths, two changes in governmental power took place. First, either by coincidence or in cause-and-effect relationship, the acceptance of the new philosophies and the rapid enfranchisement of the masses developed together. The combination led to a belief that:

> The meaning of free government was the dictatorship of the majority.
> Thus, freedom ceased to be the polestar of the human mind. . . .
> After 1870 or thereabouts men thought instinctively . . . in terms of organization, authority, and collective power.[8]

With the assurance that his natural goodness was sufficient to sustain him in his community, man rejected as undue restrictions the laws which regulated the obligations inherent in his liberty. But because men are not gods, they cannot live without law based upon truth which transcends opinion. To make up the deficiency, increased organization and faith in public opinion were substituted for individual acceptance of responsibility with respect for law. The results have been a catastrophic "derange-

---

[7]Lippmann, *The Public Philosophy*, p. 124.
[8]Lippmann, *The Good Society*, p. 47.

ment of the true functions of power and an enfeeblement, verging on paralysis, of the capacity to govern."[9]

A second effect of the shifting philosophy of the nineteenth century has to do with the relegation of the law to economics. With the consolidation of economic power a keen interest arose in throwing off political restraint. As a result, "economic . . . power has become a significant coercive force of modern society. Either it defies the authority of the state or it bends the institutions of the state to its purposes."[10] Both the dictatorship of public opinion and the supremacy of economics have worked toward an unhealthy stereotyping of opinion.

Thus, we have come to a situation in which strong government is preferable to free government. The masses vascillate between the fear of losing their rights and the desire to be relieved by arbitrary leadership of the responsibility of governing. Public opinion born of this vascillation has emerged as the prevailing force. Much lip-service has been paid to preserving the "American way of life," but there seems to be no clear definition of what is to be preserved. The directing force of civilization seems to be a fear of disaster which seeks to preserve the twilight zone that is the *status quo* rather than a strong conviction based on the public philosophy.

Since public opinion is the prevailing force, those who have private thoughts contrary to it usually keep such thoughts to themselves. Gone is the quest for truth that fostered dialogue through which men could discover laws to form the basis of good government. Abroad in the land is a notion that each man has a right to whatever private beliefs comprise truth for him. This notion has given rise to an assumption that any search for truth of public significance would be futile. The critical question is how modern man can rediscover and espouse that truth upon which all men by virtue of their humanity will tend to agree.

III.

Considerations in renewal of the public philosophy. If the public philosophy is to be renewed, dialogue between individuals and groups of differing points of view must be reopened. The modern spirit of tolerance of all things with no clear definition of what is being tolerated has brought about an appalling vagueness of positions. Because of the high premium placed on pseudo-intellectual respectability and upon the relativity of all things moral, people are afraid to commit themselves to

---

[9]Lippmann, *The Public Philosophy,* p. 19.
[10]Reinhold Niebuhr, *Moral Man and Immoral Society* (New York: Charles Scribner's Sons, 1932), pp. 14-15.

any definite position. Without some commitment, there can be no dialogue, and without dialogue there can be no testing of ideas and clear formulation of thought. The reopening of rational dialogue must take place before any meaningful return to those principles which embody truth and transcend differences can take place.

If dialogue is to be productive, the participants must have availed themselves of information which can lend content to the debate. Otherwise, dialogue will degenerate into that ambiguous inertia which results from groups intoxicated with the idea that discussion *per se* is the panacea for finding solutions to human problems. The kind of information which is needed for significant dialogue has been summed up by Toynbee:

> Neither the human race nor any member of it can afford to ignore the present human situation. We must cope with it if we are not to destroy ourselves; in order to cope with it we must understand it; and trying to understand it commits each and all of us to making some acquaintance with at least three vast realms of knowledge; a knowledge of non-human nature; a knowledge of human nature; and a knowledge of the characters and histories of the local and temporary cultures . . . that man has created and transmitted and modified and discarded in the course of the ages.[11]

This statement implies broader and deeper requirements of education than most people assign to it or attempt to derive from it. Certainly it points out the need for education to extend far beyond the twelve to sixteen years usually given over to formal education. The constant rise of automation has increased the number of leisure hours available to adults. It is, therefore, feasible to expect that man will avail himself of greater understanding. But he must actively realize that (1) the study of man is more important than the study of matter and (2) the search for truth is more satisfying than ephemeral sensory titillation. Otherwise, there is little hope that he will be any better off than before.

Paradoxically, the lessening of the number of hours needed for earning a living has not as yet produced a more relaxed and reflective humanity. Since the increase of leisure has come simultaneously with the great emphasis on economic power and the worship of sensory pleasure, man has thrown himself into a more frenzied, less reflective existence than ever before. Those things which are by nature economic, empirical, and tangible have been crowned with supreme value. The position of the intangible has been described by Niebuhr as follows:

---

[11]Arnold J. Toynbee, "*Education: The Long Views,*" *Saturday Review,* XLIII (November 19, 1960), p. 76.

> . . . all the highest ideals and tenderest emotions which men have
> felt through the ages . . . seem from our perspective to be something
> of a luxury. . . . We live in an age in which personal moral idealism
> is easily accused of hypocrisy and frequently deserves it. It is an age
> in which honesty is possible only when it skirts the edges of cynicism.
> All this is rather tragic. For what the individual conscience feels when
> it lifts itself above the world of nature and the system of collective
> relationships . . . is not a luxury but a necessity of the soul.[12]

The search for truth must be taken up if the public philosophy is to be
renewed.

IV.

The speech teacher's role and responsibility. We have surveyed briefly
the tremendous problems which stand in the way of a renewal of the
public philosophy. It behooves everyone who believes in liberal democracy and has some awareness of the current situation to try to make a
contribution to the revitalization of the public philosophy.

For the person involved in education, the challenge is overwhelming.
None but the most romantic idealist would assume that either he or his
field of instruction alone can make any great dent in the obstacles which
lie in the way of renewing the public philosophy. However, the field of
speech has as significant an opportunity to make a worthwhile contribution as any other discipline. The shifting of public thought has always
been dependent upon the communication of ideas by articulate persons.
Spoken words are forceful in a way that written words are not. To
ignore the spoken word, one must reduce the speaker to something
less than a person. In the making of this reduction, a basic universal law
is broken because personality is, by its nature, inviolate; and to ignore is
to violate passively. Ignoring the written word may, in a sense, amount
to the same thing. But the author is rarely present when his work is
being ignored, and his absence makes of him an abstraction which need
not be confronted. Hence, with the exception of action, which is the
most concrete form of expression, speech is the most powerful activating
force available to man.

Courses in speaking and writing have been as much the victims of
galloping specialization as have courses in any other discipline. As other
fields have become increasingly specialized in their content, the people
in speech have become increasingly alarmed about their alleged lack of
content. Among the attempts to solve this dilemma are two chief lines

---

[12]Niebuhr, pp. 276-277.

of action. One is to draw content from the study of form, usage, and meaning of words. The other approach, which was considered by Hunt to be the most effective, is to have work in communication given not separately but in conjunction with courses in general education. The objection to this approach has been that if teachers of speech tried it they would find themselves working in fields in which they would not be professionally competent. In answer to this objection, Hunt said:

> This never seemed to me a fatal objection. . . . If courses in general education are to include the greatest, most universal, most essential human preoccupations . . . then they should be within the range of interests and eventually of the competence of instructors in writing and speaking.[13]

The content of the courses in general education includes—in whatever context—the ideas on which the public philosophy is built. Students may, therefore, be expected to come to courses in public speaking with some raw materials for dialectic on subjects that are fundamental to the public philosophy. Emphasis in these courses should be placed on thinking through and articulating positions on significant issues; thus, the role of the speech teacher in the renewal of the public philosophy begins to emerge.

It would be foolish to assume that students are going to bring knowledge of the great ideal of liberal democracy from, say, their history class into the speech class; select from their learnings a topic such as "The True Nature of Liberty"; and, as a result of their work in speech, come up with the inviolability of man as a basic premise. Given students steeped in the patterns of a culture which has departed from the public philosophy, only the teacher who is blind to the complexities of the problem could expect such a progression. If a student should exhibit such apparent progress toward the goal, one would have to assume that either shallow hypocrisy or other influences had been at work along with the speech course.

What is possible in speech courses is that students bring to class information which they may have memorized for a test or hopefully have been led to think about in their general liberal arts courses. In the speech class they should be expected to make speeches using some of this material having universal human significance. In preparing and making speeches, students should be expected to develop some sensitivity to ethical values. As they work through the process of selecting topics and preparing speeches, they should be brought to define and assess

---

[13]Everett Lee Hunt, "Rhetoric and General Education," *Quarterly Journal of Speech*, XXXV (October 1949), 277.

their own values. Given the conditions that (1) our educational system is dependent on teacher and text for truth and (2) it is taboo for the teacher to lay his own moral judgments before his students, a student may proceed through his entire educational career without defining his own position on any matter of either public or private significance. If he does not arrive at some defined positions on significant issues, he will never become a responsible citizen.

Before the student can responsibly define and express his position on any issue which has significance for him, he must overcome some of the prevalent pressures which impel him toward making a calculated guess at majority opinion and joining the herd. To give him some help with this problem, the speech teacher should seek to cut away fear of dialectic by making it necessary for students to defend the statements they make.

By creating a situation in which the student must try to think through and form some conclusions about even one or two significant problems, the teacher of speech can help him toward responsible citizenship. The person who never learns to think his way through to some position on issues of importance fails to assume the responsibility which goes with freedom. People with this kind of responsibleness are imperative to the life and health of a liberal democracy.

Another facet of the role which the speech teacher may have in the renewal of the public philosophy is in his attempt to re-create what Rice called the "questing curiosity"[14] which children bring to kindergarten and frequently lose shortly thereafter. Encouraging dialectic and challenging unquestioned obedience to verbal and written symbols is one way in which the teacher may work toward this goal. Also, questions should be raised which will sharpen the student's awareness of his world and, hence, increase the scope and intensity of his interest in that world. The Jacobin philosophy eliminated the inner struggles which must take place within man before he can obtain his true humanity. It thus led to the assumption that any morality that might conceivably not be intrinsic to man's nature could be absorbed from his culture by some process akin to osmosis. This notion has been proven by experience to be a fallacy. The problem and the responsibility for its solution belong to our educational institutions:

> Helping each generation to discover the meaning of liberty [and] justice . . . is a perennial task of any society. . . . One of the most difficult problems we face is to make it possible for young people to

---

[14]George P. Rice Jr., "The Teacher and Political Morality," *Vital Speeches of The Day,* XVIII (November 15, 1951), 79.

participate in the great tasks of their time. We have designed our society in such a way that most of the possibilities open to adolescents are
either bookish or frivolous. And all too often we do not evoke his moral
strivings. The best we can do is to invite him to stand sentinel over a
dry reservoir.

Instead . . .we should be telling them the grim and bracing truth
that it is their task to re-create those values continuously in their own
behavior facing the dilemmas and catastrophes of their own time.[15]

By requiring the student to take what he has learned from book and
lecture and put it in the practical social context, the speech teacher may
start him on the way to fulfilling this task.

If speech courses are to turn out students who can be expected to
make some active contribution, the courses should help them gain a
better command of the tools of oral communication. Without extraordinary natural ability, students cannot be expected to produce speeches
of Churchillian eloquence after one or two semesters of speech. However,
they should have gained a conception of what eloquence is and should
have learned to view it as something for which to strive. Since there is
a dearth of artistic use of language in most contemporary speeches, some
study of the great speeches in history should be included.

In speech courses some attempts should be made to bring the student
to an awareness of the complex problem of finding a universal language
in this age of specialization. Ours is a culture which has become so highly
specialized that each academic discipline has developed its own technical
language. The barriers which are created by this condition are more
subtle but almost as great as the barriers which exist between people who
cannot speak the same tongue. If, as has been suggested, courses in
speech are seen as related to courses in other fields, then speech as a discipline may ultimately have the catalytic effect upon technical language
which is needed to minimize the barriers. Because the renewal of the public philosophy is largely dependent upon communication among people
with widely varying perspectives and interests, anything which can be
done to remove barriers to communication will be of positive significance.
Although speech teachers alone are not going to remove these existing
barriers, they can be of real service if they can produce in students an
awareness of the language problem and one or two embryonic ideas
concerning its solution.

Finally, the person who is working to help bring about a renewal of
the public philosophy should be a good receiver as well as a good transmitter in the communicative process. The speech teacher should strive

---

[15]John W. Gardner, "Moral Decay and Renewal," *Saturday Review* XLVI
(December 14, 1963), 18.

to help students listen to and evaluate speeches which they hear. Many speeches heard in class and throughout life will be almost, if not entirely, devoid of information, exhortation, inspiration, or any other worthwhile reason for presentation. Because of this condition, the habit of not listening to speeches is prevalent. However, the responsible citizen should learn to keep his attention on what is being said. If it is devoid of significance, he ought to know why. Besides, once a person becomes entrenched in the habit of turning off his attention after the first three minutes, he may miss some content which is of value. The responsible citizen is the alert citizen.

V.

Summary and conclusion. It is difficult to see objectively the age of which we are a part. The best we can do is to try to discern and evaluate present trends in the light of those historical events which have brought us to the present. In this essay a limited attempt has been made at such a discernment and evaluation. Since the last half of the nineteenth century the trend of the prevailing philosophies has been away from what we have been calling the public philosophy. If these philosophies continue to prevail, the decline of Western society, which has been based on the public philosophy, will continue. Since philosophies are born of philosophers and since philosophers are sometimes bred in our educational institutions, the future of the public philosophy may depend upon the teachers who work in those institutions.

In the field of speech the key words are information, dialogue, and articulation. Without proper information the process of communication becomes shallow and hypocritical. Who has not sat in a lecture hall, political convention, or church and heard popular cliches of the day strung together in empty sequence only to come away with the feeling that the speaker did not really know what he was talking about and hence said nothing? Words and phrases are the stuff upon which much communication must depend; but if the user of words has not taken the trouble to make concrete, insofar as is necessary for his own understanding, the words and phrases which he uses, there will be little or no communication.

Dialogue is the tempering fire for information and opinion. Lippmann said: "The highest laws are those upon which all rational men of good will, when fully informed, will tend to agree."[16] But how shall valid agreement be reached without dialogue? Dialogue is difficult be-

---

[16]Lippmann, *The Public Philosophy*, p. 123.

cause it requires that people commit themselves. When one makes a commitment, he exposes himself and his position to the possibility of rejection. Rejection is rarely a sought-after experience, but some rejection is imperative in the pursuit of truth. Dialogue ultimately involves a struggle with one's fellows and with one's own thoughts. That dialogue which seeks truth is difficult because it requires faith in the existence of truth and in the possibility of man's finding it.

Articulation is imperative to community: "In the maintenance and formation of a true community the articulate philosophy is, one might say, like the thread which holds the pieces of the fabric together."[17] The man who can use words but has no informed basis for his words will have little to contribute toward the renewal of the public philosophy. The man who is informed but inarticulate may have something to contribute, but what he has to give may be lost because of his lack of communicative ability. The public philosophy is *ipso facto* a community affair. Thus, the informed person who has the courage to participate creatively in dialogue and the ability to articulate ideas distilled through this process will be best equipped to propagate it.

As speech teachers work with the legions of students who pass through their classrooms each year, they should seek to bring them to to a good beginning in pulling together these three areas of information, dialogue, and articulation. Herein lies a distinctive and significant contribution to the renewal of the public philosophy.

EXERCISES

1. Define speech as an academic discipline. In what ways is it similar or dissimilar to activities found in other disciplines?
2. Can speech training be effectively offered in typically nonspeech courses? List five disciplines which might effectively employ speech activities as a learning tool. Suggest a minimum of three activities they might engage in.
3. Define speech education. How does your definition compare with lay definitions? Can you account for the difference?
4. Speech instruction may be content or performance oriented. Describe the proper proportionment of learner performance and lecture-discussion periods. Do you believe instruction in theory or performance is of more importance?
5. Why is training in speech necessary to today's youth? Describe the correlation, if any, between success in professional and personal life and instruction in speech.

---

[17]Lippmann, *The Public Philosophy*, p. 104.

6. What problems do you foresee with fellow teachers or administrators concerning the relevance of speech to the total school curriculum? How will you answer their questions?
7. Should speech training be required of all students? Why?
8. List the essential ideas, concepts, principles and skills you believe a student should acquire in the basic speech course. Can you expect reasonable retention of these goals by students? Are these "essentials" commensurate with educational psychology and behavioral objectives?
9. If training in speech did not exist, would students be any the less for it?
10. Describe all the doubts you have concerning speech instruction.
11. How may your local, regional and national speech associations influence the discipline of speech? To what extent should each teacher of speech participate in the activities of such organizations?
12. What Greco-Roman influences are visible in speech education today? How do these influences affect an understanding of speech and its instruction?
13. Is it necessary that speech be thought of as a distinct and separate academic discipline? Where do you view speech in today's secondary school?
14. Should speech education be offered in the elementary school? In what ways can the elementary school teacher foster oral communication in her classroom?
15. What, if any, are the distinguishing differences that exist between introductory speech courses on the secondary and collegiate level?

PROJECTS

1. Examine the curriculum guidelines of fifteen high schools within your state. Choose five schools located in small communities, five medium sized, and five from large city schools. What courses are offered in speech? Do any of the schools require training in speech? How many electives may a student choose in speech? Did you find any differences in the amount or kind of courses offered in relation to the size of school? What accounts for this?
2. Secure a list of individuals having recieved instruction in speech within the past two years. Interview these individuals. Ask each to describe the advantages and/or disadvantages speech instruction has had for him. Build a small quiz and test their retention of essen-

tial speech concepts and principles. In light of your data evaluate and justify the training in speech these individuals received.

3. Visit a local college or high school and discuss with the teacher of speech the following question: "If you were to begin your teacher training anew, what would you do differently?"

4. Attend a local P. T. A. meeting (or its equivalent) and suggest to several parents that what is needed in their school curriculum are additional teachers of speech and language. Describe to your classmates the opinions and statements of those you interview. Describe and interpret the implications of their remarks.

5. Conduct a survey of several teachers in a local high school who do not teach speech to determine the extent speech related activities are practiced or employed in their classrooms. If considerable oral activity is evidenced, justify the need for a course or teacher of speech.

Chapter 2

Teaching,
Teaching Strategies,
and the Teacher of Speech

Often educational researchers upon data analysis expand their findings into universals generalizable to every learner and learning climate. While certain principles of learning or methodologies may be generalizable to many classrooms, each teacher nonetheless must question and evaluate research in terms of its suitability and applicability to his course subject matter, students, teaching style and ability. While hypothesizing generalizations to the whole is the principle occupation of the theoretician, putting theory into practice remains the province of the teacher.

The most difficult challenge a teacher faces is the necessity for constantly examining, testing, and (potentially) incorporating methodologies, strategies, and materials coming to his attention via research monographs or hearsay. All teachers seeking a philosophy of education which best facilitates the learning process engage in this endeavor. There are, however, many pitfalls into which the unwary teacher may fall if he does not exercise the greatest of care. A word of caution is noted. The first premise any teacher in search of improved teaching methodologies must agree to is that the learner comes first. Students are learners, not guinea pigs. Secondly, teachers must not allow their search for better teaching methodologies to be dictated out of a need to reduce whatever boredom or difficulty they might perceive. Such a light-hearted search is unlikely to engender pedagogical advantages for the learner. The facilitation of learning demands that attention be attuned to the needs, problems, aspirations and general education of the learner—not to an easing of one's work load.

There is a vast amount of literature classified under the genre of "education." The amount of research and reporting in education is staggering. The number of magazines, books, and scholarly journals produced each month concerned in one form or another with the learning process almost precludes an editorial attempt to collate in one chapter sample readings describing the learning and teaching processes. Rather than insert an *apologia,* the editor wishes to make clear that the readings which follow suggest a logical framework upon which a teacher-in-training may begin to build a foundation of knowledge leading to a better understanding of the teaching and learning processes.

William Clark Trow, "Role Functions of the Teacher in the Instructional Group," notes with disappointment that while research investigating the nature of the individual abounds, there is an apalling lack of experimental data reporting the dynamics of social interaction characteristic of an instructional group. While in recent years educational researchers have made a concerted effort to close this gap, there is still much to be learned. Trow structures the concept of these interrelationships and clarifies some of the principle concepts that are of prime importance in education.

Without reducing the concepts of interpersonal relationships to absurdity, these interrelationships may be tentatively classified as personality, position, role and skill. Personality in the generic sense is "the generalized aspects of the characteristic response-patterns of an individual, whether native or acquired, and however they may be socially or morally evaluated." Position refers to an individual(s) particular place (in respect to time) in a particular system. Behavior which is expected of an individual is known as that individual's role. Skill is the ability of an individual to perform well some complex behavior.

Trow's theme is that an effective facilitator of learning is influenced by not only teaching skill (*technē*) but personality, role factors, and extra-class roles as well. All teachers are participants in roles such as faculty member, liaison officer and learner. Trow explains how each of these roles affect a teacher's behavior in the classroom, and emphasizes that the teacher-in-training must not only be prepared to meet such roles but understand their influences upon his instructional style.

The administrative and executive roles of disciplinarian, measurer and record-keeper, learning aids officer, and program director are analyzed independently, distinguishing their respective skills and responsibilities. Each of the teacher's roles quickens questions that must of necessity be answered, and carried effectively and efficiently into practice. For upon the posture of the teacher and the learning climate generated by his influence the efficacy of instruction balances.

Teachers exist in our culture out of respect for their knowledge and ability to transmit their learning to society's children. While at times it may be necessary to act as janitor, baby-sitter, or clerical help in order to insure a maximum learning environment or experience, the superstructure of our educational system is based upon the instructional roles of the teacher. Instructional roles may be classified and differentiated as evaluator, adapter, resource person, and motivator. Each of these tasks require of the teacher distinct pedagogical approaches and techniques.

Many conscientious and dedicated teachers, however, fail as effective facilitators of learning because they misperceive the functions or requirements of one or more roles demanded of them. Trow examines a few of the conditions which confound a teacher's role perception, and offers corallary information by which teachers-in-training may avoid such mistaken identity. To do so, he analyzes the root cause of perception discrepancies affecting role behavior.

The background of the teacher often colors his perceptions in such a manner as to make an objective analysis of another's cultural background and the problems related to it most difficult. Many teachers fail to appreciate the significance of this fact. The organizational climate initiated and formulated by the school administration may, likewise, influence the teacher's role perception and the learning climate within the instructional group. Student and teacher expectations are also of major import since instructors and learners have, unfortunately, come to stereotype each other's behavior. There is, after all, nothing sacrosanct about these roles. Finally, the teacher's personality will be received differently by each member of the instructional group. There is a potential for evoking either hostile or genuinely warm reactions toward the facilitator of learning. Trow concludes his paper by suggesting means by which teachers-in-training may be adequately trained to meet these role functions.

Harry S. Broudy, "Two Exemplars of Teaching Method," confines his discussion of instructional modes to that of rhetorical and dialectical. Socrates, an anti-sophist, employed dialectical instruction while such notables as Isocrates and Quintilian have been equated with rhetorical instruction.

Rhetorical instruction, born out of sophistry, was employed to teach young men in Greece to speak well before the courts and assemblies. Basically, the study of oratory at this time involved (1) analyzing literature as models for speech composition and (2) instruction in the art of speech writing and speaking.

Rhetorical instruction had for this time certain virtues as a method. First, it was most definite. The teacher was always sure of where he was since everything was taught in systems and categories. Secondly, rhetorical instruction exploited the reliability of habituation: practice and imitation played a central theme. Thirdly, as a formal discipline it prepared individuals for the type of situations they would likely encounter.

Such a teaching strategy, however, probably has little relevance for the modern educator since it is not suitable for the development of thinking. Analysis will indicate that the objective of rhetorical instruction was to make thinking unnecessary. In reviewing rhetorical instruction we may say of it that it was completely methodized, without ambiguity, and capable of replication.

The dialectical instruction of Socrates was quite different. Put in a time perspective we might conclude that the pattern of motivation was different. Socrates, the personification of the generation gap of his day, had to convince his followers of the saneness of abandoning conventional attitudes and commitments. This he did by exhortation and self-examination, as is apparent in the *Apology* and *Protagoras* respectively.

"The Socratic dialogue or dialectic was a joint logical venture into a problem of proper definition and soul therapy." In this vein Socrates, unlike rhetoricians, was attempting to prepare individuals for citizenry by placing a heavy relevance upon philosophical training as opposed to eloquence. He felt that logical critical thinking was more important than simply modeling speakers into persuasive elements.

Central to dialectical instruction was the necessity of the learners awareness of his own ignorance. With this starting point the outcome sought was a manner of feeling and thinking. The learner had to be, in effect, jolted into anger with both himself and his mentor. Dialectical instruction accomplished this by openly criticizing those values, mores and opinions held by the learner and regarded as beyond disbelief.

Carl R. Rogers, "The Interpersonal Relationship in the Facilitation of Learning," sketches another approach to teaching. Rogers advocates utilization of the dynamics of interpersonal communication possible between teacher and learner. This, Rogers suggests, is central to the facilitation of learning.

The article will sharply arouse the reader's attention by boldly announcing "teaching, in my estimation, is a vastly over-rated function." To Rogers the traditional conception of teaching raises all the wrong questions, such as "What shall we teach?" "What needs to be known?" "What shall the course cover?" Rather, since it may be said of man that he lives in a state of environmental flux, the types of questions asked and the goals sought should be the "facilitation of change and learning." Teachers must assist individuals in how to learn, to adapt and change. Students must become cognizant that a reliance upon process instead of inert knowledge is the real mark of an educated man.

There are many who may take exception to Rogers' essay. To the old tried-and-true-formula teacher it may be a bitter pill. The life style, educational philosophy and classroom climate of Rogers conception of the facilitation of learning cannot be indexed and catagoried by a systems analysis expert. At times the unleashing of learner curiosity and creativity—as Rogers advocates—may result in seeming havoc and chaos. The classroom must not be thought of as a sterile, neatly arranged row of desks occupied by submissive, unchallenged minds. Interpersonal relationships between the teacher and learners demand that the classroom be viewed as a community of learners.

The essay cites evidence documenting the effectiveness of such instruction. Many student reactions to Rogerian instruction are included as indices of learner opinions toward such methodology. But most important, in the editor's opinion, is Rogers' outline of the characteristics and attributes necessary in becoming a facilitator of learning.

First, the facilitator of learning must be a real and genuine person. Learners irregardless of I.Q. are extremely adept at spotting phonies. The facilitator of learning in entering into interpersonal communication with a learner must be himself, unabashedly honest at showing his feelings, attitudes, and emotions, when appropriate to the encounter.

Secondly, the facilitator of learning must be capable of prizing (non-possessive caring, accepting) and trusting the learner. The facilitator must be capable of recognizing the learner as an individual of worth, possessing attitudes, feelings and emotions toward the instructor, his classmates, course subject matter and other pertinent variables which may affect the learning outcome of the student. The facilitator of learning can accept these feelings. "The facilitator's prizing or acceptance of the learner is an operational expression of his essential confidence and trust in the capacity of the human organism."

Thirdly, the facilitator of learning must be capable of empathic understanding. Empathic understanding is the ability to project oneself into the position of another individual: reacting, feeling, and thinking much the same about things as that other individual. The facilitator must be sensitive to the needs, values, beliefs and feelings of the learner. As the reader is surely aware, there is little else as annoying as a teacher paying lip service to your questions and/or problems with a reply such as "Well, I know how you feel." Students readily recognize such banter and pay it little heed, but when they honestly believe a teacher wishes to and can understand, a tremendous releasing effect may follow, causing the learner to be more eager to learn.

Rogers closes his article with citations of evidence supporting his thesis.

Wallen and Travers "Relationship of some Teaching Methods To Some Principles of Learning," and W. J. McKeachie, "Research on Teaching Methods" relate the findings of current thought and research to instructional methodologies and principles of learning. In short briefs they outline the findings of experiments designed to test various relationships and variables in the teaching and learning process. Each article is extremely valuable in measuring the relative strength of one's educational philosophy. These two articles ought to be studied carefully.

Wallen and Travers develop six principles of learning and demonstrate the limitation of most teaching methods in meeting these principles. The six principles developed are not extensive in the sense that they are comprehensive of the accepted principles of learning. The authors have purposely limited their discussion to six in order to illustrate their thesis.

The first principle examined is "Behavior which represents achievement or partial achievement of an educational objective should be reinforced." Secondly, "The introduction of cues which arouse motivation toward the achievement of an educational objective will increase the effectiveness with which that objective is achieved." The third principle discussed, particularly significant to teachers of speech is "practice in applying a principle to the solutions of problems will increase the probability of transfer of training to new problems which require the use of the same principle for solution." Fourth, "Since learners differ in their capacity to make the responses required, learning will be most efficient if it is planned so that each learner embarks on a program commensurate with his capacity to acquire new responses." Principle five is that "If a pupil has had training in imitation, then he is capable of learning by observing demonstration of skills to be acquired." The final principle under observation is "The learner will learn more efficiently if he makes the response to be learned than if he learns by observing another make the response or make some related response."

The objective, suggest Wallen and Travers, of developing instructional methodologies and strategies should be to incorporate and make use of as many and as wide a scope of learning principles as possible. Only then may we hold final allegiance to a teaching method.

McKeachie's article "Research On Teaching Methods" reviews research conducted on the effectiveness of lecturing techniques, discussion, laboratory, project methods, independent study, and automated techniques. McKeachie develops his analysis by illustrating differences between (1) lecture versus discussion (2) time distribution of lecture and discussion (3) lecture versus automation (4) methods of lecturing

(5) student-centered versus instructor-centered (6) variations in teaching by discussion (7) homogeneous versus heterogeneous grouping (8) automation (9) television and others. Rather than review McKeachie's conclusions the editor leaves that opportunity to the reader.

Samuel L. Becker and Carl A. Dallinger, "The Effects of Instructional Methods Upon Achievement and Attitudes in Communication Skills," asks the following questions of the discipline of speech: "(1) Can we compensate for limitations in the preparation of instructors, provide better 'on the job' training for staff members, and raise the level of instruction in communication skills courses by utilizing experts to present the basic principles of communication to students? (2) Can we maximize the use of instructional resources by making each student more directly responsible for his own training, without reducing the quality of the education he receives?"

In an attempt to sufficiently answer these questions three methods of teaching communication skills were tested experimentally to determine their effectiveness. The methods studied were (1) instructor responsible for dispensing content areas, (2) a self-study program presented in bibliographic form, and (3) the "kinescope method."

Becker and Dallinger clearly state the procedural methodologies employed to test their hypotheses. The results of their experiment are most interesting in that they suggest students are equally capable of acquiring a knowledge of communication and communication skills when exposed to each of the teaching methods. It appeared to the experimenters that the bibliographic method was the most efficient while remaining equally effective as a means of instruction.

Balcer and Seabury, "The Teacher of Speech," describe the attributes and qualifications of effective teachers of speech. This essay, reprinted from *Teaching Speech in Today's Secondary Schools,* presents an excellent overview of desirable teacher behaviors and illustrates that the success of a speech education program in high school is largely dependent upon the teacher of speech. Activities, students, principle, or modern equipment are poor substitutes for an able teacher. The teacher, after all, determines the socio-emotional climate of the classroom and the efficacy of learning which ensues.

Balcer and Seabury in outlining behaviors characteristic of competent teachers, cite a study by Hart indicating teacher behaviors thought most effective and ineffective by high school students. A faculty panel is also cited which came to common agreement as to what facilitators of learning must be able to demonstrate as effective teachers. These attributes were (1) a sense of mission (2) love of people (3) love of his work (4) intellectual honesty (5) thorough knowledge of his subject (6) a nonauthoritarian attitude (7) understanding of students, and (8) the ability to create student interest.

The opinions of school principals concerning what constitutes an effective teacher of speech demonstrate administrative practicalities occasionally overlooked by teachers. Some of the qualities sought by administrators in teachers of speech are "(1) personability, (2) social competence (3) liberally and professionally educated (4) an ability to motivate students (5) enthusiasm for teaching (6) the maintenance of professional standards."

Balcer and Seabury also discuss factors guiding administrative policy decisions involving the teacher of speech. Since administrators obviously have the right to inquire as to a teachers attitudes, capabilities, potentials, opinions and conception of the discipline of speech, the teacher of speech must be capable of answering such inquiries intelligently and eruditely. Some of the typical questions asked by administrators are (1) "What is your philosophy of speech and speech education?" (2) "How does speech act as an integral part of the total school curriculum?" (3) "What do you believe are the effects of speech and speech standards upon learners, parents, etc.?" (4) "How are you qualified for the position of teacher of speech?" and many other questions demanding careful prior analysis and consideration from the teacher of speech.

Summarizing, Balcer and Seabury demonstrate to the reader the necessity for fulfilling certain qualifications, having an aptitude and feeling for teaching speech, and finally, possessing the ability to communicate effectively an educational philosophy concerning a great number of items relative to teaching and the learning process.

Frederick W. Haberman tackles a proposition which has eluded definition by many educators in speech. In his article "Toward The Ideal Teacher of Speech" Haberman attempts to classify those behaviors and attributes characteristic of an "ideal" teacher of speech. The educational philosophies and methodological strategies of instruction which abound and are espoused by teachers of speech vary so greatly as to make nearly impossible a consensus as to what constitutes an "ideal" teacher of speech. All of us, hopefully, aspire to that somewhat nebulous nomination, but do so under teaching frameworks often more characteristic of chaos and confusion than perfected methods, materials, and philosophies.

If a teacher evaluation scale were available so as to measure Haberman's ideal teacher of speech it might reveal him a "middle of the road" teacher basing his subject matter and instructional methodologies on sound pedagogical principles. Here, in the editors opinion, lies the significance of Haberman's article. He has not outlined rarified attributes capable of practice by only spiritual leaders or automated robots. Rather, Haberman suggests that any teacher can become an "ideal" teacher of speech. "Ideal," therefore is not used in the singular sense to connote oneness or some unobtainable model of perfection. Such descriptive effort, perhaps, would be of interest to the philosopher but extremely futile to the teacher trying to improve his teaching.

The teaching of speech offers challenges to the teacher perhaps unparalleled by any other discipline or occupation. It is from these challenges and opportunities that Haberman has inferred the necessary qualities an ideal teacher of speech should possess. Perhaps the most challenging contribution a teacher of speech can make is the furtherance of a student's intellectual integrity. A moment's reflection upon the intellectual process involved in writing and delivering a speech— the movement from irrelative lines of thought to an integrated speech— demonstrates how close a speech teacher is to the crucial moments of creativity exhibited by learners.

The teacher of speech contributes as well to the psychological adjustment of the learner. Many students are totally unprepared for speaking in public. These students are very much aware, however, of the importance of making a good impression, competition, saying things intelligently, and of course, the symptoms of stage fright. In short, hundreds of seemingly unconnected factors may bombard the thinking and nervous system of the student while preparing his first speech. This first speech, as with all subsequent speeches, constitutes a major stepping-stone in the maintenance of psychological integrity. To be able to stand before an audience and speak one's own thoughts, with one's own voice, and exhibition of one's own body is a major accomplishment. More than simple tension release overcomes the speaker completing his initial public presentation. A sense of pride and accomplishment flood his senses. To the extent, then, that the teacher of speech has positively affected the learner's progress at communicating orally, he will have afforded the learner invaluable aid in the solidification of his psychological adjustment.

In addition, Haberman suggests, the teacher of speech contributes to the development of stylistic awareness. Words have such a utilitarian purpose to so many that the significance, beauty, and meaning of words are often misunderstood and/or ill-used. The teacher of speech in stressing the importance of style and its relationship to the communicative act, may evoke in his learners a new awareness of the creative process and implications for the manipulation of language.

The teacher of speech provides as well direction in developing skills important in personal, social, and national life. Isocrates was not far off when he equated public speaking and the ability to communicate effectively with preparation for citizenship. This proposition holds true today. No individual in a society as great and as complex as ours should be "handicapped" by inarticulation, slovenly delivery, or the inability to order and structure ideas in a clear and logical manner. Training in speech aids an individual to function unfearful of the inability to express his ideas, opinions, feelings or desires effectively to other members of society. Speech training viewed in this context is indispensable to the intellectual, psychological, and social growth of our citizenry.

In recognizing this, Haberman drew from the aforementioned benefits and potentials of speech training, characteristics typical of an "ideal" teacher of speech. Haberman cleverly summarizes his paper by hesitating to offer comment upon whether the posture of his "ideal" teacher of speech can be realized. Let it suffice to say it should.

Role Functions of the Teacher in the Instructional Group

WILLIAM CLARK TROW

Psychological studies of educational processes have, until recently, related primarily to the nature and behavior of the individual. Inferences from the animal laboratory have helped interpret his learning and, from the clinic, his personality, while measurement devices have been invented to quantify various aspects of his basic reaction patterns, his capacities, his growth, and his academic achievement. Such studies must be continued, for there is much that we still need to know in all these areas. But investigations based on the obvious fact that education is a matter of social interaction have tended to lag behind the others.

The reason for this lag may well be ascribed to the early lack of an adequate conceptual framework. Such contributions as the "group-minded theory," expounded by LeBon[1] and others, and Trotter's[2] "instincts of the herd" were stimulating but inadequate. More recent sociological concepts of the society, the culture, the organization, and the group, with the subsumed role, position, and status, and their related psychological concepts of attitude and personality have made possible a scientific study of group processes. Implications for education[3] began to appear as investigations explored the regularities and variations in group climate, cohesiveness, control, and leadership, and the conditions influencing communication, decision-making, social locomotion, and conformity. The results obtained from these investigations clarify the number of educational tasks and have already begun to have an important influence on matters of discipline and pupil adjustment as well as on instructional procedures. They can undoubtedly make further contributions to the teacher-education program in general and to educational psychology in particular if the latter is viewed, as it should be, as the study and practice of social as well as individual psychology in an educational setting.

From *Dynamics of Instructional Groups* NSSE yearbook, Part II, 1960. pp. 30-50.

[1]Gustave LeBon, *The Crowd: A Study of the Popular Mind.* London: T. Fisher Unwin, 1896.

[2]Wilfred Trotter, *Instincts of the Herd in Peace and War.* London: T. Fisher Unwin, 1917.

[3]William Clark Trow, Alvin E. Zander, William C. Morse, and David H. Jenkins, "Psychology of Group Behavior: The Class as a Group," *Journal of Educational Psychology,* XIL (October, 1950), 322-38.

INDIVIDUAL AND SOCIAL PSYCHOLOGY IN EDUCATION—
FOUR CONCEPTS

At the risk of oversimplification, four basic concepts will be used here to categorize certain interrelationships that are of prime significance in education. These are personality, position, role, and skill. Others derive from them or relate closely to them in one way or another, some of which are elaborated in other chapters of this yearbook.

Personality

While the term *personality* has many meanings, as Allport[4] and others have shown, it is here used in its generic meaning to refer to the generalized aspects of the characteristic response-patterns of an individual, whether native or acquired, and however they may be socially or morally evaluated. The response-patterns are generalized from what the individual has done, and therefore may be expected to do, under any given set of circumstances. In the vernacular, it is "what comes naturally." Various dimensions may be measured; for example, dominance-submission, anxiety-confidence, rigidity-flexibility, and extraversion-introversion.

Whatever dimensions are considered, personality is presumably based on genetic factors and derived from environmental identifications, sanctions, and conditionings. In the classroom it may be revealed by various kinds of teacher behavior—punitive, defensive, exacting, conciliatory, co-operative, and so on, which may reflect the influence of previous teachers and perhaps the theory and practice of the training program.

Position

The term *status* is sometimes used instead of *position*, though it is a narrower term and is better restricted to mean *location* in a prestige hierarchy. Position, according to Linton's generally accepted interpretation,[5] is a recognized place in a particular social system accorded to one or more individuals at a particular time with respect to that system. It implies a collection of duties, rights, privileges, and responsibilities. It may be one's social class, an office he holds, or membership in an organization, his identification with an institution or profession, or just a job. While a position is an objective fact, attitudes in regard to it may vary at least in one important respect, namely, that of prestige, social acceptability or desirability.

---

[4]Gordon W. Allport, *Personality: A Psychological Interpretation*, chap. ii. New York: Henry Holt & Co., 1937.
[5]Ralph Linton, *The Cultural Background of Personality*. New York: Appleton-Century Co., 1945.

The prestige hierarchy may be roughly measured by the amount of pay the position commands, the deference accorded it, or its ascribed value to the social system of which it is a part. Thus, if among the number of individuals it is known only that there is a congressman, a foreman, a surgeon, a millionaire, a teacher, a hobo, a mechanic, a day-laborer, a lawyer, a school superintendent, a salesman, and a college professor, most people would be able to rank them fairly easily in a prestige hierarchy. The rankings of different people might vary somewhat, and some judges would want to know more about them, as, for example, is the salesman of the door-to-door variety, or is he vice-president in charge of sales? In contrast, the position of the teacher is likely to have relatively low prestige in wealthy communities and relatively high prestige in more deprived areas where sometimes, in accord with the European tradition, few have received the benefits of higher education.

If position is thought of diagrammatically, not as a point on a vertical line but as a circle at one place or another on it, not only may the whole circle have a high or low prestige position but dots in it, representing persons, may have high- or low-ascribed status as compared with others in that circle or position. The factors that contribute to these differences are matters of sociometric choice and derive from the criteria that determine individual acceptance anywhere, such as age, seniority, training, personal attractiveness, friendliness, competence, and the like. But the vertical line of status ascription stops at the top of the circle that defines the individual's position. It will go higher only if he successfully affects a disguise of some sort, as some try to do "so as not to be taken for a schoolteacher." Social locomotion to a higher position is, of course, possible by marriage, acquired wealth, or some significant accomplishment.

Role

Role is the behavior expected of or characterisic of an individual in a given position. According to Sargent,[6] a person's role is the pattern or type of social behavior which seems to him appropriate in a given situation in view of the demands and expectations of those in his group. Or, as Linton[7] puts it, role is the sum total of the culture patterns associated with a particular position—the attitudes, values, and behavior ascribed by society to any and all persons as occupants of that position.

---

[6]S. Stansfield Sargent, "Conception of Role and Ego in Contemporary Psychology," in *Social Psychology at the Crossroads*, pp. 355-70. Edited by John H. Rohrer and Muzafer Sherif. New York: Harper & Bros., 1951.

[7]Linton, *op. cit.*

It is a pattern of activity—what a person has to do (or thinks he has to do) in order to validate his eligibility for the position he holds.

Group members may be a bit vague about the duties and responsibilities of a particular role, or there may be a difference of opinion among them, or between them and the individual concerned, as to what they are, thus leading to confusion and conflict. On the other hand, there may be rules of order or by-laws, which set forth clearly the duties of officers and committees and the rights and privileges of the membership, a plan which is usually followed in classrooms and student-body organizations where democratic processes are being taught. In industry there are often job analyses or job specifications. But in education, while there are plenty of suggestions or even directions, there is little concensus regarding the role of the teacher.

Confusion is likely if, as sometimes happens, the role is taken to refer to an individual instead of to a position. For example, John Doe may seem to have separate roles as a businessman, head of a family, lodge member, and committee chairman. Actually he has these positions, with more or less well-defined roles in each. As a businessman he may have the roles of hiring and firing, keeping accounts, and waiting on customers; as family member he is husband, younger children's playmate, older children's helper and adviser; as lodge member he may have the duties assigned to the role of treasurer; and as committee member he may play one of a number of informal, functional roles.

It is of advantage to be able to identify the group functional roles[8] for, although they grow out of individual personal characteristics, they suggest ways of perceiving individuals and of making group action more effective. Accordingly, they are delineated as:

1. *Group task roles*: initiator, contributor, information and opinion seeker and giver, elaborator, orienter, evaluator-critic, energizer, and procedural technician.
2. *Group building and maintenance roles*: encourager, harmonizer, gatekeeper, and expediter, standard-setter, group observer and follower.
3. *Individual negative roles*: aggressor, blocker, recognition-seeker, self-confessor, playboy, dominator, individual-help seeker, and special-interest pleader.

Most, if not all, of these roles are visible to those who look for them in faculty meetings, in committees, in student councils, and wherever matters have to be decided and actions taken.

---

[8]Kenneth D. Benne and Paul Sheats, "Functional Roles of Group Members," *Journal of Social Issues*, IV (Spring, 1948), 41-49.

We shall limit our discussion here to the roles of the teacher as teacher and not consider the roles of persons who are teachers in other positions, say as members of a family or of other groups. But, first, it is important to differentiate role and skill.

Skill

Skill refers to the degree of excellence with which a person performs some complex act. The criteria may be speed, precision, or, more generally, success in attaining individually or socially approved objectives. A skill may be quite an individual matter, as when a man goes into his back yard and shoots at a target. However, if he instructs his son in marksmanship, the situation changes—in his position as family member, he assumes the role of instructor. Whatever his skill in marksmanship, his skill as an instructor is not an individual matter but one of social interaction.

Most skills are themselves, in part at least, matters of social interaction between opponents or among participants, as in team games in which what one does depends on what others do. This seems to be a case of what Skinner[9] calls operant discrimination, in which only certain responses in certain contingencies are appropriate, and these, when reinforced, are learned. The instructor, in such situations, must not only develop the individual skills of the team members but must also teach them to perceive the contingencies or social cues and the way to respond to them. The formula is: Under these conditions, when you see this, do that. (For example, in basketball, when the other team has the ball, guard your man; i.e., when he runs off, take after him!)

Is a person who engages in some skillful activity merely practicing a skill, or is he playing a role? And in social situations, if he improves his skill so that he develops a more acceptable pattern of responses, does that mean that his personality has changed?

A nurse in training was rated sociometrically at the bottom of her class by her fellow trainees. Conferences with her revealed the nature of the behavior, which produced this result, as well as the causal factors. The nurse was not particularly happy about the situation, and the counselor suggested that, as a try-out, she greet her classmates in a cheerful way. He pointed out that talk about the weather, which irritated her, was an example, not of judgments of natural phenomena but of a means of social contact with others. She agreed to try and reported somewhat later that, at first, she felt silly but that the responses of the others were so different and so pleasant, she wanted to keep it up. At the

---

[9]B. F. Skinner, *Science and Human Behavior,* chap. vii. New York: Macmillan Co., 1953.

end of the year, her rating was well up in the middle range, well out of the rejectee category. As her role-playing gradually became her own role, and as she acquired a social skill, had her personality changed? Or had she merely developed more skill in the social role of her position as a student nurse?

Some college students objected to the practice of a group dynamics expert, complaining that he was trying to change their personalities. Presumably they came to college to learn, not to change! Is the teacher an instructor or actually a change agent? How much can one learn without changing? Or is learning social skills, but not others, equivalent to personality change? And should the regular teacher-training program merely improve certain skills in the teacher's various roles, or should it seek to change the personalities of those who are to assume or have assumed the position of teacher?

Personality, Role, and Skill in the Teaching Position

The hypothesis presented in this chapter is that quality of teaching is a function not only of the degree of development of skill but also of the intrusion of personality and role factors into the teacher's classroom behavior. Personality factors modify the individual's ability to recognize and to assume the appropriate role in a particular situation, and, as a consequence, the development of the needed skill may be accelerated or retarded.

By implication, then, the teacher-training program should either use or seek to change the personality of the neophyte, or of the teacher in service, if he is to acquire the necessary skill in the appropriate teaching roles. To avoid misunderstanding, it should be emphasized first, that personality change, if that is what it is, may not be necessary in many cases; and, second, that competence in subject-matter areas is assumed for the purposes of the present discussion.

Clearly, it becomes necessary, first, to delineate the roles for the performance of which appropriate skills must be developed. Then, we can consider the personality factors that may interfere with the recognition and acceptance of these roles and the development of skill in their performance.

EXTRACLASS ROLES OF THE TEACHER

The teacher's instructional and administrative roles are predominant and will be considered separately. In addition, there are other important roles which, though practiced outside of class, nevertheless influence classroom behavior. Failure to recognize them and lack of skill in their performance may result in various kinds of misfortune. These may be called the roles of the faculty member, the community liaison officer, and the learner.

Faculty Member

Typically the beginning teacher has never before been a member of an organizational hierarchy. His position has gradually shifted from that of son or daughter in a family to student in a college or university with few responsibilities except those of passing courses. His relationship to his peers has been his own concern and of no particular significance so far as his college work was concerned.

However, as a staff member he suddenly finds himself close to the bottom of an organizational hierarchy, one now to be judged, not so much by what he knows as by what he does. Will he be able to perceive the organizational patterns, the attitudes toward the ideas he may have acquired in his training, whether they are sought or regarded as impractical ("When you've been in this game as long as I have, you'll realize . . ."), and where the power lies—whether in the administration, in the board of education, or perhaps in a clique of older teachers?

He and other staff members should be shrewd enough not to be caught off guard by plausible but disruptive elements and be able to promote authentic communication both up and down in the hierarchy in order to provide a general understanding of administrative policy, and of their own attitudes, with an appreciation of the implications of each. In meetings of the faculty and of faculty committees, members should be able to recognize the functional roles of their colleagues, whether constructive, supportive, or disruptive, and to make their contributions on the positive side. Social perception of a rather high order is needed, and those who fail in this will probably find out not only that they are unhappy but also amid the jealousies and dissatisfactions that sometimes permeate a school faculty, they may also find that they are blocked in various ways, even to the extent of not being able to conduct their own teaching as they would like.

Community Liaison Officer

Patterns of community relationship differ widely in different schools. In the narrower role functions that are directly related to the classroom, primarily those of utilizing community resources and of parent-teacher relations, there are wide differences in role expectations. In some places, the school walls virtually shut out the community, and parent contacts are reduced to the traditional report card; in others, outside resource persons and frequent excursions supplement instruction, and parent-teacher conferences and home visitations are the rule.

Sometimes, in these matters, the teacher's role expectations differ from those of his colleagues and of the administration. If they do, to follow the school pattern is, of course, the safe way since innovations which change the nature of parent or community contacts will be likely to be unpopular. This is particularly true in the case of any change in the traditional report cards, to which the parents are the ones who will be likely to object. Conducting parent conferences and arranging for resource persons and for excursions are skills which can be readily acquired. But introducing them where they are not practiced requires a different set of skills.

Learner

It is generaly recognized that the undergraduate program for teacher education and training is only a beginning to get the young teacher started. In most states further formal instruction is required before the life certificate is granted. But this requirement is not always viewed with enthusiasm nor are other upgrading devices—unless sugar-coated with graduate degrees and pay increases—while individual, self-directed study seems not to be the rule. Of course, a perceptive teacher can learn from his pupils and students,[10] for in a sense they are the laboratory from which a knowledge of the processes of development and learning is obtained. But whether a teacher learns from his students, from formal or informal courses and workshops, or from his own reading and study, one of his important roles is necessarily that of learner, not only to make up for weaknesses in his education and training but also to keep abreast of new discoveries. He needs to learn more about his subject matter, about method, about young people as individuals and in groups, and about the work in general. A number of factors may reduce a teacher's zest for learning. The teaching load, the nature of professional and academic courses, and costs might be among the factors to be investigated as possible deterrents.

ADMINISTRATIVE AND EXECUTIVE ROLES OF THE TEACHER

Other chapters of this yearbook deal with the leadership function of the teacher. It will, therefore, be sufficient here merely to identify some of the administrative tasks which should be differentiated and

---

[10]Marie I. Rasey and J. W. Menge, *What We Learn from Children*. New York: Harper & Bros., 1956.

which can advantageously be considered as separate roles, since they involve separate patterns of skills and responsibilities.

Disciplinarian (Policeman)

Probably no aspect of the teaching position is of greater concern to young people preparing for the profession than that of discipline. Will they be able to keep order? In a real sense, though few of them realize it at first, this is not a separate role at all but a part of the total instructional process. As a rule, when the teaching is good, there is no problem of discipline. Individual misbehavior of a mild sort is handled by class organization, directions, questions, and the like, within the pattern of the ongoing instruction. In such cases, and when the deviation is more severe, the teacher as evaluator and adapter takes care of it by conferences, special help, reassignment, counseling, or referral. But still, the problem of control remains, not only in the classroom but also in the corridors, lunchroom, library, and study hall. Shall autocratic or democratic methods be employed? If the latter, will the youngsters get out of hand? Should punishment be used? Corporal punishment? And back of it all is the realization that the more disciplinary measures the teacher uses the more anxiety and aggression are aroused and the less learning goes on. Here, even more perhaps than in other roles, it is clear that personality factors enter into the teacher's decision as to what to do and may even interfere with the development of skill.

Measurer and Record-Keeper (Clerk)

The abilities required for maintaining records, and even for administering standardized group tests, are largely clerical. In this connection, tasks of the evaluator role—selecting tests, devising examination questions, and rating pupils—are not included. Apart from such matters requiring professional judgment, some teachers seem unable to maintain records systematically, if one is to judge by the condition of the record forms in many school offices. A little skill-training would presumably overcome the influence of personality factors in this area.

Learning-Aids Officer (Librarian)

A third administrative role of the teacher involves the selection and preparation of learning aids, whether books, apparatus, films, recordings, pictures, displays, exhibits, or other matter. Some courses require a good deal of apparatus—shop, art, and science, for example. Others could be improved by more adequate supplementation. Many learning aids have been developed but may not be easily accessible. Some can be had for the asking; others can more suitably be devised for special purposes. Concepts are based primarily on sensory experiences. When these have been supplied, the shorthand of verbal symbols is usually sufficient. But in the rapid piling up of new concepts that takes place during the school days, the teacher can well be aware of the need for sensory referents and modify his approach accordingly.

Program Director (Planner)

School grades and classes are made up of individuals who attend school to learn. Learning is an activity, whether it is taking part in a project, reading a book, or just thinking. But there are many activities in which pupils frequently engage that have little relation to the course of study. The teacher is the director, or should be, of the activity that takes place, whether he runs the whole show himself or participates democratically with the pupils in planning and in carrying out what they have planned together. It is not necessary to discuss here the various techniques involved in maintaining a desirable group climate or in making decisions. But democratic control is control not only of the conduct of pupils but also of their learning. It involves planning—preplanning if one likes the term—and flexibility to meet the possibly unexpected events that may occur. Here again, personality factors may intrude into the performance of learned skills, but the skills are necessary.

INSTRUCTIONAL ROLES OF THE TEACHER

In addition to the administrative and executive roles of the teacher, there are the more purely instructional roles, the activities for which the whole superstructure of the school is provided. They may be differentiated as motivator, resource person, evaluator, and adapter. While they are basically all a part of the same general task, they require different perceptions and different skills.

Motivator

The task of the teacher as motivator is to discover whether the pupils are emotionally ready to learn and, if not, to take such steps as may be necessary to develop that readiness. This sometimes appears to be a hopeless task. It has been said that you can lead a horse to water but you can't make him drink. The statement is obviously false, for it all depends on how you go about it. He will drink if the conditions are right—a sufficient number of hours of water deprivation, for example. What are the conditions which will insure a thirst for knowledge? Many have been tried—forcing methods, rewards and punishments, encouragement of various sorts, and the sugar-coating devices of a generation ago. Suffice it to say that the successful methods seem to include reducing fear and anxiety and providing for group participation, intrinsic rewards, recognition of individual progress, and the satisfaction of individual needs. If there are the guide lines, some teachers may be constitutionally unable to follow all of them, but in any case skill-training is indicated.

Resource Person

The role of the teacher as resource person is a complex one and should perhaps be broken down into smaller parts.

Telling. Most simply, telling consists of supplying the information needed or suggesting where it may be obtained. The latter may be sufficient when a project has been planned, or when the available references are adequate. However, a teacher is naturally expected to teach, which usually means more than supplying information when it is asked for. One teacher reportedly, after giving a little talk about something or other, concluded with the declaration: "Now that is clear, whether you understand it or not!"

Explaining. On surveys of pupil attitudes toward their teachers, one usually finds the commendatory statement often repeated, "She explains things." The teacher's function as explainer and clarifier goes beyond mere telling and is fundamental though often overlooked even by the teacher himself. The oft-quoted statement, "If you know a thing, you can teach it," breaks down in every field of instruction. The foreman knows how, but he can often say little more than, "Do it like I do." The teacher of literature reads poetry to a class and may be the only one to be thrilled by it; his explanations have all the sad futility of explaining a joke. The mathematician shows how, but his explanations may be unsuccessful because he does not realize what the parts are that his students do not understand since he had never found them difficult himself. And so it goes or is likely to go.

Demonstrating. Explaining things so that pupils understand is sometimes all that is necessary. But often there is the further requirement that they be able to do something—solve the problems, use the tools, play the instrument or the game, or speak the language. In such situations, to explanation must be added demonstration. Cues of one sort or another must be indicated and mistakes corrected so that the student's performance tends to approximate more and more closely the criterion of correctness. Explaining and demonstrating, repeating and repeating again require patience and probably other personality characteristics that many do not have. Can they be acquired through practice?

Evaluator

As evaluator, the teacher is expected to determine the level of performance of the pupils in comparison with expectations based on age, grade, intelligence, and previous experience. This is done by means of both standardized and teacher-made tests, by observation and interpretation of the pupils' day-to-day activities, and by notations indicating the detection of errors which pupils are mature enough to be able to correct. On the basis of this information, the teacher resumes his roles of motivator and resource person in order that the needed learning may take place.

Adapter

Thus far, the class has been thought of largely as a unit. But the teacher in his instructional role must also be able to adapt his instruction and materials to the varying interests, abilities, aptitudes, and needs of those in his classroom. As evaluator, he judges their abilities and recognizes their physical and mental handicaps and also their special talents, not only for classwork but also for participation in various group activities. And as therapist—or perhaps mental hygienist would be a better term—he creates the best kind of climate possible for the different personalities, challenging some, encouraging others, and giving help where help is needed. This role, perhaps more than any of the others, seems to be dependent on personality factors, though the skills needed for its proper performance can undoubtedly be developed.

INFLUENCES ON ROLE BEHAVIOR

Having indicated the several roles of the teacher, we are now ready to consider the factors which lead to success or failure in performing these roles. First would be those factors which influence in one way or another the perceptions of the teacher's role, as a consequence of which they might, or might not, be performed to everyone's satisfaction. Then we should consider the extent to which personality factors intrude in such ways that perception of a role as well as the development of skills in performing it are interfered with. Such factors can only be suggested since there is as yet no generally accepted personality theory. But the most useful personality constructs will be those which discriminate role behaviors and so point most clearly to the acceptance or rejection of skill-training.

Conditions Affecting Discrepancies in Perceiving Role Behavior

We have seen that a role is the behavior expected of or characteristic of an individual in a given position. It would, therefore, follow
that for the teacher's roles there would be discrepancies between the
expectations of those who assume the role and the expectations of
others concerned, primarily the administration and the students. A few
conditions which produce discrepancies in perceiving teaching roles
may be suggested.

Social Class. Allison Davis[11] and a number of other writers have
pointed to the importance of social class differences in education. To
the middle-class teacher, the language habits and the aggressions of
lower-class children suggest moral obliquity, and as a consequence
he perceives his role as that of the disciplinarian, employing punishment for misdeeds instead of using his skill in the instructional roles
that presumably would be more helpful to the pupils in acquiring new
responses.

It is sometimes said of such a pupil, "The only language he understands is punishment," when it might be expected that at school he
could receive instruction in some other language! But this is not easy.
One can imagine the bafflement of the teacher who, in exasperation
told a mother about the mischief her offspring was up to in school.
Instead of being overwhelmed by the enormity of his evil ways, she
burst into delighted laughter exclaiming, "Just like his old man!" On
the other hand, for some of the same offenses, upper-class youth are
likely to be treated quite differently, perhaps in part because of the
influence their parents have on them or the wider influence of these
parents in the community.

Student Ability. For those of high and of low intelligence, the role
of adapter may be played in different ways, but the pupils are likely
to be the losers. True, the feeble-minded are often encouraged by
being placed in separate classes or institutions. But the dull normals
usually lead a dreary academic existence, often rejected by their age
group as "dumb bunnies," and by the teacher through the traditional
marking system, while the superior are forced to follow the weary
treadmill routine. Some teachers perceive their role as one of devotion
to the slow learners because "the rest can take care of themselves."
Others adapt to the bright because "the rest can't get it anyway."
Modern practices aim at adapting instruction to the total wide range
of ability to be found in almost any classroom, but this may be asking
too much of the teacher.

---

[11]Allison Davis, *Social Class Influences upon Learning.* Cambridge, Massachusetts: Harvard University Press, 1948.

Organizational Climate. Teacher roles are influenced in various ways by the administration. It is said that an autocratic principal or superintendent produces autocracy in the classroom, while a democratic form of administrative leadership encourages democratic classroom practices. The Andersons[12] have shown that dominative and integrative teacher behaviors tend to produce their like in the pupils. On the other hand, when there are discrepancies in the perception of teacher and administrative roles with respect to organizational climate, there will tend to be conflict. It is quite likely that this fact lies at the root of the objections to using administrative devices for merit increases.

Student and Teacher Expectations. If a teacher meets his first class of the term with the question, "Well, what shall we do today?" the students are likely to be baffled, since they expect to be told what will be required of them. Their expectations are based on their previous school experiences not only in instructional but also in disciplinary matters. They usually try out a new teacher in order to discover how far they can go with impunity. They know what to expect within limits, but they are not sure of the limits. In other words, they are testing the role behavior of their new teacher. After a while, both they and the teacher know what to expect—whether they like it or not. The teacher may be thus forced into a pattern of role behavior which he may not like and from which he will be unable to extricate himself unless he can develop different attitudes and, hence, different role expectations in the students.

Personality. It is natural that any teacher should affect the different personalities in his class differently, whether because of his own personality pattern, the roles he assumes, or his skill in their performance. For example, a college instructor who started to employ democratic processes in his class was surprised when three students walked out. They reported afterwards in conference that they did not want any of this democratic stuff, that they were not interested in hearing from the other students who didn't know any more than they did, and that they preferred the instructor to decide what should be studied and to do the talking, since that was what he was paid for. Other class members were neutral on the subject while many were enthusiastic about being able to follow up some of their own interests and to work on projects with other class members.

It is not intended here to analyze individual student personalities but merely to suggest the probability[13] that the quest for the good teacher

---

[12]Harold H. Anderson and Others, "Studies in Teachers' Classroom Personalities," *Applied Psychology Monographs*, VI (1945); VIII (1946); XI (1946).
[13]John D. McNeil, "Toward Appreciation of Teaching Methods," *Phi Delta Kappan*, XXXIX (March, 1958), 295-301.

as such, like the quest for the good leader, is a fruitless one unless the interaction of teacher and class is considered. And, even when this is done, one is bound to lose, since what is acceptable to some students is rejected by others. However, losses may be of varying amounts, and it should be possible to reduce their size.

Personality and Skill

For the purposes of this chapter, personality is considered as the generalized characteristic response patterns of the individual, whether native or acquired, as of any stated time. Such characteristic response patterns have not yet been delineated or classified to everyone's satisfaction. However, a few examples should provide a basis for the hypothesis that they affect not only the teacher's choice of roles and his role expectations but also the skill that can be acquired in playing the teacher's roles.

The Teacher's Motivational Needs. It is well recognized that any vocation satisfies certain needs of the person who chooses it. Lists of needs vary, but security and affection, have long held an established place on most of them, and some persons in whom these needs are strong find satisfaction in teaching. The more extreme form is delineated by Horney[14] as the complaint type, those who move toward people and will secretly dominate them under the guise of loving. Such persons would tend to be overpermissive and overindulgent. Their attitude is personal rather than professional, and they would presumably seek to avoid the disciplinary, punitive role and to play down those of measurer and evaluator. Others may feel a need for recognition and status and, if they are at all insecure, would be expected to emphasize discipline, marks, and standards. These are the martinets, the "tin Hitlers," whom everyone has encountered. Any skill-training to correct for such behavior would tend to fall flat so long as those who practice it cling to these personality patterns.

Dominance-Submission. Sometimes the needs are not so obvious as the characteristics that have developed to satisfy them. The dominant personality types will presumably leave no doubt as to "who's boss around here," and will probably find it difficult to acquiesce in pupil choices and to submit to administrative rulings. In the classroom, their domination may be aggressive and punitive, or it may be sublimated to other forms including the more standard, "Now-what-I-want-you-to-do" pattern. It may even look very democratic until the students discover that they have to be democratic "or else." How submissive a

---

[14]Karen Horney, *The Neurotic Personality of Our Time* (New York: W. W. Norton & Co., 1937) and *Our Inner Conflicts* (New York: W. W. Norton & Co., 1945).

teacher can be and yet be effective is a matter of opinion. The "yes man" may be skillful in his role, but much depends on whether he says "yes" only to the boss or to everyone who talks to him. Certainly moderate amounts are helpful, at least to the extent of a willingness to try to follow the suggestions of a supervisor or psychologist in order to help solve pupil learning or behavior problems.

Anxiety-Confidence. Whether or not there is an anxious personality type, Horney makes much of the attitude of basic anxiety. It is, no doubt, true that some people are more anxious and fearful than others even when the amount of threat is approximately constant. It may well be that a moderate amount of anxiety serves to motivate people to take steps to remove it, at least when they suspect the causes. It seems certain, however, that the anxious, fearful person, the "worrier," will find it hard to develop role skills because he will be unable to trust his own judgment, or even believe in his own successes. In contrast would be the confident, self-sufficient individual who carries himself and the group along with him, whether successfully or not, depending on his skill.

Rigidity-Flexibility. It may be that the rigidity-flexibility dimension of personality is the most important of all, at least as it relates to the ease or difficulty with which personality patterns may be modified. A great deal of work has been done on it, ranging from the clinical interest in Freud's anal type (the pedantic, frugal, obstinate, and orderly) to the F Scale of Adorno *et al.*[15] and their followers. However, relatively little is known about it as it relates to the ability of the teacher to adapt his procedures to the needs of the ongoing activities of the classroom and of other groups. The rigid type might be expected to be something of a perfectionist in the administrative and executive roles; but if his natural ways of operating in the instructional roles were inadequate, as they might well be, he might have difficulty in acquiring better ones and also in changing his routine to adapt to various learning situations as they arise. The flexible person, on the other hand, if his skills were adequate, could presumably shift his role behavior and techniques, as needed, as easily as a dentist or surgeon selects his instruments for different purposes.

PREPARING TEACHERS FOR THEIR ROLE FUNCTIONS

It may seem that if a knowledge of group processes, including role functions, is added to the professional training program, it would be more than the traffic would bear. However, it is at least equally prob-

---

[15]T. W. Adorno, Else Frenkel-Brunswik, and Associates, *The Authoritarian Personality.* New York: Harper & Bros., 1950.

able that a clarification of roles would actually simplify the training program and also make the demands on the teacher less confusing. Further, it may seem that, if the roles are spelled out and training is provided for each, the profession would be changed into a skilled trade. But there is no danger of this inasmuch as the factor of choice (the need for rendering a professional opinion) appears at every turn— in deciding which is the appropriate role, almost from minute to minute, and in selecting the appropriate skill.

Knowledge of Roles

The introductory course in educational psychology can properly provide a knowledge of the several educational roles as they operate in instructional groups. More fundamental training in group dynamics, if a student wishes it, can easily be postponed for graduate study after a period of teaching experience. But beginning teachers can easily be equipped not only to recognize the need for performing quite distinct, identifiable roles, but they can also learn that some of their students— and their colleagues—are not merely objectionable characters or personable people, as the case may be, but that consciously or unconsciously these teachers are playing recognizable roles and, therefore, may deal more effectively with whatever situation may arise.

Developing Role Skills

Any program of teacher training, with its methods courses and practice teaching, aims to develop teaching skills. In the process, however, the trainee is likely to be confused so that he might quite naturally ask, "How do I know when to do what?" A differentiation of roles would help to answer this question, with practice in the appropriate skills of each. While some of these skills are verbal, some of them go deeper.

Assessing Personality Factors

Promoting Role Acceptance. It is too early yet to say just which personality factors intrude in such ways as to promote the acceptance of different roles and which ones produce rejection. Some of the possibilities have been suggested in connection with the discussion in the preceding section. The "born teacher" has the needed characteristics, whatever they are, and requisite skills will be acquired easily and rapidly, since there is no avoidance or rejection of the several roles. His administrative routines, including discipline, will run as smoothly as his instructional roles. He may later become a professor of education.

But, like the brilliant subject-matter specialist, he may find it hard to help beginners over difficulties he himself has never encountered.

Interfering with Role Acceptance. The majority of student teachers will have some difficulty with one role or another, or perhaps with several. If they are not "born teachers," can they be trained to become good teachers? Presumably they can. For some, to be able to understand a role or to practice a teaching skill will be sufficient. For others, something more fundamental may be needed, analogous to removing a fear of water before some youngsters can be taught to swim.

Whether or not the needed changes should be called a change in personality, or in attitude, or in social response patterns is perhaps not important. What is important is that the trainee learn to behave in a different way—not play a different role but live it; not merely learn to say different words in a training situation, but to feel differently and be able to generalize both the situation and the response.

For some, this may be impossible, and if their deviation from what is needed is too great, they should probably never be permitted to teach. Some might require a period of clinical therapy, while the majority could no doubt acquire the needed response patterns in the regular training program.

REFERENCES

ARGYLE, MICHAEL. "The Concepts of Role and Status," *Sociological Review,* XLIV (Sec. 3, 1952), 39-52.

Group Dynamics, Research, and Theory. Edited by Dorwin Cartwright and Alvin F. Zander. White Plains, New York: Row, Peterson & Co., 1953.

LIPPITT, RONALD, and OTHERS. *The Dynamics of Planned Change.* New York: Harcourt, Brace & Co., 1958.

NEWCOMB, THEODORE M. *Social Psychology.* New York: Dryden Press, 1950.

SARBIN, THEODORE R. "Role Theory," in *Handbook of Social Psychology,* Vol. I, pp. 223-58. Edited by Gardner Lindzey. Cambridge, Massachusetts: Addison-Wesley, 1954.

STILES, LINDLEY J. *The Teacher's Role in American Society.* Fourteenth Yearbook of the John Dewey Society. New York: Harper & Bros., 1957.

TROW, WILLIAM CLARK. "Group Processes," *Encyclopedia of Educational Research.* New York: Macmillan Co., 1960.

Two Exemplars of Teaching Method

HARRY S. BROUDY

Theories of learning and of teaching take their cues from the kind of competence needed to achieve success in a given social order. Because oratory was a sure road to success at certain junctures in the history of Athens and Rome, educational theorists directed their search toward methods, rules, and principles of learning and teaching rhetoric. In the courts of chivalry, on the other hand, educators were concerned with other outcomes, so their "research" took a different direction. We can imagine that they cherished and debated theories about teaching horsemanship, the use of arms, and the finer points of gallantry. In our time the paradigm of success learning is scientific understanding, hence current interest is riveted to cognition, concept attainment, and the kind of creative transformations that produce new scientific theories and technological solutions. Hence, also, the attempt to derive teaching models from communication systems, administration, information theory, and computer programming.

I think it is also true that at any given time, at least in Western culture, a countercurrent to the current success type of learning also operates. For the most part, this protest movement appeals to ideals of personality and conduct that the success pattern either threatens or obscures. Not infrequently the instigators of this protest are teachers only in the larger sense of being social reformers, teachers of the people, for example, Moses, Solon, or Jesus. However, some, like Pythagoras and Plato, did formalize and institutionalize their instruction. The former is believed to have conducted a fellowship or society in which his doctrine was taught and practiced, while Plato founded a long-lived academy in which he himself was a teacher.

It may be the case, therefore, that the life style of an age can be discerned in the style of teaching exemplified by men who taught the young for success in their time and those reformers who relied upon teaching to change that life style. For this purpose it is more profitable to choose figures who were teachers by profession and who were reflective about the educative process; in other words, teachers who were self conscious about method and articulate enough about their reflection to have said or written something about it.

Reprinted with permission of the Association for Supervision and Curriculum Development and Harry S. Broudy, from *Theories of Instruction*, James B. Macdonald and Robert R. Leeper, eds. Washington, D. C.: Association for Supervision and Curriculum Development, 1965, pp. 8-17. Copyright 1965 by the Association for Supervision and Curriculum Development.

I shall confine myself to two of these modes of teaching, that of rhetorical instruction, and the dialectical instruction of Socrates which may be regarded as a protest against the Sophists. I have not confined myself to one figure in the rhetorical field, e.g., Isocrates or Quintilian, although either would certainly serve as an examplar. My reasons for this are that the developments of the method from the Greek Sophists do need to be mentioned and that its architectonic is more impressive even than so notable a figure as Quintilian himself.

RHETORICAL INSTRUCTION

In order to teach young men to speak well and persuasively before juries and assemblies, the Sophists and the later rhetoricians had to analyze examples of good speaking and writing so as to formulate rules. Prodicus of Ceos studied synonyms in an attempt to clarify the meaning of words. Gorgias of Leontini (483-375 B.C.) is said to have devised the figures of antithesis, balance of clauses, and final assonance. Isocrates (436-338 B.C.), the foremost rhetoric teacher of his time, brought the rules of rhetoric to a high order of perfection and created the set speech as an instrument of political action.

The teaching of oratory comprised (a) a study of literature which was to furnish material and models of style for the composing of speeches and (b) study of the art of speech making, although the literary part might have been completed in the school of the grammarian.

As to the teaching of literature, the procedure that Protagoras exemplified in the Great Speech in Plato's dialogue of that name was formalized as early as 166 B.C. by Dionysius of Thrace as follows:

1. Give the selected passages an exact reading with respect to pronunciation, punctuation, and rhetorical expression.
2. Explain the figures of speech.
3. Explain the historical and mythological references.
4. Comment on the choice of words and their etymology.
5. Point out the grammatical forms employed.
6. Estimate the literary merit of the selection.

This is about as explicit a set of directions as a teacher could want—perhaps more explicit than some would want. It fixed the form of the prelection and *exposition de texte*. In the hands of a Quintilian this lesson could be an impressive display of erudition, ingenuity, and originality, but the steps could also be executed by a hack who, with the help of glosses and commentaries, could give a fair imitation of Quintilian. This is the strength and weakness of method—almost any method.

The more strictly oratorical part of the teaching also was methodized to an extraordinary degree. By the fourth century B.C., it was pretty well agreed by Aristotle and others that the teaching of rhetoric involved three factors: nature, art, and exercise. Then as now teachers could only wish for a high order of talent and docile temperament. Hence, most of the attention had to be given to art and exercise.

The art was summed up in sets of definitions, precepts or rules, and classifications. These were to be learned by heart. The exercises consisted of practice tasks in imitating the best models the instructor could set before his pupils.

An idea of the complexity of the subject can be gained by noting that the art of speaking and writing as well was divided by Cicero (*De partitione, oratoria,* 46 B.C.; Clark, 1957, p. 69ff.) into the following tasks:

> *inventio*: to find out what one should say
> *dispositia*: to arrange what one has found
> *elocutio*: to clothe it with language
> *memoria*: to secure it in one's memory
> *pronuntiatio*: to deliver it.

So much for the resources needed by the speaker. As to the oration or speech itself, six divisions were recognized:

> *exordium*: opening
> *narratio*: statement of the facts colored to favor the speaker's argument
> *divisio*: forecast of the main points the speaker plans to make
> *confirmatio*: the argument in favor of the speaker's contentions
> *confutatio*: rebuttal of possible objections
> *peroratio*: conclusion or summation.

Within these large divisions were numerous subdivisions. Cicero classified 17 sources of arguments for the *inventio*. As to style, Cicero himself came to be recognized as the model *par excellence* but models also were sought in other standard Roman authors: Virgil, Horace, Ovid, Lucan, Statius, Persius, Martial, Catullus, Juvenal, and Sallust. Clark quotes Marrou to the effect that Latin was taught as a dead language as early as the days of Jerome and Augustine (Marrou, 1938, p. 14; Clark, 1957, p. 86).

The actual teaching procedure both in the school of the grammarian and in the higher school of the rhetors was as follows:

1. The pupil would memorize the definitions, classifications, and rules as embodied in textbooks.
2. The teacher would analyze the models to be imitated by a prelection.
3. The pupil was directed to apply the precepts and imitate the model in practice declamations or compositions on hypothetical themes.

The imitation, which was the heart of the method, was obviously not a simple duplication of the model. Good imitation involved:

1. Giving the student the results of careful study of the model by the teacher to reveal how the author achieved his effects. This analysis was offered by the teacher either in a lecture or by assigning material covering this point in a textbook (cf. Quintilian, *Institutio*, II, v, 6-16).
2. Asking the student to write sentences that exhibited the stylistic characteristics of the model: periodic sentences, certain figures of speech, etc. Exercises in imitation included learning by heart, learning by translation from Greek to Latin, and paraphrasing poetry into prose.

Even the exercises in the earlier phases of composition study were not left to chance. There were collections of graded exercises (*progymnasmata*) to guide the writing and speaking practice. Other exercises called for retelling fables, plausible fictions, and stories from history; narrations dealing with persons; amplifying proverbs into a moral essay; refuting an argument; taking a set of facts typical of a class of situations and applying them to a particular case; praising or dispraising a thing or person (one writer treated of this exercise alone in 36 divisions and subdivisions); making comparisons; composing imaginary speeches that might have been given by some historical or mythological figure; describing objects and events vividly; arguing on set questions (e.g., Should a man marry?); and speaking for or against a piece of legislation.

Harsh things have been said about the rigidity and artificiality of this method, especially when applied to the study of other subjects. However, as a method it was not without its virtues.

In the first place, the method had the virture of definiteness. Provided he was not mired in the sea of classifications and sub-classifications, the teacher always knew what to do next and, after a fashion, could provide a reason to himself and his pupil for doing it.

In the next place, the method exploited the reliability of habituation. Quintilian believed that the pupil could form habits even of meditation and improvisation. Above all, counseled Quintilian, keep writing:

> We must write, therefore, whenever possible; if we cannot write, we must meditate: if both are out of the question, we must still speak in such a manner that we shall not seem to be taken unawares nor our client to be left in the lurch (Quintilian, *Institutio*, X, vii, 3-29).

In the third place, the method illustrates a type of formal discipline that is quite different from what is usually called by that name. The forms were speech-types suited for all standard occasions, e.g., for defending a client charged with treason, or for accusing a public official of taking bribes. A properly trained orator knew by heart a well-developed speech for every occasion, and all he had to do was substitute

in the blanks the appropriate names, places. The orator could be ingenious and original, but he did not have to be. For most situations the
student had a stock of model responses learned by assiduous imitation.
He had models for subject, style of composition, and delivery. He had
achieved a discipline of forms. One relied for transfer on an ample
repertoire of interchangeable formulae, rather than on the strengthening
of intellectual powers or on the explanatory potency of theory.

Does such a teaching strategy have any relevance for the modern
classroom? Probably not in its totality, because very little of our curriculum is devoted to training orators. Nevertheless, in legal training,
medical training, and certainly in teacher training, mastering type-
responses by imitation and repetition is still important. Judgment in
standard cases is reduced to choosing the appropriate response type. It is
not suitable to develop thinking, because its objective is to make thinking unnecessary. Nor is thinking an unmixed blessing in professional
practice. One would hardly entrust one's body to a surgeon who had
to think his way through every step of an operation, just as one would
not entrust one's body to a craftsman who could not think his way
through the atypical situation. As a profession utilizes more theory to
justify and guide practice, its training program is bifuricated into theoretical and performance components for which the same teaching method
may not be suitable. All attempts to reduce them to one method are
to me, at least, unconvincing.

The method is still not easily dispensed with for appreciative teaching. The development of standards and appreciation in literature and
the fine arts involves introjection of models, and imitating models is
one way of introjecting them. They then become internal standards
instead of external ones. Of course, the method assumes that the teacher
has the temerity to select models for imitation. In an age when, as
a matter of principle, to accept standards of excellence is academically
not respectable this method is inapplicable, not because it is imitative,
but rather because there is nothing one dares to imitate wholeheartedly.

The thoroughness of a teaching method can be estimated by the
degree to which each phase of the teaching transaction is subjected to
analysis and rules.

1. *Motivation* or acts designed to secure and hold the attention of the
   learner to the learning task.
2. *Presentation of the learning task* or those acts designed to instruct
   the learner as to the expected response and the means of achieving it.
3. *Elicitation of a trial response* or those acts designed to test whether
   or not the learner is performing in accordance with (2) and has
   mastered the given cues.

4. *Correction of trial response* or those acts which inform the learner of the adequacy of the trial response.
5. *Elicitation of the test response* or those acts which assign unpracticed tasks to be performed with fewer cues than those supplied in the learning task.[1]
6. *Fixation of desired response by practice into habit.*

If one reviews the apparatus developed by the rhetoricians, it becomes evident that they left none of the above phases to chance. The act was completely methodized, it could be described without ambiguity, and could be replicated by appropriate training.

DIALECTICAL INSTRUCTION

A quite different way of carrying out the instructional sequence is examplified in the Socratic teaching. In the first place, the pattern of motivation was different. While the rhetor could appeal to the student's desire to succeed in the life of his day, Socrates could not, because he intended to convince his pupil that the success standards of the day were false standards. Hence the strategy had to consist of shaking the youth loose from conventional attitudes and commitments. This he did in two ways: by *exhortation* and *self-examination.*

In the *Apology,* Socrates said:

> Men of Athens . . . while I have life and strength I shall never cease from the practice and teaching of philosophy, exhorting any one whom I meet and saying to him after my manner: You, my friend . . . are you not ashamed of heaping up the greatest amount of money and honor and reputation, and caring so little about wisdom and truth and the greatest improvement of the soul, which you never regard or heed at all?

The frequent use of exhortation to become concerned about the state of one's values (one's soul) has been noted by Jaeger (1943, II, p. 39). It is illustrated in the *Protagoras* (313 B.C.) when Socrates, accompanying Hippocrates to the house of Callias to hear Protagoras, asks the excited young man:

> Well, but are you aware of the danger which you are incurring? If you were going to commit your body to some one, who might do good or harm to it, would you not carefully consider and ask the opinion of your friends and kindred, and deliberate many days as to whether you should give him the care of your body? But when the soul is in question, which you hold to be of far more value than the body, and upon the good or evil of which depends the well-being of your all—

[1] For a more detailed discussion of these phases of the teaching act, see Broudy, 1961, p. 340-48.

about this you never consulted either with your father or with your brother or with any of us who are your companions. But no sooner does this foreigner appear, than you instantly commit your soul to his keeping.

Next, the learner had to be jolted into anger with his teacher and himself. This was accomplished by beginning with the criticism of a conventional and traditional view of courage, temperance, wisdom, or justice that his respondent regarded as beyond question. Such a sortie is the examination of the idea that justice is more or less a matter of helping one's friends and injuring one's enemies in the first book of the *Republic*.

Socrates explores the consequences of this definition. The learning task is beginning to unfold, but it will emerge only as the learner makes some trial responses and is corrected by Socrates.[2] The critical point in the learning episode is the moment when the learner "sees" that his original view is mistaken, that he is ignorant in matters about which he had regarded himself as knowledgeable. He is now ready for further explorations into self-knowledge and further exasperation.

The Socratic dialogue or dialectic was a joint logical venture into a problem of proper definition and soul therapy. The method was to show that "If A is defined as X, unacceptable consequences C would follow." Other definitions, B C . . . N, were then tried until the quest was achieved or given up.

It will be noted that as far as Socrates was concerned, he, too, was trying to turn out good Athenian citizens, but, unlike the rhetoricians, he was relying on philosophical training rather than eloquence to achieve it. Rather than the skills of persuasion he was hoping to form skills of logical critical thinking, that by abstraction could produce valid generalizations about value, that is, about the good life. But he was trying to change attitudes at the same time.

The main point of the dialogue *Meno* is the persuasion of Meno, the wealthy young Thessalian who has had some training at the hands of Gorgias, the Sophist, that if virtue can be taught it cannot be the kind of knowledge that is picked up conventionally or by ordinary experience (for then everybody would be teaching it and virtuous fathers would not have delinquent sons). But if we do not know what virtue is how can we ever know when and if we come across it?

How we can recognize what we do not already know is then illustrated by the famous mathematics lesson to the slave boy, which, in turn, leads to the speculation that in a previous life the slave boy had

---

[2]As will be noted below, this interchange is better described as a long argument in which each step is presented to the pupil for agreement or disagreement.

known the ideas which under Socrates' questioning he now recollects.

It is somewhat puzzling to have programmed instruction and teaching machines claim Socrates as an ancestor. But perhaps the programmers have been influenced too much by the mathematical episode in the *Meno*. Although Plato in that dialogue chose an illustration that lent itself to step-by-step programming as well as to the introduction of the doctrine of reminiscence, Socrates was not noted for the teaching of mathematics. In most of the Socratic dialogues, it is the pupil who gives the reinforcing answers rather than Socrates. Socrates makes long speeches and explanations that are only formally questions, whereas the pupil answers with a brief "yes" or "no." Furthermore, the reinforcement of the programmed text is more like that of the rhetorical exercises than that of the inner self-examination that served as motivation for Socrates' pupils. Finally, the Socratic methodology depended on having the pupil become aware of his own ignorance and the outcome was a way of thinking and feeling. Most of our programmed instruction, on the other hand, stresses positive content which also serves as a check on the pupil's logical processes (Broudy, 1963).

The short-term Socratic teaching method can be described as a critical search for adequate definition that follows a fairly clear sequence regulated by logical rules. It was not designed to teach the ordinary symbolic skills, factual infomation or what we today would call science, but it can be used wherever the problem of definition arises and where critical examination of theory is concerned. As a mode of teaching it stresses logico-linguistic materials and operations (Smith, 1960).

The long-term teaching was more than an exercise in logical thinking. It was a training series on successively higher levels of abstract thinking, best described in the metaphor of the ladder of knowledge and the divided line (*Republic* vi).

The lowest of these levels represented a traditional, fictional, almost mythological account of things (*eikasia*). Next higher was a kind of common sense knowledge or opinion based on experience (*pistis*). Higher still was the attempt to know *why* in terms of some general theory, knowledge typical of well-developed science (*dianoia*), and finally one reached a kind of knowledge that is certain (*noesis*) because the knower has apprehended the form and scheme of reality itself.

Obviously, the general method for reaching the highest stage of knowledge is abstraction, the road to theory, but at the end of the road, one needs a vision or intuition, an illumination that replaces scientific conjecture with utter conviction. The educational strategy, therefore, is broader than the teaching of any subject or the practice of logical operations. This is so because the last stage is not a cognitive maneuver.

It is a conversion of the soul possible only to a soul that has been nurtured to cherish courage, temperance, and wisdom by careful rearing in a wise society. Exhortation appeals to exemplars, and even speculative mythology would be needed if the cognitive training were to achieve the long-term goal. The methodology as well as the curriculum for this type of education is described by Plato in *Republic,* ii. We would call it conditioning.

Conditioning the pupil without his consent and often without his full awareness of what was happening to him, on the one hand, and the refinement of these habits and attitudes by intensive and systematic cognition, on the other, are still the major problems of formal and informal education. Plato and Socrates realized with utmost clarity that (a) without a base of conditioned dispositions (what to hate and what to love) verbal approaches to value education were useless, (b) that one had better be sure of one's rationale for a value pattern before imposing it on the unsuspecting young, and (c) that without the control of all the value-forming factors in the environment, formal training in value education was bound to limp.

These styles of teaching are only two of many that have been exemplified in the history of education. They may throw some light on our current attempts to understand and formulate the structure of the teaching act, because they represent the extremes of a continuum of emphasis. At one end is schooling for professional competence in a given period of history; at the other, is schooling for human development in its broadest meaning. Both utilize maneuvers that motivate, present, correct, test, and fix the responses of the learner, but the specific nature of these maneuvers varies with the outcomes that are sought as well as with other variables too numerous to enumerate. The attempts to isolate a sequence or structure for all teaching may, therefore, be interesting but not very illuminating until the outcomes are unpacked and carefully analyzed. Inasmuch as each epoch is characterized by its own success routes and its own ground rules for awarding power and prestige, it will probably evolve its own characteristic syndrome of curriculum and method, and our own time is no exception.

If our own time is unique at all, it is only because the requirements for vocation, citizenship, and self-development entail such a high order of cognitive and evaluative competence for such a large proportion of the people. Symbolic skills, basic concepts in rapidly proliferating sciences, value exemplars, and skills of group deliberation—each demands its own strategy of teaching. The various ways in which one uses results of schooling in our society—the replicative, associative, interpretive, and applicative—also require variations in teaching method. There is little danger that educational research will run out of problems.

Perhaps our greatest danger is that research will be so captivated by the type of study that pays off in terms of current success that it neglects other types. Thus at a time when the sciences are so important for the national interest, it is tempting to forget that the associative and interpretive uses of knowledge are still important to a wholesome life in a tolerable society, and the problem is aggravated if we wish that society to remain democratic. The relative neglect of the humanities and, to a lesser extent, of the social sciences in the expenditure schedules of the federal government and private foundations in favor of research in the physical sciences is an example of this. Education follows suit insofar as its slow rate of change permits it to do so.

If we are to be shrewd about the history of teaching styles, we ought to encourage research and study that run counter to the fashion of the moment—the fashionable moments will be supported by the social forces in which they originated. If this is so, this is a time to encourage the study of how values are taught and learned; how general education can be fashioned so as to provide the cognitive and evaluative maps needed for life in the modern mass society; how men and women can exploit the fine arts to develop the imaginative modes of perception, and finally, how men can preserve individuality and significance in a world that threatens both.[3]

REFERENCES

HARRY S. BROUDY. *Building a Philosophy of Education.* Second edition. Englewood Cliffs, N. J.: Prentice-Hall, 1961.
—————. "Socrates and the Teaching Machine." *Phi Delta Kappan* 44:243-47; 1963.
D. L. CLARK. *Rhetoric in Greco-Roman Education.* New York: Columbia University Press, 1957.
W. F. FROEBEL. *The Education of Man.* Translated by W. N. Hailmann. New York: Appleton, 1911.
N. L. GAGE, editor. *Handbook of Research on Teaching.* Chicago: Rand McNally & Co., 1963. p. 1-44.
W. W. JAEGER. *Paideia: The Ideals of Greek Culture.* Translated by G. Highet. New York: Oxford University Press, Vol. I, (2nd ed.), 1945; Vol. II, 1943; Vol. III, 1944.
H. I. MARROU. *Saint Agustin et la Fin de la Culture Antique.* Paris, 1938.
F. B. QUINTILIAN. *Institutio Oratoria.* Translated by H. E. Butler. London: Loeb Classical Library, 1953. 4 vols.
B. O. SMITH. "*A Concept of Teaching.*" *Teachers College Record* 61:229-41; 1960.

---

[3]Portions of this paper are adapted from the author's chapter, "Historic Exemplars of Teaching Method." *Handbook of Research on Teaching.* N. L. Gage, editor. Chicago: Rand McNally & Company, 1963, and H. S. Broudy and John S. Palmer, *Exemplars of Teaching Method.* Chicago: Rand McNally & Company, 1965.

The Interpersonal Relationship in the Facilitation of Learning

CARL R. ROGERS, PH.D.

Western Behavioral Sciences Institute, La Jolla, California

> ". . . It is in fact nothing short of a miracle that the modern methods of instruction have not yet entirely strangled the holy curiosity of inquiry; for this delicate little plant, aside from stimulation, stands mainly in need of freedom; without this it goes to wrack and ruin without fail."
>
> ALBERT EINSTEIN

I wish to begin this talk with a statement which may seem surprising to some and perhaps offensive to others. It is simply this: Teaching, in my estimation, is a vastly over-rated function.

Having made such a statement, I scurry to the dictionary to see if I really mean what I say. Teaching means "to instruct." Personally I am not much interested in instructing another. "To impart knowledge or skill." My reaction is, why not be more efficient, using a book or programmed learning? "To make to know." Here my hackles rise. I have no wish to *make* anyone know something. "To show, guide, direct." As I see it, too many people have been shown, guided, directed. So I come to the conclusion that I *do* mean what I said. Teaching is, for me, a relatively unimportant and vastly overvalued activity.

But there is more in my attitude than this. I have a negative reaction to teaching. Why? I think it is because it raises all the wrong questions. As soon as we focus on teaching the question arises, what shall we teach? What, from our superior vantage point, does the other person need to know? This raises the ridiculous question of coverage. What shall the course cover? (Here I am acutely aware of the fact that "to cover" means both "to take in" and "to conceal from view," and I believe that most courses admirably achieve both these aims.) This notion of coverage is based on the assumption that what is taught is what is learned; what is presented is what is assimilated. I know of no assumption so obviously untrue. One does not need research to provide evidence that this is false. One needs only to talk with a few students.

Lecture given at Harvard University, April 12, 1966.

Reprinted with permission of the Association for Supervision and Curriculum Development and Carl R. Rogers, from *Humanizing Education: The Person in the Process,* Robert R. Leeper, ed. Washington, D. C.: Association for Supervision and Curriculum Development, 1965, pp. 8-17. Copyright 1965 by the Association for Supervision and Curriculum Development.

But I ask myself, "Am I so prejudice against teaching that I find no situation in which it is worthwhile?" I immediately think of my experience in Australia, only a few months ago. I became much interested in the Australian aborigine. Here is a group which for more than 20,000 years has managed to live and exist in a desolate environment in which a modern man would perish within a few days. The secret of his survival has been teaching. He has passed on to the young every shred of knowledge about how to find water, about how to track game, about how to kill the kangaroo, about how to find his way through the trackless desert. Such knowledge is conveyed to the young as being *the* way to behave, and any innovation is frowned upon. It is clear that teaching has provided him the way to survive in a hostile and relatively unchanging environment.

Now I am closer to the nub of the question which excites me. Teaching and the imparting of knowledge make sense in an unchanging environment. This is why it has been an unquestioned function for centuries. But if there is one truth about modern man, it is that he lives in an environment which is *continually changing*. The one thing I can be sure of is that the physics which is taught to the present day student will be outdated in a decade. The teaching in psychology will certainly be out of date in 20 years. The so-called "facts of history" depend very largely upon the current mood and temper of the culture. Chemistry, biology, genetics, sociology, are in such flux that a firm statement made today will almost certainly be modified by the time the student gets around to using the knowledge.

We are, in my view, faced with an entirely new situation in education where the goal of education, if we are to survive, is the *facilitation of change and learning*. The only man who is educated is the man who has learned how to learn; the man who has learned how to adapt and change; the man who has realized that no knowledge is secure, that only the process of *seeking* knowledge gives a basis for security. Changingness, a reliance on *process* rather than upon static knowledge, is the only thing that makes any sense as a goal for education in the modern world.

So now with some relief I turn to an activity, a purpose, which really warms me—the facilitation of learning. When I have been able to transform a group—and here I mean all the members of a group, myself included—into a community of *learners*, then the excitement has been almost beyond belief. To free curiosity; to permit individuals to go charging off in new directions dictated by their own interests; to unleash curiosity; to open everything to questioning and exploration; to recognize that everything is in process of change—here is an experience I can never forget. I cannot always achieve it in groups with which I am associated but when it is partially or largely achieved then it becomes a never-to-be-forgotten group experience. Out of such a context arise true students, real learners, creative scientists and scholars and practitioners, the kind of individuals who can live in a delicate but ever-changing balance between what is presently known and the flowing, moving, altering, problems and facts of the future.

Here then is a goal to which I can give myself wholeheartedly. I see the facilitation of learning as the aim of education, the way in which we might develop the learning man, the way in which we can learn to live as individuals in process. I see the facilitation of learning as the function which may hold constructive, tentative, changing, process answers to some of the deepest perplexities which beset man today.

But do we know how to achieve this new goal in education, or is it a will-of-the-wisp which sometimes occurs, sometimes fails to occur, and thus offers little real hope? My answer is that we possess a very considerable knowledge of the conditions which encourage self-initiated, significant, experimental, "gut-level" learning by the whole person. We do not frequently see these conditions put into effect because they mean a real revolution in our approach to education and revolutions are not for the timid. But we do find examples of this revolution in action.

We know—and I will briefly describe some of the evidence—that the initiation of such learning rests not upon the teaching skills of the leader, not upon his scholarly knowledge of the field, not upon his curricular planning, not upon his use of audio-visual aids, not upon the pro-grammed learning he utilizes, not upon his lectures and presentations, not upon an abundance of books, though each of these might at one time or another be utilized as an important resource. No, the facili-tation of significant learning rests upon certain attitudinal qualities which exist in the personal *relationship* between the facilitator and the learner.

We come upon such findings first in the field of psychotherapy, but increasingly there is evidence which shows that these findings apply in the classroom as well. We find it easier to think that the intensive re-lationship between therapist and client might possess these qualities, but we are also finding that they may exist in the countless interpersonal interactions (as many as 1,000 per day, as Jackson [1966] has shown) between the teacher and her pupils.

What are these qualities, these attitudes, which facilitate learning? Let me describe them very briefly, drawing illustrations from the teach-ing field.

Realness in the Facilitator of Learning

Perhaps the most basic of these essential attitudes is realness or genuineness. When the facilitator is a real person, being what he is, entering into a relationship with the learner without presenting a front or a facade, he is much more likely to be effective. This means that the feelings which he is experiencing are available to him, available to his awareness, that he is able to live these feelings, be them, and able to communicate them if appropriate. It means that he comes into a direct personal encounter with the learner, meeting him on a person-to-person basis. It means that he is *being* himself, not denying himself.

Seen from this point of view it is suggested that the teacher can be a real person in his relationship with his students. He can be enthusiastic, he can be bored, he can be interested in students, he can be angry, he can be sensitive and sympathetic. Because he accepts these feelings as his own he has no need to impose them on his students. He can like or dislike a student product without implying that it is objectively good or bad or that the student is good or bad. He is simply expressing a feeling for the product, a feeling which exists within himself. Thus, he is a person to his students, not a faceless embodiment of a curricular requirement nor a sterile tube through which knowledge is passed from one generation to the next.

It is obvious that this attitudinal set, found to be effective in psychotherapy, is sharply in contrast with the tendency of most teachers to show themselves to their pupils simply as roles. It is quite customary for teachers rather consciously to put on the mask, the role, the facade, of being a teacher, and to wear this facade all day removing it only when they have left the school at night.

But not all teachers are like this. Take Sylvia Ashton Warner, who took resistant, supposedly slow-learning primary school Maori children in New Zealand, and let them develop their own reading vocabulary. Each child could request one word—whatever word he wished—each day, and she would print it on a card and give it to him. "Kiss," "ghost," "bomb," "tiger," "fight," "love," "daddy"—these are samples. Soon they were building sentences, which they could also keep. "He'll get a licking." "Pussy's frightened." The children simply never forgot these self-initiated learnings. But it is not my purpose to tell you of her methods. I want instead to give you a glimpse of her attitude, of the passionate realness which must have been as evident to her tiny pupils as to her readers. An editor asked her some questions and she responded:

"'A few cool facts' you asked me for . . . I don't know that there's a cool fact in me, or anything else cool for that matter, on this particular subject. I've got only hot long facts on the matter of Creative Teaching, scorching both the page and me" (Warner, 1963, p. 26).

Here is no sterile facade. Here is a vital *person,* with convictions, with feelings. It is her transparent realness which was, I am sure, one of the elements that made her an exciting facilitator of learning. She doesn't fit into some neat educational formula. She *is,* and students grow by being in contact with someone who really *is.*

Take another very different person, Barbara Shiel, also doing exciting work facilitating learning in sixth graders.* She gave them a great deal of responsible freedom, and I will mention some of the reactions of her students later. But here is an example of the way she shared herself with her pupils—not just sharing feeling of sweetness and light, but anger and frustration. She had made art materials freely available, and students often used these in creative ways, but the room frequently looked like a picture of chaos. Here is her report of her feelings and what she did with them.

> "I find it (still) maddening to live with the mess—with a capital M! No one seems to care except me. Finally, one day I told the children . . . that I am a neat, orderly person by nature and that the mess was driving me to distraction. Did they have a solution? It was suggested they could have volunteers to clean up . . . I said it didn't seem fair to me to have the same people clean up all the time for others—but it *would* solve it for me. 'Well, some people *like* to clean,' they replied. So that's the way it is" (Shiel, 1966).

I hope this example puts some lively meaning into the phrases I used earlier, that the facilitator "is able to live these feelings, be them, and be able to communicate them if appropriate." I have chosen an example of negative feelings, because I think it is more difficult for most of us to visualize what this would mean. In this instance, Miss Shiel is taking the risk of being transparent in her angry frustrations about the mess. And what happens? The same thing which, in my experience, nearly always happens. These young people accept and respect her feelings, take them into account, and work out a novel solution which none of us, I believe, would have suggested in advance. Miss Shiel wisely comments:

> "I used to get upset and feel guilty when I became angry—I finally realized the children could accept *my* feelings, too. And it is important for them to know when they've 'pushed me.' I have limits, too" (Shiel, 1966).

---

*For a more extended account of Miss Shiel's initial attempts, see Rogers, 1966a. Her later experience is described in Shiel, 1966.

Just to show that positive feelings, when they are real, are equally effective, let me quote briefly a college student's reaction, in a different course. ". . . Your sense of humor in the class was cheering; we all felt relaxed because you showed us your human self, not a mechanical teacher image. I feel as if I have more understanding and faith in my teachers now . . . I feel closer to the students too." Another says, ". . . You conducted the class on a personal level and therefore in my mind I was able to formulate a picture of you as a person and not as merely a walking textbook." Or another student in the same course, ". . . It wasn't as if there was a teacher in the class, but rather someone whom we could trust and identify as a 'sharer.' You were so perceptive and sensitive to our thoughts, and this made it all the more 'authentic' for me. It was an 'authentic' *experience,* not just a class" (Bull, 1966).

I trust I am making it clear that to be real is not always easy, nor is it achieved all at once, but it is basic to the person who wants to become that revolutionary individual, a facilitator of learning.

Prizing, Acceptance, Trust

There is another attitude which stands out in those who are successful in facilitating learning. I have observed this attitude. I have experienced it. Yet, it is hard to know what term to put to it so I shall use several. I think of it as prizing the learner, prizing his feelings, his opinions, his person. It is a caring for the learner, but a non-possessive caring. It is an acceptance of this other individual as a separate person, having worth in his own right. It is a basic trust—a belief that this other person is somehow fundamentally trustworthy. Whether we call it prizing, acceptance, trust, or by some other term, it shows up in a variety of observable ways. The facilitator who has a considerable degree of this attitude can be fully acceptant of the fear and hesitation of the student as he approaches a new problem as well as acceptant of the pupil's satisfaction in achievement. Such a teacher can accept the student's occasional apathy, his erratic desires to explore by-roads of knowledge, as well as his disciplined efforts to achieve major goals. He can accept personal feelings which both disturb and promote learning—rivalry with a sibling, hatred of authority, concern about personal adequacy. What we are describing is a prizing of the learner as an imperfect human being with many feelings, many potentialities. The facilitator's prizing or acceptance of the learner is an operational expression of his essential confidence and trust in the capacity of the human organism.

I would like to give some examples of this attitude from the classroom situation. Here any teacher statements would be properly suspect, since many of us would like to feel we hold such attitudes, and might have a biased perception of our qualities. But let me indicate how this attitude of prizing, of accepting, of trusting, appears to the student who is fortunate enough to experience it.

Here is a statement from a college student in a class with Mr. Morey Appell:

> "Your way of being with us is a revelation to me. In your class I feel important, mature, and capable of doing things on my own. I want to think for myself and this need cannot be accomplished through textbooks and lectures alone, but through living. I think you see me as a person with real feelings and needs, an individual. What I say and do are significant expressions from me, and you recognize this" (Appell, 1959).

One of Miss Shiel's sixth graders expresses much more briefly her mispelled appreciation of this attitude, "You are a wonderful teacher period!!!

College students in a class with Dr. Patricia Bull describe not only these prizing, trusting attitudes, but the effect these have had on their other interactions.

> ". . . I feel that I can say things to you that I can't say to other professors. . . . Never before have I been so aware of the other students or their personalities. I have never had so much interaction in a college classroom with my classmates. The climate of the classroom has had a very profound effect on me . . . the free atmosphere for discussion affected me . . . the general atmosphere of a particular session affected me. There have been many times when I have carried the discussion out of the class with me and thought about it for a long time."
>
> ". . . I still feel close to you, as though there were some tacit understanding between us, almost a conspiracy. This adds to the in-class participation on my part because I feel that at least one person in the group will react, even when I am not sure of the others. It does not matter really whether your reaction is positive or negative, it just *IS*. Thank you."
>
> ". . . I appreciate the respect and concern you have for others, including myself. . . . As a result of my experience in class, plus the influence of my readings, I sincerely believe that the student-centered teaching method does provide an ideal framework for learning; not just for the accumulation of facts, but more important, for learning about ourselves in relation to others. . . . When I think back to my shallow awareness in September compared to the depth of my insights now, I know that this course has offered me a learning experience of great value which I couldn't have acquired in any other way."
>
> ". . . Very few teachers would attempt this method because they would feel that they would lose the students' respect. On the contrary. You gained our respect, through your ability to speak to us on our level, instead of ten miles above us. With the complete lack of communi-

cation we see in this school, it was a wonderful experience to see people listening to each other and really communicating on an adult, intelligent level. More classes should afford us this experience" (Bull, 1966).

As you might expect, college students are often suspicious that these seeming attitudes are phony. One of Dr. Bull's students writes:

". . . Rather than observe my classmates for the first few weeks, I concentrated my observations on you, Dr. Bull. I tried to figure out your motivations and purposes. I was convinced that you were a hypocrite . . . I did change my opinion, however. You are not a hypocrite, by any means . . . I wish the course could continue. 'Let each become all he is capable of being.' . . . Perhaps my most disturbing question, which relates to this course is: When will we stop hiding things from ourselves and our contemporaries?' (Bull, 1966).

I am sure these examples are more than enough to show that the facilitator who cares, who prizes, who trusts the learner, creates a climate for learning so different from the ordinary classroom that any resemblance is, as they say, "purely coincidental."

Empathic Understanding

A further element which establishes a climate for self-initiated, experiential learning is empathic understanding. When the teacher has the ability to understand the student's reactions from the inside, has a sensitive awareness of the way the process of education and learning seems *to the student,* then again the likelihood of significant learning is increased.

This kind of understanding is sharply different from the usual evaluative understanding, which follows the pattern of, "I understand what is wrong with you." When there is a sensitive empathy, however, the reaction in the learner follows something of this pattern, "At last someone understands how it feels and seems to be *me* without wanting to analyze me or judge me. Now I can blossom and grow and learn."

This attitude of standing in the other's shoes, of viewing the world through the student's eyes, is almost unheard of in the classroom. One could listen to thousands of ordinary classroom interactions without coming across one instance of clearly communicated, sensitively accurate, empathic understanding. But it has a tremendously releasing effect when it occurs.

Let me take an illustration from Virginia Axline, dealing with a second grade boy. Jay, age 7, has been aggressive, a trouble maker, slow of speech and learning. Because of his "cussing" he was taken to the principal, who paddled him, unknown to Miss Axline. During a free work period, he fashioned a man of clay, very carefully, down to a hat and a handkerchief in his pocket. "Who is that?" asked Miss Axline. "Dunno," replied Jay. "Maybe it is the principal. He has a handkerchief in his pocket like that." Jay glared at the clay figure. "Yes," he said. Then he began to tear the head off and looked up and smiled. Miss Axline said, "You sometimes feel like twisting his head off, don't you? You get so mad at him." Jay tore off one arm, another, then beat the figure to a pulp with his fists. Another boy, with the perception of the young, explained, "Jay is mad at Mr. X because he licked him this noon." "Then you must feel lots better now," Miss Axline commented. Jay grinned and began to rebuild Mr. X (Adapted from Axline, 1944).

The other examples I have cited also indicate how deeply appreciative students feel when they are simply *understood*—not evaluated, not judged, simply understood from their *own* point of view, not the teacher's. If any teacher sets herself the task of endeavoring to make one non-evaluative, acceptant, empathic response per day to a pupil's demonstrated or verbalized feeling, I believe he would discover the potency of this currently almost non-existent kind of understanding.

Let me wind up this portion of my remarks by saying that when a facilitator creates, even to a modest degree, a classroom climate characterized by such realness, prizing, and empathy, he discovers that he has inaugurated an educational revolution. Learning of a different quality, proceeding at a different pace, with a greater degree of pervasiveness, occurs. Feelings—positive and negative, confused—become a part of the classroom experience. Learning becomes life, and a very vital life at that. The student is on his way, sometimes excitedly, sometimes reluctantly, to becoming a learning, changing being.

THE EVIDENCE

Already I can hear the mutterings of some of my so-called "hardheaded" colleagues. "A very pretty picture—very touching. But these are all self reports." (As if there were any other type of expression! But that's another issue.) They ask "Where is the evidence? How do you know?" I would like to turn to this evidence. It is not overwhelming, but it is consistent. It is not perfect, but it is suggestive.

First of all, in the field of psychotherapy, Barrett-Lennard (1962) developed an instrument whereby he could measure these attitudinal qualities; genuineness or congruence, prizing or positive regard, empathy or understanding. This instrument was given to both client and therapist, so that we have the perception of the relationship both by the therapist and by the client whom he is trying to help. To state some of the findings very briefly it may be said that those clients who eventually showed more therapeutic change as measured by various instruments, perceived *more* of these qualities in their relationship with the therapist than did those who eventually showed less change. It is also significant that this difference in perceived relationships was evident as early as the fifth interview, and predicted later change or lack of change in therapy. Furthermore, it was found that the *client's* perception of the relationship, his experience of it, was a better predictor of ultimate outcome than was the perception of the relationship by the therapist. Barett-Lennard's original study has been amplified and generally confirmed by other studies.

So we may say, cautiously, and with qualifications which would be too cumbersome for the present paper, that if, in therapy, the client perceives his therapist as real and genuine, as one who likes, prizes, and empathically understands him, self-learning and therapeutic change are facilitated.

Now another thread of evidence, this time related more closely to education. Emmerling (1961) found that when high school teachers were asked to identify the problems they regarded as most urgent, they could be divided into two groups. Those who regarded their most serious problems, for example, as "Helping children think for themselves and be independent"; "Getting students to participate"; "Learning new ways of helping students develop their maximum potential"; "Helping students express individual needs and interests"; fell into what he called the "open" or "positively oriented" group. When Barrett-Lennard's Relationship Inventory was administered to the students of these teachers, it was found that they were perceived as significantly more real, more acceptant, more empathic than the other group of teachers whom I shall now describe.

The second category of teachers were those who tended to see their most urgent problems in negative terms, and in terms of student deficiencies and inabilities. For them the urgent problems were such as these: "Trying to teach children who don't even have the ability to follow directions"; "Teaching children who lack a desire to learn"; Students who are not able to do the work required for their grade"; "Getting the children to listen." It probably will be no surprise that when the students of these teachers filled out the Relationship Inventory they saw their teachers as exhibiting relatively little of genuineness, of acceptance and trust, or of empathic understanding.

Hence we may say that the teacher whose orientation is toward releasing the student's potential exhibits a high degree of these attitudinal qualities which facilitate learning. The teacher whose orientation is toward the shortcomings of his students exhibits much less of these qualities.

A small pilot study by Bills (1961, 1966) extends the significance of these findings. A group of eight teachers were selected, four of them rated as adequate and effective by their superiors, and also showing this more positive orientation to their problems. The other four were rated as inadequate teachers and also had a more negative orientation to their problems as described above. The students of these teachers were then asked to fill out the Barrett-Lennard Relationship Inventory, giving their perception of their teacher's relationship to them. This made the students very happy. Those who saw their relationship with the teacher as good were happy to describe this relationship. Those who had an unfavorable relationship were pleased to have, for the first time, an opportunity to specify the ways in which the relationship was unsatisfactory.

The more effective teachers were rated higher in every attitude measured by the Inventory: They were seen as more real, as having a higher level of regard for their students, were less conditional or judgmental in their attitudes, showed more empathic understanding. Without going into the details of the study it may be illuminating to mention that the total scores summing these attitudes vary sharply. For example, the relationships of a group of clients with their therapists, as perceived by the clients, received an average score of 108. The four most adequate high school teachers as seen by their students, received a score of 60. The four less adequate teachers received a score of 34. The lowest rated teacher received an average score of 2 from her students on the Relationship Inventory.

This small study certainly suggests that the teacher regarded as effective displays in her attitudes those qualities I have described as facilitative of learning, while the inadequate teacher shows little of these qualities.

Approaching the problem from a different angle, Schmuck (1963) has shown that in classrooms where pupils perceive their teachers as understanding them, there is likely to be a more diffuse liking structure among the pupils. This means that where the teacher is empathic, there are not a few students strongly liked and a few strongly disliked, but liking and affection are more evenly diffused throughout the group. In a later study he has shown that among students who are highly involved in their classroom peer group, "significant relationships exist between actual liking status on the one hand and utilization of abilities, attitude toward self, and attitude toward school on the other hand" (1966, p. 357-8). This seems to lend confirmation to the other evidence by indicating that in an understanding classroom climate every student tends to feel liked by all the others, to have a more positive attitude toward himself and toward school. If he is highly involved with his peer group (and this appears probable in such a classroom climate), he also tends to utilize his abilities more fully in his school achievement.

But you may still ask, does the student actually *learn* more where these attitudes are present? Here an interesting study of third graders by Aspy (1965) helps to round out the suggestive evidence. He worked in six third-grade classes. The teachers tape-recorded two full weeks of their interaction with their students in the periods devoted to the teaching of reading. These recordings were done two months apart so as to obtain an adequate sampling of the teacher's interactions with her pupils. Four-minute segments of these recordings were randomly selected for rating. Three raters, working independently and "blind," rated each segment for the degree of congruence or genuineness shown by the teacher, the degree of her prizing or unconditional positive regard, and the degree of her empathic understanding.

The Reading Achievement Tests (Stanford Achievement) were used as the criterion. Again, omitting some of the details of a carefully and rigorously controlled study, it may be said that the children in the three classes with the highest degree of the attitudes described above showed a significantly greater gain in reading achievement than those students in the three classes with a lesser degree of these qualities.

So we may say, with a certain degree of assurance, that the attitudes I have endeavored to describe are not only effective in facilitating a deeper learning and understanding of self in a relationship such as psychotherapy, but that these attitudes characterize teachers who are regarded as effective teachers, and that the students of these teachers learn more, even of a conventional curriculum, than do students of teachers who are lacking in these attitudes.

I am pleased that such evidence is accumulating. It may help to justify the revolution in education for which I am obviously hoping. But the most striking learnings of students exposed to such a climate are by no means restricted to greater achievement in the three R's. The significant learnings are the more personal ones—independence, self-initiated and responsible learning; release of creativity, a tendency to become more of a person. I can only illustrate this by picking, almost at random, statements from students whose teachers have endeavored to create a climate of trust, of prizing, of realness, of understanding, and above all, of freedom.

Again I must quote from Sylvia Ashton Warner one of the central effects of such a climate. ". . . The drive is no longer the teacher's, but the childrens' own . . . the teacher is at last with the stream and not against it, the stream of childrens' inexorable creativeness" (Warner, p. 93).

If you need verification of this, listen to a few of Dr. Bull's sophomore students. The first two are mid-semester comments.

". . . This course is proving to be a vital and profound experience for me. . . . This unique learning situation is giving me a whole new conception of just what learning is. . . . I am experiencing a real growth in this atmosphere of constructive freedom . . . the whole experience is very challenging. . . ."

". . . I feel that the course has been of great value to me . . . I'm glad to have had this experience because it has made me think. . . . I've never been so personally involved with a course before, especially *outside* the classroom. It's been frustrating, rewarding, enjoyable and tiring!"

The other comments are from the end of the course.

". . . This course is not ending with the close of the semester for me, but continuing . . . I don't know of any greater benefit which can be gained from a course than this desire for further knowledge. . . ."

". . . I feel as though this type of class situation has stimulated me more in making me realize where my responsibilities lie, especially as far as doing required work on my own. I no longer feel as though a test date is the criterion for reading a book. I feel as though my future work will be done for what *I* will get out of it, not just for a test mark."

". . . I have enjoyed the experience of being in this course. I guess that any dissatisfaction I feel at this point is a disappointment in myself, for not having taken full advantage of the opportunities the course offered."

". . . I think that now I am acutely aware of the breakdown in communications that does exist in our society from seeing what happened in our class. . . . I've grown immensely. I know that I am a different person than I was when I came into that class. . . . It has done a great deal in helping me understand myself better . . . thank you for contributing to my growth."

". . . My idea of education has been to gain information from the teacher by attending lectures. The emphasis and focus were on the teacher. . . . One of the biggest changes that I experienced in this class was my outlook on education. Learning is something more than a grade on a report card. No one can measure what you have learned because it's a personal thing. I was very confused between learning and memorization. I could memorize very well, but I doubt if I ever learned as much as I could have. I believe my attitude toward learning has changed from a grade-centered outlook to a more personal one."

". . . I have learned a lot more about myself and adolescents in general . . . I also gained more confidence in myself and my study habits by realizing that I could learn by myself without a teacher leading me by the hand. I have also learned a lot by listening to my classmates and evaluating their opinions and thoughts . . . this course has proved to be a most meaningful and worthwhile experience. . . ." (Bull, 1966)

If you wish to know what this type of course seems like to a sixth grader, let me give you a sampling of the reactions of Miss Shiel's youngsters, misspellings and all.

". . . I feel that I am learning self abilty. I am learning not only school work but I am learning that you can learn on your own as well as someone can teach you."

". . . I have a little trouble in Socail Studies finding things to do. I have a hard time working the exact amount of time. Sometimes I talk to much."

". . . My parents don't understand the program. My mother say's it will give me a responsiblity and it will let me go at my own speed."

". . . I like this plan because thire is a lot of freedom. I also learn more this way than the other way you don't have to wate for others you can go at your on speed rate it also takes a lot of responsibility" (Shiel, 1966).

Or let me take two more, from Dr. Appell's graduate class.

". . . I have been thinking about what happened through this experience. The only conclusion I come to is that if I try to measure what is going on, or what I was at the beginning, I have got to know what I was when I started—and I don't . . . so many things I did and feel are just lost . . . scrambled up inside. . . . They don't seem to come out in a nice little pattern or organization I can say or write. . . . There are so many things left unsaid. I know have only scratched the surface, I guess. I can feel so many things almost ready to come out . . . maybe that's enough. *It seems all kinds of things have so much more meaning now than ever before.* . . . This experience has had meaning, has done things to me and I am not sure how much or how far just yet. I think I am going to be a better me in the fall. *That's one thing I think I am sure of*" (Appell, 1963).

". . . You follow no plan, yet I'm learning. Since the term began I seem to feel more alive, more real to myself. I enjoy being alone as well as with other people. My relationships with children and other adults are becoming more emotional and involved. Eating an orange last week, I peeled the skin off each separate orange section and liked it better with the transparent shell off. It was jucier and fresher tasting that way. I began to think, that's how I feel sometimes, without a transparent wall around me, really communicating my feelings. I feel that I'm growing, how much, I don't know. I'm thinking, considering, pondering and learning" (Appell, 1959).

I can't read these student statements—6th grade, college, graduate level—without my eyes growing moist. Here are teachers, risking themselves, *being* themselves, *trusting* their students, adventuring into the existential unknown, taking the subjective leap. And what happens? Exciting, incredible *human* events. You can sense persons being created, learnings being initiated, future citizens rising to meet the challenge of unknown worlds. If only one teacher out of one hundred dared to risk, dared to be, dared to trust, dared to understand, we would have an infusion of a living spirit into education which would, in my estimation, be priceless.

I have heard scientists at leading schools of science, and scholars in leading universities, arguing that it is absurd to try to encourage all students to be creative—we need hosts of mediocre technicians and workers and if a few creative scientists and artists and leaders emerge, that will be enough. That may be enough for them. It may be enough to suit you. I want to go on record as saying it is *not* enough to suit me. When I realize the incredible potential in the ordinary student, I want to try to release it. We are working hard to release the incredible energy in the atom and the nucleus of the atom. If we do not devote equal energy—yes, and equal money—to the release of the potential of the individual person then the enormous discrepancy between our level of physical energy resources and human energy resources will doom us to a deserved and universal destruction.

I'm sorry I can't be coolly scientific about this. The issue is too urgent. I can only be passionate in my statement that people count, that interpersonal relationships *are* important, that we know something about releasing human potential, that we could learn much more, and that unless we give strong positive attention to the human interpersonal side of our educational dilemma, our civilization is on its way down the drain. Better courses, better curricula, better coverage, better teaching machines, will never resolve our dilemma in a basic way. Only persons, acting like persons in their relationships with their students can even begin to make a dent on the most urgent problem of modern education.

I cannot, of course, stop here in a university lecture. An academic lecture should be calm, factual, scholarly, critical, preferably devoid of any personal beliefs, completely devoid of passion. (This is one of the reasons I left university life, but that is a completely different story.) I cannot fully fulfill these requirements for a university lecture, but let me at least try to state, somewhat more calmly and soberly, what I have said with such feeling and passion.

I have said that it is most unfortunate that educators and the public think about, and focus on, *teaching*. It leads them into a host of questions which are either irrelevant or absurd so far as real education is concerned.

I have said that if we focused on the facilitation of *learning*—how, why, and when the student learns, and how learning seems and feels from the inside, we might be on a much more profitable track.

I have said that we have some knowledge, and could gain more, about the conditions which facilitate learning, and that one of the most important of these conditions is the attitudinal quality of the interpersonal relationship between facilitator and learner. (There are other conditions too, which I have tried to spell out elsewhere [Rogers, 1966b]).

Those attitudes which appear effective in promoting learning can be described. First of all is a transparent realness in the facilitator, a willingness to be a person, to be and live the feelings and thoughts of the moment. When this realness includes a prizing, a caring, a trust and respect for the learner, the climate for learning is enhanced. When it includes a sensitive and accurate empathic listening, then indeed a freeing climate, stimulative of self-initiated learning and growth, exists.

I have tried to make plain that individuals who hold such attitudes, and are bold enough to act on them, do not simply modify classroom methods—they revolutionize them. They perform almost none of the functions of teachers. It is no longer accurate to call them teachers. They are catalyzers, facilitators, giving freedom and life and the opportunity to learn, to students.

I have brought in the cumulating research evidence which suggests that individuals who hold such attitudes are regarded as effective in the classroom; that the problems which concern them have to do with the release of potential, not the deficiencies of their students; that they seem to create classroom situations in which there are not admired children and disliked children, but in which affection and liking are a part of the life of every child; that in classrooms approaching such a psychological climate, children learn more of the conventional subjects.

But I have intentionally gone beyond the empirical findings to try to take you into the inner life of the student—elementary, college, and graduate—who is fortunate enough to live and learn in such an interpersonal relationship with a facilitator, in order to let you see what learning feels like when it is free, self-initiated and spontaneous. I have tried to indicate how it even changes the student-student relationship—making it more aware, more caring, more sensitive, as well as increasing the self-related learning of significant material.

Throughout my paper I have tried to indicate that if we are to have citizens who can live constructively in this kaleidoscopically changing world, we can *only* have them if we are willing for them to become self-starting, self-initiating learners. Finally, it has been my purpose to show that this kind of learner develops best, so far as we now know, in a growth-promoting, facilitative, relationship with a *person*.

Relationship of Some Teaching Methods to Some Principles of Learning

NORMAN E. WALLEN AND ROBERT M. W. TRAVERS

The two previous sections of this chapter have been devoted to the design of teaching methods and the general nature of the procedures that should be followed. Although, in the past, knowledge available for the planning of teaching methods has been very meager, there are reasons for doubting that available knowledge has been used systematically. If teaching methods from the past are evaluated on their consistency with current knowledge of learning, they appear even more inadequate. But the interesting task of making such a comprehensive analysis would require major research. Nonetheless, to indicate the general lack of relationship between teaching methods and current knowledge of learning, a less extensive analysis will be presented. In this analysis, we shall not attempt to list a comprehensive set of widely accepted principles of learning and then study the extent to which each of a number of methods utilizes the principles involved. Rather, we will limit our discussion to six principles, as against the broad categories of variables used in our earlier discussion. The six principles are sufficient to illustrate the limitations of most teaching methods and perhaps also the difficulties involved in designing a method consistent with many principles.

Principle 1: Behavior which represents the achievement or partial achievement of an educational objective should be reinforced.

Significance of the principle for classroom learning. This principle means that there are known events which, if they occur subsequent to a response, facilitate the learning of the response, at least for some learners. The principle has great potential importance for education, because many of the common reinforcers are at least partially under the control of the teacher. Beginnings have been made in research on the identification of reinforcers. That such research is likely to be fruitful is evident from the studies that have been undertaken on the effects of praise and blame (Forlano & Axelrod, 1937; G. G. Thompson & Hunnicutt, 1944), a simple classification of potential reinforcers. These studies suggest that although praise may, in most cases, be a better reinforcer, blame is better for some students, and that the efficiency of each type can be predicted with some accuracy even with a fairly crude questionnaire measure of student personality. It is also known

---

From *Handbook of Research on Teaching*, N. L. Gage, ed., (New York: Rand McNally, 1964), pp. 494-501.

that certain kinds of information may serve as reinforcers, at least under some conditions.

A special class of reinforcers is described by the phrase "knowledge of results." Whenever the learner has a clearly defined goal toward which he is striving, and when the attainment of the goal depends upon the comparison of the learner's behavior with some kind of standard, such comparisons may function as reinforcers. This aspect of reinforcement, easily demonstrated in the laboratory, has also been demonstrated in educational settings.

Despite the excellent beginnings that have been made in research in this area, little is known about the reinforcing effect of the following practices which are frequently observed in schools:

1. Public display of the accomplishments of the student.
2. Providing new problems to be solved after the student has shown some skill in solving a particular class of problem.
3. Physical contact with the teacher.
4. Praising a child for good behavior but with an implied reprimand for the other children.
5. The smiles or laughter of the teacher.
6. Gestures of approval from fellow students.
7. Meeting standards set by the pupil himself.
8. Disagreement of the teacher with the student.

Utilization of the principle by different teaching methods. Teaching methods show substantial differences in the presumed reinforcers which they introduce and also in the extent to which they recognize and utilize reinforcement at all. For example, what is commonly referred to as the lecture method of teaching assumes that information can be communicated without making any provision for reinforcement. The transmission is strictly an intellectual process. Other traditional forms of teaching rely upon grades, release from the learning situation ("You may go as soon as you have the right answers"), reduction in anxiety, or the promise that the results of learning will be appreciated later in life. Recitation methods appear to rely either on direct approval as a reinforcer or on silence, as when the teacher indicates only when a pupil is wrong and moves on to the next question when he is right. Newer methods rely more upon "intrinsic" reinforcers which are assumed to derive from the learning activity or the response itself. Group approval, teacher approval, and self approval are also mentioned as reinforcers in some descriptions of modern teaching methods. Skinner (1958) used a concept similar to that of "intrinsic" reinforcers when he stated that some activities are self-reinforcing. Discussion methods of conducting classes, in which the pupils interact with one another, would appear to rely upon social conditions such as approval of another's response.

Since we do not know which set of reinforcers or which combination is most effective, differences in method must represent differences in personal preferences. Perhaps a person is likely to recommend the use of those reinforcers which are effective for him.

Principle 2: The introduction of cues which arouse motivation toward the achievement of an educational objective will increase the effectiveness with which that objective is achieved.

Significance of the principle for classroom learning. An important corollary should be added to this principle—*an optimum level of motivation exists at which learning is facilitated to a maximum degree.* Motivation energizes action and also gives direction to action. Many who have studied the problems of effective teaching hold that the main function of the teacher is to arrange conditions so that the pupil directs his energies toward worth-while goals. The doctrine of interest which preceded modern conceptions of motivation recognized that some objects in the environment were more capable than others of arousing a positive affective response, but the relationship between affective responses and goal-directed action systems was never clear. Implicit in most discussions of interest was the idea that pupils learn most when they like what they do. The doctrine had difficulty in coping with the fact that a pupil will sometimes voluntarily devote large amounts of time to distasteful activities which enable him to achieve a goal important to him. Modern conceptions of motivation have overcome this basic difficulty in the doctrine of interest, though many other difficulties remain. Of special interest to the understanding of classroom behavior are the concepts of motivation developed by McClelland, Atkinson, Clark, and Lowell (1953) and by Spence and Taylor (1951). McClelland's type of theory recognizes that the level of motivation depends partly on the cues provided by the environment and partly on internal capacity to respond to those cues. It implies that teachers may be able to supply cues which arouse activity, but also that the structures which permit these cues to operate may not exist in all pupils. The theory does not exclude the possibility that all environmental stimuli or variations in such stimuli may have arousal properties.

Of particular importance is the variable denoted "anxiety." Although defined in various ways, it generally connotes a condition of observable agitation accompanied by such physiological observables as sweating palms, increased heartbeat, etc., and verbal statements of "unpleasantness." In short, "anxiety" connotes a response pattern similar to what is often called fear. Although it was once fashionable to speak of anxiety as unequivocally undesirable in an educational setting, present thinking and research do not support this generalization. Excessive anxiety may indeed hinder learning; a great body of evidence shows that extreme, persistent anxiety hinders at least certain types of learning in both subhuman species and man. Yet some data suggest that anxiety facilitates very simple forms of learning, wherein previously learned responses are of slight importance. Furthermore, some theorists consider reinforcement—in this case anxiety reduction—to be the crucial variable. They argue that the deliberate arousal of anxiety is desirable (particularly if it can, through learning, come to be elicited by any problem situation) provided that the anxiety is reduced subsequent to certain behaviors. Perhaps activity directed at the problem can itself become reinforcing—such would seem to be the case with at least some scientists. From this point of view, the undersirable features of anxiety result when anxiety is allowed to persist too long (Bugelski, 1956, pp. 460-463). It is also possible that excessive motivation may hinder learning when the motivation is other than anxiety.

Despite the growing body of knowledge about motivational conditions related to learning, we lack much information vitally needed for the design of teaching methods. No method exists for determining which cues will produce arousal in a particular child. A clear picture of the development of motives is lacking. What to do about the child who typically shows a very low level of arousal or a very high one is still largely speculative. Numerous other problems could be listed.

Utilization of the principle and its corollaries by different teaching methods. The state of knowledge in this area is unsatisfactory. The fact that the most significant work is of recent origin is reflected in the vague and confused thinking about motivation which characterizes most teaching methods. The methods which derive from the Rousseau tradition are based on the assumptions that the world surrounding the child is full of cues adequate to arouse motivation and that the teacher must take great care not to remove these cues or inhibit their effect. The progressive education movement after World War I followed this tradition and attempted to fill the classroom with objects and materials which would raise the level of arousal. Individual differences in the arousal produced by different classes of cues were taken into account by the variety provided. Visitors to such classrooms generally agreed that they witnessed a high level of activity among the pupils, though some would question whether it was directed toward desirable goals.

Traditional education has tended to adopt the reverse policy of avoiding distracting elements in the classroom so that the pupil would devote more attention to either the teacher or his books. Where the moving about of the pupils was restricted, as it was in such classrooms, a rich range of materials would have little value. In this situation great reliance was placed on the arousal value of the teacher and the printed materials. In some cases the teacher was able to perform this arousal function with great success, but in others the teacher had to fall back on the utilization of anxiety as a motive. To some extent, the policies of the progressive education movement represented a revolt against the use of anxiety as a motive manipulated by the teacher.

Other teaching methods disregard to a great degree the operation of motivational variables. The typical lecture method assumes that a lecturer can transmit information and that whatever motivation is necessary has to be inherent in the student. Still, even the most ardent protagonist of the lecture method would agree that some lecturers are much more capable than others of "arousing interest." How a lecturer is to do this is not generally specified. Advocates of self-selection teaching methods (Olson, 1959) assume that a rich environment will provide cues which arouse a pupil in such a way that worth-while long-term goals are eventually achieved.

Undoubtedly, the designer of a teaching method may have considerable choice concerning what motives to invoke. The same educational goal may be achieved through the operation of many different motivational variables. Choice may depend also on factors other than the efficiency of the learning process. Objections to the use of anxiety as a motive are based more on ethical than on psychological issues.

Principle 3: Practice in applying a principle to the solution of problems will increase the probability of transfer of training to new problems which require the use of the same principle for their solution.

Significance of the principle for classroom learning. This is the principle which emerges from the work on learning sets conducted by Harlow (1949) and his associates. Most educators would agree that the learning of principles such as Newton's laws of motion cannot be considered an end in itself, and that the importance of learning lies in the possibility that the principles may be applied to the solution of numerous problems. Just how such transfer of training was to take place was a complete mystery until Harlow demonstrated that transfer to novel situations would occur most readily if certain training practices were followed. These demonstrations do not imply that all is known concerning the most effective ways of teaching broad problem-solving skills. A particularly important problem is whether principles which are "self-discovered" are better retained and more easily transferred than those which have been handed to the student. That relationships of learning conditions in the area of problem-solving to subsequent performance are complex is well illustrated in a study by Kersh (1958). In this study three groups learned the "rules" necessary for solving mathematical problems. The groups consisted of a "no help" group which was supposed to discover the rules, a rule-given group, and a group given an intermediate amount of assistance. The "no help," or "self-discovery," group developed a greater postexperimental interest in the problems than either one of the other two groups. But the intermediate group was superior to the other two groups in application of the rules to new problems.

Utilization of the principle by different teaching methods. Long before current knowledge of methods of teaching problem-solving, the protagonists of particular teaching methods adopted policies for teaching problem-solving skills. Some of these practices were based on practical experience and have subsequently been justified by research. For example, teachers of mathematics in a traditional framework of education commonly gave their students large numbers of problems to solve related to each principle that was studied. Physics teachers have done likewise. Experience in teaching in these areas seems to justify this practice, and it is also largely in accordance with recent research on problem-solving. In contrast, the project method of Kilpatrick assumed that the kind of problem-solving involved in working on large projects would develop the required problem-solving skills. Furthermore, lecture and demonstration methods of teaching problem-solving assume that the process can be learned efficiently by vicarious experience, though in fairness one must state that lecture methods have often been coupled with problem-solving assignments given as homework. In recent years, those who have proposed that teaching be centered around the use of teaching machines have seen the possibility of exposing the pupil to carefully planned programs of problems. Mechanized teaching equipment offers the possibility of developing learning sets much more systematically than is possible with the typical recitation method. Indeed, they are ideally suited to making use of the operation of this particular principle.

Principle 4: Since learners differ in their capacity to make the responses to be acquired, learning will be most efficient if it is planned so that each learner embarks on a program commensurate with his capacity to acquire new responses.

Significance of the principle for classroom learning. The principle is stated in general terms and could be stated in a series of separate and distinct principles, each specifying some known variable which is related to the capacity of the individual to acquire or manifest par-

ticular categories of response. This principle excludes variables in the
motivational and affective categories. Under ideal conditions a teacher
should be able to measure the capacity of each child to learn a range
of responses before instruction is initiated. In the absence of such a
procedure, the possibilities of individualized teaching are limited. If
individual differences are to be taken into account, the only alternative to systematic assessment is the adoption of some procedure for
the study of the child under conditions as they exist in the school.
Despite the widespread claim that child-study methods are going to
solve this problem, the failure of the leader of this movement to evolve
and set of validated techniques for observing children under typical
school conditions has led to skepticism about the value of this approach
to the assembly of individual differences.

While much research has already been undertaken on the intellectual
capacities related to individual differences in the capacity to learn,
many fundamental issues still have to be explored. For example, little
is known about the generation of the various psychological "factors" that
have been demonstrated to represent measurable variables related to
learning in the young adult. To what extent early learning, in the sense
used by Hebb (1958), generates some of the "factors" that are measured is an important question which still needs to be investigated.

Utilization of the principle by different teaching methods. Emphasis
on individual differences and on differences within the same individual
over a period of time has been largely responsible for the development
of many of the "methods" mentioned previously, such as the activity,
progressive, and laboratory approaches. Carried even further it has led
to the propagation by Olson (1959) of an interesting approach to teaching method called "self-selection." In essence, the child is allowed a
great deal of freedom in structuring his learning situation whether it be
in terms of books to read, arithmetic workbooks, or presumably the
broader areas of what responses are to be learned. This approach places
great reliance on the child's seeking those experiences which will develop
desired responses. Thus, the role of the teacher, according to Olson
(1959, p. 404), is to "guarantee that every classroom situation, or its
immediate surroundings, will have in it tasks which are interesting in
terms of the intrinsic content, and which also cover a range of difficulty
as great as the variability in the human material with which he deals.
Research with this technique is virtually nonexistent, though Olson does
mention a study in arithmetic at the third- and fourth-grade level which,
he believed, indicated that on the whole the children were sound in the
judgment of their abilities and that the gains under a considered self-
selection plan seemed somewhat better than under a more laissez-faire

procedure maintained in previous years. Inasmuch as this technique assumes that arousal of motivation and reinforcement will occur without any specific planning by the teacher and that the student will adequately assess his readiness—assumptions which many psychologists would not be willing to grant—further research is imperative.[1]

Principle 5: If a pupil has had training in imitation, then he is capable of learning by observing demonstrations of the skills to be acquired.

Significance of the principle for classroom learning. The nature of imitative activity and the conditions under which it occurs have long been matters of interest to education. The frequently voiced notion that the teacher should set a good example and perhaps behave according to standards far above those demanded of other members of the community is based upon the assumption that children will imitate teachers. In the classroom many teachers have doubted the efficacy of imitation as a mechanism for development of skills. Little was known about the phenomenon of imitation until it was systematically studied by Miller and Dollard (1941) within a framework of reinforcement learning theory. Their research with animal and human subjects showed that imitation is a learned behavior tendency, and without the learning of the tendency, imitation does not occur. This finding suggests that there may be individual differences in the ability to imitate produced by differences in previous training in imitation. Insofar as this is the case, the teacher may either have to develop imitative skills in some children or plan for them a learning program which does not involve imitation. Certainly, the inability of many children in kindergarten or first grade to learn from demonstrations suggests that substantial individual differences do exist in this area.

Utilization of the principle by different teaching methods. Few teaching methods have been clear in the application of this principle. Despite general agreement that many attributes of character are learned by an imitative process, there is little agreement that intellectual skills are learned by a similar process. Indeed, the concept that has found its way more and more into education during the last half-century has been that learning is most effective when the learner performs directly the response to be learned. One claim of progressive education was that traditional education involved learning by vicarious experience and that greater activity on the part of the learner was desirable. In the new

---

[1]Since the writing of this chapter, *Summerhill*, by A. S. Neill, has appeared and requires comment. Although not a research report, this description of the techniques and results of 40 years of experience with self-selective procedures in a small residential school is a persuasive argument for their effectiveness. It is to be hoped that further work meeting the more rigorous definition of research advocated here will be done and reported.

education, learning by imitation was not to be a central method of intellectual development. A similar emphasis is seen in many "plans" such as the Winnetka Plan and the Morrison Plan. Such approaches to education and the teaching methods which they imply leave little place for the application of the principle under consideration. Perhaps the "learning by doing" concept of education has had an undue influence on educational planning. Certainly other methods of learning have value and these include learning by imitation and learning by being shown, as when the teacher takes the hand of a child and guides it in the writing of his name. The latter process, studied in a variety of situations, has been shown to produce learning, sometimes of a kind that is hard to produce by other means.

Principle 6: The learner will learn more efficiently if he makes the responses to be learned than if he learns by observing another make the response or makes some related response.

Significance of the principle for classroom learning. This principle does not exclude the possibility that learning may be accomplished by imitation, i.e., by means other than doing. It does emphasize the importance of the learner's own attempt to make the response to be learned. As has been emphasized in the discussion of the principle involving imitation, there are circumstances under which the learner may profit by observing the performance of another. Nevertheless, the actual performance of the learner permits aspects of learning to take place which are not, and often cannot be, acquired by vicarious means. This has led many psychologists, notably Skinner (1958), to emphasize the importance of the learner's making the full and complete response. A distinction must also be made between the learner's making the full response and the learner's making certain substitute responses, often of a verbal nature. A child's expressing his attitude toward, say, religious or racial minorities in a classroom situation may differ vastly from what emerges in a real problem situation.

Utilization of the principle by different teaching methods. Many traditional forms of teaching relied heavily on learning occurring through the learner's observing the response of another. In the lecture method, as it has been used in teaching mathematics and the physical sciences, the teacher often solves a problem in front of the class and expects the pupils to learn thereby the problem-solving technique. Doubts concerning the efficiency of this approach were highly influential in bringing about educational change during the first half of the present century. Another common approach to education has been for the pupil to make, not the response to be learned, but some substitute or related response. Thus the student may discuss how he would behave in certain situations involving moral issues and indicate the moral stand he might take. For years, Sunday schools relied upon this method of teaching moral values. The assumption was that verbal behavior which reflected high moral values would be followed by other forms of behavior which reflected the same values. The classic research of Hartshorne and May (1930) demonstrated that this assumption was not sound. The project method of Kilpatrick was an attempt to abandon the method of learning by indirect experience or by substitute verbal responses. Some educators trained in group dynamics have also suggested teaching methods where the learner practices responses or aspects of responses to be learned rather than practicing verbal responses. The danger of designing a teaching method around single principles is seen in many of these efforts to apply a "learning by doing" concept of education, to the neglect of other approaches to learning or other variables.

IMPLICATIONS FOR RESEARCH AND PRACTICE

The preceding discussion is not a comprehensive analysis of the relationship of learning principles to teaching methods. Only a few principles of learning have been discussed. Teaching methods have been discussed in terms of broad categories, and particular viewpoints within these categories have been overlooked. The object has not been to present a complete blueprint of these relationships; rather it has been to show that different teaching methods emphasize different principles and neglect others. Since this is the case, there is little likelihood that any one is superior to any other when the over-all effects of teaching are appraised. The best one might hope for would be slight differences in teaching effectiveness within narrow aspects of the learning process, and this is roughly what is found by empirical research.

The writers see the great need at the present time for an attempt to design a teaching method which makes as much use as possible of a wide range of learning principles. When this is done, there may be some hope of finding a teaching method which is definitely and markedly superior to others which have not been thus systematically designed. There is a possibility that many different teaching methods might be designed which would make full use of many principles, differences between them being a product of the objectives that each is designed to achieve. Also, the same goals may be achieved with equal efficiency by each one of a number of different teaching methods, efficiency being measured as a function of learner time. These are problems which will have to be explored before research of a scientific nature can be expected to make a major contribution.

Research on Teaching Methods

W. J. MCKEACHIE

This review is organized in terms of traditional categories of teaching method—lecturing, discussion, laboratory—and also in terms of fairly recent approaches to college instruction—project methods, independent study, and automated techniques.

LECTURING

College teaching and lecturing have been so long associated that when one pictures a college professor in a classroom, he almost inevitably pictures him as lecturing. The popularity of the lecture method probably derives from a conception of the instructor's primary goal as that of transmitting knowledge.

Since students typically have few opportunities to make responses during lectures, they seldom receive feedback from their efforts to learn during lectures. Delay of feedback may not, however, seriously hinder the learner in acquiring knowledge if he is motivated and the material is not too difficult. We would expect lack of feedback to be a greater handicap if the lecturer's goal is to develop concepts or problem-solving skills. There is experimental evidence that, when this is the goal, active participation on the part of the learner is more effective than passive listening or observing.

Lecture Method versus Discussion Method

The effectiveness of lecture and discussion methods has often been compared. Since discussion offers the opportunity for a good deal of student activity and feedback, it could, in theory, be more effective than the lecture method in developing concepts and problem-solving skills. However, since the rate of transmission of information is slow in discussion classes, we would expect lecture classes to be superior in helping students acquire knowledge of information.

Although many studies have been made comparing the lecture method with discussion or other methods, few have used independent measures of these different types of outcome. The results of these studies are generally in line with our hypotheses but are certainly not conclusive. For example, using tests of information, Remmers (1933) found slight

From *Handbook of Research on Teaching,* N. L. Gage, ed., (New York: Rand McNally, 1964), pp. 1125-1149.

but nonsignificant differences favoring learning in large lecture groups as compared with that in small (35-40) recitation sections. Spence (1928) obtained similar results comparing lecture and discussion technique in classes of over a hundred students. In one of the earliest comparisons of lecture and discussion methods, Bane (1925) found little difference between the methods on measures of immediate recall but a significant superiority for discussion on a measure of delayed recall. Ruja (1954), however, found that the lecture was superior to discussion as measured by a test of subject-matter mastery in a general psychology course. In the other two courses in his experiment there were no significant differences in achievement, nor were there differences in changes in adjustment in any of the courses. Eglash (1954) found no difference between a discussion class and lecture class in scores on the final examination, in scores on an achievement test administered several weeks after the course had ended, or in scores on a measure of tolerance. Husband (1951) also found no significant difference in achievement of students in large (200-student) lecture and in "small" (50-student) recitation classes, but in five out of six semesters the lecture group was nonsignificantly superior. In all these experiments, the information measured by the examination could be obtained from a textbook, and in only one was a discussion group of less than 35 used.

When we turn to measures of more complex outcomes, the results are somewhat different. Hirschman (1952), using a measure of concept learning, compared the effectiveness of presenting material by dictation with that of presenting written materials followed by discussion and rereading. The reading-discussion method resulted in superior ability to identify examples of the concepts presented. In quite a different type of experiment, Barnard (1942) compared the effectiveness of a lecture-demonstration teaching method with that of a problem-solving developmental discussion in a college science course. In this experiment the lecture-demonstration method proved superior on a test of specific information, but the discussion method proved to be superior on measures of problem solving and scientific attitude. Similarly Dawson (1956) found problem-solving recitation and lecture-demonstration methods to be equally effective in a course in elementary soil science as measured by a test of recall of specific information, but the problem-solving method was significantly superior as measured by tests of problem-solving abilities. Other evidence favoring discussion was the experiment of Elliott, who found that students in his discussion groups in elementary psychology became more interested in electing additional courses in psychology than did students in a large lecture.[1] The results of DiVesta's (1954) study of a human relations course tended to favor a discussion method over the lecture method in improving scores on a leadership test. Similarly, Casey and Weaver (1956) found no differences in knowledge of content but superiority in attitudes (as measured by the Minnesota Teacher Attitude Inventory) for small-group discussions as compared to lectures.

Despite the many findings of no significant differences in effectiveness between lecture and discussion, those studies which have found differences make surprisingly good sense. In only two studies was one method superior to the other on a measure of knowledge of subject matter; both studies favored the lecture method. In all six experiments finding significant differences favoring discussion over lecture, the measures were other than final examinations testing knowledge.

When one is asked whether lecture is better than discussion, the appropriate counter would seem to be, "For what goals?"

Distribution of Lecture and Discussion Time

Many universities and large colleges divide class meetings between lectures and discussions. This administrative arrangement is supported by a study in the teaching of physiology, in which discussion meetings were substituted for one-third of the lectures (Lifson, Rempel, & Johnson, 1956). Although there were no significant differences in achievement, as compared with all lectures, the partial discussion method resulted in more favorable student attitudes which persisted in a follow-up study two years later. Warren (1954) compared the effectiveness of one lecture and four recitations with that of two lectures and three demonstrations per week. In one out of five comparisons, the one-lecture plan was superior, while the other comparisons found nonsignificant differences. Superior students tended to prefer the two-lecture plan while poorer students did not. On the other hand, in Remmers' (1933) comparison of two lectures and one recitation versus three recitations, the poorer students tended to do better in the lecture-recitation combination, although students in both groups preferred the three-recitation arrangement. In Klapper's study (1958) at New York University, most students preferred a combination lecture-discussion method to one employing all lectures or all discussions. Students at the State University of Iowa also preferred all group discussion or a combination of lecture and discussion to lectures alone (Becker, Murray, & Bechtoldt, 1958).

---

[1]D. Beardslee, R. Birney, & W. J. McKeachie, *Summary of Conference on Research in Classroom Processes* (Dept. of Psychology, University of Michigan, 1951) (Unpublished).

In a course in which the instructors wish not only to give information but also to develop concepts, the use of both lectures and discussions would thus seem to be a logical and popular choice. The lecture can effecitvely present new research findings; the discussion can give students opportunities to analyze the studies, find relationships, and develop generalizations. By participating actively in discussion, the students should not only learn the generalizations but should also begin developing skill in critical thinking.

The Lecturer versus Automation

Since we have hypothesized that the lecturer is particularly effective in transmitting information, it is in order to ask how the lecturer in the ordinary classroom compares with other means of transmitting information. As has already been suggested, if the learner is motivated, a good deal of communication of knowledge apparently can take place with relatively infrequent checks on the progress of the learner and relatively few extrinsic rewards. From Hebb (1949) it could be inferred that relatively fresh ideas would be motivating, but that experiences too far removed from the student's past experience would produce anxiety. This suggests that the generalization of materials should be of great importance in learning.

Skinner and his students have recently popularized teaching machines which present course materials in well-organized step-by-step fashion with questions (Skinner, 1958). When a student misses a question on some machines, the question is later repeated, but when the correct response is made, the learner proceeds. It seems that the teaching machine should have advantages over the lecturer, for the sequence can be carefully planned to utilize research on the method of successive approximations, on concrete to abstract sequences in problem solving, and on building up generalizations from varying specifics. Lecturers, on the other hand, vary greatly in the degree to which they organize their materials systematically. Probably few lecturers use optimal sequences of presentation.

Moreover, the learner in a lecture is largely passive, while the learner using a teaching machine is continually active. Many studies of different types of learning and concept-formation demonstrate that active learning is more effective than passive learning (e.g., Ebbinghaus, 1913; Wolfle, 1935). Further, the lecturer presents material symbolically. For learning involving perceptual or motor responses, verbal descriptions should be less effective than actual sensorimotor experiences.

Because the lecture provides little feedback, does not always present material in an optimum sequence, allows the student to be passive, and provides little direct experience, lectures may be inferior to other teaching media in achieving certain goals. In fact, if instructors become extinct, they will probably first disappear from the lecture hall.

The chief competitor of the lecturer is not the teaching machine, television, or film, but a much older invention—printing. If rate of transmission of knowledge is important in teaching, a good book is hard to beat. Not only can the reader control his own rate, but the motivated, skilled reader can traverse the printed page much more rapidly than even the faster lecturer can deliver the material. Over a generation ago, Greene (1928) demonstrated that college students learned as much from reading a passage as from hearing the same material in a lecture.

Although printed materials have been almost as popular as television and have existed for a much longer time, lectures have survived. Even the advent of picture-book textbooks did not dislodge the lecturer. If we stop to think about this, we probably should not be surprised that dozens of research studies have not had much impact upon lecturers' attitudes toward television.

Perhaps the lecturer's arguments are rationalizations, for there is little research to support them. Nevertheless, psychologists may have underestimated important factors in their usual analyses of the learning situation. To maintain good experimental controls, we carefully control rate and sequence of presentation in most of our experiments. The materials used are meaningless to the learner. The results lead us to stress the importance of feedback to the learner.

Lecturing, however, is largely devoted to communicating meaningful materials to somewhat motivated learners. Apparently such learning can take place with relatively infrequent checks on the progress of the learner. In fact, the learner can to some extent obtain feedback by himself. Our experimental controls lead us to overlook the important fact that when knowledge is presented by a teacher he is able to respond to feedback from the learners. This may be an important asset of the instructor. Films and television present material at a relatively fixed rate, but an instructor can go faster or slower when he gets cues of inattention, irritation, or confusion from his class.

The reader too can pace himself, but the inexperienced student may not be able to separate the important from the unimportant. Even though lecturers speak more slowly than books can be read, a good lecturer may be able to give his students all they need from a book in much less time than it would take them to read it.

Textbooks, films, and teaching machines must be organized to fit average students if they are to be economically feasible. The lecturer can not only plan his lecture for his own class but he can respond to feedback from his class as he delivers it. This responsiveness to cues from the class is probably the reason that material can be covered less rapidly in "live" classes than in television classes. Because the instructor responds to feedback, his presentation may appear to be unorganized. Yet one might hypothesize that this very responsiveness makes for greater effectiveness than does a carefully organized, inflexible presentation.

Although there is little relevant research evidence on this matter, we would expect live lecturing to be most effective in situations where there is considerable variation between groups in ability, relevant background, or motivation and where flexible adjustment to the group is therefore important.

Most lecturers avow aims beyond transmission of information. College instructors often say that they provide the integration lacking in the text. Again one would expect that other means of communication could also provide integration. Probably what the instructor really does is to provide his own system of integration. Whether or not this is preferable to the integration provided by a textbook, acceptance of the frame of reference of the instructor does at least make a difference in the grade received by the student. Runkel (1956) measured the structure of instructors' and students' attitudes in beginning college courses in psychology and zoology. He found that *agreement* with the instructor's position *did not* predict students' grades, but students whose attitudes were *colinear* (i.e., who used the same dimensions) with the instructor *did* earn higher grades. In short, students who structured the field as the instructor did, tended to earn higher grades. What we do not know yet is whether or not the instructor can communicate his structure to students who do not already have it.

Probably the most careful attempts to measure attitudinal and motivational outcomes have been those comparing live instruction with television instruction in the research programs at Pennsylvania State University and Miami University. In neither case did the live instructor seem to be superior. Still, if the students' tendency to identify with the instructor has anything to do with personal interaction with the instructor, it may be ominous that students did not seek personal conferences with television instructors as much as with "live" instructors.

Methods of Lecturing

Few experiments have compared the effectiveness of classroom lectures with other teaching methods in achieving attitude change, but if we turn from classroom experiments to other research dealing with change of attitudes, we find a substantial and growing literature relevant to differing techniques of lecturing.

The research of Hovland and his associates at Yale (1953) indicates that such variables as credibility of the lecturer, order of presentation, presentation of one side of an issue versus presentation of both sides, and emotionality of argument are factors in determining the effect of a lecture. For example, the Hovland group found that a group of college students were more likely to change their opinions (at least temporarily) when they received a persuasive communication from a source which they considered highly credible than when the same communication came from a less credible source. Although we assume that students perceive their instructors as credible sources, faculty rating scales including an item such as "Knowledge of Subject Matter" have revealed that students do discriminate between professors on this dimension. It has been argued, against inclusion of this item, that students are not competent judges of the instructor's knowledge. Regardless of the validity of the student ratings, however, they may indicate the students' credence in the instructor's statements and thus his effectiveness in bringing about attitude changes.

In most of the Yale experiments comparing communication sources with differing credibilities, the actual information gained from the communication was not different for different communicators. In one study, however, a communication from a neutral source resulted in greater informational learning than did the same communication emanating from either an expert or a biased source. Should teachers try to be neutral laymen?

Sometimes even college professors try to reinforce their points by waving the flag or preaching academic hell-fire and brimstone. The Yale studies suggest that this type of teaching is ineffective, for they indicate that the greatest change in reported behavior occurred in those groups to which a minimally fear-arousing lecture was given. This difference persisted at least a year, even though all presentations resulted in equal factual learning.

In presenting controversial points the lecturer often wonders whether he should present the evidence on both sides of the issue or simply present that favoring the position he accepts. Aside from the ethical problems involved, the Yale experiments indicated the greater effectiveness of presenting both sides for (1) an intelligent audience, (2) those initially disagreeing with the lecturer's position, and (3) those who come into contact with the opposing arguments in some setting other than the lecture.

If he wishes to present two sides of an issue, the lecturer is faced with the problem of choosing the order in which to present them. An extensive series of studies has illuminated the effects of differing orders. The most relevant results have been summarized as follows:

When contradictory information is presented in a single communication, by a single communicator, there is a pronounced tendency for those items presented first to dominate the impression received (Hovland, 1957, p. 133).

The primacy effect found in presenting contradictory information in the same communication was reduced by interpolating other activities between the two blocks of information and by warning the subjects against the fallibility of first impressions (Hovland, 1957, p. 134).

Placing communications highly desirable to the recipient first, followed by those less desirable, produces more opinion change than the reverse order (Hovland, 1957, p. 136).

When an authoritative communicator plans to mention pro arguments and also nonsalient con arguments the pro-first order is superior to the con-first order (Hovland, 1957, p. 137).

Research on organization of materials is also relevant to lecturing aimed at cognitive changes. In organizing a lecture the professor frequently is guided by the maxim "Tell them what you're going to tell them. Tell them. Then tell them what you've told them." In a classroom experiment in a course in physics (Lahti, 1956), the instructor first stated a principle and then illustrated and applied it. He compared this with a technique in which he developed principles by demonstration and analysis of application situations and then stated the principle. For students with poor backgrounds the results showed the latter (inductive) method to be superior to the former method on tests of ability to apply the principles. On the other hand, Hovland and Mandell (1952) found that opinions were more likely to change in the direction advocated by the speaker if he drew the conclusion appropriate to his argument rather than leaving it to the students. As we shall again see later in our consideration of laboratory teaching, research on this topic is not clear-cut. Probably it is important for the instructor to point out the conclusion if most students would not arrive at it by themselves. On the other hand, as we have seen, discovery of a conclusion by oneself may have considerable motivational value for a student.

Katona's (1940) classic studies of college student learning supported the importance of organization in learning and retention and also pointed toward the importance of the learner's own organization. Katona found that learning by organization results both in superior retention and in superior application when compared with learning by rote memorization. Such findings make apparent some of the ways in which lecturers are not as effective as they might be.

Size of Lecture Class

Our examination of research on class size led to the conclusion that more meaningful research on this variable must take into account the methods used in teaching classes of different sizes. Thus, it seems illogical to treat class size separately from method; we will consider class size under the general topics of lecture and discussion.

Among the earliest and most comprehensive programs of research on college teaching were the monumental studies of class size conducted at the University of Minnesota in the 1920's. These studies pointed to the conclusion that large classes are actually superior to small classes. Fifty-nine well-controlled experiments were reported by Hudelson (1928). These experiments involved such widely varying subject matter as psychology, physics, accounting, and law. In 46 of the experiments, results favored the large classes. Although many of the differences were not statistically significant, the majority of significant differences favored large classes. In these experiments small classes averaged 25 to 30 students, but they ranged from 12 to 60 in size while large classes ranged in size from 35 to 150. Extreme differences in size were no more favorable to small groups than were small differences. Although most of the criterion measures were tests of knowledge, some experiments also attempted to measure higher-level intellectual changes, with similar results.

More recent experiments have been less favorable to large classes. Rohrer (1957) found no significant differences. The Macomber and Siegel experiments at Miami University (1956, 1957a, 1957b, 1960) are particularly important because their measures included, in addition to conventional achievement tests, measures of critical thinking and problem solving, scales measuring stereotypy of attitudes, and tests of student attitudes toward instruction. Although the only statistically significant differences favored the smaller classes (particularly for high-ability students), most differences were very small. Significant differences favoring small classes were found on measures of change in misconceptions in psychology, on a case test of problem solving in marketing, and on measures of student attitudes toward all the courses. When retention of knowledge was measured one to two years after completion of the courses, large classes did not prove to be significantly inferior to small classes in any one course. However, in eight of the nine courses compared, differences favored the small class (Siegel, Adams, & Macomber, 1960). As we saw earlier, Nachman and Opochinsky (1958) found a small class to be superior to a large class in performance on surprise quizzes, but the two classes were not significantly different on the final examination for which students prepared.

At Grinnell College, students gave instructors higher ratings in smaller classes (Lovell & Haner, 1955); at Brooklyn (Riley, Ryan, & Lifshitz, 1950) and Purdue (Remmers, 1927), there was no significant difference in ratings of instructors by small and large classes generally, although Remmers (1933) reported that students involved in a controlled experiment at Purdue preferred a small recitation to a large lecture. The weight of the evidence seems to favor small classes if one uses student or faculty satisfaction as a criterion.

Despite the lack of conclusive experimental support for their position, most college professors still believe small classes to be superior to larger ones. For example, the Miami University professors involved in the Macomber-Siegel experiments felt that large classes were about equal to small classes in covering content but inferior in achieving other objectives. In view of the research results, is this simply academic featherbedding or are there good reasons for the professors' distrust of the research results?

Let us briefly return to theory. We have stressed the role of the lecturer as an information communicator. Insofar as information-giving is a one-way process, size of group should be limited only by the audibility of the lecturer's voice. In fact, as Hudelson suggests, a large class may have sufficient motivational value for an instructor to cause him to spend more time in preparation of his lectures and thus to produce better teaching and greater student achievement. But if, as we suggested in our discussion of automation, the effective lecture involves interaction between instructor and students, the large class may be inferior even for lectures, for laboratory experiments suggest that fewer students raise questions or interpose comments in large classes than in small (J. R. Gibb, 1951).

If there is less participation in large classes, the Minnesota research may suggest that we hark back to the criterion problem mentioned earlier. Were the achievement tests used biased against teaching which introduced varying points of view? If our tests place a premium upon exact recall of the materials presented by the teacher or textbook, the student who hears other points of view may be at a disadvantage.

To sum up: large lecture classes are not generally inferior to smaller lecture classes if one uses traditional achievement tests as a criterion. When other objectives are measured, large lectures tend to be inferior. Moreover, both students and faculty members feel that teaching is more effective in small classes. Regardless of the validity of these feelings, any move toward large classes is likely to encounter strong resistance. Probably of more significance than class size per se is its relation to the teaching method used. For example, one would expect class size to be of minimal relevance in television teaching, of slight importance in lecturing, but of considerable significance in discussion teaching. One unplanned consequence of increasing class size may be a restriction upon the teacher's freedom to vary his methods to fit his objectives.

What is the role of the lecturer in higher education? The research results we have cited provide little basis for an answer. They do not contradict—sometimes they support—our earlier notions that the lecture is an effective way of communicating information, particularly in classes where variations in student background, ability, or interest make feedback to the lecturer important. We have also seen that the organization and presentation of lectures may influence their effectiveness in teaching students how to apply knowledge or in influencing attitudes. However, a suspicion, supported by bits of evidence, arises that other methods of teaching may be more effective than lecturing in achieving some higher cognitive and attitudinal objectives.

DISCUSSION METHODS

In our review of research comparing the effectiveness of lecture and discussion methods, we implied that discussion may be ill-suited for communicating information because the rate of communication from instructor to student is slow. However, we should point out that not all information is eagerly received. When information encounters intellectual or emotional resistance, discussion methods may be necessary to bring the source of resistance to light.

Moreover, if students are to achieve application, critical thinking, or some other higher cognitive objective, it seems reasonable to assume that they should have an opportunity to practice application and critical thinking and to receive feedback on the results. Group discussion provides an opportunity to do this. While teaching machines and mock-ups may also be designed to provide prompt and realistic feedback, a group discussion permits presentation of a variety of problems enabling a number of people to gain experience in integrating facts, formulating hypotheses, amassing relevant evidence, and evaluating conclusions. In fact, the prompt feedback provided by the teaching machine may actually be less effective than a method in which students are encouraged to discover solutions for themselves with less step-by-step guidance (Della-Piana, 1957). Since problem solving ordinarily requires information, we might expect discussion to be more effective for groups with more information than for those lacking in background. Some support for this hypothesis is provided by a study of the learning of children in visiting a museum. Melton, Feldman, and Mason (1936) found that lectures were more effective than discussions for children in Grades 5, 6, and 7, but discussions were more effective for eighth-graders.

We noted that lectures usually place the learner in a passive role and that passive learning is less efficient than active. We would expect discussions to promote more active learning, and for once we have some relevant evidence. Bloom and his colleagues (1953) at the University of Chicago used recordings of classes to stimulate students to recall their thoughts during class. As predicted, they found that discussion did stimulate more active thinking than did lecture classes. Krauskopf (1960) substituted written for oral responses to the tape recordings and found that rated relevance of thoughts was positively correlated with achievement, accounting for variance in achievement beyond that accounted for by ability.

The idea that discussion methods should help overcome resistance to learning is also difficult to verify. Essentially, the argument is that some desired learning encounters emotional barriers which prevent it from affecting behavior. For example, a psychology student may learn that distributed practice is effective, but not change his study methods because his anxiety about grades is so great that he doesn't dare try anything different. In such circumstances, experiments on attitude change suggest that the instructor must either bring about changes in underlying attitude and motivation or change the individual's perception of the instrumental relationship between his belief and his motives. Psychotherapists believe that expressing one's attitude in a nonthreatening situation is one step in the process of change. A group discussion may provide such opportunities for expression as well as give opportunities for other group members to point out other instrumental relationships.

In addition, most attitudes influencing learning have some interpersonal antecedents and are stabilized by one's perception of the attitudes of liked persons. Group discussion may facilitate a high degree of liking for the instructor and for other group members. It also permits more accurate assessment of group norms than is likely to occur in other techniques of instruction. Consequently, change may follow.

In fact, while individual instruction would be advantageous for many teaching purposes, group processes can provide a real advantage in bringing about changes in motivation and attitudes. Lewin (1952) showed in his classic experiments on group decision that it is sometimes easier to change a group than an individual.

Whether or not discussions actually are superior in these respects cannot be easily determined, for discussions range from monologues in which occasional questions are interposed to bull sessions in which the instructor is an interested (or bored) observer. Nevertheless, a good deal of research has been attempted to compare the effectiveness of differing discussion techniques.

Student-Centered versus Instructor-Centered Teaching

The theories of client-centered counseling and of Lewinian group dynamics have led to an increased interest in discussion techniques. A wide variety of teaching methods are described as "student-centered," "nondirective," "group-centered," or "democratic" discussion. Nevertheless, they have in common the desire to break away from the traditional instructor-dominated classroom and to encourage greater student participation and responsibility. In Table 1 are listed some of the ways in which the student-centered method has been supposed to differ from the traditional "instructor-centered" method.[2]

From the standpoint of theory, student-centered teaching in its more extreme forms might be expected to have some serious weakness, at least in achieving lower-level cognitive goals, such as knowledge of facts. With the instructor's role as information-giver reduced, his role as source of feedback virtually eliminated, his opportunity to provide organization and structure curtailed, it is apparent that a heavy burden falls upon the group members to carry out these functions. We expect that these functions could best be assumed by groups which not only have some background in the academic discipline involved but also have had experience in carrying out these functions in "democratic" groups.

Since student-centered teaching attempts to reduce dependence upon the instructor, it would be expected to diminish his influence as a prestige figure, and possibly to reduce his power to bring about attitudinal changes. However, this may be more than compensated for by increased freedom of expression and increased potency of group norms as sources of influence. Participation in discussion gives students an opportunity to gain recognition and praise which should, according to learning theory, strengthen motivation. Thistlethwaite (1960) found that National Merit Scholars checked as one of the outstanding characteristics of teachers who contributed most to their desire to learn, "allowing time for classroom discussion." Other characteristics mentioned include "modifying course content to meet students' needs and interests," "treating students as colleagues," and "taking a personal interest in students." However, in line with our earlier discussion of feedback, another trait mentioned was "providing evaluations reassuring the student of his creative or productive potentialities."

---

[2]A good summary and critical evaluation of studies in this area may be found in R. C. Anderson (1959).

TABLE 1

Dimensions upon which Student-Centered and Instructor-Centered Methods May Differ

Student-Centered	Instructor-Centered
Goals	
Determined by group (Faw, 1949)	Determined by instructor
Emphasis upon affective and attitudinal changes (Faw, 1949)	Emphasis upon intellectual changes
Attempts to develop group cohesiveness (Bovard, 1951b)	No attempt to develop group cohesiveness
Classroom Activities	
Much student participation (Faw, 1949)	Much instructor participation
Student-student interaction (McKeachie, 1951)	Instructor-student interaction
Instructor accepts erroneous or irrelevant student contributions (Faw, 1949)	Instructor corrects, criticizes, or rejects erroneous or irrelevant student contributions
Group decides upon own activities (McKeachie, 1951)	Instructor determines activities
Discussion of students' personal experiences encouraged (Faw, 1949)	Discussion kept on course materials
De-emphasis of tests and grades (Asch, 1951)	Traditional use of tests and grades
Students share responsibility for evaluation (Ashmus & Haigh, 1952)	
Instructor interprets feelings and ideas of class member when it is necessary for class progress (Axelrod, 1955)	Instructor avoids interpretation of feelings
Reaction reports (Asch, 1951)	No reaction reports

The advocates of student-centered or group-centered teaching also introduced another category of objectives not usually considered in traditional classes—development of skills in group membership and leadership. The group-centered teacher might often argue that even if his method were no more effective than traditional methods in achieving the usual course objectives, it is so important that students learn to work effectively in groups that it may even be worth sacrificing some other objectives in order to promote growth in this area.

Student-centered teachers often stress group cohesiveness. Hence, a possible explanation for the contradictory results on student achievement in the experiments considered below may be found in the studies of group cohesiveness and productivity in industry (e.g., Seashore, 1954).

These studies indicate that it is not safe to assume that a cohesive group will be a productive one. Cohesive groups are effective in maintaining group standards, but may set either high or low standards of productivity. Since strongly cohesive groups feel less threatened by management than do less cohesive groups, it may be more difficult to change their standards. Thus in creating "groupy" classes an instructor may sometimes help his students develop strength to set low standards of achievement and maintain them against instructor pressures, or at least to develop group goals different from their normal academic goals.

Another factor may account for the fact that some researchers report student enthusiasm for student-centered teaching while others report hostility. Horwitz (1958) found that aggression toward the teacher increased when the teacher exercised his authority arbitrarily, i.e., refused to abide by the students' decision about teaching methods after telling them that their vote would count. The same method was not resented when the instructor indicated that he would make the final decision. This is important because the limits of student power are often ambiguous in student-centered classes. Also relevant was Horwitz's finding that the more hostility was inhibited, the less learning took place on a type-setting task.

Experiments on student-centered teaching. With this introduction, let us review experimental attempts to demonstrate the effectiveness of student-centered teaching.[3] One of the best known comparisons of student-centered and instructor-centered instruction is that made by Faw (1949). Faw's class of 102 students met two hours a week to listen to lectures and two hours a week in discussion groups of 34. One discussion group was taught by a student-centered method, one by an instructor-centered method, and one group alternated between the two methods.

As compared with the instructor-centered class, the student-centered class was characterized by more student participation, lack of correction by the instructor of inaccurate statements, lack of instructor direction, and more discussion of ideas related to personal experiences.

Faw's major measure of attainment of objectives was in the intellectual area. Scores on the objective course examination based on the textbook showed small but significant differences favoring the student-centered method. In the area of his major interest, emotional growth, Faw's method of evaluation was to ask students in the student-centered and alternating method classes to write anonymous comments about the

---

[3]Much of the following material on student-centered discussion is based on Birney and McKeachie (1955) and is used with the permission of the American Psychological Association.

class. Generally Faw thought that these comments indicated that the students felt that they received greater social and emotional value from the student-centered discussion groups than from an instructor-centered class.

A very similar experiment was carried out by Asch (1951). Like Faw, Asch taught all the groups in his experiment. Three sections of about 30-55 students were taught by an instructor-centered method which was half lecture and half discussion. One section of 23 students was taught by a nondirective method quite similar to that of Faw. However, there were certain differences between the two experiments. In Faw's experiment both student-centered and instructor-centered classes spent two hours a week listening to lectures. While Faw did not mention grading, one assumes that grades were determined by the instructor on the basis of the course-wide examination. In Asch's experiment, students in the student-centered class were allowed to determine their own grades.

Asch's results do not completely agree with Faw's. On the final examination in the course, students in the instructor-centered class scored significantly higher than members of the student-centered class on both the essay and objective portions of the test. Note, however, that the student-centered class was specifically told that this examination would in no way affect their grades in the course, and therefore the two groups were probably not equivalent in motivation. Haigh and Schmidt (1956), however, found no significant difference in a similar comparison.

As measured by the Bogardus Social Distance scale, attitude change in the two sections was not significantly different. Yet, in comparison with the instructor-centered class, a greater percentage of members of the student-centered class improved in adjustment as measured by the Minnesota Multiphasic Personality Inventory.

Asch's students, like Faw's, had a different perception of their achievement from that shown by the course examination. Faw's student-centered class did better on the course examination than the instructor-centered class section but thought they would have learned more if they had been in an instructor-centered class. Asch's students, however, rated the student-centered class higher than the instructor-centered class in helping them to learn the subject matter of the course even though they actually scored lower than the instructor-centered class.

Following the model of Lewin, Lippitt, and White's (1939) study of authoritarian, democratic, and laissez-faire group climates, the staff of the University of Michigan's general psychology courses set up an experiment using three styles of teaching: recitation, discussion, and group tutorial (Guetzkow, Kelly, & McKeachie, 1954). As compared to discussion and tutorial methods, the more autocratic recitation method proved not only to produce superior performance on the final examination, but also to produce greater interest in psychology, as measured by the election of advanced courses in psychology. Furthermore, students liked the recitation method better than the other methods. The greater gains in knowledge produced by the recitation method fit in with the general principle that feedback aids learning, for students in the recitation sections had weekly or semiweekly quizzes. McKeachie (1951) suggests that the popularity of this method is related to student anxiety about grades, which is most easily handled when students are in familiar, highly structured situations.

Another factor in these results may be the inexperience of the instructors involved, most of whom had had less than a year of previous teaching experience. It is possible that skillful discussion or tutorial teaching requires greater skill than do more highly structured methods.

Despite the superiority found for the recitation method in producing achievement measured immediately after the course, two results dealing with motivational outcomes favored the other methods. The discussion sections were significantly more favorable than the other groups in their attitude toward psychology; a follow-up of the students three years later revealed that seven men each from the tutorial and discussion groups majored in psychology and none of those in the recitation sections did so.

One of the most comprehensive experiments on student-centered teaching was that of Landsman (1950). He contrasted a student-centered type of teaching with a more direct type of democratic discussion organized around a syllabus. His experimental design involved eight classes in a course sequence of "Human Development," "Adjustment," and "Learning." Three instructors took part in the experiment, and each instructor used both methods. Outcome measures included the Horrocks-Troyer test (an analysis of case histories), a local case-history analysis test, the group Rorschach, the MMPI, autobiographies, and students' reactions. His results showed no significant difference between methods on any of the measures.

Other experiments have also been carried out with negative results. For example, Johnson and Smith (1953) also found no significant difference in achievement test scores between small "democratic" and large lecture classes. An interesting sidelight of their experiment was that one democratic class evaluated their procedure very favorable, while the other democratic class tended to be less satisfied than lecture classes. Bills (1952) also found no difference in achievement between psychology classes taught by lecture-discussion versus student-centered methods, but did find that the students in the student-centered class were significantly more favorable in their attitude toward psychology.

Maloney (1956) found no differences in achievement between two types of discussion groups but did find gains in group cohesiveness, participation, and other indices of effectiveness in groups in which the leader specifically tried to establish acceptance and other characteristics of the student-centered group. In a graduate course in counseling, Slomowitz (1955) found no significant differences between nondirective and problem-oriented discussions in achievement or application to a case-study test. The nondirectively taught student did, however, change in self concept more (at the .10 level of confidence) than did students in the other group. Like Slomowitz, Deignan (1955) was concerned not only with achievement but also with emotional changes. Although there were no other significant differences between the groups on follow-up tests a semester later, the student-centered group evaluated the course more highly. Rasmussen (1956) also reported no difference in achievement but higher morale among groups of in-service teachers electing student-centered extension courses as compared with students taught by instructor-centered methods. Krumboltz and Farquhar (1957) compared student-centered, instructor-centered, and eclectic teaching methods in a how-to-study course. There were no significant differences between methods on an achievement test or on self-ratings of study habits. Burke's results (1956) are similar.

In an attempt to teach critical thinking, Lyle (1958) compared a problem-oriented approach with conventional lecture-discussion-text procedures. Apparently he found that the conventional group was superior to the problem-oriented group in achievement. Gains in critical thinking were not greater in the problem-centered classes. When students were asked to write a question for the final examination, the conventional group wrote factual questions and the problem-centered group wrote "thought" questions.

In an experiment in teaching written and spoken English, Jenkins (1952) found that a teaching role in which the instructor acted as resource person in a democratic class was not significantly superior to traditional methods on three measures of communication skills.

The Johnson and Smith study (1953) is one of the few to support our earlier suggestion that the success of student-centered teaching depends upon the previous group experience of the students. They suggest that the critical factor in the success of one democratic class was the enthusiastic participation of one student who happened to be a member of a student cooperative.

Wispé (1951) carried out an interesting variation of the student-centered versus instructor-centered experiment. Instead of attempting to control the instructor personality variable by forcing instructors to teach both instructor-centered and student-centered classes, Wispé selected instructors who were rated as naturally permissive or directive. He then compared their sections of the Harvard course in "Social Relations." He found no difference in final examination scores between students taught by the different methods. Students preferred the directive method, and the poorer students gained more in directive classes.

In a methodological aside, it is worth noting that analysis of covariance and multiple correlation were used in Wispé's study. As indicated in our introduction, one reason why statistically significant differences are so rare in this research may be that the researchers commonly use "weak" statistics in which the error estimates are inflated by failure to take account of known sources of variance such as individual differences in previous knowledge or intelligence.

As a counterpoint to Wispé's study with teachers using their preferred method, we have the Springfield College experiment (Ashmus & Haigh, 1952; Haigh & Schmidt, 1956) in which the students were given their choice of group-centered or instructor-centered teaching. Students choosing either type did not differ significantly in intelligence. The results showed no difference in the achievement of the two groups on a test not counted toward the course grade. Those in the nondirective classes were more highly satisfied with the course.

Moore and Popham (1959) reported that three student-centered interviews with students produced greater gains on the college Inventory of Academic Adjustment than did three content-centered interviews conducted outside of class in an educational psychology course. Similarly, Zeleny (1940) found not only greater gain in knowledge but also greater self-rated change in personality in a group-discussion class than in a traditional recitation discussion class.

While scores on objective final examinations seem to be little affected by teaching method, there are in addition to the changes in adjustment reported by Asch, Faw, Zeleny, and Moore and Popham, other indications that student behavior outside the usual testing situation may be influenced in the direction of educational goals by student-centered teaching. The classes compared by Bovard (1951a, 1951b) and McKeachie (1951) differed in the degree to which interaction between students was encouraged and in the degree to which the class made decisions about assignments, examinations, and other matters of classroom procedure. Like other experimenters, Bovard and McKeachie found that the groups did not differ in achievement measured by the final examination. However, two clinical psychologists evaluated recordings in the class discussions which followed the showing of the film, "The Feeling of Rejection." Both clinicians reported that the "group-centered" class showed much more insight and understanding of the problems of the girl in the film.

Patton (1955) felt that an important variable in group-centered classes was the students' acceptance of responsibility for learning. In his experiment he compared traditional classes with two classes in which there were no examinations, no lectures, and no assigned readings. Students in the experimental classes decided what reading they would do, what class procedure would be used, what they would hand in, and how they would be graded, so that they had even more power than had previous experimental groups. At the end of the course, these classes, as compared to the control group, felt that the course (1) was more valuable, (2) showed greater interest in psychology, and (3) tended to give more dynamic, motivational analyses of a problem of behavior.

But giving students power cannot work if they will not accept responsibility; so Patton also obtained individual measures of acceptance of responsibility within the experimental classes. As hypothesized, he found that the degree to which the student accepted responsibility was positively correlated with gain in psychological knowledge, gain in ability to apply psychology, rating of the value of the course, and interest in psychology. The effect of giving students additional responsibility seemed to depend upon the student's readiness to accept that responsibility.

Although the Bovard, McKeachie, and Patton experiments suggested that student-centered classes promoted transfer of learning, D. E. P. Smith (1954), comparing three methods varying in degree of directiveness, found no differences in their effects upon students' abilities to make "applicational transfer" of their learning.

The most impressive findings on the results of small-group discussion come from the research on the "Pyramid Plan" at Pennsylvania State University (Carpenter, 1959; Davage, 1958, 1959). The basic plan may be represented by a description of their experiments in psychology. Each "Pyramid Group" of psychology majors consisted of six freshmen, six sophomores, two juniors, who were assistant leaders, and a senior, who was group leader. The Pyramid groups met weekly for two-hour periods to discuss personal-professional goals, requirements for entering their selected professions, skills needed for academic success, the significance of their courses for their goals, issues in higher education, and the central concepts of psychology. The group leaders worked with a faculty supervisor in defining objectives, discussing small-group theory and techniques, and defining issues to be considered by the Pyramid groups. One control group consisted of students who simply took pretest measures; another control group received comparable special attention by being given a special program of lectures, films, and demonstrations equal to the time spent in discussion by the Pyramid groups. The results on such measures as attitude toward psychology, knowledge of the field of psychology, scientific thinking, use of the library for scholarly reading, intellectual orientation, and resourcefulness in problem solving were significantly favorable to the Pyramid Plan. Moreover, a follow-up study showed that more of the Pyramid students continued as majors in psychology. Such an array of positive results, little short of fantastic, testifies not only to the effectiveness of the Pyramid program but also to the resourcefulness of the Pennsylvania State research staff.

L. M. Gibb and Gibb (1952) reported that students who were taught by their "participative-action" method were significantly superior in role flexibility and self-insight to students taught by traditional lecture-discussion methods. In the participative-action method class, activities centered around "sub-grouping methods designed to increase effective group participation."

> The instructor, who played a constantly diminishing role in the decisions and activities of the groups, gave training in role playing, group goal setting, problem centering, distributive leadership, evaluation of individual performance by intra-group ratings, process observing, and group selection, evaluation, and revision of class activities (L. M. Gibb & Gibb, 1952, p. 247).

Gibb and Gibb also supported the assumption that group-centered teaching can facilitate development of group-membership skills. They found that in nonclassroom groups the participative-action students were rated higher than other students in leadership, likeableness, and group-membership skills. DiVesta's results tend to support this (1954), and R. P. Anderson and Kell (1954) reported that members of student-centered groups were characterized by positive attitudes toward themselves as participants in the group.

Although McKeachie (1954) reported significant changes in attitudes of students toward Negroes and toward the treatment of criminals, differences between leader-centered and group-centered classes were not significant. As predicted, however, group decision did produce more accurate perception of the group norm and more conformity to the norm than lecture or discussion without decision. While no direct attempt was made to change the group norm, the experiment suggests that the instructor who wishes to change attitudes might find the group-decision technique useful. Wieder (1954) found that a nondirectively taught psychology class tended to reduce prejudice more than did conventional classes.

One final bit of support for less directive teaching is Thistlethwaite's (1959) finding of a significant negative correlation between a college's productivity of Ph.D.'s in natural science and the directiveness of the teaching methods used.

In the Guetzkow, Kelly, and McKeachie (1954) experiment reported earlier, none of the males in the very popular highly structured recitation sections majored in psychology. At least seven males in the sections taught by each of the other two methods completed a psychology major. Since the three methods had been equated in terms of the number of students intending to major, this is a surprising finding. Such results are shocking to conventional theory. Most psychologists have thought that prompt feedback and well-structured sequences of presentation were conducive to learning. Yet the Thistlethwaite studies indicate that the top colleges in production of scholars are those where tests are infrequent and where students don't know what to expect next. If this is so, maybe we need to throw some random elements into our lectures and teaching machines. In any case, these results suggest that techniques most suitable for teaching knowledge may not be those most effective for developing motivation and high-level achievement.

The results of the spate of research on student-centered teaching methods are not conclusive, but tend to support the theory with which our discussion began. We had suggested that student-centered teaching might be ineffective in achieving lower-order cognitive objectives. Experiments reporting losses and gains in this area seem to be balanced. Students apparently can get information from textbooks as well as from the instructor.

We had also predicted that any superiority of student-centered discussion methods would be revealed in high-level outcomes. In 11 studies, significant differences in ability to apply concepts, in attitudes, in motivation, or in group membership skills have been found between discussion techniques emphasizing freer student participation compared with discussion with greater instructor dominance. In 10 of these the differences favored the more student-centered method. The eleventh (Guetzkow, Kelly, & McKeachie, 1954) had mixed results.

In short, the choice of instructor-dominated versus student-centered discussion techniques appears to depend upon one's goals. The more highly one values outcomes going beyond acquisition of knowledge, the more likely that student-centered methods will be preferred.

Variations in Discussion Teaching

Buzz sessions. One popular technique for achieving student participation in groups is the buzz session (McKeachie, 1960). In using this procedure, classes are split into small sub-groups for a brief discussion of a problem. Although many teachers feel that this technique is valuable as a change of pace or as a way of getting active thinking from students, little research has tested its effectiveness. Vinacke (1957) found that, in comparison with their performance on a pretest, students in two- and three-man groups wrote more new ideas after a five-minute discussion than did students working alone. It is possible, however, that similar changes could have been produced by a general discussion or a lecture.

Leadership. Laboratory and field studies of group processes may shed some light on factors which condition the effectiveness of groups and which thus may help account for the lack of effectiveness of many discussion classes.

For example, one problem faced by the discussion leader is the student who dominates discussion or the clique who carry the ball. In some discussion classes, the instructor's fear of exerting too much control over the class may result in failure to give minority points of view an adequate hearing. Research suggests that effectiveness of group problem solving depends upon the leader's ability to obtain a hearing for minority opinion (Maier & Solem, 1952).

Some student-centered teachers assume that all decisions should be made by the group. Hence, they feel, the instructor should not determine objectives, make assignments, or give tests, but should ask the group to make these decisions. If the group does this, can the time they lose from academic work in making decisions be compensated for by the increased motivation of the students? Democratic methods permit formation of group norms and more acute perception of group norms, but as in industry these norms may not necessarily be conducive to high productivity or learning. The general question of the areas in which the instructor should make decisions is one which different instructors have answered in different ways and one well worth further discussion and research. One hunch based on research on business conferences is that the instructor should make most procedural decisions, leaving the class time for problems related to the content of the course (Heyns, 1952).

Even in discussion of course content, however, it appears that some instructor direction may be useful if the goals are the learning of relationships and the ability to apply this learning. In comparing groups given more versus less instructor direction in discovering the basis of solutions of verbal problems, Craig (1956) found that the directed group not only learned faster but retained their learning better than the group given less help. This result is supported by Corman's research on guidance in problem solving (1957).

Studies of business conferences have also shown that one of the commonest causes of dissatisfaction is the member's failure to understand the purpose of the conference. It is little wonder that a student with a high need to achieve success may be frustrated and often aggressive in a democratic class in which he is confused about the purposes of the teacher's procedures and, at the same time, subject to the stress involved in getting a good grade. Bloom's studies (1953) of student thought processes show that on the average 30 per cent of the student's time in discussion classes is spent in thinking about himself and other people as compared with 18 per cent of the time in lectures. With members of the group thus concerned about their own needs, it is no wonder that discussion groups are not always productive.

Grading. Another important problem in conducting student-centered (or other) classes is that of grades. Not only does the instructor control the pleasantness or unpleasantness of a good many student hours, but because of his power to assign grades he can block or facilitate the achievement of many important goals. The importance of this aspect of the teacher's role is indicated by studies of supervision in industry. In one such study it was discovered that workers were most likely to ask a supervisor for help if the supervisor was not responsible for evaluating his subordinates (Ross, 1956). This suggests that as long as students are anxious about the grades the instructor will assign, they are likely to avoid exposing their own ignorance.

The student's anxiety about grades is likely to be increased if his instructor's procedures make him uncertain about what he must do to attain a good grade. Although we have already seen that a high degree of structure may not lead to better education, it is nevertheless worth noting that for many students democratic methods seem unorganized and ambiguous. In an ordinary course the student knows that he can pass by reading assignments and studying lecture notes, but in a student-centered class the instructor does not lecture, does not make assignments, and leaves the student ignorant of what the instructor is trying to do.

Some instructors have thought that the grade problem might be solved by using a cooperative system of grading. Deutsch (1949) found no differences in learning between students in groups graded co-operatively and those graded competitively, although the cooperative groups worked together more smoothly. Following up Deutsch's work, Haines (1959) also found no significant achievement advantages for students working cooperatively as compared with those working competitively for grades, but he did find marked differences in group morale. Haine's work suggests that cooperative grading in the discussion group can be successfully combined with individual grading on achievement tests.

In comparing a "teamwork" class using group incentives with a lecture class, H. C. Smith (1955) did not find differences in satisfaction comparable to those found by Haines and by Deutsch in their experiments.

Complicating the problem of grading is the probability that low grades produce different effects upon different students. Waterhouse and Child (1953) found that frustration produced deterioration in performance for subjects showing high "interference tendencies" but produced improved performance for those with low "interference tendencies." "Interference tendencies" were assessed by a questionnaire in which the subjects were asked to check on a six-point scale the degree to which 90 responses to frustration were characteristic of them.

Considering the importance of grading for both students and instructors, it is regrettable that there is so little empirical research on it. How do students learn to evaluate themselves? How do they learn to set goals for themselves? Do differing grading procedures facilitate or block such learning? Can more educational substitutes for grades be devised? To these questions we have no answers at the present time.

Size of Discussion Group

One of the earliest experimental studies of college teaching was that of Edmonson and Mulder (1924) on class size. This study was conducted in an education course in which there were two sections—one of 45 students and the other of 109. Both sections were taught by the same instructor in order to control the possible effect of instructor differences, and both sections used the same text and took the same tests. The discussion method was used in each section. Forty-three students in each class were paired on the basis of intelligence and past experience. This pioneer study led to the conclusion that size of class is not a significant variable in effecting student learning as measured by usual course achievement tests, although students preferred the small class (if 45 can be considered a small discussion group).

As in the size experiments reported in our discussion of the lecture method, there seemed to be little theoretical reason for the choice of class sizes in this experiment. There is, in fact, some doubt whether either size is optimal for discussions. However, similar results were reported by Hudelson (1928) when using classes of 20 and 113 in an education course, and by Brown (1932) in psychology classes. In fact, using special team procedures, Brown produced slightly better achievement in groups of 60 than were obtained from discussion classes of 25.

Support for small classes, however, comes from the studies on teaching French conducted by Cheydleur (1945) at the University of Wisconsin between 1919 and 1943. With hundreds of classes ranging in enrollment from 9 to 33, Cheydleur found the smaller classes to be consistently superior on departmental examinations, with reliabilities of .72 to .95. These departmental examinations correlated about .8 with standardized tests of achievement in French. The only thing unclear in Cheydleur's report is whether or not some selective factor could have been operating.

Mueller (1924) in a pioneer study also found the smaller class to be more effective in an experiment comparing elementary psychology classes of 20 and 40 students. A study by Schellenberg (1959) in a Western civilization course suggested that even the smallest groups in these studies may be above optimal sizes. Working with discussion groups of 4, 6, 8, and 10 students, he found higher satisfaction and higher instructor grading in the smaller groups. While Schellenberg recognized that grades are an unsatisfactory criterion since the instructor's judgment may shift from section to section, he referred to laboratory studies of group problem solving which point to optima in the range of 4- to 6-person groups.

From the standpoint of theory one might expect increasing size to have two effects. One of these would be an increase in the resources of the group in knowledge, different approaches to the problem, and ability to provide feedback. The second consequence of size, however, is likely to be a decreasing ability to exploit the total resources of the group because of the difficulty in obtaining contributions from everyone. Further, with increasing size, group members are likely to feel restraints against participation (J. R. Gibb, 1951). The consequence of increasing feelings of threat in larger groups is that group participation is increasingly dominated by a few people. In Princeton classes of 4 to 12 students, Stephan and Mishler (1952) reported that increasing group size was related to increasing instructor dominance. Thus group size becomes a much more relevant variable in classes taught by discussion than in those taught by lecture.

Homogeneous versus Heterogeneous Grouping

One common criticism of discussion classes is that class time is wasted either by discussion of problems raised by the able students which are beyond the ken of the other students or by problems raised by poor students which the other students feel are too elementary. One answer to such criticism is to use homogeneous groupings so that each student is discussing problems with students of his own ability.

Recently, concern about America's resources of high-level talent has resulted in the proliferation of honors programs featuring homogeneous classes for students with high academic aptitude and achievement. The logic of such programs is evident, and research evidence supports their educational value. Nevertheless, an earlier college experiment on ability grouping showed no significant advantages for homogeneous grouping by intelligence and even a trend toward the opposite result in psychology classes (Longstaff, 1932).

Briggs (1947), on the other hand, found that special intensive seminar classes meeting less often than conventional classes produced greater achievement for superior students than did the conventional class for a control group matched in ability. Unfortunately, in this study the seminar students volunteered and were selected by interview so that they probably had higher motivation than their controls.

The two earliest publications in this area (Burtt, Chassel, & Hatch, 1923; Ullrich, 1926) reported results which seem very reasonable. They both concluded that homogeneous groups were not superior to heterogeneous groups when given standard material but did superior work when the bright students were pushed. Similarly, Tharp (1930) found homogeneous grouping to be superior in foreign language classes and Taylor (1931) found it to be superior in analytic geometry. All in all, it seems safe to conclude that homogeneous grouping by ability is profitable, if teaching makes use of the known characteristics of the groups.

Homogeneous grouping by personality proved to be ineffective in Hoffman's (1959) experiment in group problem solving. Comparing groups of four students who were similar in personality profiles on the Guilford-Zimmerman Temperament Survey with groups made up of dissimilar students, he found that the *heterogeneous* groups produced *superior* solutions. Hoffman accounts for this difference by suggesting that heterogeneous groups are more likely to propose a variety of alternatives permitting inventive solutions.

On the other hand, in a study by Stern and Cope (Stern, 1960, pp. 315-316), groups of "authoritarian," "antiauthoritarian," and "rational" students in a citizenship course were segregated into homogeneous groups in which the instructor was unaware of which group he was teaching. Authoritarian students in the experimental group achieved more than comparable authoritarians did in conventional classes.

It is apparent that we need further analysis to determine what kinds of homogeneities or heterogeneities contribute to what objectives. If we omit from consideration the general adjustment problems of segregated groups, the idea that one should be able to do a better job of teaching a group with known homogeneous characteristics than a heterogeneous group seems so reasonable that it is surprising that the results of research on this idea are not uniform. It may be that the potential advantages of carefully planned grouping have not been realized simply because we have not yet learned optimal teaching procedures for such groups.

From a theoretical point of view the importance of group size and heterogeneity probably depends upon the purpose of the discussion. If, for example, one is interested in using group members as sources of information or differing points of view, the larger and more heterogeneous the group, the greater its resources. On the other hand, the degree to which a group uses its resources depends upon communication; fewer group members can participate in a large group and members are less likely to volunteer their contributions in large groups.

A final problem is that of group pressures toward consensus and conformity. As we saw in our consideration of discussion techniques, one barrier to effective group problem solving is the tendency of a group to accept the majority view without sufficient consideration of minority views. Since group members may be less likely to express divergent opinions in large groups than in small groups, we might venture the paradoxical hypothesis that the larger the group, the more effect a few outspoken members are likely to have in determining the success of discussion.

LABORATORY TEACHING

The laboratory method is now so widely accepted in scientific education that it may seem heretical to ask whether laboratory experience is an effective way to achieve educational objectives.

Laboratory teaching assumes that firsthand experience in observation and manipulation of the materials of science is superior to other methods of developing understanding and appreciation. Laboratory training is also frequently used to develop skills necessary for more advanced study or research.

From the standpoint of theory, the activity of the student, the sensorimotor nature of the experience, and the individualization of laboratory instruction should contribute positively to learning. Information cannot usually be obtained, however, by direct experience as rapidly as it can from abstractions presented orally or in print. Films or demonstrations may also short-cut some of the trial and error of the laboratory. Thus, one would not expect laboratory teaching to have an advantage over other teaching methods in amount of information learned. Rather we might expect the differences to be revealed in retention, in ability to apply learning, or in actual skill in observation or manipulation of materials. Unfortunately, little research has attempted to tease out these special types of outcomes. If these outcomes are unmeasured, a finding of no difference in effectiveness between laboratory and other methods of instruction is almost meaningless since there is little reason to expect laboratory teaching to be effective in simple communication of information.

In a course on methods of engineering, White (1945) found that students taught by a group-laboratory method achieved more than those taught by a lecture-demonstration method. However, Balcziak (1953), comparing (1) demonstration, (2) individual laboratory, and (3) combined demonstration and laboratory in a college physical science course, found no significant differences between them as measured by tests of information, scientific attitude, or laboratory performance.

Kruglak (1952) compared the achievement of students in elementary college physics laboratories taught by two methods—the demonstration and the individual method. The individual method proved superior not only in student learning of techniques but also in solving simple laboratory problems. Another experiment on methods of laboratory instruction found that a problem-solving method was superior to traditional laboratory-manual methods in teaching students to apply principles of physics in interpreting phenomena (Bainter, 1955). Lahti (1956) also found a problem-solving method to be superior to more conventional procedures in developing ability to design an experiment. Because many laboratory teachers have been interested in teaching problem-solving methods, this may also be an appropriate place to note Burkhardt's finding (1956) that students who are taught calculus with an emphasis on the understanding of concepts learn concepts better than students taught with conventional emphasis upon solving problems. On the face of it this might appear to be in opposition to the results of Kruglak, Bainter, and Lahti. Actually all of these studies point to the importance of developing understanding rather than teaching students to solve problems by going through a routine series of steps. Whether or not laboratory is superior to lecture-demonstration in developing understanding and problem-solving skills probably depends upon the extent to which understanding of concepts and general problem-solving procedures are emphasized by the instructor in the laboratory situation.

PROJECT METHODS AND INDEPENDENT STUDY

The recent interest in independent study as a means of utilizing faculty time more efficiently has brought to the fore a teaching method which has been used in some form for many years. If one goal of education is to help the student develop the ability to continue learning after his formal education is completed, it seems reasonable that he should have supervised experience in learning independently—experience in which the instructor helps the student learn how to formulate problems, find answers, and evaluate his progress himself. One might expect the values of independent study to be greatest for students with high ability and a good deal of background in the area to be covered since such students should be less likely to be overwhelmed by difficulties.

Independent study programs frequently involve the execution of projects in which a student or group of students undertakes to gather and integrate data relative to some problem.

The results of research on the effectiveness of the project method are not particularly encouraging. One of the first "independent study" experiments was that of Seashore (1928). His course consisted primarily of guided individual study with written reports on eight projects, each of which took about a month to complete. Final examination scores, however, were no different for these students than for students taught by the usual lecture-discussion method (Scheidemann, 1929). In a college botany course, Novak (1958) found that students in conventional classes learned more facts than did those taught by the project method. The project method was particularly ineffective for students in the middle third of the group in intelligence. Similarly, Goldstein (1956) reported that students taught pharmacology by a project method did not learn more than those taught in a standard laboratory.

Unfortunately, measures of achievement such as those used in the studies just noted are probably not sufficient measures of the objectives of project instruction. Presumably the real superiority of the project method should be revealed in measures of motivation and resourcefulness. Novak's experiment was laudable in its inclusion of a measure of scientific attitude, but neither conventional nor project classes made significant gains from the beginning to the end of the semester. Similarly, in a class in mental hygiene, Timmel (1954) found no difference in the effectiveness of the lecture and project methods in changing adjustment. One morsel of support comes from Thistlethwaite's (1960) finding that National Merit Scholars checked requirement of a term paper or laboratory project as one characteristic of their most stimulating course.

With the support of the Fund for the Advancement of Education, a number of colleges have recently experimented with more elaborate programs of independent study. As with other comparisons of teaching methods, few differences have been found between achievement of students working independently and those taught in conventional classes. Moreover, the expected gains in independence have also often failed to materialize. Students taught by independent study do not always seem to develop greater ability or motivation for learning independently.

One of the most comprehensive research programs on independent study was that carried out by Antioch College (Churchill, 1957; Churchill & Baskin, 1958). The Antioch experiment involved courses with varying periods of independent study in humanities, social science, and science. A serious attempt was made not only to measure cognitive and affective achievement but also to evaluate the effect of independent study upon "learning resourcefulness." In addition, the Antioch staff, recognizing that not all students are ready to work independently, planned programs of training for independent work.

The results of the experiments, however, do not point clearly to any conclusion. For example, in one experiment, independent small groups learned more subject matter in physics than students working independently as individuals. But in art, students working individually learned more than those in independent small groups. As in most experiments on teaching methods, the predominant results were of "no significant difference." An exception to this may be found in various indices of student satisfaction in which several significant differences favor lecture-discussion over independent study and especially over independent small groups.

In the Antioch College study, however, one method of saving faculty time was found effective as measured by both student learning and student attitudes. This method, used in teaching French, increased the students' time in class from six to eleven hours a week, but eight of the instructional hours were in charge of a student assistant who used visual materials prepared by the instructor (Baskin, 1960).

In another well-controlled experiment, carried out at Oberlin College (McCollough & Van Atta, 1958), students in introductory science, psychology, and mathematics were required to work independently of the instructor in small groups. This independent work occupied one-third of the college year following several weeks of preliminary training. As in the Antioch experiment, no significant differences in learning appeared either as measured by the usual achievement tests or by a test of learning resourcefulness. Generally, the Oberlin students seem not to have been unhappy about the independent study experience although they indicated that they would have preferred several two-week periods of independent study to the single longer period.

The most favorable results on independent study were obtained at the University of Colorado by Gruber and Weitman (1960). In a course in freshman English in which the group met about 90 per cent of the regularly scheduled hours and had little formal training in grammar, the self-directed study group was significantly superior to control groups on the test of grammar. In a course in physical optics, groups of students who attended class independently of the instructor but were free to consult him learned fewer facts and simple applications but were superior to students in conventional classes in difficult applications and learning new material. Moreover, the latter difference was maintained in a retest three months later while the difference in factual knowledge disappeared (Weitman & Gruber, 1960). In a class in educational psychology an experimental class meeting once a week with the instructor and twice a week in groups of five or six students without the instructor was equal to a conventional class hearing three lectures a week in mastery of content, but tended to be superior on measures of curiosity. In another experiment, students in self-directed study paid more constant attention to a lecture than did students in conventional classes.

The experiment by McKeachie, Lin, Forrin, and Teevan (1960) also involved a fairly high degree of student-instructor contact. Students normally met with the instructor in small groups weekly or biweekly, but they were free to consult the instructor whenever they wished. The results of the experiment suggest that the "tutorial" students did not learn as much from the textbook as students taught in conventional lecture and discussion section classes, but they did develop stronger motivation both for course work and for continued learning after the course. This was indicated not only by responses to a questionnaire administered at the end of the course but also by the number of advanced psychology courses later elected.

Independent study experiments have varied greatly in the amount of assistance given students and in patterning instructional versus independent periods. For example, merely excusing students from attending class is one method of stimulating independent study. The results of such a procedure are not uniform but suggest that classroom experience is not essential for learning. However, the kinds of learning that take place out of class may be different from those that take place in class.

Jensen (1951) compared four groups, including one in which students were completely excused from class attendance. The results showed no difference in gains among the four groups, but students who had worked independently were more willing than others to volunteer for further independent study. Wakely, Marr, Plath, and Wilkins (1960) compared performance in a traditional four-hours-a-week lecture class with that in a class which met only once a week to clear up questions on the textbook. In this experiment the traditional classes proved to be superior. Similarly, Paul (1932) found 55-minute class periods to be superior to 30-minute periods as measured by student achievement.

The results of studies in a child development course by Parsons (1957) and Parsons, Ketcham, and Beach (1958) were more favorable to independent study. In the latter experiment four teaching methods were compared—a lecture, instructor-led discussions, autonomous groups which did not come to class, and individual independent study in which each student was sent home with the syllabus and returned for the final examination. All groups were chosen randomly. In both experiments students working independently made the best scores on the final examination, which measured retention of factual material in the textbook. The instructor-led discussion groups were the lowest in performance on the final examination. There were no significant differences between groups on a measure of attitudes toward working with children. The authors explain their results on the grounds that the independent group was not distracted by the interesting examples, possible applications, or points of view opposing those in the text, all of which were presented in the other groups.

However, in the latter experiment one group of students was made up of teachers commuting to campus for a Saturday class. The results for these students were quite different from those for resident students. In this case students in independent study performed significantly worse than other groups on the examination, perhaps because they were less committed to regular study and may also have experienced more frustration in not having class.

Although the Parsons, Ketcham, and Beach results were favorable to independent study, they are not satisfying to the advocate of this method. These results lead to the conclusion that if a student knows that he is going to be tested on the factual content of a particular book, it is more advantageous for him to read that book than participate in other educational activities. In fact, one might suggest that even better results could be obtained if the desired facts could be identified by giving the students test questions in advance. But knowledge of specific facts is not usually the major objective of an independent study program. What we are hoping for is greater integration, increased purposefulness, and more intense motivation for further study. That independent study can achieve these ends is indicated by the Colorado and Michigan experiments. But the paucity of positive results suggests that we need more research on methods of selecting and training students for independent study, arranging the independent study experience, and measuring outcomes. Note that the Colorado results came in courses in which a good deal of contact with the instructor was retained.

AUTOMATED TECHNIQUES

The impending shortage of college teachers has sparked several hotly contested skirmishes about the virtues or vices of various techniques of teaching with devices substituting for a portion of the usual face-to-face interaction between instructors and students. Since some college faculty members anxious about technological unemployment resist innovations, research has often been used as a technique of infiltration rather than as a method of developing and testing educational theory.

Along with many inconsequential studies, a few carefully executed programs of research have emerged. Representative of these are those described in the following section.

Television[4]

Before reviewing the research on teaching by television, let us consider two hypotheses that may help in analyzing the research results.

Television is not a method of instruction in the sense that discussion and lecture are methods of instruction. Rather it is a means of giving the student a clear view of the instructional situation. Therefore, we would expect that (1) the relative effectiveness of teaching via television will vary depending on the importance of being able to see clearly. For example, we would expect television to be effective when it is important for students to see demonstrations, visiting lecturers, or films, but to have little advantage when communication is primarily verbal.

---

[4]Some portions of this section were previously published in W. J. McKeachie, TV for college instruction, *Improving Coll. & Univer. Teaching*, 1958, 6, 84-89, and are used by permission of the publisher.

Television reduces the opportunity for students to communicate with teachers and for teachers to interact with students. We would thus expect that (2) the effectiveness of television will vary inversely with the importance of two-way communication not only for feedback to the student but particularly for feedback to the teacher.

In 1954, Pennsylvania State University (Carpenter & Greenhill, 1955, 1958) received a grant from the Fund for the Advancement of Education to study the effectiveness of conventional courses taught for a full semester over closed-circuit television as compared with the same instruction given in the usual manner. With these funds, a program of research was initiated on the courses entitled General Chemistry, General Psychology, and Psychology of Marriage. In 1957 the research program was expanded to (1) extend the project to additional courses; (2) study instructional variables, and (3) work on methods of improving instruction on television.

The results of this research may be used either to extol or damn television. Essentially they indicate that there is little loss in student learning in courses taught by television as compared with classes taught conventionally. For example, the first experiment dealt with the lecture portion of courses in general chemistry and general psychology. In the chemistry course the differences between methods on objective measures of information were not significant. In the psychology course the conventional class did prove to be slightly superior in knowledge to the television class.

Students learned the information needed to pass examinations, and most did not object strongly to the televised classes although they preferred live instruction. Students in psychology were asked (1) how much they liked psychology, and (2) how much it contributed to their education as compared with other courses they were taking. On both counts, ratings of the students in the television classes were lower than those of students who were in the same room as the instructor. The psychology students were also asked if they would like to take another course in psychology. About the same percentages of students signed up from lectures, television originating rooms, and television receiving rooms, but when asked if they would prefer taking it in a large class or by television, a plurality preferred television. While students at other colleges do not rebel at television either, research findings quite consistently report less favorable attitudes toward courses taught by television as compared with conventional classes (e.g., Lepore & Wilson, 1958; Macomber & Siegel, 1960).

The effectiveness of television is particularly astonishing to one who has seen the apparent inattention in many television classes. If students who are obviously inattentive learn as much as those who appear to be attentive, one might suspect that many students have developed the ability to appear attentive in conventional classes even though their minds are wandering. In the latter case, television students may simply be exposing the reactions to lectures which polite students ordinarily hide from their instructor. The New York University research staff (Klapper, 1958) used student observers to classify television students into high-, middle-, and low-attention groups. In none of their courses was attention level related to achievement, although their evidence suggested that students who had more previous knowledge of the subject paid less attention than those who had less.

Factors unimportant in using television. The heading of this section would normally be "Factors Conditioning the Effectiveness of Educational Television," but the results of the research are more clearly indicated by the title chosen. For example, recognizing that instructor-student interaction is sometimes important in learning, the Pennsylvania State group installed "two-way" microphone communication in the receiving rooms so that students in the receiving rooms could ask questions. This technique has been used even more extensively at the State University of Iowa (Stuit, *et al.*, 1956) and at Case Institute of Technology (Martin, 1957a, 1957b). The Pennsylvania State group found that this method of instruction was not superior to simple one-way communication, although students prefer two-way communication (Carpenter & Greenhill, 1958). Similar results were found in the research on television instruction in the Army and at Case (Fritz, 1952; Martin, Adams, & Baron, 1958).

Another attempt to combine the value of interaction with that of television was an experiment in presenting a 35-minute television lesson followed by a 15-minute discussion period in each of the receiving rooms. Other students in the same course observed by means of television the 15-minute discussion conducted by the instructor with the eight students in the origination room. Still other students were allowed to leave or to study their notes. As in the other attempt to provide interaction, results showed no significant differences in test performance between students taught by each of these three methods.

The Effect of Instructional Methods upon Achievement and Attitudes in Communication Skills

SAMUEL L. BECKER AND CARL A. DALLINGER

The method used to communicate the "content" of a course in communication skills has little effect upon the acquirement of skills or on the knowledge which the student gains of the principles of speaking, writing, reading, and listening. Hearing the regular classroom instructor in the face-to-face situation, viewing television recordings made by "experts" in each subject area, and reading comparable material in textbooks and journals seem to be equally effective as methods for handling this aspect of the course. Instructor differences are, in general, independent of the teaching methods compared.

Colleges and universities which attempt to integrate the teaching of reading, writing, speaking, and listening in courses in communication skills face two major problems in the years immediately ahead: (1) the instruction of many more students without a proportionate increase in staff; (2) obtaining instructors adequately prepared in all of the four areas named.

A few institutions give graduate students "on the job" training as teaching assistants in communication skills courses, but graduate programs specifically designed to prepare persons to handle all of the phases of instruction with equal competence have not been developed. That such programs will be developed in the immediate future is unlikely because there is little opportunity for professional recognition and advancement for those so prepared. Rather, the prospect is that for some time the majority of instructors teaching communication skills will continue to be trained either in English or in speech. Hence, their preparation will be one-sided, and lacking in certain of the basic subject areas they are called upon to teach.

In view of this situation, these questions may be asked: (1) Can we compensate for limitations in the preparation of instructors, provide

From *Speech Monographs*, Vol. XXVII, (March, 1960), pp. 70-76.

Mr. Becker is Associate Professor of Speech and Head of the Division of Radio, Television, Film at the State University of Iowa. Mr. Dallinger is Associate Professor of Speech and Co-ordinator of the Communication Skills Program at the same institution.

This paper summarizes the monograph, *Communication Skills: An Experiment in Instructional Methods* (Iowa City: The State University of Iowa, 1958), of which these writers were senior authors. It also includes the results of certain analyses completed after the appearance of the original publication. The study was supported in part by the Fund for the Advancement of Education.

better "on the job" training for staff members, and raise the level of instruction in communication skills courses by utilizing "experts" to present the basic principles of communication to students? (2) Can we maximize the use of instructional resources by making each student more directly responsible for his own training, without reducing the quality of the education he receives?

In an effort to provide at least partial answers to these questions, during the academic year 1957-1958 the State University of Iowa compared experimentally the effectiveness of three methods of teaching the communication skills course. These were: (1) the method then and presently in use—hereafter called the "normal" method—which makes the individual instructor directly responsible for training his students in all of the skills and content areas covered in the course; (2) a method of teaching—hereafter called the "bibliography" method—designed to make the student more self-reliant by reducing from four to three the number of formal class meetings each week, and presenting the basic principles of the course as normally covered in lectures and discussions in a bibliography of assigned and optional readings; (3) the presentation of the basic principles of the course by "experts," through the use of kinescopes, supplemented by the discussion of the principles so presented and their application in performances under the guidance and criticism of the classroom instructor. This third method will hereafter be called the "kinescope" method.

PROCEDURE

The experiment was conducted with the two major communication skills courses at the State University of Iowa, the two-semester "main" course and the one-semester "accelerated" course. Each year between 15 and 20 per cent of the freshmen admitted to the university are permitted to take the accelerated course. These are freshmen who are high in academic aptitude and who have a reasonably high level of skill in speaking and writing. In this experiment only the normal and bibliography methods were used with accelerated students. In the two-semester main course all three methods were used.

In both the main and the accelerated course students were randomly assigned to one of the sections scheduled at the hour for which they had registered. Each section was then assigned one of the three instructional methods. In the case of the sixty-three main course sections, one-third of the classes held at each of the six hours the course was offered were assigned to the normal method of instruction, one-third to the bibliography method, and one-third to the kinescope method.

Accelerated course students were assigned in a like manner to normal and bibliography sections. Instructors were randomly assigned to sections, except for the following considerations: (1) instructors teaching more than one section of the course were assigned to sections within the same treatment group (all normal, all bibliography, or all kinescope); (2) an effort was made to achieve a balance of experienced and inexperienced instructors among the three methods.

Since the main course extended throughout the year, a method of preregistration was arranged so that each student would continue in the same section and under the same instructor. If a student found it necessary to change to another hour, he was required to enroll in a section taught by the same method as the one in which he had previously been enrolled. In so far as possible, instructors continued with the same classes.

In order to facilitate the measurement of instructor differences, all but one of the classes taught by any instructor who had more than one section of the course were eliminated by a random selection method. Also, classes in which the same instructor did not continue into the second semester were eliminated, since the achievement of students in these sections might have been influenced by the change of instructors rather than by the teaching method. Students for whom complete pre-examination and achievement examination scores could not be obtained were likewise eliminated. This left for the main course study 582 students distributed among 36 sections, taught by 36 different instructors. Twelve of these sections were taught by the normal method, 13 by the biblography method, and 11 by the kinescope method. The accelerated course analyses were based upon 176 students in nine sections taught by nine different instructors. Of these sections, four were taught by the normal method, and five by the bibliography method.

Included in the planning of the experiment was the preparation of syllabi for the bibliography sections of the accelerated course and for the bibliography and kinescope sections of the main course. No syllabi were prepared for the normal sections of either course, since one of the assumptions underlying this method is that instruction is more effective when the individual teacher has full responsibility for his class, adapting materials, methods, and rate of presentation to student needs.

Twenty-eight half-hour kinescopes were used in the kinescope sections. Twenty-six of these were produced at the State University of Iowa and two were made by the late Irving J. Lee of Northwestern University. Since the kinescopes were viewed as projected films, and not on television monitors, classrooms were provided which could be darkened in such a way as to permit note-taking during the projection of the kinescopes.

At least one copy of each of the items assigned for required or optional reading in the bibliography sections was put on "reserve" circulation in the university library. Methods of stimulating and checking on the reading done by students in these sections were left to the classroom instructors.

Criterion Measures. Eight instruments were used in the pre-test and post-test evaluations:

1. "English Composition." A multiple-choice examination covering punctuation, capitalization, grammar, choice of words, appropriateness of usage, sentence sequence, and the organization of ideas.
2. "Reading Comprehension." A power test of reading comprehension.
3. "General Vocabulary."
4. "Brown-Carlson Listening Comprehension Test."
5. "Principles of Communication Skills." A mutliple-choice examination covering the principles of writing and speaking, with emphasis on purpose, organization, support of ideas, language, and basic bibliographical and footnote forms.
6. "Expository Theme." An original theme, at least 450 words in length. Each student was given two hours in which to write the theme, which was judged on the basis of purpose, content, organization, sentence structure, diction, and mechanics. Each pre-test theme was rated by one experienced staff member; each post-test theme by two or three staff members, with an additional reader added in those cases where disagreement among the original judges was marked. Different topics were used for the pre-test and post-test themes.
7. "Argumentative Speech." A four-minute extemporaneous speech for which each student was given fifty minutes to prepare. The speech was judged on the basis of central idea, analysis, supporting material, organization, language, adjustment to speaking situation, bodily action, voice, articulation and pronunciation, fluency, and general effectiveness. Each pre-test speech was rated by one or two staff members, each post-test speech by three to five staff members.
8. "Attitudes Toward Communication." A multiple-choice questionnaire designed to measure how important the respondent felt various aspects of the communication skills to be. In order to minimize response bias, an attempt was made to disassociate this questionnaire in the minds of respondents from the communication skills course and from this experiment.

These tests were supplemented by questionnaires designed to elicit from instructional staff and students their reactions to the three methods of instruction.

Treatment of Data. Simple analyses of variance[1] were made to test the homogeneity of the main course sections and the accelerated sections on each of the pre-test measures and also on the Entrance Composite Percentile Rank, which has been found to be a reliable measure of academic aptitude.[2] In these and all other analyses or tests of significance, the five per cent level of confidence was pre-set as the level at which to reject the hypothesis of no difference.

To test the difference between methods of instruction and between sections using the same method, a groups-within-treatments analysis of covariance design, with the individual as the unit of measurement, was used.[3] Separate analyses were made for the accelerated course and the main course, and for each criterion measure. In each case, the post-examination was the criterion measure and the corresponding pre-examination the control variable. The groups-within-treatments design, with the individual student as the unit of measurement, permitted some measurement of instructor differences. Where analysis indicated that the hypothesis of no differences in achievement between sections within each method was not tenable, the test for differences between methods of instruction was made with a groups-within-treatments design with the section mean, rather than the individual, as the unit of measurement.[4]

In order to test whether the achievement of students of varying academic ability was differently affected by the three methods of instruction, achievement in speaking, theme writing, listening, and knowledge of the principles of communication for each method of instruction and for different levels of academic aptitude was tested with analyses of variance, utilizing a treatments-by-levels design.[5] To set the levels of academic aptitude, separate frequency distributions on the Entrance Composite Percentile Rank were obtained for both main course and accelerated course students. Each group was divided into four approximately equal-sized levels. Scores were randomly eliminated in such a way that for each analysis, there were the same number of students from each method at each level.

Chi-square tests were run on the student questionnaire data to see whether experience with one method affected student attitude toward

---

[1]E. F. Linquist, *Design and Analysis of Experiments in Psychology and Education* (Boston, 1953), p. 56.

[2]The Entrance Composite Percentile Rank of a student indicates the per cent of students whose total scores fell below his total score. The composite score is obtained by summing a student's percentile ranks on English placement, vocabulary, reading comprehension, and mathematics tests. This composite has been found to correlate highly with academic achievement in college as measured by overall grade point average.

[3]Lindquist, *Design and Analysis*, p. 177.

[4]*Ibid.*

[5]*Ibid.*, p. 123.

this and other methods. Theoretical cell frequencies were not great enough to permit the calculation of chi-squares with the faculty attitude data.

RESULTS

In order to minimize redundancy, we shall concentrate here on the results of the main course experiment, except in those instances where the accelerated course results were essentially different or where it appears important to contrast the results obtained in the two courses.

Evidence supports the assumption that none of the main course sections differed significantly on any of the pre-test measures. At the end of the year, significant *instructor* differences were found for all but the vocabulary measures. Significant differences between *methods of instruction* were found for none of the criterion measures.

Since more of the variance was attributable to differences between instructors than to differences between methods of instruction, an attempt was made to find whether *systematic* differences between instructors existed. The two instructor variables examined were academic background (graduate work in speech vs. graduate work in English) and teaching experience (no experience, experience not in communication skills, experience only in communication skills, experience elsewhere and in communication skills). These variables of experience and background appeared to have a consistent effect only on the *theme* criterion. Experience in teaching communication skills or a background in English or literature seemed to increase the probability that a teacher's students would do better in writing. Unfortunately, there were not enough experienced speech or inexperienced English instructors to permit a further breakdown in order to isolate whether the differences found could be attributed solely to academic background or teaching experience.

In the methods-by-levels analysis of the scores on the examination over principles, no significant interaction was found between level of student aptitude and method of instruction, nor were significant differences found between methods of instruction. Table I shows the mean for each level and method on this examination. As expected, significant differences were found between levels of academic aptitude. These differences consistently favored the higher levels. The same results were found for the listening data and essentially the same results for the theme data. Quite different results were found, however, for the speech data. These are summarized in Table II. Again no significant interaction was found, nor were significant differences found between methods of

TABLE I

Principles Post-Examination Means by Levels and Methods

	Normal Method	Bibliography Method	Kinescope Method	Total
Level of Academic Aptitude:				
1.	19.98	20.80	20.74	20.51
2.	18.77	18.93	19.40	19.03
3.	17.71	18.20	18.55	18.15
4.	16.26	15.87	16.08	16.07

TABLE II

Speech Post-Examination Means by Levels and Methods

	Normal Method	Bibliography Method	Kinescope Method	Total
Level of Academic Aptitude:				
1.	45.20	45.22	44.61	45.01
2.	47.17	44.53	43.77	45.16
3.	44.12	44.31	45.25	44.56
4.	44.26	43.26	43.31	43.61

instruction. Significant differences were found between levels of academic aptitude. However, it was found that the lowest level was significantly lower than each of the other levels on the speech post-test, but that the other levels did not differ significantly from each other.

In the levels analyses of the accelerated course data, there were the important differences from the results of the main course analyses: Students receiving instruction by the normal method scored significantly higher on the principles post-examination and the theme post-examination than did students receiving instruction by the bibliography method.

Analyses of the attitude toward communication measures secured near the end of the experiment showed no significant differences between instructors within each method or between methods of instruction. Significant differences were found, however, between main course and accelerated course students, with the latter group displaying more favorable attitudes toward the importance of the skills of communication. It is interesting to note that students in the accelerated course also averaged significantly higher attitude scores prior to the experiment and *before* they knew that they would be in the accelerated course.

Just before the end of the year students in the main course were asked their opinions concerning the three methods of instruction. Table III shows their reactions. The normal method of instruction was most

TABLE III

If the Communication Skills Course is Offered Next Year in Three Different Ways and a Friend of Yours has a Choice, Which of the following Types of Sections Would You Advise Him to Take?

Response	Group			Total
	Normal	Biblio.	Kine.	
Section which meets four times a week, with approximately one class period a week devoted to lectures and discussion. [Normal]	78.8%	51.2%	27.2%	53.1%
Section which meets three times a week, rather than four, and has extra reading assigments to take the place of the lecture material. [Bibliography]	5.9	35.7	6.9	14.9
Section which meets four times a week, with approximately one class period a week devoted to viewing and discussing a film of a television lecture. [Kinescope]	15.3	13.1	65.9	32.0
	100.0	100.0	100.0	100.0

favored and the bibliography method least favored. However, students who had been in a section taught by a particular method tended to be far more favorably disposed toward that method than students who had received other types of instruction. These differences among the three groups of respondents were statistically significant. When students were asked the type of instruction which they believed "would be easier" and from which they believed they "would gain most," they again tended to favor the type used in the section in which they had been enrolled. Comparable results were obtained from the students in the accelerated course.

At the end of the experiment, the instructors clearly preferred the normal method. As in the case of the student responses, however, there was some tendency for those instructors who had taught by a particular method to look upon that method more favorably. Whether these differences were significant was not tested.

CONCLUSIONS

Within the limitations of this study, one may retain the hypothesis that students can acquire a knowledge of the principles of communication and achieve skill in speaking, writing, reading, and listening equally well from each of the methods of instruction tested. Because it permits the saving of classroom space and instructional time, the bibliography method would appear to be the most efficient, while being at least as effective as the other methods.

Except for speech, students of greater academic aptitude tend to acquire knowledge and skill in communication better than do students of lesser ability. At none of the levels, however, do different methods of instruction appear to have differential effects.

The hypothesis that the attitude of students toward communication is affected in the same way by each of the methods of instruction may be retained. The hypothesis that attitudes of students towards these methods of instruction are affected equally by each method must, however, be rejected. Though students, in general, seemed to prefer the normal method of instruction, experience with either of the other methods tended to make them much more favorably disposed toward that method.

If it is important to faculty morale that instructors favor the method of instruction which is used, the bibliography method of teaching communication skills will undoubtedly have a difficult time being adopted in the near future. The kinescope method would have only slightly less trouble. The choice would almost certainly be the normal method. Teachers feel that ample time is needed for class discussions. They apparently have little faith in the ability of freshman students to read, evaluate, and retain written material. The evidence would indicate, however, that much of this bias grows out of the fact that most instructors have had experience in teaching only some variation of what we have here called the normal method. Experience with the other methods would undoubtedly bring about more favorable attitudes toward them. This would seem to be consistent with research in other areas which has shown that legislation can lead, rather than follow, popular sentiment.

Planning Speech Courses and Curricular Programs

KARL F. ROBINSON AND E. J. KERIKAS

The first chapters of this book have discussed the broad factors that affect the teaching of speech in the high school or college. Whether speech instruction is organized as courses in the regular curriculum pattern, is conducted in activities outside the classroom, or, as usually happens, is a combination of both patterns, these seven *general* factors influence it: (1) a clear understanding of the goals and objectives of speech training in the secondary school; (2) a thorough knowledge of the needs, interests, and abilities of the students; (3) a trained teacher with suitable personal qualities to handle the program; (4) the cooperation of the administrator; (5) facilities that at least meet the minimum essentials; (6) satisfactory community-school cooperation; and (7) compatible relationships with other departments in the school.

Before the teacher can proceed to plan a program or deal with classroom problems, he must have a basic approach to instruction upon which courses, activities, and methods of teaching depend.

BASIC APPROACHES IN TEACHING SPEECH

Since a *mastery of fundamentals* of speech underlies success in any speech situation, no matter what the type of speech may be, *a sound teaching approach must insure such mastery.* In addition it must *follow up such fundamentals,* stressing them in activities and more specialized types of performance; further, it must *allow the addition of theoretical principles and techniques necessary in meeting the more complex speech situations.*

Three basic approaches are possible; all are in use in high school speech instruction. Predominance of any one over the others depends upon the character of the speech courses and the local conditions affecting them. These three approaches will be designated as (1) the *elements* approach, (2) the *activities* approach, and (3) the *combination* approach.

The Elements Approach

In the elements approach the mastery of fundamental processes is considered so important that it is made the *end* of speech instruction,

From *Teaching Speech: methods and materials,* Karl F. Robinson and E. J. Kerikas. New York: David McKay Company, Inc., 1963, p. 99-116.

rather than merely the *means* of meeting various types of speech situations.

In this text these fundamentals are treated in Part Two, and include poise and emotional adjustment, communicativeness, bodily action, voice and articulation, language, speech preparation, and listening. Becker and others[1] found that 100 per cent of Michigan high school speech teachers include such fundamentals as their basic course content with the use of talks the chief exercise for teaching them. Evelyn Konigsberg,[2] formerly Chairman of the Department of Speech, Jamaica High School, and now Principal, Washington Irving High School, New York City, supports an elements approach through the use of functional drill in the teaching of voice and articulation. She attacks the stress upon merely "communicating ideas" and "practicing speaking in functional situations" as ways of insuring effective speaking. "Voice and articulation are two very basic elements of communication through speech," she states, and indicates that they must be *taught directly* by the teacher of speech.

The elements approach requires goals, units, and methods to be planned so that fundamentals are taught through drill, talks, oral reading or any other suitable vehicle, but with stress upon the mastery of the element or fundamental habits to be developed. In no case, however, should this approach be used without a satisfactory synthesis of the element with the whole act of speech.

An elements approach is also found in many college beginning courses. Jones[3] in his study of the basic course in colleges and universities in the United States, reported many schools which organized their fundamentals or voice and diction courses on this basis.

The Activities Approach

The activities approach rests upon the selection of an experience (activity) such as conversation, discussion, and so on, as a vehicle by means of which the fundamentals are taught. The emphasis is upon the theory and technique of the activity as an end. Fundamentals are involved as *means* of performing the activity. Such activities are developed later in this text.

Quite often the particular techniques of the activity dominate such work, any emphasis upon the basic elements of speech being by-passed

---

[1]Albert Becker, Charles Brown, and Jack W. Murphy, "Speech Teaching in Michigan High Schools," *Speech Teacher,* I (March, 1952), 137-45.

[2]Evelyn Konigsberg, "Making Drill Functional," *Speech Teacher,* I (March, 1952), 128.

[3]H. Rodman Jones, "The Development and Present Status of Beginning Speech Courses in the Colleges and Universities in the United States" (unpublished doctoral dissertation, Northwestern University, 1952).

in the stress upon successful communication in the activity. The activities approach has much to recommend it: it is an accepted educational approach through everyday speech experiences; it is easily motivated; it *can* be used successfully to teach fundamentals. However, unless the teacher is on his toes, the total activity and its techniques will crowd out the individual pointing-up and repeated experience (drill) necessary to set desirable speech habits. No teacher should delude himself that he is doing his basic job if he teaches activities *only,* and never "nails down" the fundamentals upon which they depend for successful oral communication.

In the majority of basic college courses, public speaking is the principal activity used, according to Jones.[4] A greater variety of activities characterizes the standard high school course.

The Combination Approach

Most usable in high school speech instruction and in many college courses is a *combination* of these two. *Motivation* for development in speech fundamentals and mastery of everyday speech situations can be secured readily through activities. Diagnosis of needs in fundamentals, pin-pointing areas for work, and repeated experience on particular basic skills in order to build *new habits* are best served by the elements approach. The desired synthesis can be secured through activities. Both approaches can serve in teaching techniques of an activity. The intelligent teacher must learn when and how the goals of his instruction are best served by the two approaches.

In this text, the fundamentals are studied with a careful analysis of elements and suitable culminating exercises in Part Two, the principal vehicle being talks or public-speaking experiences. The forms of speech are treated in Part Three as extraclass or classroom activities. They can be taught *within* regular classroom work, as well as in extraclass programs of speech instruction without any emphasis upon contest speech. Necessary adaptations should be made by the teacher. Course outlines suggested in this chapter rest upon a combination approach with fundamentals or elements stressed first and activities following.

FACTORS UNDERLYING ORGANIZATION

In addition to the *general* factors influencing the speech program in any school, the instructor must consider certain *specific, organiza-*

---

[4]Jones, *ibid.*

tional factors that determine the exact courses, their content, sequence, and relationship in the whole program. A discussion of these follows.

1. Adequate Class Time for Speech

High school and college speech instruction invariably stresses improvement of personal speech habits and development of speaking skills. To achieve these ends time is needed for (1) individual performance, (2) careful evaluation and criticism by the teacher, (3) repeated performance under supervision to allow application of suggestions given. The student must *do* the thing he wishes to develop. Reading books, hearing lectures, or writing *about* speech is not enough. Each student should have as many actual performances as possible in every course.

Skills courses meeting every day are best. They allow wide participation, keep interest high, and permit benefits of cumulative experience. If a five-hour course per week is not possible, a three-hour plan is next best. Teaching efficiency and results go down in the two-hour or one-hour per week class. This is especially true when enrollments run thirty to forty pupils in a class. In a one-hour class, especially, ten to fifteen students is a top figure. Even then a teacher needs careful planning to achieve his goals. A better plan usually is to have a shorter course with more frequent meetings.

2. Optimum Class Size

As noted above, class size directly affects efficiency in teaching speech, more than in other subjects, because individual performance is essential. Large classes and short teaching time frustrate both pupil and teacher. Administrators not acquainted with the nature of speech instruction often use the same measuring stick for speech classes that they employ in social science or English classes; the result is overcrowding and ineffective work. Speech teachers who inadvertently or deliberately admit too many students jeopardize their program.

Best results in basic skills courses are achieved when classes do not run over twenty-five students. A three-hour or five-hour class permits a given assignment to be covered in about three periods, assuming eight recitations are heard daily. The teacher must see that maximum class size limits are respected.

Experiments with closed-circuit television and/or team teaching have shown it is possible to instruct larger speech classes, sometimes of sixty to seventy students, using lectures and demonstrations of skills assignments. However, all such experiments employ smaller groups of about twenty students when individual pupil performances are conducted and teacher critiques are given to each person.

3. Length of Performance

Length of performance is another important variable. Beginning assignments usualy are short, running one, two, or three minutes. Standard course patterns indicate longer performances as pupils develop and as projects become more difficult or principles of composition are applied. If speeches averaged three minutes in a five-hour semester course with an enrollment of twenty students per class, each student might have a total of ten appearances. This would be most desirable. Gardner[5] found a combination of three, six, and nine minute speeches a popular one in beginning college classes. Most instructors prefer more frequent, short talks to few, long ones.

4. A Class Schedule Permitting Students to Program Speech

Regardless of time, class size, or speech length, the teacher must reach as many students needing speech training as he can. If speech is *required*, class schedules will be organized to permit students to take it. However, when speech is an *elective subject* it must compete with other subjects which are required. The speech instructor should always clear schedule with the principal or department head to see that there are no such conflicts. He should also try to avoid scheduling against other popular electives.

5. Full Accreditation of Speech Classwork

Speech classwork taught as an elective or requirement should always be accredited on the same basis as any other academic subject. Any other plan penalizes the student and teacher. Noncredit speech, either as a requirement or as an elective, places an unfair burden of motivation upon speech instruction.

6. Sufficient Instructional Budget

The speech teacher should never hesitate to make his budgetary needs known. Texts, equipment, supplies, library materials—all these are standard curricular items. They affect course sequences, teacher planning, and classroom work. The speech teacher should consult with his administrator regarding his needs and budget practices.

7. Application beyond the Classroom

Speech training must function beyond the class assignments and exercises. It should be applied in school and community life. The teacher should survey these two fields for possibilities that affect the courses

---

[5]Wofford Gardner, "The Relationship of Improvement in Public Speaking Skill to the Length and Frequency of Classroom Performance" (unpublished doctoral dissertation, Northwestern University, 1952).

he teaches, the subject matter of speech assignments, audiences to be met, and so on. Thus he lays the foundation for a broad and functional program.

8. Suitable Coordination with Extraclass Speech Activities

A reciprocal relationship should exist between classroom instruction in speech and activities outside the classroom. A knowledge of the *whole* school speech outlook permits carefully planned courses that will help to feed the extraclass program and provide basic training and specialized skills useful to both. Similarly, these activities can serve the courses in speech. They introduce students to speech, they let them taste the benefits and enjoyment of participation, they motivate them to desire more work in the field presented in a continuing, organized form in class. Activities are often the beginning of an organized classroom program growing from a demand for more speech education.

Thus speech classes and activities serve each other. Intelligent organization and planning of the *total* program make for good coordination and effective work.

All of these factors underlie sound organization of speech instruction. They are fundamental to the more detailed planning of course outlines and lesson plans that follow.

BASIC PRINCIPLES UNDERLYING PLANNING AND TEACHING

Realistic and successful planning of speech instruction rests upon certain basic principles of teaching. The list below and the subsequent teaching pattern furnish such a foundation for the beginning teacher.

1. He must know (through diagnosis) the speech interests, needs, and abilities of his students.
2. He must realize that speech is a complex form of behavior, that it is habituated, and that the speech habits he observes are of long standing.
3. He must provide suitable motivation for students if they are to make the desired changes in speech behavior.
4. He must set up the long-term or remote goals (objectives) that he wishes the students to achieve in the course.
5. He must determine the immediate, tentative, readily achievable goals for the various steps in development leading to the remote goals of the course.
6. He must provide satisfactory theory and training experiences for the accomplishment of both immediate and remote goals. These experiences should not be isolated drills used only as exercises for teaching fundamentals or basic skills. They should be chosen to permit elements to be *taught* and *synthesized* in relation to the *whole* configuration of speaking.

7. He must guide the students toward goals through his criticism and suggestions, tactfully and effectively given.
8. He must allow sufficient time for maturation in the learning process, and repeated performance to permit the "setting" of the new habits.

A TEACHING PATTERN

In practice these principles indicate a teaching pattern or "instructional ladder," which characterizes high school speech instruction:

I. LONG RANGE OR REMOTE *COURSE* GOALS
(Determined by teacher in terms of desired information, attitudes, personal speech habits, basic and specialized speech skills to be developed in the course.)

II. NEEDS, INTERESTS, ABILITIES OF STUDENTS
(as related to I above. Revealed through testing and diagnosis by the teacher.)

III. IMMEDIATE GOALS FOR CLASS AND INDIVIDUALS (tentative)
(Based on II, within limits set by I. Set by the teacher for the particular class and pupil to achieve.)
Achieve via IV: *organized* units of instruction in course.

VI. CONTINUED UNTIL, IDEALLY, EACH REMOTE GOAL IS REACHED BY EACH STUDENT
(Within the limits of his abilities.)

V. NEW IMMEDIATE GOALS
(Set by the teacher after III goals are reached. The goals in V are tentative, also, more difficult of achievement, always moving towards I, the long range course goals.)
Achieved by using suitable units such as in IV, suited to the *new* goals.

IV. UNITS IN THE COURSE including
A. *Suitable motivation*
B. *Selected individual and group experiences and activities, needed theory*
C. *Evaluation: suggestions and criticism by teacher and class*
D. *Application of criticism and suggestions*
E. *Repeated experience* (until first immediate goals [III] are reached)

PLANNING THE BASIC COURSE

The first course is the most important and most common course in the secondary school or college. Since it is often the only speech course offered in high school, it necessitates careful planning. As has been noted earlier, it is peculiarly subject to conditions in the local situation. However, certain general trends and patterns are helpful to the teacher as a plan that can be adapted to meet conditions in a given situation. A guide of this type is useful in the statement of objectives.

Objectives in Basic Speech Skills

The speech program should be based upon a comprehensive set of objectives. In Chapters I and II we have discussed the broad aims of secondary and higher education and the needs of students. The list of goals[6] that appears below is designed to meet student needs. It indicates the possible scope of a program in basic speech skills and reading that is the chief concern in a first course in speech. Additional and more specialized courses, quite obviously, have more specialized objectives.

1. The speech needs and abilities of every student should be tested and diagnosed.
2. Students who possess speech defects such as stuttering, lisping, dialects, or speech maladjustments should be provided opportunities for correction.
3. *The large group having "inadequate" and normal speech should be given the chance to profit from systematic education in such fundamental speech processes as:*
   a. Adjustment to the speaking situations of everyday life so that social adaptions of this type can be made without fear and with confidence and poise.
   b. Development of a speaking personality characterized by attitudes of sincerity, friendliness, and communicativeness.
   c. Skill in developing a subject, in using one's ideas and in knowing the sources of information to supplement them with ample and relevant materials.
   d. Analysis of the audience which is addressed.
   e. Organization and arrangement of content to insure the desired response from the audience.
   f. Mastery of an effective technique of delivery.
   g. Expressing one's ideas in simple, acceptable, and effective spoken language.
   h. Articulating and pronouncing words intelligibly.
   i. Using the voice effectively.

---

[6]Karl F. Robinson and W. Norwood Brigance, "The Program of Basic Skills in Speaking," *Bulletin of the National Association of Secondary School Principals,* XXIX, No. 133 (November, 1945), 19-29.

j. Communication of ideas with expressive and well-coordinated bodily activity.

k. Ability to select and arrange content for reading aloud.

l. Effective use of fundamental processes in reading aloud ordinary material from the printed page.

m. Cultivation and acquisition of suitable listening habits that will enable the individual to give respectful attention to speakers for purposes of learning, evaluating, and criticizing.

4. Students who are superior in basic speech skills should be given opportunities to develop special skills directly associated with their life interests and in keeping with their needs and abilities.

5. Basic speaking skills should be implemented through a balanced program of functional speech experiences. These should be directly related to school and community problems, practical situations, and educational experiences which form a framework for participation in a democratic society.

6. Evaluating the growth and development in basic speech skills.

A Simplified Plan for Constructing Courses of Study in Speech

Knowing the goals of the basic speech course gives an orientation to the teacher who is planning the courses of study for a particular situation.

The average speech teacher who undertakes to build a course of study or to construct a curriculum in speech faces an unusual predicament. Logically, such a teacher may turn for help to readings on curriculum building in textbooks on education, but in them he will find little specific help. For the most part, they concern themselves with building the curriculum for an entire school system, or with the reorganization of courses of study in the school as a whole. Too often they suggest a series of detailed steps in procedure that makes the process complicated and confusing for one seeking a comparatively short and easy solution.

The following plan, which has been evolved from years of teaching summer and regular term courses in problems and methods of teaching speech in the secondary school and college, is presented as a suggested practical procedure. It has been employed by thousands of teachers. The steps are set down in order below:

I. *Determine the philosophy of speech education, stating it in terms of broad objectives.*

The question to be here decided is what one believes to be the broad objectives of education and what place speech has in the objectives of education. One's philosophy may be stated in terms of them.

II. *Determine the specific course objectives.*

These will be refinements of the broad objectives and in many cases will be the result of analysis of them. The objectives for a basic course have been stated above.

III. *Choose the content: speech experiences and activities that will accomplish the objectives.* These can be listed in outline form.

A. Content should always be selected with respect to the objectives and the student needs, etc. (see IIIB below and II above).

1. A knowledge of available sources of platform assignments, information, materials, teaching aids, and equipment is essential to proper selection. (Consult methods books, speech texts, bibliographies, textbook reviews, course notes, personal experience, and issues of the *Quarterly Journal of Speech* and *The Speech Teacher* for assistance.)

2. Examine and note the content of courses of study and curricula in speech that are available.

a. Courses of study published by various states and municipalities.

b. Curriculum projects in colleges and universities.

c. Courses of study in English and the language arts often include usable speech materials.

d. College and university courses may be summarized in catalogues of the particular department or school. They are available in the school or public library. Catalogues may also be obtained from the registrar of a college or university.

3. List *all of the content* that might be included in the program.

B. *Select, refine, and restrict that which fits the local situation* (most of these factors have been developed in Chapters I-III).

1. *The training and preparation of the teacher,* including particular abilities and weaknesses.

2. *The students to be enrolled in the class.*

a. Age; year in school; grade or class.

b. Elective or required subject.

c. Mental, physical, racial, social, and emotional characteristics; their nationality.

d. Interests and abilities in speech, as well as in other areas.

3. *Facilities in the school for speech work.*

    a. Classroom: furniture, lighting, equipment.

    b. Auditorium; stage—its size, shape, usability; lighting; paint shop; amplifying system and sound equipment.

    c. Library facilities.

    d. Recording apparatus.

    e. Transportation: school bus, cars, railroads, etc.

4. *Attitude of the administrator.*

    a. His ideas about speech education.

    b. The budget for speech work.

5. *Attitude of other departments in the school toward speech.*

    a. English

    b. Languages

    c. Science: Physics, Chemistry, Biology

    d. Music

    e. Commercial

    f. Athletics

    g. Manual Arts

    h. Social Studies

    i. Art

    j. Counselors and home-room teachers; deans

6. *The attitude of the community toward speech.*

    a. Parents

    b. Church groups

    c. Dinner clubs: Kiwanis, Rotary, Lions, etc.

    d. Community resources: recreation center, theater, etc.

    e. Services expected by the community

7. *Extraclass speech activities and contests.*

    a. Forensics

    b. Plays

    c. Operettas

    d. Assembly programs; convocations

8. *The textbook to be used* (if one is used).

    a. General textbook in speech

    b. Specialized or supplementary books

9. *The course or courses to be offered.*

    a. Relationship to all points above must be considered

    b. Relationship to the extraclass program in particular

    c. Number of semesters

    d. Number of meetings each week

    e. Number and kind of speech performances

    f. Year offered

    g. Elective or required; credit

IV. *Organize the content as units, having specific objectives for each.*
    In the first course, representative units might be Introduction and Orientation, Voice and Articulation, Bodily Action, Speech Composition, Discussion, etc.
 V. *Determine the teaching order, or the arrangement of the unit.*
    Consider the logical and psychological factors that will affect the *arrangement* of the units.
        Check principles that should govern:
        1. Simple to complex
        2. Part to whole
        3. Chronological
        4. Easy to difficult
        5. Immediate to remote developments
 VI. *Plan the units specifically.*
VII. *Break down the units into daily lesson plans. Carefully develop the lesson plans.*
VIII. *Provide for evaluation of the work taught and the course of study planned.*
    A. Recordings, tests, rating scales, other methods.
    B. Descriptive evaluations of course content and organization by teacher and students.

How to Plan a Unit of Work

A further important consideration is the organization and planning of the content of the units that have been selected for the course. The unit outline should be carefully conceived and should precede the daily lesson plans in a course syllabus or curriculum guide. Below are some suggested steps for planning the units:

1. Write the specific objectives of the unit.
2. List the subject matter sources from the textbook or from reference books. State exact chapters and pages to be used.
3. Write such materials as will be needed to supplement textbook information. If no text is used in a speech course, lecture notes should be prepared.
4. List the activities of the students; include
    a. Facts and theory to be learned.
    b. Performance activities.
5. Prepare any guide or study sheets needed to aid the student in the preparation of his written work or platform performance. Be sure to distribute these well in advance for speaking assignments.
6. Indicate the plan of procedure or method by which the theory and practice are to be developed.

7. List any special equipment or facilities that are needed.
8. Plan any test, evaluation, or criticism scheme for appraising the work to be taught. In the case of an evaluation scheme, be sure that it is understood by the students and has been previously used successfully in a teaching situation.
9. Indicate the estimated time in days or hours for the unit.

So that the teacher may note applications of these principles, a sample of a unit plan prepared by a teacher in the field is included.

Unit Two[7]
Bodily Action (Time: 7 days)

I. *Specific Objectives*
   A. To give the students an understanding of bodily action and the importance of action in communication.
   B. To develop free, spontaneous, and abundant action that springs from inner impulses.
   C. To provide situations that demand the use of bodily action.
   D. To show the relationship of body and voice as an integrated part of speech presentation.
   E. To develop through lecture and discussion an understanding of the principles of bodily action.

II. *Evaluation of Unit Work*
   A. Class participation in discussion.
   B. Evaluation of speeches presented.
   C. Effort and interest shown in bringing in and presenting outside materials.
   D. Teacher's observation.
   E. Speech activities showing use of bodily action as a whole.

III. *Student Activities*
   A. Read chapters 5 and 6 in Sarett and Foster.
   B. Outside reference reading.
   C. To determine what good bodily action entails from the use of pictures brought to class.
   D. Discuss phases of bodily action (gesture, movement, posture), arriving at good definitions as well as understanding and use.
   E. Reading of paragraphs to demonstrate movement.
   F. Round-robin story telling.
   G. Speeches of demonstration.

IV. *Sources of Material for the Student*
   A. Text: Sarett, Lew, W. T. Foster, and J. H. McBurney. *Speech —A High School Course.* Boston: Houghton Mifflin Co., 1956.

---

[7]This unit outline and the lesson plans that follow were prepared by Miss Elizabeth Hubbs, Highland Park (Ill.) High School.

B. Outside readings:
  1. Griffith, Nelson, Stasheff. *Your Speech*. New York: Harcourt Brace and Co., 1955, pp. 132-35.
  2. Adams, H. M. and Thomas Pollock. *Speak Up*. New York: The Macmillan Co.; 1956, pp. 436-42.
C. Newspapers
D. Magazines
E. Radio and TV
F. Personal experiences
V. *Supplementary Materials*
  A. Lectures
  B. Additional text references
    1. Griffith, Nelson, Stasheff
    2. Adams and Pollock
VI. *Special Facilities*
  A. Round-robin stories
  B. Reading of paragraphs from magazines
VII. *Plan of Procedure*
  First day—Definition of bodily action and what it includes.
  Second day—Application of bodily action to pictures and stress on posture.
  Third day—Study of movement.
  Fourth day—Study of gesture.
  Fifth, Sixth, and Seventh day—Demonstration speeches.

Preparing the Lesson Plan

In order to reach the final stage of implementing a course of study, the units should be broken down into daily lesson plans. These are the teacher's blueprints for daily class instruction. In order to aid the teacher, the following suggestions are given for the organization of daily work:

1. Know the *criteria* for a good lesson plan:
  a. It has a definite aim or goal.
  b. It includes specific questions designed especially for the class to be taught.
  c. It states specifically what facts, skills, or attitudes are to be learned.
  d. It allows for and makes necessary correlation of the day's lesson with previous work and with pupils' out-of-class experiences and interests.
  e. It provides for a variety of motivations, approaches, methods, drills, exercises, etc.

    f. It is designed to evoke *pupil activity.*

2. Prepare the *content* and *form* of the plan carefully:
   a. Indicate the *date, subject,* and *classroom.*
   b. List the *specific aims* for the day's work.
   c. *Link the new work to the old,* or to the students' previous experience and background.
   d. *Include the materials for instruction* (texts, charts, models, pictures, references, etc.).
   e. State specifically the *knowledge, skills,* and *attitudes to be taught.* This can be outlined carefully and clearly.
      (1) Determine a teachable order for the content.
      (2) Prepare adequate examples, illustrations, models, sketches, etc., to support main ideas.
      (3) Write out and develop key questions that will determine or unify activities for the day.
      (4) Try to individualize the work as much as possible.
   f. Develop *practical procedures* and methods for teaching the content. Include:
      (1) Approach and motivation.
      (2) A sequence of questions.
      (3) Drills and applications.
      (4) Summary.
   g. Plan the *evaluation* of the day's teaching.
   h. Give the *next day's assignment.* Make it clear and definite. Present it early in the hour, as a general rule.

Using Sources of Motivation in Teaching

A vital part of the teacher's planning and teaching rests upon his motivating the students to learn. This is especially true in a speech class where both knowledge and skill must be mastered. Although this step need not be written into the lesson plan, it should be carefully developed by the teacher in relation to the interests, abilities, and needs of his students. The speech class and activity program have many distinctive sources of motivation:

a. The personality of the teacher. He should be friendly, fair, enthusiastic, sympathetic, and understanding. Often his personal attitude is sufficient to insure the success of a lesson. His skill, learning, and experience also enter in.

b. The goals and objectives of the student: his personal improvement and skill, professional career, grades, credit, basic drives for action. One or all of these may be utilized in an assignment.

c. The content of the unit or lesson: a particular platform assignment or theory.

d. Special methods or unusual procedures in teaching content. Class programs, student planned lessons, and mild competitive methods are examples.

e. The classroom atmosphere that is created by the teacher and students.

f. The physical conditions in the classroom. The traditional desk setup may be modified by the use of movable chairs, tables for conference, and so on; soundproofing, restful wall color, and attractive decoration of the room also help. Sometimes classes are held in the auditorium, on the stage, in a radio studio or recording room. Students look forward to class time because of the room.

g. Special awards including credit, honor roll, medals, letters, trophies, scholarships, money, and certificates.

h. The use of special equipment such as a public-address system, recording apparatus, motion pictures, television, slides, films, charts, or models.

i. Special trips or public appearances in other communities.

j. Approval of the class; praise, favorable comment, or constructive criticism by the teacher.

k. Publicity in the school or local newspaper, play programs, over radio, television, or public-address system.

l. Pictures of school representatives, play casts, festival and contest winners, and so on. These can be displayed in the speech classroom or hall.

m. Participation and public performance in speech activities, plays or contests—local, state, national.

n. Particular responsibilities in the speech program: director, program chairman, presiding officer, discussion leader, etc.

o. Membership in speech or drama clubs or societies.

The Teacher of Speech

CHARLES L. BALCER AND HUGH F. SEABURY

The success of a program of speech education in a high school depends largely on the teacher of speech.

Modern classrooms, the latest textbooks, ample audio-visual aids, an alert and able group of students, interested and cooperative parents, and an understanding and able administrator do not make a successful program of speech education, important as these factors are. They are not a substitute for an able teacher of speech, who sets the tone of the class and the spirit of the program. He, together with the administrator and other teachers, sets the tone and spirit of the high school.

Reactions to teachers and to their teaching by students, teachers, and administrators can help all teachers determine for themselves what constitutes a "successful" teacher.

Some twenty years ago, Hart collected, compiled, and analyzed the reactions of 10,000 high school seniors who were given the opportunity to tell teachers what students like and dislike in teachers and their methods. These high school seniors were asked to think of the teacher they "liked best" and set down their reasons; similarly, to think of the teacher they "liked least of all"; and, finally, to indicate if the "best liked" teacher was also the "best" teacher. If, in their judgment, the "best liked" teacher was not the "best" teacher, the students were to indicate how the "best" teacher differed from the "best liked" teacher. Their reactions can help the teacher of speech to determine for himself what makes for success or failure in teaching. The ten most frequently mentioned reasons for liking a teacher best are listed in the order most frequently cited by the 10,000 high school seniors:[1]

1. Is helpful with school work, explains lessons and assignments clearly and thoroughly, and uses examples in teaching.
2. Cheerful, happy, good-natured, jolly, has a sense of humor, and can take a joke.
3. Human, friendly, companionable, "one of us."
4. Interested in and understands pupils.
5. Makes work interesting, creates a desire to work, and makes class work a pleasure.
6. Strict, has control of the class, and commands respect.
7. Impartial, shows no favoritism, and has no "pets."
8. Not cross, crabby, grouchy, nagging, or sarcastic.

From *Teaching Speech in Today's Secondary Schools* by Charles L. Balcer and Hugh F. Seabury, pp. 42-62. Copyright © 1965 by Holt, Rinehart and Winston, Inc. Reprinted by permission of Holt, Rinehart and Winston, Inc.
[1]Frank W. Hart, *Teachers and Teaching by Ten Thousand High School Seniors.* New York: The Macmillan Company, 1934. p. 131.

9. "We learned the subject."
10. A pleasing personality.

In contrast to these attributes of the "best liked" teacher, the following were the ten most frequent reasons for their disliking a teacher:[2]

1. Too cross, crabby, grouchy, never smiles, nagging, sarcastic, loses temper, and "flies off the handle."
2. Not helpful with school work, does not explain lessons and assignments, not clear, and work not planned.
3. Partial, has "pets" or favored students, and "picks on certain pupils."
4. Superior, aloof, haughty, snooty, overbearing, and does not know you out of class.
5. Mean, unreasonable, hard-boiled, intolerant, ill-mannered, too strict, and makes life miserable.
6. Unfair in marking and grading and unfair in tests and examinations.
7. Inconsiderate of pupils' feelings, bawls out pupils in the presence of classmates, and pupils are afraid and ill-at-ease and dread class.
8. Not interested in pupils and does not understand them.
9. Unreasonable assignments and homework.
10. Too loose in discipline, no control of class, and does not command respect.

Eighty percent of these high school seniors reported that the teacher they liked best was also the best teacher, that is, the one who taught them most effectively. The twenty percent who indicated some other teacher as best gave the following differences between the best-liked teacher and the best teacher:[3]

1. More exacting in standards of work, stricter in marking, and "we learned more."
2. Better at explaining lessons and assignments and work is better planned.
3. Knows the subject matter and can 'put it over' better.
4. Stricter, more rigid discipline.
5. Makes the work more interesting.
6. Is less friendly.
7. More serious, more businesslike, keeps closer to the subject, and more conscientious.
8. Less understanding of pupils and less interested in pupils.
9. More sarcastic.
10. Less attractive.

The teacher needs the cooperation of his students if they are to learn effectively. The students' viewpoint of what an effective teacher is can help the teacher to understand his task better.

Teacher's Judgment of an Effective Teacher
Not only have students indicated their idea, but teachers themselves have tried to determine what they believe an effective teacher is. A

---

[2]*Ibid.*, pp. 250-251.
[3]*Ibid.*, pp. 278-279.

panel of faculty members at Macalester College in Saint Paul, Minnesota, stated, during a discussion at a convocation in the summer session of 1957, what they believed to be eight basic qualifications of an outstanding teacher. They agreed that, at any level of instruction, a "top" teacher must have (1) a sense of mission, (2) love of people, (3) love of his work, (4) intellectual honesty, (5) thorough knowledge of his subject, (6) a nonauthoritarian attitude, (7) understanding of students, and (8) the ability to create student interest.

Most teachers and most teachers of speech probably agree that these eight basic qualifications suggest necessary characteristics of a teacher of speech, a director of plays, and a coach or director of forensics.

Administrators' Concepts of a Superior Teacher of Speech

The concepts by administrators in the secondary school of a superior teacher of speech offer helpful suggestions as any teacher of speech attempts to evaluate himself. Eye reported in *The Quarterly Journal of Speech*[4] the following concepts by two superintendents and two principals on what constitutes a superior teacher of speech:

1. The good speech teacher should have the personal qualities that would make him or her welcome and desirable company for others of the same age group. . . .
2. The teacher should be capable of establishing and maintaining good social relationships in the community without apparent strain upon either the teacher or the community.
3. There should be evidence of a broad liberal education and thorough professional training. . . .
4. The instructional skill of the teacher should be of the quality that brings pupils eagerly to class and leaves them reluctant to have the period end. The teacher should be able to identify pupil development, measure the degree of progress, and interpret the results to professional colleagues and lay people.
5. The good teacher should recognize that pupil development depends in part upon experience other than class activities.
6. The speech teacher should work toward the broadest possible offering in his own field but he should not permit his enthusiasm for the field of speech to stifle cooperation with his colleagues in other fields of teaching.
7. The teacher should be as concerned for the development of the slow pupil as for that of the bright pupil.
8. The good speech teacher should not
   a. falsely believe that making speech a required course is a terminal achievement,
   b. assume that speech is a cure for all educational, social, economic, national, and universal ills,

---

[4]Glen C. Eye, "What Constitutes a Superior Teacher of Speech?"; L. M. Fort, "The Qualifications Necessary"; Matthew L. Dann, "The Superior Teacher of Dramatics"; and A. E. Rupp, "The Superior Teacher of Debate," *The Quarterly Journal of Speech*, April 1948, pp. 216-221.

   c. look upon the auditorium as private domain, indestructible, and un-
       contestable, and
   d. blame the administrator for all obvious shortcomings of the speech
       program.

Fort, a superintendent, added some specific qualifications he felt necessary for an effective teacher of speech:

1. The ability to make a good speech.
2. A teacher who insists upon speech for the average boy and girl—a philosophy that speech is for everybody.
3. A teacher who has initiative—who is continually discovering ways and means for promoting speech activities in the community.
4. A speech teacher who is so thoroughly informed in his field that I can turn to him for the answers to the questions that continually arise in speech studies.

Dann enumerated qualities of a superior teacher of dramatics:

> Understanding of . . . young people. Skill in presentation of ideas. . . . Willingness to work hard in preparation. . . . Enthusiasm for working with youths coupled with enthusiasm for his subject. Judgment of literary material. . . . Ability to select the best participant for each part in a play. Capability . . . of superior demonstration whenever needed. Capable and willing to maintain high professional standards. . . .

Rupp, in discussing the ideal teacher of debate, emphasized the need by the teacher of debate for a sound foundation in speech, in the social sciences, and in other areas. He stated that the ideal teacher of debate must be

> . . . alert, open-minded, ready to re-evaluate the evidence at any time . . . well-read . . . possess a keen, analytical mind . . . must like young people . . . and also be a good teacher of speech.

Some Factors Which Guide Administrators

Some administrators keep in mind factors which guide them in employing teachers of speech and in helping these teachers to improve "on the job" through in-service training. An understanding of these factors can help prospective teachers of speech and teachers of speech who are in service:

    1. An administrator looks for evidence that the teacher of speech has a philosophy of speech education and the ability to express it. He has a right and an obligation to know the teacher's philosophy. It will influence and probably determine the objectives and practices of the teacher in his classes and in his direction and supervision of extra-class and interscholastic speech activities. Likewise, it will indicate the impact of the teacher on the program of speech education and the impact of both teacher and his program on the total program of the school.

The administrator may ask the teacher of speech for a statement of his philosophy or he may ask questions whose answers will reveal it. From his interview with the teacher, the administrator may learn much of the teacher's philosophy. Later, the teacher's philosophy of speech education will be revealed by his actual work. Answers to such questions as the following will probably reveal the teacher's philosophy of speech education:

a. What is his chief concern as a teacher of speech? Speech education for all students? For the gifted? For the handicapped? For the "average" student?

b. What is his conception of the role of speech in society? In everyday living? In the school? In the community?

c. What is his attitude toward his place and the place of speech education in the total program of the school? Is he a teacher, first and foremost, as he thinks of himself? Is he a "coach"? Is he a "director"? Does he seem to see any difference in the functions of the three?

d. What is his conception of speech education? Required course for all? If so, in what grade or grades? Elective courses for whom? In what grade or grades? For what purposes? Emphasis on content or "delivery"? Does he seem to visualize speech education as a program of student performances only? What relationships does he seem to see between speech education and other programs of study and activities in the school?

e. What is his attitude toward extra-class and interscholastic speech activities? Valuable experiences for students? Related to courses in speech education? Success dependent on a record of winning interscholastic speech contests? Publicity? Overly interested in trying to make a name for himself?

f. What is his conception of the place of play production in the high school? Class project? Public performances in an auditorium? An indoor or outdoor spectacle?

g. What is likely to be the kind and quality of the plays he selects for production? Plays that make possible artful production and performance by a few students only? Plays that provide opportunity for many students to achieve excellence of performance and to develop the maximum level of their capacities? Plays that are inherently worthwhile for the educational growth and enjoyment of students and an audience?

h. How well is he likely to handle students in debate practice? In play rehearsals? How many rehearsals will he need, how long will he rehearse, and how late will he rehearse the students? Will he have a rehearsal schedule publicized in advance? Will he be concerned about demands on students' time? Is he likely to manage debate practices and play rehearsals in a businesslike way? How will he manage the extra details connected with play production and travel for participation in interscholastic forensic events? Money? Transportation? Lodging? Recordkeeping?

i. Will he likely be a cooperative, dependable, and considerate teacher of speech who will exercise high integrity and judgment? What evidence does he present to indicate that he is well prepared and certified to teach in a high school or junior college?

j. What will likely be his attitude toward his students? Other teachers? Administrators?

These questions and many others concerning the teacher of speech and his function in the school are fair questions to which the administrator has a right and an obligation to know the answers.

Also, the teacher of speech has a right to know the attitude of the administrator toward speech education. If the administrator is one who wants an outstanding record in declamation, debate, and drama, and is interested in the number of "superiors" won at speech contests, the teacher of speech should know it. If the teacher of speech accepts the position, he is obligated to give the administrator of the high school what he wants, because the administrator is responsible for the school program and its success, and therefore should have commensurate authority. If the philosophy of the administrator is that speech education is to provide a valuable experience for as many students as possible—which is the generally accepted view by administrators—then the teacher of speech should take that fact into consideration when accepting the position and in guiding the extra-class and interscholastic program.

The philosophy of the administrator who evaluates the program in relation to the number of "superiors" may be altered by the teacher of speech as he works toward an acceptance of speech taught as a significant communicative experience for all students rather than as an exhibition by a few. The teacher of speech may well utilize at first the wishes of the administrator in regard to "winners" or high ratings. However, even if the success of a program of speech education, a program of athletics, or a program of music education is measured in ribbons or medals or trophies, there may be a noticeable increase in the interest and participation by students during the following year. Conversely, no awards result oftentimes in a noticeable decrease in the interest and participation during the following year. Of course, much depends on how the awards are acquired. If the teacher of speech and his students seek the awards by limiting the number of participants, using the same participants many times for the purpose of winning, conniving in any questionable manner to beat other students with less than excellence of participation and complete honesty and integrity, or driving themselves beyond reason simply to win, the teacher of speech had better take stock of his motives and procedures and those of his students. On the other hand, neither the teacher of speech nor his students are justified in doing less than their best in achieving excellence of participation in whatever events, curricular or interscholastic, they may be engaged. If excellence of performance is evident, the teacher of speech and his students should be proud to accept awards. What better argument than that supported by excellence of interest, effort, performance, achievement, and growth of students can be offered by an alert teacher of speech for the inclusion of a course in speech education in the curricular offerings of the high school? When a curricular base for speech education has been achieved, it is often possible to obtain approval for broadening the program to include additional courses. This takes time. The teacher of speech should be prepared to work patiently, persistently, and effectively for what he believes is the best program of speech education in his school.

2. A very important factor which the wise administrator keeps in mind when employing teachers of speech and in helping them improve "on the job" through in-service training is the relationship of speech education to the total program of the school. The administrator of a high school tries to keep the faculty working together in the best interests of the education of all the students. His job, in this respect, is quite easy when each faculty member accepts willingly the fact that he or she is a member of the whole group and that the goal of the whole group is primary. At the same time, the wise administrator considers it important to help in the organization of situations so that each teacher can teach, and each group of students within the whole group can learn, all or more than the teacher teaches. The speech teacher must realize that speech education is an integral part of, but not more important than, the total program. The teacher of speech needs to consider also that speech education is one of many important, integral parts of secondary education and that some other part of the total program may be just as important as speech education in its contribution to the objectives of secondary education. Teachers are, in a sense, crusaders for a better school and a better community, but teachers of speech should not be "crusaders" who believe that speech education is first and foremost in the program. An ardent "crusader" for a strong department of speech education can easily kill his chances for building up cooperation by the administrator and other faculty members and any chances for his realization of their interests in speech education. Cooperation by the teacher of speech with other faculty members and

his good human relations with them are important. Since many students interested in speech education will also be involved in other activities, there must be a give-and-take for their interests, time, preparation, and achievement. Thus, the teacher of speech must be willing to cooperate with the director of the band, the director of the choir and chorus, the advisors of the newspaper and annual, the coaches of athletics, and with the administrator and all other teachers in the high school.

3. The speech habits of the teacher of speech can well be a concern of the administrator. The teacher of speech whose speech reflects good thinking, worthwhile ideas based on knowledge in breadth and depth, and ability to engage in cooperative sharing of ideas and thinking is likely to be an asset. If his voice is clear, flexible, well-modulated, unobtrusive, and responsive to meaning, he tends to stimulate a favorable reaction to a program of speech education. Such qualities make a difference in the attitude of students, other teachers, and people in the community toward the teaching of speech as well as toward the teacher. Students are likely to be acutely aware of the speech of the teacher of speech. They are likewise increasingly aware of the speech habits of their other teachers and of other people as they are conscious of excellence of speech by their teacher of speech. He should serve as a model for his students. To some degree the community will judge the program of speech education by his speech.

The effective teacher of speech should have had a variety of speech experiences prior to the time he began to teach, and he can go on participating in a variety of speech experiences during his tenure as a teacher. Too often teachers do not make use of the opportunities available.

The teacher of speech can be one of the most important public relations persons on the staff of the high school. As such, he can do much through his speaking to promote the school and the total educational program of the school and, at the same time, the program of speech education in the school. Prospective teachers of speech should make every effort to prepare themselves by participating, while in college, in speech activities such as discussion, oral interpretation, debate, drama, radio, and television. Thus, as members of the faculty of a high school and as members of communities they will be more effective as a result of their practical knowledge of speech situations.

4. Another factor the administrator considers is the teacher's preparation. Speech education for the teacher is important if he is to be in a position to give his students real help in their pursuit of the objectives of speech education. No longer should the administrator assign

classes in speech and extra-class work in speech to a teacher who is not well prepared for it. Obviously, preparation in teaching English per se does not qualify a teacher to teach speech. Teachers of English would be the first to admit that they are not qualified to teach speech unless they have successfully completed courses, or the equivalent, in fundamentals of speech, oral interpretation, discussion and debate, dramatics, stagecraft, speech science, speech pathology, and parliamentary procedures which are usually included in the preparation of teachers of speech.

Teachers who are assigned to teach speech, discussion and debate, or play production in the high school, and who feel that they are inadequate for the task, can find worthwhile opportunities for preparation in colleges and universities. These opportunities may lie in workshops in speech and dramatic art for teachers during summer sessions. These workshops are usually aimed at giving them some help to do an effective job of teaching speech and directing students in dramatic art and forensic activities. Workshops in speech and dramatic art for high school students are, in some colleges and universities, closely allied with workshops for teachers, so that teachers can engage in laboratory practice in teaching dramatics, forensics, speech, voice and speech development, and radio and television with the supervision by faculty members in departments of speech and dramatic art. However, teachers and high school students who participate in these workshops are probably helped most by realizing that they can learn much more by working in the area of speech education than during the workshops.

Most administrators are concerned about the prospective teacher or the teacher who has "specialized" in only one aspect of speech such as debate, acting, or speech on radio and television. The teacher of speech in a high school needs background in *all* aspects of speech education. Administrators would be happy to have in their high schools dedicated and able teachers who have specialized in speech and speech education. True, in some of our larger high schools the administrators are able to bring to their high schools teachers who have specialized in one aspect of speech, but even in these schools, the teacher who has specialized is in a better position to succeed if he has prepared in all areas of speech education.

A committee of the Speech Association of America, in its recommendation to the North Central Association, summarized the training which the members of the committee believed necessary for teaching speech:

The educational record of the teacher who develops and participates in the speech program should disclose specialized college or university training in the seven topics: Fundamentals, Reading Aloud, Discussion, Debate, Public Speaking, Drama and Theatre, Radio and Television, and Motion Picture. If speech is the major teaching subject, the teacher may have emphasized (1) oral reading, theatre and drama, or (2) public speaking, discussion, and debate, or (3) radio and television; nevertheless, the teacher will have had supporting courses in all areas of speech. In semester hours, the record will show 20-26. If speech is the second teaching field, the teacher will have had at least one course in each of the areas of speech; in terms of semester hours, the teacher's record will show 16-20.[5]

In 1960 the Secondary School Interest Group of the Speech Association of America recommended to the Legislative Assembly of the Association certain minimum requirements for certification of teachers of speech in secondary schools. The Legislative Assembly adopted, on Decemeber 28, 1960, the resolution entitled "A Resolution Adopted by the Legislative Assembly of the Speech Association of America:"

Resolved: That the Legislative Assembly endorses the following statement of minimal requirements for certification of teachers of speech in secondary schools:

Section I. *General Requirement.* For permanent certification in speech, the teacher should offer at least twenty-four semester hours in speech, taken at an accredited college or university, and distributed as specified in Section II. For provisional, temporary, or "second field" certification, the teacher should offer at least eighteen semester hours in speech, taken at an accredited college or university, and distributed as specified in Section II.

Section II. *Subject Area Preparation.* To insure breadth of preparation each certified teacher of speech should have completed at least one course in each of these divisions: (A) *Speech Sciences and Processes,* such as phonetics, physiology of the voice mechanism, basic speech development, voice, articulation, et cetera; (B) *Theatre and Oral Interpretation,* such as oral interpretation, acting, directing, technical theatre, play production, radio, television, et cetera; (C) *Speech Correction,* such as speech correction, speech pathology, clinical practices in speech correction, et cetera; (D) *Public Address,* such as public speaking, discussion, argumentation, debate, radio, television, et cetera.

Section III. *Professional Preparation.* In addition to the preparation specified above, the teacher certified in speech should offer at least one course in methods of teaching speech in the secondary school, together with appropriate student teaching.

Certification of speech correctionists or therapists should follow the certification requirements of the American Speech and Hearing Association.

---

[5]Committee of the Speech Association of America, "Recommendation to the North Central Association," *Quarterly Journal of Speech,* October, 1951.

Orville A. Hitchcock, Executive Secretary of the Speech Association of America from 1951 to 1954 and Director of the Association's placement bureau during those years, gave this advice to teachers of speech:

> . . . prepare yourself thoroughly. To me, thorough preparation means that you should be broadly educated, both generally and within the field of speech. As Aristotle and other classical writers pointed out long ago, rhetoric deals with all subject matter. So does poetics. Assuming adequate preparation in speech itself, the wider your knowledge beyond the field, the better teacher of speech you will be. . . . It is a basic truth that "you can't speak speech." What you speak is the knowledge and experience of mankind.
>
> You must also remember that in speech we are concerned with people, helping them to improve. To do so, you must really understand people, know what motivates them, what makes them what they are. A speech teacher must not only know about such things; he must also be a student of human nature.[6]

Hitchcock also advocated "breadth within the field of speech," and said that "It is dangerous to become too much of a specialist." He cited as one reason for his belief the large percentage of teaching positions that are combination positions—speech combined with another field such as English or social studies, or a combination of a number of different areas within the province of speech. Another practical reason for breadth within the province of speech education is the close relationship between the various phases of speech. Each supports the others. Hitchcock stated:

> I do not see how you can be a good teacher of public speaking without having had work, for example, in speech pathology and dramatic interpretation. By the same token, I do not see how you can be an effective speech pathologist without having studied the various types of speaking (public speaking, discussion, reading aloud) that your students are certain to be called upon to do.[7]

All evidence indicates that at least a major, or the equivalent, in the field of speech education is desirable. A minor appears to be an absolute minimum.

In 1959 a special committee of the North Central Association on the certification requirements by the Speech Association of America supported the viewpoint that there is danger in

> . . . the incorrect assumption that the fields of English and speech are the same and that the teachers do the same kind of job. Speech is not Oral English. Speech instruction consists of much more than

---

[6]Orville A. Hitchcock, "How to Get a Job as a Teacher of Speech," *The Speech Teacher*, vol. 4, no. 4 (November 1955), pp. 225-230.

[7]*Ibid.*, p. 227.

having the student stand up and vocalize. Speech teachers must be trained to cope with student problems of emotional adjustment in all kinds of audience situations. They need to know how to teach strong preparation and logical structure as the basis for "thinking on one's feet," or extemporaneous speaking from notes; they are obliged to teach and insure clarity in oral communication through careful attention to the language of *practical discourse* (they are not primarily concerned with the language of fine literature); they must stress simple, clear sentence structure for *instant* intelligibility; they are obliged to teach audience analysis, usable means of vocal emphasis and bodily action to gain and hold the attention of the audience. Furthermore, they must know how to help boys and girls make effective voices out of ineffective ones, substitute standard for substandard diction, and train the body to aid and not hinder in all communication.

The English teacher does not do these things as a regular part of English instruction. Typical preparation patterns for English and speech teachers of necessity are different and, in the opinion of the Speech Association of America, these differences should be recognized in teacher certification requirements. Handling students in speech learning situations demands good preparation specific to that job. Such responsibility should not be handed to just anyone with inferior training.[8]

The committee of the Speech Association of America assumed, and stated the assumption boldly for the purpose of making the point obvious, that most teachers of English who teach speech are not prepared to teach it. The teaching of English can be a full-time job. If it is a full-time job and if teachers of English are conscientious and dedicated to teaching English as most of them are, they have neither a primary interest in teaching speech nor the time to teach it. If teachers of English were to teach speech by choice, as some of them do, it would appear that they would do so because they believed the teaching of speech to be more important than the teaching of English or else because the teaching of English could be taught better by teaching speech.

Similarly, if teachers of speech are conscientious and dedicated to teaching speech as most of them are, they have neither a primary interest in teaching English nor the time to teach it. If teachers of speech were to teach English by their choice, as apparently few of them do, it would appear that they would choose to teach English either because they believed the teaching of English to be more important than the teaching of speech or because the teaching of speech could be taught better by teaching English.

Some teachers of English have prepared to teach speech and some teachers of speech have prepared to teach English. In both cases, the preparation appears to serve these teachers well in helping them to

[8]*The Speech Teacher*, vol. 8, no. 2 (March 1959), p. 118.

be more effective teachers of English and speech, respectively. Every teacher recognizes his need for much more and much broader preparation, and is probably the first to admit it. Of course, every teacher in the secondary school is a teacher of speech, consciously or unconsciously. The problem of the teacher of speech, like that of other teachers, is to prepare himself to make a significant contribution as an effective teacher.

5. An administrator is interested in the attitude of the teacher of speech toward his students and their attitudes toward the teacher. Without good student-teacher relationships, students are likely to learn little in the classroom. If students like and respect the teacher, they are likely to learn and to conduct themselves well in his classroom and in his presence outside of class. If they respect the teacher but do not like him, they may learn in spite of their not liking him. If they like the teacher but do not respect him, they can hardly be depended on to learn and are likely, sooner or later, to embarrass the teacher with their antics of friendship and their lack of learning. If they neither like nor respect the teacher, they will probably learn nothing in his class. Perhaps one of the most serious mistakes a teacher can make, especially during his first year of teaching, is to be too friendly with his students in an effort to have them like him. After they are out of control, it is difficult, and sometimes impossible, for the teacher to regain control of the same group of students again, even though it has been done with the help of the administrator. The teacher should be friendly with his students but never sentimentally so, and never so friendly that he cannot take charge of them in a situation where his supervision is needed. If he has the respect of his students, his ability to take charge at once is considerably enhanced.

Students may respect a teacher for any of several reasons, such as their respect for his knowledge of his subject, his standards of achievement by his students, his ability to teach, his fairness, his efficiency, his sincerity, and, perhaps above all, his sincere interest in his students, their problems, their achievement, and their all-round and continuous development. It is difficult for many teachers of speech, as well as for other teachers, to determine what is the best proportion of friendliness, fairness, and firmness to maintain so as to do their best as teachers. And yet, friendliness, fairness, firmness, enthusiasm, and sincerity reflect the attitude of the teacher of speech toward his students and help to determine the student-teacher relationships in and out of his classroom. Firmness with students at the beginning of a course may be helpful in establishing good student-teacher relationships. Firmness may be modified as rapport in the classroom permits relaxation and greater friendliness, but fairness, enthusiasm for students' learning, and sincerity should always prevail.

The teacher of speech often has excellent opportunities for guidance in his relationships with students. If the teacher is interested in his students, he is likely to be interested in their problems. One teacher of speech, in working with a student in original oratory, discovered in the course of conversations with the student a home situation that was causing the student such anxiety as to impair his scholastic achievement. Other members of the faculty seemed to be "riding" the boy unfairly about his poor work, his laziness, and other faults. When these members of the faculty were informed of the impending break-up of the student's home, they could better appraise his work and understand why he was failing. Also, the teacher of speech helped the student by referring him to the guidance counselor for assistance in adjusting to the crisis.

6. The inability of a teacher of speech to direct extra-class activities satisfactorily is one of the biggest problems of the principal of a high school. Some teachers of speech manage extra-class dramatic and forensic activities very well and, at the same time, teach effectively students in their classes. Some direct the extra-class activities well but neglect their classroom activities, which constitutes a problem for both the principal and the teacher. But the teacher of speech who is unable to cope with the antics of the play cast, the debate squad, or members of the radio club presents a problem of concern to the principal. Since many of these extra-class activities are conducted after school or in the evening, the problem can become serious. Many principals have had to report to the auditorium to help maintain order while a play was being rehearsed. Obviously, the director of a play should not allow such a situation to develop. The director who needs help in supervising his play rehearsals finds himself in this position because he does not insist upon the cast's cooperation from the very first rehearsal. The director needs to have definite plans made for students not on stage during rehearsal. Many directors of plays can learn from basketball and football coaches who are often masters at making use of practice time in an organized fashion. These directors and all teachers in a high school should acquaint themselves with school policies and regulations covering after-school and evening meetings and make sure that rules are observed. They should assume vigorous leadership in their special extra-class responsibilities.

7. The teacher of speech should be a competent bookkeeper and recordkeeper. Almost all modern extra-class activities involve the handling of money. Royalty payments for plays and ticket sales for plays and

festivals can become bothersome if the teacher neglects such matters. Efficient keeping of records so that information is quickly available for Awards Day, newspaper articles, and similar uses is a responsibility of the teacher who sponsors extra-class and interscholastic events in a high school. Every teacher of speech should be prepared for such duties as ticket sales, information for newspaper stories, and awards assemblies. The efficient and wise teacher will closely supervise student assistants who can, and should, handle the "leg work" of ticket sales; insist upon accurate records; check up frequently on ticket sellers; and deposit daily in the office of the principal the cash received. A special note-book for keeping a record of the speech contests and festivals attended and of the names of students who participated and their ratings and awards can save much time.

8. Probably all principals of high schools feel that it is important that the teacher of speech organize the program of speech education so that the administration, the students, the teacher of speech, and all other teachers affected by the program of speech education know where they are going. Again, the basketball and football coaches have well-planned seasons for both practice and performance. Teachers of speech, directors of plays, and directors of forensic activities should also organize their activities so that as many students as possible can participate and so that other teachers know when to schedule their activities to minimize conflicts and to use efficiently the time allotted. Also, parents of students involved in extra-class and interscholastic speech activities need to know such things as where their sons and daughters are and why, when they are going and returning, arrangements for transportation and supervision, and what money is to be paid by the students or parents. The wise teacher of speech may plan with the principal to obtain parental approval, as well as approval by other teachers, of students' participation in extra-class events and especially for their travel and participation in interscholastic events. The teacher of speech seems to be shocked sometimes when parents and other teachers display a strong interest in his plans for "his" students' activities. Sometimes he imagines that other teachers in the school, including the basketball and football coaches, are not required to obtain advance approval of their plans. Unfortunately, not all such plans are approved in advance by all concerned. Sometimes these unapproved plans are executed with resulting conflicts and even more serious consequences. Most plans for curricular, extra-class, and interscholastic activities in a high school are the result of the combined judgment of teachers, parents, and students under the leadership of the administrator of the high school.

Although it is impossible at times for teachers of speech to determine far enough in advance the details of interscholastic forensic programs, opportunities, and responsibilities, each teacher of speech should be alert and responsible for obtaining this information as soon as possible and sharing it with the students, teachers, and parents who are involved in the program or affected by it. Furthermore, the teacher of speech, together with the principal, as necessary and possible, should seek the cooperation of teachers of speech and principals in other high schools to set up in advance of the beginning of the school year a schedule of interscholastic events. In fact, many states have organizations, consisting of administrators and teachers, to set up an annual school calendar of extra-class and interscholastic activities in which schools plan to participate. The trend in coordinating and planning these school events seems to be toward determining the events to be published on the calendar at least one school year in advance. Copies of the calendar of school activities are made available to the administrators of the high schools in the state. Teachers of speech may well be, and oftentimes are, alert and foresighted enough to work with their high school administrators to have listed on the calendar for state-wide distribution the forensic and dramatic art events planned in their high schools.

Obviously, the principal of a high school should be completely informed on all plans for extra-class and interscholastic activities. His office will undoubtedly keep a calendar of events, in addition to the calendar by the state-wide organization, on which all extra-class and interscholastic events are to be listed at the suggestion of his teachers and after they are approved. The efficient and wise teacher should provide the principal with opportunity to approve or disapprove all plans for extra-class activities, especially interscholastic activities. Principal and teacher may both arrive at the point at which the office of the principal needs and wants only to be informed of all that is going on in the school, except possibly in the case of special innovations which may best involve the combined judgment of the teacher and the principal. In the case of special innovations, the principal has a right and an obligation to exercise his judgment in the planning of the event and in affirming the plan or rejecting it.

The teacher of speech may well be concerned with the soundness of his philosophy of his rights and responsibilities in a high school. It would probably be fruitful for him to check aspects of his philosophy against what other teachers of speech have indicated as their philosophies. In order to do this best, it could be to the advantage of each teacher of speech, present and prospective, to write out his "Philosophy of Teaching Speech" and evaluate it.

In 1958 the Central States Speech Association inaugurated "Outstanding Speech Teacher Awards" for young teachers with less than five years of teaching experience, so as to promote effective speech education in the Central States area. As one of the requirements, applicants for these awards were invited to submit a statement of their philosophies of teaching speech. Such statements may offer valuable help to potential and prospective teachers of speech as well as to teachers with much experience in speech education.

Arthur L. Housman, Professor of Speech and Drama at Saint Cloud, Minnesota, State College, wrote:

> I believe fundamentally that speech is a learned process; that the process of speechmaking is complex and is related to all activities of man in social intercourse; that the act of speech is unified; that good speech is dependent upon the worthiness of the speaker, his objectives, and his ability to organize and deliver intelligently a sum of worthwhile material; that good speech demands great mental and physical effort; that good speech demands vocal and physical skill developed through the discipline of training; that good speech depends upon the speaker's sense of responsibility to himself, to his audience, and to his society; that good speaking results best from the integrated and related activities of public speaking, debate, discussion, drama, and oral interpretation which utilize the same basic technical tools, and which are provided fundamentally with the same set of circumstances in the speech situation: a body of content, and agent of oral delivery, and an audience.
>
> I believe, further, that the pressing increase of modern man's need for speech education in a society responsive to instantly available media of mass communication imposes upon the teacher of speech the greatest personal responsibility which he must understand and accept if he is to fulfill himself personally and professionally.

Ronald F. Reid, Assistant Professor of Speech and Director of Forensics at Washington University, Saint Louis, Missouri, replied:

> My philosophy of speech education requires that both content and skill be taught. Public speaking, for example, should include a study of content—the principles of persuasion, the history of rhetorical theory, and the like. It should also teach public address as a skill; in other words, it should produce speakers who are clear and persuasive. Teaching either content or skill alone is not enough.
>
> My philosophy also requires that a speech teacher be broad in outlook, that he consider himself a *teacher* first, a *speech teacher* second. This principle has several implications:
>
> 1. A speech course should be a liberal arts course in the broadest sense, one concerned with the whole student. The teacher, therefore, should prevent, as best he can, speeches on trivial subjects and those which are exclusively 'occupation centered.' He should encourage, for example, engineering students to grapple with political issues and political science majors to concern themselves with, say, literary questions.

2. The speech teacher should look beyond his particular specialty into other areas of speech, and indeed other disciplines, for knowledge. Psychology, literaure, history, rhetoric, logic—all these fields, and many others, have relevance for speech training.

3. The speech teacher should feel free, indeed obligated, to consider ethics. We must be candid enough, both privately and in our classes, to acknowledge that some insidious techniques are persuasive and that speech can be used to help an evil cause; but we must never overlook ethical considerations.

My philosophy requires, furthermore, that speech education be available to all students. The speech therapist works with the speech handicapped. All speech teachers—whether their specialty be public speaking, dramatics, radio, or something else—have a responsibility to cooperate with the therapist. Superior students should be encouraged to participate in co-curricular activities.

Finally, my philosophy requires that the speech teacher also be a student. He must study, especially in speech and the fields most closely allied to this area of speech. And he should make some scholarly contribution to research in his field. His study is in reality a part of his teaching, for the good teacher must know much and must be constantly stimulating himself intellectually in order to stimulate his students.

Another Award Winner of the 1958 Central States Outstanding Speech Teacher Award was F. Fulton Ross, then a high school teacher of speech in the Central Senior High School at Davenport, Iowa. His philosophy of speech was embodied in a series of objectives listed as desirable for achievement in the teaching of speech:

I should like to express my personal philosophy of the teaching of speech by setting forth objectives listed as desirable for achievement in the teaching of speech. . . .

1. To develop an awareness of the significance of speech as our fundamental means of communication.
2. To develop an appreciation for freedom of speech and the responsibility of the individual in using it.
3. To develop within the individual self-confidence, poise, and control in speech situations.
4. To develop within the student a realization of the importance of the quality and integrity of ideas expressed in speaking situations.
5. To help the individual develop proficiency in pronunciation, articulation, and enunciation.
6. To develop the ability of the individual to organize ideas clearly for oral presentation.
7. To help the student increase his vocabulary and thereby develop his ability to choose words and use language in speaking.
8. To develop the individual's ability to express himself through voice and bodily action.
9. To develop in the individual the ability to listen and observe courteously, analytically, and discriminatingly.

Elizabeth Moodie, then Instructor in the Speech and Hearing Laboratories of the University of Nebraska, formulated her philosophy of speech education from her experiences in the area of speech correction:

> My training and experience are limited to the area of speech therapy. Thus, my beliefs in regard to the teaching of speech have developed with reference primarily to this area. I feel that the techniques of teaching are less important than the atmosphere which is built between the student and teacher. One begins to teach by accepting the student where he is and respecting his ability to grow. An atmosphere where the student is free to experiment with new ideas, to make mistakes, and to evaluate his performance seems to me to lead to effective teaching. We do not actually teach a person to change his manner of speaking; rather we assist the child or adult in making new observations which enable him to make the changes.

Judging from these statements, teachers of speech agree on certain basic aspects of a sound philosophy. Effective teachers of speech seem to have incorporated into their teaching these beliefs:
1. *All* students can be helped by speech instruction: those with defects, those "normal," and those with talent.
2. Speech education and training should provide for social integration.
3. The proper program of speech education is personal and practical.
4. The purpose of speech is not "exhibitionism."
5. Concern for the individual in the classroom is mandatory.

Summary

The teacher of speech determines largely the caliber, quality, and success of speech education in a high school. As a human being living and working among other human beings, he necessarily strives to be liked and respected by students, teachers, administrators, parents, and others in his sphere of influence.

Effective teaching seems to be the best criterion by which most high school students judge a teacher to be their "best" teacher. However, the "best-liked" teacher, even when students judge him not to be their "best" teacher, seems to be "best-liked," because he is exacting in his standards, stricter in marking, and more effective in helping them to learn.

Teachers have agreed that a "top" teacher is one with a sense of mission, who loves people, his work, who is intellectually honest, thoroughly knows his subject, is not authoritarian, understands his students, and is able to create student interest. A "top" teacher of speech is probably one who has all eight of these basic qualifications.

Administrators have expressed their belief that the "superior" teacher of speech is (1) personable, (2) socially competent, (3) liberally and professionally educated, (4) skillful in the motivation of students and in the evaluation of their achievement and development, (5) cognizant of the relationship of student development and student experiences outside of class, (6) enthusiastic about speech and speech education without stifling his cooperation with other teachers and their fields of teaching, (7) mindful of the value of speech education for all students, (8) reasonable in his conception of the domain, role, and effect of speech education in the high school, (9) hesitant to blame the administrator for shortcomings in the speech program in the high school, (10) able to make effective speeches in the school and community, (11) familiar with the findings of research in speech and speech education as well as in teacher education, (12) understanding and enthusiastic in working with high school students, (13) sound in judging the value and suitability of subject matter for the educational development of high school students, (14) capable of injecting demonstration, when needed by students, in teaching dramatics, forensics, and speech, and (15) interested in developing and maintaining high professional standards.

Factors considered by wise and conscientious administrators who have a right and an obligation to know the attitudes, capabilities, and potentialities of teachers of speech in high schools are: (1) the teacher's philosophy of speech and speech education including extra-class and interscholastic dramatic, forensic, and speech activities, (2) the relationship of speech education, as an integral part of the total educational program of the high school and to each of its other integral parts, (3) the effect of the speech abilities, speech habits, and speechmaking on students, other teachers, parents, and others who are influenced by the teacher and who influence him, (4) the breadth and depth of preparation within the field of speech, liberal arts, and professional teacher education, (5) attitude of the teacher toward high school students and their attitude toward the teacher with assurance of mutual respect and fondness, (6) the ability of the teacher to direct at least satisfactorily extra-class and interscholastic dramatic, forensic, and speech activities to serve sound objectives of speech education, and (7) preparation and ability as a bookkeeper and recordkeeper to assume responsibility for budgets, receipts, expenditures, information for newspaper stories, names and ratings of students in interscholastic events, information for awards assemblies, et cetera, related to activities within the scope of the program of speech education in the high school. These factors of administrative concern are indicative of judgments which may be exercised by principals of high schools. However, the teacher of speech has a right to know the attitude of the principal toward speech and speech education and an obligation to cooperate with him in working toward acceptance of speech taught as a significant communicative experience for all students.

A teacher of speech is responsible for evaluating periodically his philosophy of speech education which affects his choice of objectives, his methodology and materials, the standards by which he evaluates student achievement and growth, and the outcomes of his efforts in a high school and community. Doing so, he will likely find fruitful the philosophies of speech education as expressed by other educators. Each prospective teacher of speech may well write and evaluate his "Philosophy of Teaching Speech."

Speech and the Teaching Personality

SETH A. FESSENDEN, R. I. JOHNSON, P. M. LARSON, KAYE M. GOOD,

The literature of education and communication is replete with references to "personality development," "personality adjustment," and "personality problems." The recognition of this aspect of educational need is increasingly evident. Counseling programs in schools and colleges have been expanded to include the "total adjustment problems" of students as well as problems of academic adjustment and course selection. Psychological clinics by the hundreds are engaged in studying the personality needs of individuals who are finding difficulty in coping successfully "as persons" with ordinary everyday problems.

Certainly, in a book addressed to teachers, the role of personality in the process of teaching should be kept in focus as an important factor in all teaching-learning relationships. The impact of a teacher's personality upon his pupils is much greater and longer lasting than the impact of his knowledge, and, in the long run, it will be an effective determinant of their future success and happiness. It is a catalytic agent in the accumulation and assimilation of experience.

THE NATURE OF PERSONALITY

To use a word is not always to understand its meaning. The word personality is a verbal "medium of exchange," but the abstract concept that it represents may not be the same in the mind of the speaker and the mind of the listener. This suggests a basic principle in communication: the importance of definition in the interest of common understanding. Each man's concept of "personality" has been built up through numerous observations and experiences and has been influenced by the various contexts in which he has heard the word used. In discussing "personality" intelligently, one must stop for a moment to consider its meaning.

The term here is used in its psychological sense: An individual's personality is his pattern of behavior—not traits or attitudes that are concealed or suppressed, but the overt self. The true picture of one's personality, therefore, is to be found in the impression that he makes upon others by what he does and the way he does it. One may, for example, acquire a reputation for calmness in dealing with troublesome situations when, as a matter of fact, he is often inwardly tense and irritated. He may conceal certain fundamental tendences (for example, the tendency toward fear) and substitute a totally different reaction pattern when he confronts the real situation. Whatever traits he manifests are the traits the observer properly ascribes to his personality.

Etymology often throws interesting light on meanings imbedded in language. *Person* (the basic part of the word *personality*) is derived from a word meaning "mask," a mask worn in a play, a mask which concealed the features of the actor but permitted his voice to "sound through."

> In the same way that in Greek tragedies *persona* was the mask worn by the actor to indicate the attitude and characteristics for which his part in the play called, so the child's expressed behavior is the true indication of his personality in that it portrays the role which he has found for himself in life. What went on behind the mask and what goes on underneath the surface of the child's conscious behavior are matters which certainly explain much of what is visible, but do not enter into the reactions set up in the audience and hence are not part of personality.[1]

Personality, then, is not the "release of self" unmodified and uncontrolled. It is not what a person is but what he shows himself to be. Therefore, the development of personality is the development of behavior patterns in many and varied situations. If the behavior patterns are consistent under different circumstances and in different situations, it can be said that the personality is unified or integrated. Similar situations will evoke similar types of reactions. But, as one may realize, the inconsistencies of behavior are sometimes more conspicuous than the consistencies. How often does someone say, "He is one person at home, another in his office"!

Every individual is a "self," and the aim of education is to assist in the expansion of that self, through the discovery and development of potentialities, to meet the expanding needs of the individual in a constantly expanding environment. It is a selective process. It seeks to develop an integrated selfhood that will help the individual to function effectively in his life role, both present and future. This leads to the psychological definition of education: the continuous accumulation and interpretation of experience resulting in desirable changes in behavior. These changes in behavior constitute the developing personality.

---

[1]From *Psychological Factors in Education* by Henry Beaumont and F. G. Macomber, p. 42. © McGraw-Hill Book Company, 1949. Used by permission of McGraw-Hill Book Company.

PERSONALITY DEVELOPMENT AS AN OBJECTIVE
IN SPEECH EDUCATION

Stated in one form or another, the objective of personality development is accepted as a logical "must" in modern education. Whether it is called education for social effectiveness, personal-social adjustment, or personality development, the means and ends are essentially the same.

Unfortunately, the acceptance of the personality objective does not always alter the practices that already prevail in the classroom. The mechanical routines persist, with the same prescribed "learning" for all. Too often, the problems of personal and social adjustment are pigeonholed in a department called a "counseling service," delegated to the "homeroom" teacher, or referred to an administrative officer for "disciplinary" treatment. The responsibility of the teacher is as broad and inclusive as the needs of the pupils—as the needs of each pupil. His philosophy is a developmental philosophy, and his concern encompasses *all* of his pupils. He can, and will if he is a conscientious teacher, be dissatisfied with his teaching unless he can observe changes in pupil attitudes and behaviors, changes in the direction of maturing personality, as a result of supervised classroom experience. In other words, he will broaden his base of evaluation to include judgments of pupil progress wherever that progress occurs, as in improved relationships with the group, increased interest and enthusiasm, a better command of language, inventiveness and originality, more effective participation, and better emotional control.

THE COMMUNICATIONAL ASPECT OF PERSONALITY

"Communication," as used here, refers to the continuous interchange of ideas through the medium of language, a process which establishes a basis for common understanding and mutual cooperation. It involves not only the formulation and expression of thought but assimilation and interpretation as well. Only through such a process can social intelligence evolve. The fact that communication can and does take place without the use of words is not to be overlooked. Sign language is not uncommon among tribes who do not speak the same tongue. To communicate by signs is a favorite "game" of children. Even adults indulge in charades, in which meaning is "acted out" instead of spoken. Drawings and other graphic symbols may be used to convey ideas. All forms of art are communicative whether verbal symbols are used or not. But the word is the basic medium that is used day by day in efforts to share experience, clarify understandings, and achieve better group rapport. The psychological implications for personal development will be discussed as the chapter proceeds.

Since this is a book for teachers, designed to reinforce good teaching through good communication, let us look at some of the relationships that exist between effective communication and effective personality. The role of language in learning has never been adequately explored by the psychologists, but it is obvious that without speech and hearing the intellectual and social development of a child would be greatly impaired. Furthermore, since the human personality is largely a product of social experience, its development will be helped or hindered by the effectiveness with which ideas are shared, expressed, and understood. Many years ago, John Dewey observed:

> There is more than a verbal tie between the words *common, community,* and *communication.* Men live in a community in virtue of the things which they have in common; and communication is the way in which they come to possess things in common. . . . Not only is social life identical with communication, but all communication (and hence all genuine social life) is educative.[2]

Many people are ineffectual because they fail in communication. This lack, or deficiency, has two possible explanations: (1) an unwillingness or inability to use accepted verbal symbols with discrimination and due concern for meaning, both the denotative and the connotative, (2) the habit of half-thought and hurried conclusions which cannot be translated into language because the thought is fragmentary and unfinished. Good communication, therefore, is an index of good thinking. "The thinking process is not complete until the solution has become communicable."[3]

Whether the view of education is from the point of view of its social objectives or, more narrowly, from the point of view of personal and individual development, language becomes the indispensable vehicle of learning, the means by which and through which educational progress is accelerated and educational goals are attained.

To understand better the role which communicational ability plays in determining personal effectiveness or ineffectiveness, one can visualize certain situations in his experience in which "good" personality or "poor" personality has been exhibited. How many of the situations involve elements of communication—perhaps a manner of speech, good taste in selecting subjects of conversation, or an attitude of intelligent listening? The following list is only suggestive. Each individual can add to it from his own experience.

The man who talks too much about himself.
The child who is overcome with fear when he is asked to "recite."

[2]Reprinted with permission of the Macmillan Company from *Democracy and Education* by John Dewey, p. 5-6. © The Macmillan Company, 1916.
[3]From *Language and Communication* by George A. Miller, p. 235. © McGraw-Hill Book Company, 1951. Used by permission of McGraw-Hill Book Company.

The too-quiet person—the tongue-tied type who allows awkward pauses to occur in social conversation.

The individual with the dominant voice who embarrasses the party with loud talk.

The man who tries to tell a story which he doesn't know too well.

The chronic interrupter.

The poor listener—the person whose attention wanders when he is not doing the talking.

The person who lacks social tact, who has the fatal gift for saying "the wrong thing."

The oversensitive person who becomes emotional in conversation.

The individual who is controversially minded, who turns all conversation into argument.

The teacher whose voice is pitched too high, who gives the impression of nervousness and irritation.

The mother who always says, "Now what have you been doing?" with an inflection of distrust and suspicion.

The person who leaves his sentences dangling because he has no clear understanding of what he wants to say—the fuzzy thinker.

The teacher whose tone and general manner make it difficult to establish a "feeling of friendliness" in the classroom.

The pupil (or the adult) who "freezes up" when he is called upon to speak before a group.

The intolerant individual who "cries down" any opinion that differs from his own.

The chronic exaggerator who distorts facts for the sake of dramatic effect.

The speaker who fails to sense the restlessness of his audience.

The monotonous individual with the "lifeless" voice whose conversation is drab and boring.

The "one-track mind," the person who always talks about the same thing whether he is making a speech or holding a conversation.

The telephone talker who strains your ears and your patience by mumbling his words and refusing to speak into the transmitter.

Now one might try looking at the other side of the coin to find positive examples of "good" personality traits as revealed by speech habits, personal attitudes, voice quality, and the like. Experience should provide numerous illustrations like the following:

The person who listens courteously while another is talking.

The teacher (or the policeman) who answers questions pleasantly.

The tactful conversationalist who "picks up the ball" before an awkward silence develops.

The listener who encourages the "shy violet" by drawing out personal interests.

The person who gracefully refuses to monopolize the conversation.

The person whose voice reflects a dynamic spirit.

The teacher with a calm voice that prevents feelings of tension and "nervousness."

The person who speaks clearly and distinctly, the person you can understand *the first* time.

The person who exhibits a sense of humor and who can use the light touch when the situation demands it.

Almost everyone has had the experience of meeting a person who makes a very favorable impression by his general appearance, his manner of dress, his pleasant facial expression before he begins to speak. What happens if his "speaking personality" contradicts the impression made by his physical personality? On the other hand, there are people whose general appearance might be characterized as commonplace. They do not "stand out" in a group because of any superior physical qualities. But when they begin to talk, they command attention and admiration. Their tone, inflection, and manner of speaking show friendliness and respect. What they say and how they say it command confidence. In such cases, the "speaking personality" erases completely the initial impression of commonplaceness.

Note that in offering these examples of the impact of speech on personal effectiveness, the authors are holding true to the definition of personality—the manifest self, not the hidden self. The man who "talks too much about himself," for example, may be a very good person, kind, just, and honest. But his personality picture is *what comes through* in his total pattern of behavior. His speech, what he says and the way he says it, is a part of that pattern and hence one of the determining factors influencing others' assessment of him.

THE TEACHER'S PERSONALITY NEEDS

It is perhaps trite to repeat the statement that the most important subject matter in the curriculum is the teacher's personality. That part of the teacher's self which he projects into action (that is, his personality) conditions every learning situation in his classroom. The teacher who shows by word and action that he distrusts his pupils (along with the rest of humankind) is likely to bring up a brood who will justify his direst suspicions. If he believes that pupils should be seen and not heard (except when ordered to speak), he will soon have an unresponsive—even if docile—group who will lock him out of their world of experience. There is no greater jeopardy to good teaching than the kind of ostracism that children know how to inflict upon their teachers.

To determine the aspects of personality that are most important in the job of teaching, it is necessary to look, for a moment, at the nature of the teacher's work.

The teacher guides classroom experiences and supervises classroom activities.
The teacher delegates certain responsibilities, makes assignments, gives directions.

The teacher explains, answers questions, discusses problems.

The teacher talks with pupils (in groups and individually), acting as friend and counselor.

The teacher often entertains (and teaches) by reading or telling stories or relating personal experiences.

The teacher often enlists the cooperation of the group in determining the type of group organization to be used and the group standards to be adopted.

The teacher studies the individual pupils in his class to discover their strengths and weaknesses, their special interests and needs.

The teacher seeks to develop a spirit of rapport in the class group.

The teacher welcomes parents to the school and talks with them about their children's work.

The teacher evaluates, striving to judge fairly each pupil's progress in all aspects of his development.

The teacher attends teachers' meetings and conferences.

The teacher studies; he reads professional books and articles; he prepares materials in advance which may be useful in teaching.

The teacher participates in certain community activities both for service and for recreation.

In discharging these responsibilities, what personal qualities are needed? Many lists of desirable teacher traits are available in pedagogical literature. It is not the present purpose of the authors to explore such lists exhaustively. Neither is it intended to suggest that the teacher-personality pattern should be uniform for all teachers. But, in the light of the work that the teacher performs and the cooperative relationships that he must maintain with pupils, patrons, and administrative personnel, certain abilities, attitudes, and personal qualities can be identified as highly desirable, if not indispensable.

Perhaps the reader can extend this list by calling to mind the personality traits of some teachers whom he would rate high on a scale of teaching effectiveness. Good teachers are remembered longer for *what they were like* than for the specific knowledge they imparted.

Ability to gain and hold the respect of others
Attitude of respect toward pupils and other associates
A sympathetic interest in pupils
A courteous manner
Enthusiasm for the work of teaching
A pleasant and cheerful disposition
A sense of humor
An effective command of language

Remember that abilities and attitudes become *qualities of personality* only as they are projected into action. Try to visualize the teacher in action as he demonstrates the characteristics listed above. Picture certain situations in which the teacher *shows or fails to show* the desired trait. Take the first item mentioned: Ability to gain and hold the respect of others.

Situation 1. The teacher is meeting with a parents' group. A parent asks why the school spends money for "visual aids," indicating that if the children would study their lessons in the books, they would learn much better than by looking at films. "They see enough picture shows anyway." Here are two types of answers. Which will command readily the respect of the group?

> *Answer 1*: Well—I don't know much about it. The supervisor brought a film out last week, and I used it because she said to use it. If they want to spend money for films, I guess they know what they're doing.
>
> *Answer 2*: I am glad to try to answer that question. It shows an interest which I believe all parents should have in finding out what the schools are doing and why they are doing it. Certainly, the purpose is not to take away from what the pupils are learning or can learn from books but to add to their learning by presenting very realistic experiences that will help them to remember and to understand better the problems which they discuss in class. As a matter of fact, some kinds of 'visual aids' have always been used in teaching. Although the use of films is a more recent innovation, it is the same in principle as the use of an apple, divided into fourths or eighths, to help the pupil understand fractions. Experimentation shows that pupils do learn more quickly by the use of such aids. The best way to convince oneself of the value of visual aids in teaching is actually to see how the teacher uses them and how the class responds to them. I shall be very happy, if you will let me know in advance, to plan such a lesson and invite you to watch the demonstration. Afterwards, I shall be glad to talk with you about your impressions.

Situation 2. The teacher in a mathematics class is explaining the work for the next day—something about money and interest. A pupil volunteers the statement: "My uncle says interest rates are too high; he can't keep up his payments on his house." Following are several reactions that the teacher might express. Which is more likely to win class respect and make for good rapport? Can you suggest some of the reasons for this?

1. What your uncle thinks about interest rates has nothing to do with these problems you are to do for tomorrow.
2. Very interesting, John, but will you please pay attention to what I am saying?
3. That's very interesting, John. Many people, like your uncle, borrow money when they buy a new home, build a new house, or need money for home repairs. How many of you have a brother, uncle or father who is building a house, or planning to build? (Eight pupils hold up hands.) Fine. With the help of you eight people, who already know something about house-building, I wonder if we

couldn't plan a house of our own, find out what it would cost, and see how much money we could borrow and how much interest we would have to pay. Maybe that could be our first problem in learning about money and interest.

Note that what the teacher says is only a partial explanation of his effectiveness. The way he says it is often more important in producing favorable or unfavorable response than the actual words he uses or the ideas he expresses. Personal attitudes are often revealed by the manner of speech, by subtle inflection, by tone, by accompanying physical movement or facial expression. Select another one of the "desirable teacher traits" and make a similar analysis in terms of actual situations and behavior patterns. For example, what trait actions tend to reveal "pleasant and cheerful disposition"?

Situation 1. A new child enters school, a girl in the second or third grade. The mother brings her to the door of the room after the session has started. The girl is obviously shy and a little frightened at the prospect of being plunged into a new school experience where everything and everybody is strange. The teacher goes to the door and meets the mother and daughter. What will be her attitude toward the newcomer?

1. She may open the door brusquely, shout over her shoulder, "Children, please be quiet! Josie, get back in your seat!" Then, to the callers: "Excuse me, please. They're worse than usual this morning. I already have thirty. I don't see how they expect me to handle another one. You have your registration slip? Hm-m—Mary Jones. Well, I guess we can crowd you in. . . ."
2. The teacher goes to the door, smiles at Mary, takes the registration slip, and says, "So you're going to be in my room. Mary. The children and I will be glad to have another little girl in our family. I am sure you can be very helpful. First, let me find a very special friend for you who will show you where to put your hat and coat. . . ."

Situation 2. The school day is beginning. The children are coming into their respective classrooms. In different rooms, a different "atmosphere" prevails. Let's listen in to detect some of the differences that help to create different atmospheres. Listen particularly for the "overtones" as the teacher speaks to the children. Some teachers talk in "smiling syllables" and some in "smiting syllables":

"Good morning. Don't block the door." (This in response to a pupil's greeting.)

"Go directly to your seat—and sit quietly!"

"A note from your mother? Put it on my desk. I'll read it when I get time."

"Good morning. You must have come bright and early today. I saw you in the playground as I came in.

"Thank you for the note, Mary. Is it an excuse for your absence yesterday?"

"Not a single person tardy today. That will give our room a good reputation."

Rap! Rap! "John! Eyes this way, please."

"How many of you think that a new song would be a good way to start the day happily? I have a new one that we can learn in a very few minutes."

If one were to continue this analysis of behavior patterns, he would find increasing evidence of the role that the teacher's speech plays in determining his teacher-personality. He is careful to speak courteously—not abruptly and offensively. He avoids ironical and "cutting" remarks. He keeps his voice well modulated—no harsh or high-pitched tones. In conversation, his voice is warm and sincere; it carries conviction. His voice is "alive"; it reveals interest and enthusiasm. His sense of humor enables him to maintain self-control, to see things in perspective, to conceal his irritation over minor disturbances, to speak calmly. He indulges in no emotional harangues.

The nature of the teacher's work is such that he is using the spoken word as a medium of communication during the major portion of the teaching day. When he is not speaking, he is usually listening, or he is guiding an experience that involves the use of speech as a major learning activity. He must, therefore, be aware of two things: (1) the importance of speech as a revealer of himself and (2) the importance of intercommunication, through speech, as a means of personal-social development. Speech is the television screen on which the acting self is projected. Through multiple self-projections, the total picture of the individual's social understandings and social values is made available for the guidance of impressionable minds. Language, therefore (speech in particular), is not a compartment of education. It is a common denominator. It is not a skill that represents an end in itself. It is a means to further self-growth, a medium through which all learning can be accelerated and improved, and it is an indispensable factor in satisfactory social adjustment. It is, therefore, a matter of concern for all teachers, at all levels of learning and in all areas of educative experience.

SOME PROBLEMS OF PERSONAL-SOCIAL ADJUSTMENT

Acceptance of personality development as a valid educational objective has already been discussed. But it is necessary to probe more deeply into the relation of adjustment patterns to speech abilities and into certain background factors in the child's experience. It is a simple matter to observe the common symptoms of poor adjustment, but it is not always easy to identify the original causes, the beginning of such behaviors. It is a fallacy, however, to assume that the cause must always be identified and removed before any remedial measures are undertaken. A broken leg may result from a fall from a horse, but the fractured limb can be successfully treated without shooting the offending animal. Naturally, persisting causes that explain the recurrence and continuation of deviant types of behavior become the logical points of attack. For example, if a feeling of inferiority has been developed through successive experiences of failure, the tasks that have been set for the child (or that he has set for himself) should be examined and modified so that they fall within the limits of his potential ability. The satisfaction of success (even in limited measure) becomes the antidote for the frustration of failure.

> A child who has developed the self concept, "I am a person who fails," will view each new experience not as a challenge and possibility for new learning, but as another difficult task where the bitterness of failure may again plague him. Such a child can hardly be expected to show much enthusiasm for learning in school or for extending his social contacts. Similarly a child whose experiences have all convinced him that the way to succeed is to be a child who always "gets there first" will view each new situation primarily as an opportunity to prove his skill and to win again. Each succeeding year adds substance and conviction to the individual's concept of self and thus serves as a framework guiding and setting limits for his personal and social adjustment.[4]

The psychological need for recognized achievement (the experience of success) in areas of pupil interest—and within the limits of the self-pattern of abilities—brings the prevailing "grading system" in the schools under severe indictment. School grades, in the main, are competitive and are geared to fixed standards for all in the mastery of a prescribed and uniform body of subject matter. If a pupil "lags behind" in long division, he may be dubbed a "failure" in the eyes of his classmates and his parents. There is no recognition of compensating factors—driving interests, personal incentives, social adaptations, citizenship qualities, or other evidences of personal growth. It is reasonable to suppose that some of these evidences of growth are more important in a child's life than his facility in manipulating divisors, dividends, and quotients. If integrated personal development is an accepted aim, the criteria for evaluating pupil progress must be as broadly based as the objective. Only by thus broadening the concept of purpose and practices of ap-

---

[4]Caroline Tryon and William E. Henry, "How Children Learn Personal and Social Adjustment," Forty-Ninth Yearbook of the National Society for the Study of Education, Part I, *Learning and Instruction,* Chapter VI, pp. 169-170. Quoted by permission of the National Society for the Study of Education.

praisal can the teacher supply the "success needs" of pupils and give them a sense of achievement that will motivate continued effort and offset much of the negativism that results, in many cases, from competitive academic marks.

More flexible reporting forms are being developed which permit the use of a "broader base" for appraising pupil progress. Many teachers prepare a supplementary report for parents describing the general adjustment of the pupil to school experience—including some comment on attitudes, interests, types of superior achievement, possible needs, specific problems that should receive attention, and the like. Furthermore, with the increased role of counseling in teaching, more attention is being given to the inclusive pattern of pupil experience in determining the kind and degree of growth that is taking place. An innovation in a number of school systems is a parents' counseling night when teachers discuss with parents the children's progress in school. No teacher need feel deterred in his desire to recognize achievement in any area of growth (academic or non-academic) by the persistence of a grading system that is too restricted to fit his philosophy of education. In many situations, people must learn to "live with" certain imperfect practices which make their tasks more difficult but which, in no sense, defeat their efforts.

TWO TYPES OF MALADJUSTED PERSONALITY

It is not the purpose here to discuss the total range of possible maladjustment patterns. Two examples will suffice to illustrate the possible relationship of speech as a causal factor or as a therapeutic experience. One is the pattern of withdrawal; the other is the pattern of aggressiveness. Many teachers consider the aggressive child the problem child and look upon the quiet child (the withdrawing child) as the better adjusted personality. The psychologist is more likely to look upon the symptoms of withdrawal as indicative of serious inner disturbance and need for educational guidance. The pattern of withdrawal manifests itself in nonparticipation in group discussion, evidence of inattention, fear of being the focus for group attention, slow and hesitating speech, refusal to answer questions, frequent "I don't know" responses, social aloofness. As has already been intimated, a feeling of inferiority developed through successive experiences of failure or social nonacceptance may produce such negative, or withdrawing, types of behavior. One can reconstruct in imagination, from actual life observations, conditions and situations that might contribute to the development of a nonparticipating, retiring, nonsocial personality. Read the following list of suggestions and add to them from your own observations.

1. A child, naturally low-voiced, habitually fails to make himself heard in a group. He feels himself ignored because his ideas never "get across."
2. A child who is somewhat slow in his speech seldom gets his ideas expressed because others, more aggressive and ready with words, usurp his opportunity.
3. A child's parents, as well as his older brothers and sisters, reprimand him for interruptions. He is constantly being "shushed" instead of being listened to.
4. A child is severely criticized for his attempts to "do his share" in a social situation. For example: "Don't you know how to speak to Mr. Smith?" "What did you mean by laughing at that? I hope Mrs. McCracken wasn't offended!" "When will you learn how to introduce me to your friends?" "Such a thing to say! You certainly didn't act as though you were ten years old. I was ashamed of you!"
5. A teacher interrupts a child who is about to ask a question: "Susan, stand up straight. Your posture is terrible."
6. The child has been subjected to other types of irrelevant interruptions in his school recitations. For example: "That word is Tuesday, Mary, not Toosday. Say it again. No, no, no! Come here and write the word on the board. Now say it: *Tuesday*. Well, go on. What was it that happened on Tuesday?"
7. A child feels embarrassed because her dress is soiled, because she is compelled to wear eyeglass-frames she doesn't like. Her emotional state makes it impossible for her to speak calmly or even to think clearly about what she is saying or should say. She seeks escape in silence. She finds it safer to "live within herself" than as a participating member of the group.

Aggressive behaviors are readily observed. They often constitute serious problems from the point of view of orderly group action. A child may project himself overzealously into a situation as an "attention-getting" device. He may resort to disruptive and socially disapproved behavior in order to satisfy an "ego" need. He may rebel against boredom by deliberate and dramatic statements designed to produce excitement, diversion, or even "shock." Aggressive behavior may also manifest itself in excessive talking, dominance of a group situation, the habit of argument (denial or disagreement), the resentment of criticism, severe negative criticism of others, intemperate and exaggerated statements. Curiously enough, certain types of aggressiveness are sometimes developed as a result of an inferiority feeling. Instead of "giving in" to a failure experience (say in mathematics) and developing a generalized attitude of failure, the child strives to compensate by attaining other types of recognition. The discerning teacher, therefore, will strive to direct pupil effort and interest into productive experiences—experiences that will be socially approved and provide opportunity for the pupil to gain favorable recognition. The dangers of overcompensation will not be discussed here. It is obvious, however, that prolonged concentration or "drive" in a single direction, purely for compensating reasons, will produce an increasing imbalance of personality.

> The history of civilization is replete with instances of greatness achieved as a result of [compensatory effort], from Demosthenes to Steinmetz. On the other hand, society may well suffer from the over-compensation in which some of its members engage as exemplified by Machiavelli, Napoleon, Hitler, and Mussolini.
>
> It is interesting to speculate how different the history of the world might have been if each of the latter had been born of healthier parents and, as adults, had reached a few inches more in stature. Their fanatical drive for power undoubtedly was related to their comparative stature and health. From the individual's point of view, compensation may serve a useful temporary purpose, but it seldom results in his achieving the well-balanced personality which might be possible through other means.[5]

The tendency to compensate does not always manifest itself in socially desirable behavior. Hence, the importance of careful guidance and direction. Defeat or frustration often sets off a burst of aggressiveness which is essentially a search for new channels, any channels, through which "ego" satisfaction can be attained. The fabrication of extravagant tales of personal adventure, cleverness in circumventing regulations, the amassing of a store of stolen articles, the organization of a "gang," daredevil behavior on the playground, the excessive spending of money, all may be efforts on the part of the child to compensate for certain academic inabilities. The teacher's cue in such cases is to discover useful tasks, commensurate with the pupil's ability, that will challenge his interest and provide an opportunity for praiseworthy recognition and success.

It is wise to keep in mind, however, that the major purpose of education is developmental. Remedial considerations enter the picture when symptoms of maladjustment are observed—or when patterns of deviant behavior have already been established. Teachers are in a position to

---

[5]From *Psychological Factors in Education* by Henry Beaumont and F. G. Macomber, p. 277. © McGraw-Hill Book Company, 1949. Used by permission of McGraw-Hill Book Company.

guide, supervise, direct, and counsel pupils in such a way as to promote a balanced pattern of growth on the part of most of their charges.

THE SPEECH OF THE TEACHER AND THE SPEECH OF THE PUPIL

Speech needs of the teacher cannot be completely dissociated from the speech needs of the pupils. Personality is a product of social experiences and is meaningful only in social relationships. Both teacher and pupil live in a social environment and are constantly reacting to it. Both are striving for certain satisfactions, certain ends that to them are important. What "blocks" may be interposed between the initial incentive and the attainment of those ends? In the case of the teacher, it may be a lack of psychological understanding of the basic principles of child growth and learning. Therefore, if the usual formula doesn't work, he is at a loss to know in which direction to move. In the case of the child, it may be a lack of compatibility between what he must do (to satisfy external pressures) and what he needs to do (to satisfy certain internal drives or to gain a certain degree of social acceptance).

One type of ability which the teacher and the pupil must use continually in striving to be more effective is the ability to communicate. As already pointed out, a community rests on common understandings, and common understandings rest on communication. Nine-tenths of the teacher's activity in the schoolroom is characterized by, or accompanied by, the sharing of ideas through speaking or listening. Likewise, the pupil's activities revolve, to an amazing degree, around the use of words. His "intake" and "output" of ideas, his status in the group, his total school achievement are conditioned, in great measure, by his ability to understand what he hears and reads and to express what he understands. The cultivation of this ability is the continuous concern of the school (and therefore of the teacher) at all levels of experience, and it is co-extensive with the total curriculum.

A final word is called for in this chapter about the effect of teacher-personality upon the developing pattern of pupil-personality. The child's tendency to imitate is nowhere more apparent than in the classroom. Values may be enunciated and reenunciated, but more teaching is done by example than by precept. The teacher who does not show emotional self-restraint will not influence children to practice emotional self-restraint. Children will not develop an attitude of courtesy and respect in the classroom unless a "climate" of courtesy and respect is created by the teacher. This impact of teacher behavior upon pupil behavior is well illustrated in the speech-personality of the teacher.

A pleasant "good morning" induces a pleasant response.

Clear, distinct speech will be unconsciously imitated by children.

A teacher who knows how to tell a good story sets an example which children will emulate.

The teacher who speaks with a scowl, points an accusing finger, issues stern commands, and pounds the desk for emphasis builds up in the minds of pupils a false impression of "good group leadership." Witness the mimicry of children when they "play school." What teacher habits do they dramatize?

From observation, other examples may be noted of speech mannerisms or teacher behavior that have a marked effect on pupil attitudes and responses. The artist-teacher is careful not to contradict in his own teaching personality those personal and social values which he envisions as educational objectives for his pupils.

REVIEW AND DISCUSSION

In your class discussion, reviewing the content of this chapter, use the following questions as guides. Try to avoid giving "yes" and "no" answers to questions like 2 and 6. Use them as "starting" points for the formulation of your own point of view, supported by your own observation and experience.

1. To what extent, in your opinion, does a teacher's success depend on his personality?
2. Do you agree that personality development is a legitimate and desirable goal of education?
3. What is your concept of personality? Is it the total of one's personal qualities, attitudes, beliefs, abilities, feelings? Or is it a pattern of behavior?
4. If a teacher accepts personality development as an educational objective, what can he do about it?
5. What does the acceptance of this objective mean in terms of evaluating pupil progress?
6. Do you agree that one's mastery of language, one's ability to communicate effectively, is an important factor in personality?
7. Why is "good speech" important in "good teaching"?
8. What are some of the things involved in good "speech personality"?
9. Think of your "best" teachers; what personality qualities contribute to their success?
10. What major types of maladjustment have you observed in pupils?
11. What do you understand by the term "compensating behavior"?
12. How does the teacher's "speech personality" affect the pupil?

If you wish to explore further the relationship of speech and personality, examine one or more of the following sources. Different members of the class may select different references and arrange a panel to present important ideas which they may discover in their reading.

SELECTED REFERENCES

ADAMS, DONALD KEITH, *The Anatomy of Personality*. Garden City, New York: Doubleday & Company, Inc., 1954.

ALLEN, ROBERT M., *Variables in Personality Theory and Personality Testing*. Springfield, Illinois: Charles C Thomas, Publisher, 1965.

ALLPORT, GORDON W., *Pattern and Growth in Personality*. New York: Holt, Rinehart and Winston, Inc., 1961.

CATTELL, RAYMOND B., *Personality, A Systematic and Factual Study*. New York: McGraw-Hill Book Company, 1950.

―――――, *The Scientific Analysis of Personality*. Chicago: The Aldine Publishing Co., 1966.

GUILFORD, J. P., *Personality*. New York: McGraw-Hill Book Company, 1959.

HAYAKAWA, S. I., "The Fully Adjusted Personality." In S. I. Hayakawa (ed.), *Our Language and Our World*. New York: Harper and Row, Publishers, 1959.

JOHNSON, WENDELL, *People in Quandaries, The Semantics of Personal Adjustment*. New York: Harper & Brothers, Publishers, 1946.

LEE, IRVING J., *How to Talk With People*. New York: Harper & Brothers, Publishers, 1952.

PEAR, TOM HATHERLY, *Voice and Personality*. London: Chapman and Hall, Ltd., 1937.

SMITH, HENRY CLAY, *Personality Adjustment*. New York: McGraw-Hill Book Company, 1961.

Toward the Ideal Teacher of Speech

FREDERICK W. HABERMAN

Teachers of speech are among the best in our public school system. This is not because they are better trained. They share equally with other teachers—teachers of physics, of English, of history—a good collegiate education. There are superb teachers in every field; and every field, including speech, has its duds. But teachers of speech are likely to possess characteristics that contribute heavily to success in teaching. They tend to be more extroverted than introverted; more often than not, they possess the physical attributes of voice, carriage, and manner so useful in teaching; and, for the most part, they are practitioners of their own art.

As speech teachers meditate on the ideal toward which they strive, they may observe that there is some new evidence that our civilization wants people proficient in speech and that teachers of speech have unusual opportunities in their classrooms.

II

Speech is a part of the curriculum or not a part of it as a locality of a nation decides on its objectives. All subjects in the curriculum, including speech, are practical projections of the objectives of the people. As the objectives of the civilization become more complex and changeable, the school system becomes more complex and changeable; in reverse, the school system is simple and stable as the objectives of society are simple and stable. In a simple, primitive society that exists by hunting and fishing there is no need for a complex school system. On a higher scale it is still possible to be simple and efficient if the society itself is simple and efficient. The monolithic state has a far easier task than the pluralistic or democratic state. Under a Mussolini, Italy knew precisely what objectives it had in training its Fascistic youth; under Hitler, Germany knew what kind of students it wished to create as Nazi youth; under Stalin and Khrushchev, the Russians know what characteristics they want in their Communist youth. But the United States is different. A democratic government is, in the nature of things, extraordinarily complex. No one person devises a single philosophy for

From *The Speech Teacher,* vol. X, no. 1 (January, 1961). Reprinted by permission.

Professor Haberman is Chairman of the Department of Speech, University of Wisconsin.

all the people to follow. On the contrary, every person in the nation is invited to devise a philosophy and even encouraged to persuade his neighbors to adopt it. The stronger and more certain a particular philosophy or objective becomes, the greater the likelihood that it will find a place in the curriculum of the school.

Since it is difficult at any given time to delineate the dominant desires of the people, we take refuge in surveys. A recent and elaborate one called "The Liberal Arts as Viewed by Faculty Members in Professional Schools," by Paul L. Dressel, Lewis B. Mayhew, and Earle J. McGrath, tells how faculty members in nine professional schools believe that speech should fare in the curriculum as a projection of the objectives of our society. The faculty members were asked their opinions on 18 subjects: would they require the subject of all students, make it optional but encourage it, make it optional only, discourage or prohibit it? It was found that there was a

> "preference shared by faculty from all fields for those subjects developing particular intellectual skills. Thus mathematics, English composition, and speech were seen as desirable requirements by substantial majorities of all professional faculty members, regardless of their specialties. . . . [These three] have reasonably clear connotations in terms of content and procedure, and they represent attempts to cultivate basic skills of communication long deemed desirable for the educated person."[1]

Table 22 shows how faculty members would rank speech on the four questions asked.

TABLE 22—SPEECH[2]

Professional Group	Required of all	Optional but Encouraged	Optional	Discouraged or Prohibited
Total	50.7	28.3	17.8	2.3
Agriculture	72.1	20.1	6.7	.6
Business	48.7	28.5	18.8	2.8
Education	48.5	27.0	20.1	2.8
Engineering	47.2	29.9	18.3	3.4
Home Economics	66.7	16.7	16.7	—
Journalism	29.0	34.5	31.5	4.0
Music	35.6	33.6	26.8	3.0
Nursing	39.3	37.1	22.3	.9
Pharmacy	46.3	38.9	14.7	—

[1]Paul L. Dressel; Lewis B. Mayhew; Earle J. McGrath, *The Liberal Arts as Viewed by Faculty Members in Professional Schools* (A Publication of the Institute of Higher Education, Teachers College, Columbia University [New York, 1959]), pp. 58-59. Used by permission.
[2]*Ibid.*, p. 29.

Of another significant chart, the authors say,

"Table 26 summarizes the composite order of importance of the liberal arts courses in the views of this sample of professional faculty members. English, composition, mathematics, history, chemistry and speech are the fields most heavily favored as required subjects."[3]

This survey suggests that speech is a worthy objective in our complex society. Inevitably the curriculum of our public schools and colleges will reflect this objective. Speech training in the schools will grow. We will need teachers of speech. The career that opens to them is a worthy one.

TABLE 26
Percentages of Combined Professional Faculties Favoring Certain Policies Toward Liberal Arts Subjects[4]

Subject	Required of all	Optional but Encouraged	Optional	Discouraged or Prohibited
English Composition	96.4	2.2	0.6	0.2
Mathematics	64.1	17.6	15.6	1.5
History	56.5	29.6	12.4	0.8
Chemistry	51.6	19.0	24.7	3.7
Speech	50.7	28.3	17.8	2.3
Physics	47.5	24.2	24.9	2.4
Economics	45.1	28.7	22.8	2.5
Literature	44.3	32.9	20.6	1.1
Psychology	42.1	31.0	24.1	1.8
Biology	42.0	22.7	29.4	4.7
Sociology	32.1	32.5	30.7	3.5
Foreign Language	30.5	34.9	30.8	2.9
Philosophy	27.0	41.1	29.3	1.6
Physiology	27.0	18.8	44.8	8.3
Political Science	26.8	36.0	32.1	4.1
Music	13.0	19.1	58.0	8.4
Art	12.1	24.7	55.0	7.1
Religion	7.7	20.9	61.7	8.7

III

The teaching of speech presents unique opportunities to a teacher. From an anlysis of these opportunities, we can infer here and perhaps state later what ideal qualities the teacher should possess.

A. The speech teacher contributes to the intellectual integrity and methodology of the student. He works at the crux of the intellectual

[3]*Ibid.*, p. 34.
[4]*Ibid.*, p. 35.

process. Think for a moment of what is involved in the whole process of making a speech. The teacher assigns a speech, saying to the student, "You are to make a speech on a subject of your choosing." This is enough to throw any student into a quandry. He can look over the entire world, not overlooking the fact that he is himself a part of that world. But as he looks into himself, it is a most astonishing person, no matter what his age, who does not see there a trackless void. Even after he has a subject, he doesn't know precisely what central idea he should evolve; he doesn't have any supporting thoughts, nor are they arranged even if he does have them; he doesn't have them in mind to deliver, even if they are arranged. The teacher in this situation helps the student to discover an idea, to shape a central conception, to analyze and synthesize ideas, to provide movement of ideas from beginning to end. In this process are intellectual method and intellectual creation at their best. There is scarcely any teacher in the entire curriculum of the public school who is so close at crucial moments to the intellectual creativity that goes on inside a pupil.

B. The speech teacher contributes to the psychological integrity of the pupil. The speech teacher encourages the pupil to stand on his own. The idea the pupil develops is his. A bit of supporting evidence derived from his personal observation takes its place alongside a piece of information taken from Schweitzer or Einstein, and suddenly he finds himself in awfully good company; the words he uses to express his idea well up from inside him and he is pleased with his resourcefulness; a quip that he invents makes people laugh and he is transported; the speech which he designs has a perceptible unity and he knows the skill of the artist. He delivers this speech all by himself. His mother and father aren't there; his teammates aren't there; his teacher isn't there; he is alone. He can use nobody's voice but his own, nobody's body, nobody's brain, nobody's courage but his own. He knows that he is alone, and he has moments of fearful misgiving. He must fight. A wise teacher gives him some weapons for the fight, some advice on strategy, and some encouragement. Still in all, he goes to the battle alone. When he wins, he is a stronger warrior for the frays ahead. He has learned some confidence. He knows that he has some power. He knows that he is something.

C. The speech teacher contributes to the development of the pupil, particularly to a stylistic awakening. In a speaking situation the words uttered by the speaker have a direct, almost visible effect upon the audience. One who experiences it for the first time is filled with a sense of awe. The experience is a heady one. The pupil learns vividly the power of words: they are not inert; they burn, crackle, delight. Here is discovery. If the pupil is bright and truly creative, he can work to achieve in writing the effect that he has observed in speaking. Writing and speaking may have certain desired effects in common, but they are two different processes.

D. The speech teacher helps the pupil to develop skills that are important in personal and national life. The growth of speech work in high schools and in colleges in the last generation is indicative of society's belief that speech work meets the need for intellectual, psychological, and physical training that is of the utmost importance to a human being functioning in a complex civilization. The "speech handicapped person" is not necessarily one who lisps or stutters. He is handicapped if he is inarticulate, if his speech is slovenly, if he is incapable of handling ideas with some semblance of clarity and interestingness, if he has no confidence in himself in an interview, discussion, or meeting. The "speech handicapped nation" is one that takes a chance on poor communication during wartime, or on communication misunderstandings between races and religions, or on inarticulateness in operating a democratic society.

IV

So the job of teaching speech is important and it is complex. The speech teacher will fall short of his goals, but no matter, he is activated by a great ideal and for this reason strives to become the ideal teacher.

1. The ideal teacher of speech must have a profound knowledge of his subject. The only substitute for breadth and depth of knowledge is great cunning and a winning smile. The substitute may pass for the genuine article for awhile, but sometime will be revealed as ersatz and shoddy.

   The speech teacher needs to know the fundamental physiological processes involved in human communication, including the sounds of the language, how they are formed, and how received.

   He needs to know the psychological processes involved in human communication, including conceptions of meaning, attention, social control, and satisfaction of wants.

   He needs to know the linguistic processes involved in human communication, including rhetoric—the art of creating meaning through direct, popular discourse; poetics—the art of creating meaning through indirect discourse; logic—the art of creating meaning through scientific discourse.

   He needs to know the aesthetic processes involved in human communications, including the form of speeches, of drama, and the like.

He needs to understand the functional processes involved in the media which carry human communication, including the platform, radio, and television.

He needs to understand the history of human communication, including the history of theory and the history of practitioners.

Along with knowledge he needs to possess some measure of above-average competence in a basic speech form: acting, reading, debating, public speaking.

2. The ideal teacher of speech has a desire to develop the talents of others. This is a dull way of saying literally what Jacques Barzun says by illustration:

> To pass from the overheated Utopia of Education to the realm of teaching is to leave behind false heroics and take a seat in the front row of the human comedy. What is teaching and why is it comic? The answer includes many things depending on whether you think of the teacher, the pupil, the means used, or the thing taught. But the type situation is simple and familiar. Think of a human pair teaching their child how to walk. There is, on the child's side, strong desire and latent powers: he has legs and means to use them. He walks and smiles; he totters and looks alarmed; he falls and cries. The parents smile throughout, showering advice, warning, encouragement, and praise. The whole story, not only of teaching, but of man and civilization, is wrapped up in this first academic performance. It is funny because clumsiness makes us laugh, and touching because undaunted effort strokes chords of gallantry, and finally comic because it has all been done before and is forever to do again.[5]

It is an attitude of mind that makes a teacher. Back-stage at the Wisconsin Union Theatre I once observed a young student come to one of the technical theatre assistants, who was a graduate student, and ask for help in the building of the upper half of a Dutch door. The student was not very skillfull with the tools of his extra-curricular trade. With the hammer he bruised the wood; with the saw he beveled its edges. The teacher assistant could witness this mutilation no longer; besides, he decided, this guy was hopeless. Taking saw and hammer in hand, he said, "Watch me." He created a fine Dutch door in jig time. He was happy and proud when all was finished; but the student was neither.

In contrast, on another occasion, I observed a teaching assistant who was asked by a student how to build something that would look like a big boulder on the stage. The assistant agreed to help. He explained when necessary, offered a guiding hand when really

---

[5]Jacques Barzun, *Teacher in America* (Boston, 1945), p. 13. Used by permission, Little, Brown and Company, publishers.

needed, but stood by most of the time and watched even when the boy made silly mistakes. But the boulder was made. Two people were proud and happy. The student had created a boulder; the teaching assistant had helped to create in another human being a skill and an appreciation of something. Both the door and the boulder that were created in that shop will be thrown away; but there is in one boy a modicum of skill and understanding and appreciation that may last a lifetime.

I shall not say that one teaching assistant was better than the other or that one will be more valuable to civilization than the other. For the one is a performing artist and the other is a teaching artist. We need both.

3. The ideal teacher of speech understands children. Not children in the abstract or children as a generalization, or children at large, but rather children the plural of one child plus another child plus another child and so on. In short, the teacher must know and understand each individual child who makes up his class. The need to understand each child can be exemplified by a story of a teacher in a Wisconsin high school. She had a boy in one of her classes named Donald Johnson. He was a recalcitrant pupil. The teacher, unable to do anything with him, decided to confer with his parents. Since there were many Johnsons in the phone book, she asked him who his parents were. Instantly, he said, "You want to report me to my mother, don't you?" "No," she replied, "but I would like to talk to her so that perhaps you and I can have a much better and more profitable time in our class." Later, at a conference in the Johnson home, Mrs. Johnson told the teacher that the boy was adopted, that she and her husband had great difficulty with him indeed, that he never seemed to succeed in anything he tried, and that wherever he went, he got into trouble. "Does he have anything that he works at, anything that he likes to do, any hobbies?" the teacher asked. "Well, yes, he has his maps." "Maps?" "He has maps all over the house." "That might be interesting," said the teacher, "May I see some of them?" Mrs. Johnson took the teacher to the recreation room, a very large room whose walls were virtually covered with maps. This was during World War II and here were maps of all the major theatres of action, and on the maps, colored pins and strings showing the disposition of forces all over the world.

Shortly afterward, this teacher was asked to make a speech at a nearby city to an education group who wanted to know what might be done with a junior high speech class. She decided that she might take with her six of her junior high school pupils to demonstrate certain speech activities. She asked Donald Johnson to bring some of his maps and come with her. He said, "I'll come, but I won't talk." "All right," she said, "that will be perfectly all right, you do just as you want to." Gasoline was rationed during World War II; so Mrs. Johnson, who had a large automobile, took all of them in her car. At the meeting, the speech teacher made some introductory remarks and then went to the back of the room while each child demonstrated something. In the course of events she asked Donald to bring up his maps. She said to him, in an off-hand way, "How many maps did you bring with you?" "I brought four." "Why did you select these particular ones?" He told why. "How did you get started on doing these maps?" and he said a few words about that. "What do these maps show?" This topic was up his alley and he talked for several minutes, until he had actually made a speech. When he had finished with his talking, the audience broke spontaneously into applause. The teacher looked around for Mrs. Johnson. She wasn't there. She found Mrs. Johnson in the ladies' rest room, sobbing. "This is the first time in my boy's life that anybody has ever given him any praise. This is the first time he has succeeded. This is the first time that anybody has said anything good or done anything good for him."

Donald had made a speech. Henceforth, in some measure, small or large, he would be a different boy.

4. The ideal teacher of speech elicits originality and creativity from pupils. The teacher of public speaking has working for him by the nature of events, a powerful force that will help make his teaching a success. That force is the motive on the part of the student to speak, the tremendous desire to be heard. The student in the public speaking class has the opportunity to say something that may become vivid—so vivid that it becomes a part of the lives of his fellow-students. When he gets up to speak, he shoulders a responsibility. He is in a sense, an educator in microcosm.

This urge to deal with subjects that are meaningful must not be blunted by the teacher. On the contrary, the teacher must continually encourage it, prod it, and elicit it. He must urge his students to achieve the utmost in perception, and the utmost in artistry. He must see to it that students deal with the significant or else that they find what is significant in what might on the surface appear to be trivial. In this sense, then, there is no trivial subject; there are only trivial people and trivial ways of handling things. But it won't do to allow the student to tell about his trip down the Mississippi River, or his most embarrassing moment, or how to put up pin-curls, unless the teacher can be assured that the student knows how to elicit from these subjects something that becomes significant. Not necessarily world-shaking, but significant in the sense that there is a principle involved or a moral that is larger than the simple recital of a set of routine sentences.

It is originality, then, for which we strive. Too often, these days, emphasis on originality takes a back seat to learning the technique of blackening a space on a true-false answer sheet which will be graded by an IBM machine. It may be necessary for the teacher to coax out of his students a subject that is important, by which I mean, a subject that is important to the student, that has some emotional content, that contains a principle or generalization that says something revealing about an event, or idea, or human conduct, and for this reason contains a germ of wisdom.

5. The ideal teacher of speech encourages straight thinking, precise expression, and emotional maturity in pupils.

The teacher of speech has not only the general job of the teacher to do, but also the specialized job in speech. The general job of all teachers is to educate a child. It is the baker who feeds him, the doctor who heals him, the tailor who clothes him, the architect who houses him. All teachers collaborate in trying to educate pupils who will have precision of thought, precision of expression, and maturity of emotions. The teacher of speech has a special and peculiar job to do within the framework of each of these three aims. He is much concerned with thought and with precision of thought. He asks students to think, to understand something which they will read orally, or which they will enact on a stage, or which they will use as a central conception for a speech. The speech teacher is quite apt to require the pupil to compose an outline. Outlining is a harsh discipline, but no better aid to thought, and for precision of thought, was ever devised. The speech teacher is intimately concerned with the development of precision of expression. The hardest job that all teachers have, and this is true of the teacher of speech, is that of teaching pupils skill in the handling of their language. The speech teacher works at it day after day. It is less clear to us how any teacher, including the teacher of speech, is able to develop maturity of emotions in pupils. But there are two ways in which the speech teacher helps. One of these is by developing in the student a sense of psychological courage. He is led to examine a social or political problem; he is led to take a point of view on this problem, a point of view which is presumably compatible with his general philosophy; and he is led to defend that point of view as well as to express it. This process from inception to completion involves a kind of courage which is different from the physical courage that might be shown on the football field, and vital to anyone who would mature in his emotional conduct. In another way, the speech teacher can contribute: he can develop in the student a sense of the significance of things. For maturity means that one has a proper understanding of what is important and of what is trivial and is willing to sacrifice for the important and to pass by the trivial.

6. The ideal teacher of speech has vitality. Vitality is action. Vitality is inherent in the teacher's way of thinking, his habitual modes of tackling problems, the very choice of problems which he selects to tackle, the friendships he has, the repose, determination, and success with which he can meet crises. It means that one has to be more than a teacher in order to be a teacher, and that the more he knows about everything that goes on in life, the more ingenious, the more fertile, the more imaginative—in short, the more vital will be his teaching.

The most devitalizing influence at work on the teacher is overwork. Teachers of speech, because of their field and because of their personalities, are magnets for extra-curricular work. It is not unusual for the teacher of speech in a high school to have a full schedule of classes in the daytime, then to return at night for rehearsal of a play; or to teach all day, work with the debate group in the evening, and then travel to a tournament on Saturday. If School Board members wish to have a debate team, they should pay to have a debate team; if they wish to have a schedule of dramatic activities, they should pay for that schedule of activities. This means that they should lighten the class load of the teacher if they are going to make extra-curricular activities a part of the work. A teacher's time is like a rack of pool balls. Once the rack is filled with 15 balls you can't put in any more, you must first take one out.

It is quite easy to be a good teacher of speech at twenty-five years of age. At that time in one's life, the teacher has a newly minted bachelor's degree or even a master's degree. He has been to school for a long time; he knows a great deal about a lot of subjects. His knowledge is new and vital; he is full of it; it is spilling over. He has had from one to three years of experience. At this age his health is good, his body is powerful. With a full mind and a full body and full enthusiasm there is no problem in being able to interest lively, inquisitive, daring, driving youngsters. But the mind and the body deteriorate. A little of the knowledge slips away every day. A little bit of energy is drained off. It is hard to be a good teacher at the age of forty-five if one has not taken care to keep his mind full and his body well functioning. An overworked teacher is one who by definition is giving out more than he is taking in. He is expending his capital funds, not the interest that the funds might earn for him. At forty-five, if he has not replenished his accounts he is an intellectual bankrupt. The only possible way that this can be avoided is by carrying on between the ages of twenty-five and forty-five with scholarly activity and with community and social activity. An average of 8 hours a day specifically spent on school work is enough. I am not suggesting that the teacher should not work hard. I am suggesting only that he should not work all the time at one single thing, but rather should engage in a variety of professional and community activities, all of which are conducive to making him a better teacher.

7. The ideal speech teacher regards himself as a member of a profession. Teachers in the public schools have not generally been faithful professional members of their chosen fields. Many of them are women who stay in teaching for a very limited number of years, usually until they are married, or if after that, until they have children. As a consequence of the enormous turnover in the teaching ranks, the beginning salaries of teachers are pegged high enough to attract able people from competing opportunities in industry and business. But since they do not stay in the profession, there is a correlative tendency to keep the top salaries quite low. As a consequence of the low ceiling on salaries it is difficult to attract able men to the public school ranks. We can become a true profession in teaching only when the top salaries are far in excess of what they are now—doubled let us say—and when merit as well as longevity determines the teacher's progress in the upper salary ranges.

Even though a woman were to stay in the profession only for a few years, she still should conduct herself as if she were truly a professional who has embarked on a life's career. The speech teacher should be a member of the Speech Association of America, or the Educational Theater Association, or the American Speech and Hearing Association. These associations were formed by courageous and persistent men and women who have bequeathed honor and dignity to us. A good professional member will subscribe to the journals in his chosen field, to the *Quarterly Journal of Speech*, or to the *Speech Teacher*, or to the *Educational Theater Journal*, or to the regional journals.

As a functioning member of his profession, the teacher should work to establish the curriculum in his school, to gain conditions of freedom and dignity for speech as well as for teaching as a whole. The teacher should contribute to his profession over and beyond being a good teacher in his own classroom. He should try to make an intellectual contribution to speech through research or through writing and publication of some sort. He should take speech, in a sense, to his community, to his state, or to the nation. He should, in effect, lead both speech and teaching in general to new glories.

V

After Plato had sketched out his ideal rhetoric, someone said in effect, "This is a splendid ideal, Plato, but it is impossible to realize." Naturally, Plato refused to answer, thus establishing a tradition in handling querulous comments that I find comforting.

EXERCISES

1. What is meant by the term "organic logic of teaching and learning"?
2. What is the ultimate goal of teaching? Does this goal influence your conception of how speech ought to be taught?
3. What are the essential differences between rhetorical and dialectical instruction?
4. What implications does the Rogerian model of instruction hold for the teaching of speech?
5. What distinguishes a "facilitator of learning" from a "teacher"?
6. What principles of learning can we be sure of? Develop a list of learning principles pertinent to the teacher of speech.
7. Has the lecture or discussion method of instruction exhibited greater evidence as being an effective pedagogical strategy? Explain.
8. How is a speech classroom a "therapeutic community"? What implications does this generate for the teacher of speech?
9. To what extent must the teacher of speech be "attuned" to the climate of the classroom? Is creativity synonymous with innovativeness and/or opportunism?
10. Describe the extent and type of interaction between teacher and student necessary in counseling his progress toward improving his communication skills.
11. To what extent do the pedagogical strategies employed by the teacher of speech affect student attitudes toward communication or their willingness to improve their communication skills?
12. What is meant by "acceptance"? What implications does accepting teacher behavior have for the teacher of speech?
13. Are self-initiated courses and study possible in the discipline of speech? In what courses might you find opportunities for "student-taught" courses feasible and advantageous?

14. What are the virtues of rhetorical instruction? Do you find any implications in rhetorical instruction pertinent for the modern educator?

15. Why does Rogers consider teaching a vastly over-rated function? What does empathic understanding mean?

16. How can television be incorporated effectively in the introductory speech course? What conditions should the instructor be aware of when employing this media?

17. Does the teacher of speech enter into a student-teacher relationship similar or dissimilar to relationships employed or manipulated by teachers in other disciplines? Explain.

PROJECTS

1. Record on a sheet of paper the names of as many teachers as you recall having taken courses from. Designate these teachers as to their effectiveness as teachers; i.e. ineffective, average, superior. What kind of criterion did you employ to arrive at your evaluations? Did the course subject matter or the grade you received color your judgment? What discernible differences can you perceive between the teaching techniques employed by those teachers labeled ineffective, effective, or superior? Would other individuals have rated these teachers similarly? Do you intend to teach your course like those teachers having made a favorable impression upon you? What is your rationale for this?

2. With each of your classmates reciprocally evaluate each other in writing as to your potential attributes as teachers of speech. Exchange your evaluations. After analyzing the written comments of your classmates, assess to what extent their evaluations and perceptions of you as an effective teacher were correct or incorrect. How do you account for the differences (be there any)? Discuss with your classmates the relationship of teacher personality to the stability of a learning climate.

3. Visit a number of classrooms and observe the teaching styles exhibited by each instructor. Discuss with each instructor his or her rationale for the instructional strategies employed. What observable effect did the instructor's methodologies have upon the learners? From your knowledge of instructional goals and learning theory, do you believe that given this particular class and its subject matter you would have duplicated the instructor's strategies? Discuss with your classmates how you might have taught the class.

Chapter 3

Principles of Criticism and Evaluation

The pedagogical necessity of evaluating and criticizing student speeches has often confused and frustrated beginning teachers of speech. Even seasoned teachers report difficulty in attempting to clarify effective and valuable methodologies of evaluation and criticism. It is in fact hard to find a teacher who at some time has not expressed uneasiness about criticism and evaluation and the implications its holds for learners.

There are any number of reasons for such concern. Research studies, for example, testing the effectiveness of criticism and evaluation techniques are for the most part shallow and inconclusive. If one were to review the reams of research monographs reporting the various effects of *grading* vs. *non-grading* upon learners he could only conclude that more research should be conducted. Likewise, speech criticism was once considered a relatively simple task of providing students feedback concerning the effectiveness of their speech. Lately, however, alarming research has demonstrated that certain forms of criticism may have negative and deleterious effects upon the psyche and personality adjustment of students. In fact, criticism and evaluation now appear open to serious question as sound pedagogical methods, while in some quarters they have already fallen into disrepute. This is small comfort to a teacher attempting to decide upon a fair methodology for criticizing and evaluating student projects and speaking assignments.

The purpose of this chapter will be to formulate guidelines clarifying for the teacher-in-training the advantages and disadvantages of employing certain criticism and evaluation techniques. There will be, in at least one instance, contradictory statements about criticism and evaluation. Since the issues examined are as yet unresolved, it would be presumptuous of the editor to take a subjective stand on the matter.

246

Criticism and evaluation often are mistakenly considered as having identical purposes and ends although each is distinct and separate pedagogically. Nevertheless both criticism and evaluation have as an overriding purpose an intent to guarantee student speakers maximum opportunity for growth and maturity as effective oral communicators through the judicious guidance of an instructor (critic-evaluator). While both criticism and evaluation involve the critical assessment of a speech, criticism implies a critic judge clarifying for students their relative strengths and weaknesses as speakers, whereas speech evaluation involves a value judgment (generally in the form of a numerical or letter grade) as to the relative worth of a speech. It is helpful to keep this distinction in mind.

Gerald M. Phillips's, "The Oral Communication Revolution," is a brilliant essay devastating the standard "tried-and-true" approach to speech education. This paper was written as a result of four years experience in Title III of the Elementary and Secondary Education Act in the states of California and Pennsylvania. This position paper and the views it endorses, perhaps unorthodox and alien to many teachers of speech, must be read carefully and conscientiously with an open mind. The author has pulled no punches. Many readers may not immediately agree with Phillips' analysis and interpretation. Some may be startled and others discount it as "foolishness." Nevertheless, the facts speak for themselves and the reader must be prepared to meet them intellectually, for Phillips posits a rational analysis devoid of any sentimentality for what we have come to know as speech education. Without hesitating he offers an alternative rationale for the development of a communication-centered classroom. Reliable hard-nosed documentation supports his thesis.

Editors are obligated to remain objective in their reporting—or so say many books on manuscript preparation. In this case, however, I can no longer remain silent. What Phillips advocates not only excites my bent for the revolutionary but satisfactorily answers many personal suspicions about the nature of criticism and evaluation. The build-up I have given "The Oral Communication Revolution" must surely titillate the reader to explore it.

Phillips states that "essentially the classroom is a therapeutic community," since effective training in speech results in cognition and behavior change which in turn brings about a change in personality. Unfortunately, very few teachers comprehend this clinical relationship. This basic tenet automatically classifies a student as client. As a result, a wholly different rationale must be adopted to approach the learner effectively. No longer is the classroom teacher-centered. It is adapted to the needs and sensitivities of the learner.

A typical public speaking course, Phillips argues, is founded upon three untenable assumptions: (1) that students can learn to speak by emulation, (2) that required performance will cultivate skill, and (3) that criticism is sufficient to bring about positive behavior change. "Despite the fact that these three premises have been shown false, they persist, consciously and unconsciously, on all levels of the educational system. They have never been formally tested; there is not one shred of evidence to indicate their efficacy. The few studies that have been made, in fact, demonstrate their falsity."

How, then, should oral communication skills be taught? First, suggests Phillips, every so-called content course must place an emphasis on communication in the classroom. Training in oral communication in grades k-9 must not occur in formal courses in oral communication. Emphasis must be taken off oral communication as an act or performance. Rather, it must be viewed as a method by which men promote understanding between each other. This approach, of course, would necessitate that each teacher be trained in the teaching of oral communication.

Phillips suggests that in order to insure a communication-centered classroom four variables must be manipulated by the teacher in the following manner: (1) teachers must not grade performance, (2) extreme care must be exercised in the use of criticism, (3) learners must have ready access to the teacher, (4) "prop structuring" must be employed as a motivational technique. In addition, innovation and opportunism on the part of the teacher is essential.

Phillips concludes his paper by pointing to what may be accomplished in a communication-centered classroom. The reader is advised to evaluate and weigh objectively the advantages of Phillips's philosophy of education against his own.

Donald Dedmon in his article "Criticizing Student Speeches: Philosophy and Principles" outlines a philosophy of speech criticism based upon supportable pedagogical principles. This reading should be of aid to beginning teachers of speech in that it stresses the serious implications and effects certain criticism techniques have upon the speaking of students.

Dedmon develops his paper with the principles that each student's speech is a unique behavior, and that criticism to be meaningful must be grounded in an intelligent view of the oral communication process. Dedmon develops an effective case for focusing criticism on each individual as a unique speaker, thus requiring the critic to offer criticism on an individual basis. Large and overwhelming generalizations cannot substitute for effective criticism geared to the needs of each learner. No student should leave a speech classroom with criticism such as "watch your introduction and conclusion, visual aids may have aided your speech, you appeared jittery at times, and, oh, before I forget, is it necessary to wear such loud ties?" Such criticism is sloppy and inconclusive and constitutes a serious neglect of responsibility. While generalizations can at times suggest areas in need of improvement, the speaker must be provided specifics in order to improve his oral communication skills. How the facilitator of learning effectively accomplishes such criticism is the subject under analysis in Dedmon's article.

In addition to criticizing individually each student's speaking behavior, Dedmon suggests the critic examine the speech as a communicative entity. As such, "communicative entity" should be viewed as an operational classroom philosophy of oral communication. This philosophy should include the following viewpoints.

Oral communication must first be seen as an ongoing, dynamic, two-way process involving a speaker and listener. Secondly, the critic must view oral communication as including several interactional elements— encoding and decoding, transmitting and evaluating messages. In addition, the influence of noise upon the message must be recognized. Clearly, it is the responsibility of the instructor-critic to facilitate a student's understanding of the elements and processes of oral communication and how he may adapt to and incorporate these interrelationships.

Functional strategies of criticism employed by the critic must follow certain guidelines. Dedmon's guidelines suggest the necessity for initiative, creativity and careful planning on the part of the instructor in order to assure valuable criticism. These suggestions include (1) criticism must include the principles of effective speech making, (2) each period of criticism must be adequate timewise, (3) criticism must be constructive, (4) criticism should be narrowed to a few topics, (5) rating scales must not supplant oral criticism, (6) oral and written criticism should be employed, (7) students should not conduct criticism, (8) criticism must include all facets of the communicative act, and (9) the critic must attempt to facilitate the improvement of his criticism.

The planning stage in the development of criticism techniques must not be taken lightly. Criticism, after all, is the turning point in a speaker's development as an effective communicator. It explicates, clarifies, develops and makes known the theory of effective speech and its adaptation to practice, and hopefully, changes undesirable speech habits. Without valuable criticism from an instructor most students are unlikely to improve their communication skills.

Paul D. Holtzman, "Speech Criticism and Evaluation as Communication," in recognizing the invaluable function of the instructor-critic describes the necessity for and significance of criticism and evaluation. Holtzman allocates his article to two main divisions: criticism and evaluation. In discussing criticism as a pedagogical strategy, Holtzman examines (1) the aim of criticism, (2) the focus of criticism, (3) the progression of criticism, and (4) criticism procedures. In developing evaluation the article explores (1) the implications of evaluation, (2) what the evaluator should look for in speeches, and (3) suggestions for improving evaluation.

Holtzman emphasizes that the primary question the critic of speech must answer is "what can I say (or write or do) that will result in improving this student's communicative ability?" This is a most intelligent view. In the opinion of the editor, all speech criticism should be developed from this premise.

The critic seeks certain desirable behavioral responses in the speaking and speeches of his students. Positive criticism must aim at achieving this end. Clearly, the ends sought by the critic must be both beneficial and applicable to the student. One should never lose sight of the fact that criticism is offered for the student's benefit. The critic must not allow himelf to use criticism as a weapon, to make example of, to illustrate, nor serve as a sounding board from which to vent his spleen. Likewise, simple analysis indicates that any student is more than capable of playing the "game" of criticism. The teacher may snap his fingers and bark his commands and the student in all likelihood will perform adequately, as would a puppet. This would be a deplorable state of affairs. The behaviors instilled by training in speech must have carry-over to real life situations. Let us face reality. The speech classroom is but a fleeting fragment of a long line of experiences the student will meet. Long after the speech teacher has been forgotten, the process of making and delivering a speech effectively must be retained by individuals. Hopefully, the teacher of speech will have aided, not hindered this ability.

In line with this thought, Holtzman indicates that the critic must adjust his level of expectation to the capabilities of beginning speakers. It is one thing to lecture students upon how to write and deliver a speech and quite another to expect polished speakers the following day. A moments reflection upon our own first speaking assignments in a speech class will undoubtedly remind us of the anguish felt at attempting to remember and incorporate the proper techniques of gesturing, eye-contact, content, organization, voice, and all the while remaining calm in the face of what seemed twenty piercing eyes each searching for some miniscule error in our performance. This recollection should serve to remind us that adjusting to the prospect of speaking formally before others is often the most frightening barrier confronting beginning speakers. The critic, then, must allow the learner to build his speaking skills a step at a time. This approach, hopefully, will avoid massive confusion on the part of the neophyte speaker. This, the editor suggests, aids the critic as well for it allows him to narrow his criticism from broad generalities to the specific concepts under consideration.

Fortunately or unfortunately high schools and colleges demand an indication of a student's course performance. A teacher would be negligent to both the student and institution if his grading (evaluation) was not conducted in a manner most indicative of the student's grasp and understanding of the effective, affective, and cognitive behaviors sought in the course.

Evaluation, like criticism, is a difficult pedagogical obligation fraught with many opposing theories and opinions. Many factors may influence a teacher's evaluation of student speeches. Obviously, it should be the goal of every teacher to be objective. Unknown to the teacher, however, confounding variables may reduce objective observation to subjective evaluation. One research study, for example, intimates that speech teachers tend to evaluate speakers in terms of their own speaking ability; i.e., "Those students whose speaking most resembles my own shall receive "A's". This unconscious and subtle force may be one of hundreds operant in our evaluations. The obvious question that each teacher must ask, then is, "How reliable and valid are my evaluations, and how may I improve upon them?"

It would be skirting the issue to suggest that since grading (whether speeches, English themes, or mathematic problems) has been discussed, debated, and debased (with as yet no real end in sight) that one should automatically throw up his hands in disgust and conclude that "What was good for my education must likewise be good for my students!" There are available many effective and efficient means by which to evaluate a student's speech. The teacher-in-training should acquaint himself with these approaches to grading and test the philosophies grounding their pedagogical legitimacy. The abundance of varying educational philosophies held by teachers of speech, though, and the grading policies adopted to meet the goals of these philosophies has led to much misunderstanding and conflicting reports as to which evaluative techniques and/or procedures best serve the interest of the student and the behavioral changes sought by the teacher.

Eugene E. White in his article "A Rationale For Grades" analyzes the grading practices of teachers of speech in introductory courses. White does not discuss the merits, morality, or competence of teachers of speech to grade student speeches. Rather, the purpose of his paper is to examine and clarify what he feels are commonly held misconceptions concerning certain grading policies and procedures.

The misconceptions examined are representative of both beginning and experienced teachers. The first misconception pinpointed is the opinion that grading is an inconsequential pedagogical practice. White suggests that to advocate the abolishment of grades or to adopt a laisse-faire attitude toward grading is naive and unprofessional. In addition, since introductory speech courses are "bread and butter" courses for nearly all departments of speech, each teacher must exhibit genuine concern over the exercise of grading procedures in these courses. Grading cannot be taken lightly.

Secondly, though common sense suggests the fallibility of man, teachers should not conclude that man is incapable of correct judgment. Obviously, correct judgment is difficult to render. Grading is a complex behavior demanding much expertise from an evaluator. The grey hairs on many a professor's head will attest to this.

There is, to illustrate this point, the story of a stock brokerage in New York concerned over the seemingly unscientific manner in which their employees made decisions concerning the acquisition of stocks and bonds. The board felt their buying and selling practices were made on a much too subjective basis, thus depriving the brokerage house of maximum profit. The chairman of the board decided to acquire the latest model in high speed computers and submit to its memory banks all available information indicating the practices, trends and quirks exhibited by the stock market in recent years. He felt assured the corporation would no longer be playing the market but rather scientifically analyzing its movements, thus insuring the organization of high profits. When the final day arrived for the computer's debut, our excited executive pushed the "on" button and waited for the miraculous data. After what seemed interminable seconds of needless whirring, the computer print-out was deposited in the executive's waiting hands. Carefully unfolding the sheets his eyes rolled over the data to its conclusion, which in rather blunt terms read, "BUY LOW, SELL HIGH." Moral: The evaluator need not make use of all the miracles of modern science to effectively make evaluative judgments.

The third misconception exposed is the notion that because of the uniqueness of the speech course it is more difficult to render reliable and valid judgments. While it is true that grading a performance of the kind normally observed in an introductory speech course is difficult, teachers of speech can be reasonably assured their evaluations are correct and indicative of student mastery of expected concepts and behaviors. Even the so-called "content" course faces similar problems in evaluation. It can be argued, though, that because of the limited class enrollment of most speech courses the teacher of speech has the advantage of knowing the student as a person rather than as an IBM number. Obviously, a class of 200 does not allow the latitude of freedom or the opportunity for face-to-face dyadic relationships between student and teacher possible in a class of twenty (typical of public speaking courses).

A fourth misconception is that grading interferes with the student's acquisition of speech skills. There is no question that in rare cases this phenomenon does occur. This type of personality, however, would in all likelihood be at variance with any pedagogical device evaluative in nature. Obviously in order to prevent this, grading must be placed in its proper perspective. The teacher may do this, suggests White, by exhibiting a sympathetic and understanding attitude, fairness, consistency and firmness. In this manner the instructor may avoid a confrontation of *grades* vs. *student learning*.

The final misconception perceived by White is that grading ought to be the sole responsibility of the instructor. As Holtzman and Dedmon suggest, however, a clear line must be drawn to distinguish where the teacher's authority ends and student license begins.

Jack Douglas, "The Measurement of Speech In The Classroom," examines the potential for reliability and validity in the measurement of speeches by teachers of speech. Although Douglas admits to the fallibility of human judgments, he nonetheless believes it fortunate that standardized tests in speech are at present unavailable. Since standardized tests are paper and pencil instruments, it is doubtful, he states, that behavior change (the objective of speech instruction) could be detected by them. No test nor machine presently available can accurately measure the effectiveness of a communicative act.

Douglas suggests that the teacher of speech, in order to improve his evaluation techniques, must have an understanding of the nature of measurement. Under this premise the article examines comprehensively (1) the nature of measurement, (2) functions of measurement, (3) objects of measurement, (4) types of measurement, (5) factors affecting judgment, and (6) procedures for improving measurement.

In describing the characteristics of measurement Douglas remarks that one dominant characteristic is that measurement is a kind of observation. When working with an observation, despite our regard for sophistication and objectivity, error (human or otherwise) is an inevitable consequence in our instrument. All statistical procedures employed in prediction, correlation or factor influence must, because of the imperfections of statistical paradigms, account for some degree of error. The statistical argot for this phenomenon is "error variance."

The nature and intent of speech evaluation demands, however, that the measurement instrument employed possess a minimum of error and a maximum of validity. Validity is the ability of a measuring device to measure what it claims to measure. The items the instrument purports to measure must, then, accurately reflect what it is the teacher wishes to evaluate.

The functions of measurement may be classified, according to Douglas, as to their educational purposes of (1) diagnosis, (2) estimating progress or achievement, (3) motivating the learner, and (4) research. No test as yet devised is capable of measuring adequately all four of these purposes, although such a test is not an impossibility.

The object of measurement cannot be so easily qualified. To a large extent the individual teacher establishes the boundaries constituting the objects of measurement. There are a number of criteria the teacher may borrow from or subscribe to in evaluating speeches. Classically, the artistic, truth, and results theories are time-accepted standards of speech evaluation. But whatever standard or criterion is employed speech measurement must be a response to the entire communication act. The speech must not be viewed as a potpourri of building blocks which culminate in an effective speech. Rather, the evaluator must view a speech as a communicative entity exerting some change or influence upon an audience.

Douglas examines as well the types of measurement, including (1) simple and controlled judgment, (2) response of the audience, (3) instrumental and subjective reporting, and (4) subject matter. With such a number of measurement approaches available, the evaluator must make a critical assessment and decision as to which evaluative instrument to employ. The measurement instrument must, as explained earlier, be capable of detecting what the teacher intends it to measure. If this criterion is not met, then there is little sense in employing the instrument.

Douglas concludes his essay by offering practical advice and warning signals in the detection of factors which negatively effect judgment. The teacher avoiding these pitfalls may improve his evaluations by employing the procedures suggested at the conclusion of Douglas' essay.

This chapter has dealt primarily with the functions of evaluation and criticism. Related to criticism and evaluation (yet distinct) is the teacher's willingness to allow between herself and her students a free flow and exchange of views and opinions toward pertinent issues of the day. William I. Gordon, "The Message of the Speech Classroom," suggests it to be imperative that all teachers (especially teachers of speech) allow learners to engage in free injuiry and to culminate such inquiry in meaningful dialogue. The teacher, suggests Gordon, must be prepared to accept this responsibility.

It is a sad commentary, however, that in many classrooms students are not allowed to speak on matters of immediate relevance and interest to them. Too often learners are saddled with the old standby "Tell us what you did last summer." And, as if to add insult to injury, these speakers are instructed to cram three months of activity into a three minute speech—with a clear introduction and conclusion no less!

It takes little wisdom to report that because of this many learners (especially in required basic speech courses) view the public speaking course with contempt and ridicule and quickly become adept at "game playing." Under normal circumstances any learner quickly perceives the personality quirks of his instructor. Having "sized up" the teacher, clever game players (which includes the majority of successful students) will not unsurprisingly choose subjects which smack of issues and positions strikingly familiar to those of the instructor. Students, it seems, waste little time in bringing to bear the expressed opinions and philosophies publicly aired by an instructor. But this is not to say an instructor should not allow his "humanness" to show. Rather, it is to openly denounce the teacher suggesting to his students that his life-style is the ultimate model of intellect and ethical conduct. It is doubtful serious learning can occur in such an environment, for in it deviant viewpoints and behavior are not tolerated but squashed. It should be apparent that the learner possessing views untested by logic and/or evidence, yet afraid to publicly expose his opinions for fear of ridicule, loss of face, or worse yet loss of grade, will not adjust his thinking or realize valuable learning. Instead appropriate smiles and head nodding (which of course we have all practiced with varying degrees of success) will become automatic reflexes conditioned in order to gain favor from the instructor.

Gordon suggests that for real learning to occur in the speech classroom learners must be guaranteed the right (even though the Constitution of the United States assures that right) to express whatever opinion on whatever issue they choose without fear of intimidation from an instructor. Pedagogically, little justification may be given, for example, to the practice of rushing a large number of speakers a day through their paces with little opportunity allowed for a discussion of ideas contained in the presentations. Time is *not* of the essence. If four speeches are given per term as opposed to perhaps a potential of eight, no great catastrophe (in the opinion of the editor) will have occurred. There is, as the reader is surely aware, a conspicuous lack of data proving that a beginning speech student will become any more of an effective oral communicator as a result of eight as opposed to four public presentations. The teacher of speech, remember, is attempting not only to facilitate in learners the physical skills of oral communication but the ability to construct cogent and meaningful messages as well.

Time, therefore, must be spent observing and criticising how each individual employs warrants and qualifiers, to borrow Toulmin's terms, to insure consistency and evidence for his claims. Open and free discussion following each individual's presentation will assist the teacher in achieving this goal. Class members, it should be noted, must only be allowed to discuss the ideas developed in a students speech. A learner's classmates, in the opinion of the editor, are in no position to offer meaningful criticism on *how* a speech was given. A lively and informative clash of ideas, however, is beneficial to both the speaker and his audience. This methodology, however, can only be practiced in a classroom climate free from an instructor's potential for "mass retaliation."

Gordon concludes by citing what he classifies as "freedom of speech rights" that ought to be granted all students. How well the average teacher will function as a representative and ambassador from the "uptight" generation will in all likelihood depend upon how she views these rights and her willingness to invest her personality and teaching skills in order to adapt and insure for them. These rights might accurately be called the *Student's Magna Carta*. They are extremely relevant to the modern student and must not be dismissed.

In summary, this chapter outlines instructional strategies which can be reasonably verified as reliable and valid approaches to criticism and evaluation. Approach your readings carefully, reflecting upon the significance and implications each article holds for your teaching.

The Oral Communication Revolution

G. M. PHILLIPS

Essentially, the classroom is a therapeutic community. The teacher seeks change in the behavior of his students. He does not deal with cognition alone, but primarily seeks changes in affect which, in turn, lead to changes in behavior. His activity is manipulation of environments to permit change to come about. But any time a change in behavior materializes, it brings about a change in personality as well. Most teachers do not realize this; they do not comprehend the clinical aspects of their profession.

The anthropologist, Ernest Becker, declares that speech is significant in the development of human personality. He regards it as the only way we humans have to express our personalities in non-animal fashion. Through the oral manipulation of symbols we declare our uniqueness from other animals and display ourselves as human beings. Other forms of communication, such as writing and music, are all based on the algorithm that enables us to use spoken symbols.

Furthermore, recent ethological studies tell us that even our communication is controlled by the four basic "drives" that motivate all animal behavior. We seek to perpetuate and protect ourselves. We seek to explain our universe. We seek pleasure and excitement. We seek position, rank, or territory. For the human being, communication is the vehicle, tool or weapon used to achieve these animal goals. Failure to use communication is regarded as mental illness. The primary task of the human therapist is to retrain the symbolic capacity and capability.

There are, indeed, a number of highly reputable psychologists who regard training in oral communication as the front line in the battle for mental health. Oral communication demands exposure of the self and it is the data on which judgements by others are based. Furthermore, oral communication is the bond between teacher and student, particularly important in light of present trends toward depersonalization and dehumanization of students. Recent studies demonstrate that communication with others may be both the source of emotional problems and the means by which they can be relieved or prevented.

Schools, to date, have made little effort to provide training in oral communication through the grades. Such training as is offered comes sporadically, almost as an afterthought. In the elementary curriculum, it is apparently assumed that children can speak and nothing more

Reprinted with permission from *Pennsylvania School Journal,* April 1968, pp. 440-442, 477, 478, 479.

need be done about it unless they display one of the known pathologies that can be treated by a speech correctionist. In the secondary school, oral communication training called "speech" is directed toward a special interest program for exceptionally talented students. The elective public speaking course, the debate team and the drama group normally draws a student who is not intimidated by self exposure and who may even have a prurient drive toward self exposure. There is little evidence of a coordinate effort to provide oral communication training across the grades designed to help students meet both their communication needs imposed by the curriculum and those that they feel on the outside. Requiring a student to recite in class or present a report presumes the ability to do so, yet nowhere in the curriculum is the child trained in technique or given the emotional strength to guarantee that he can cope with the assignment. The suspicion which exists between young people and the "over thirty's" is largely a sign of a communication gap. Students cannot communicate well with each other, let alone with the authority figures they encounter, and the school does nothing about this either.

Apparently the schools are not sensitive to the oral communication needs of their students. It is tacitly assumed that every child will develop capability on his own and without formal training. The speech therapist, however, knows that for some exceptional children, this is not possible. Excluding the truly pathological children they see, the number of children with articulation problems and stuttering disabilities found in a typical speech clinic program indicates that about five per cent of elementary children do not have adequate speech and need formal remediation. Add to this the sizable population of students who, according to classroom teachers, cannot cope with the normal oral demands of the classroom, and it becomes clear that approximately 20% of the total school population is in need of training in oral communication. A survey of some 20,000 students in California and Pennsylvania showed that teachers can identify an average of 18% of their students who do not have speech pathologies and yet cannot and will not participate in the oral work required in the classroom. Subsequent depth study indicates that this phenomenon is rooted in the child's self esteem, i.e., he has never learned that it is possible for him to exert an influence by speaking aloud with others. If we add to this the testimony of most speech teachers that very few of those who come to them voluntarily for training can be considered capable, and deepen this finding with clinical information from psychiatrists who can identify children whose disturbed speech is a sign of deep emotional disorders, we discover an appalling picture of inadequacy in training generalized throughout our schools.

The problem of development of a rapprochement with black Americans confronts the schools with another kind of communication problem. The black child stands stigmatized by the fact that his communication patterns differ grossly from the pattern affected by the white majority. While difference does *not* mean inferiority, the difference is often so regarded. Mutual training is needed to enable blacks and whites to begin to talk with each other again, and further to condition employers and employees to the language differences that will be characteristic of black men and women as they enter the labor market in increasing numbers.

Vocational-technical education offers another problem. The "Vo-tech" student is generally regarded as the dregs of the educational system. He is not a member of the academic main stream, and as a result suffers from the attendant loss of self esteem to the point where the gap between those who "work" for a living and those who "think" or "push papers" has widened. Intensive training is needed in communication skills for "Vo-tech" students with a particular eye to increasing their sense of self-worth so that they can become fully aware of their value to society. In simplest terms when the drain is plugged, a plumber is emminently more valuable than a philosopher, despite the fact that the schools are concentrating on producing philosophers-of-sorts in ever-increasing numbers.

In spite of these and other pressing needs, the typical unit in oral communication, if it is offered at all, is still based on the principles of public declamation, where diction, gesture, posture and eye contact are the focus of treatment and where little or no attention is given to the problem of interpersonal relationships and the role communication plays in them. The situation could be compared to what would exist if teachers of "creative writing" devoted the bulk of their time to teaching calligraphy, under the assumption that better handwriting would produce better prose. Furthermore, instruction focused on such behavioral characteristics has been found to be fundamental in reducing the capability of people to communicate. Matters of voice, diction and gesture are about as personal as general physical appearance. When teacher demands change in these areas she is attacking the whole personality and intimidating the student seriously enough to impel him to withdraw from communication.

With all the stress placed on writing in the schools and with the limited success achieved by those teachers, it appears imperative to consider more basic levels of communication, namely those involved in direct, face-to-face communication with one another. Because of the enormous number of problem speakers in the classroom, a reexamination of the principles of instruction is warranted and new approaches to the teaching of oral communication must be generated. Furthermore, it is now clear to everyone that our society places more emphasis on oral than on written communication, and at least as much attention must be devoted to learning oral skills as is presently being given to the art of writing.

PEDAGOGICAL RATIONALE FOR A NEW SYSTEM

Presently, formal instruction in oral communication is offered in courses officially designated as "speech" or "public speaking," and is based on three *untenable* assumptions.

1. Everyone can learn to speak adequately by emulating parents, teachers and peers.
2. Skill can be cultivated by *requiring* performance under supervision.
3. Calling attention of students to their "problems" is sufficient to bring about improvement of performance.

None of these premises is acceptable. First, there is no guarantee that children will be exposed to appropriate models of interpersonal communication. Poverty class children illustrate this, for the mode in their group is considered sub-standard and inadequate by the schools. Yet, to demand conformance on the part of these children without sensible training and more important, a reason for change, is entirely unreasonable for it represents a threat by the "system" to their life style and hence, to their individual personality. It is no wonder so many of these kinds of children are alienated by the school, for to take part in it means that they must cast off everything that has ever had meaning for them.

Furthermore, there is no guarantee that any teacher will provide a viable model of communication for any child. Teachers are not trained in communication, and the fact that so many school systems demand "speech improvement" of their teachers indicates that probably some of them are quite inert as communicators. Thus, despite the fact that emulation is a major element in learning oral communication, there is no control in the system to guarantee worthy models to emulate. It is the rare teacher indeed who can speak clearly, with warmth and intelligence.

Systematic study of the etiology and remediation of neurosis negates the second premise. If a child is fearful or inept in speech, exposure to the stresses of speaking *does not* cure the ineptitude. Anxiety about potential academic failure, i.e., an "F" on the assignment, may impel the child to suppress his fears temporarily and do the performance. The evidence is that his anxiety about speaking will be even greater on subsequent occasions when he faces forced performance. Eventually, if we force him enough, we will render him unfit to communicate with his society.

The third premise, criticism brings about improvement, should be considered in the light of the teacher's emotions when she is visited and critiqued by her superiors. Unless there is a solid commitment to "improvement," and unless the critic is regarded as a person who knows how to bring improvement about, hostility and resistance are the most frequent responses to criticism, even when it is sincerely offered by people qualified to give it. To criticize performance, for example, confronts the child with a personal inadequacy about which he can do little or nothing. To tell a child his voice is too soft is very much like telling him he is too tall. He can remedy neither.

The premise that identification of weakness is sufficient to bring about improvement has been shown clinically to be patently false. It is baesd on out-moded concepts of therapy. The underlying assumptions are that given a "sound mind in a healthy body," a person can change with the direction of the teacher. He must "will" change, and if he does not, then he is a failure, wilfully disobedient, and consequently to be accorded no worth. The sophisticated clinician, however, knows that even after a problem is identified by both therapist and patient, it is quite possible that it cannot be remedied and in most cases painstaking assistance is necessary to bring about what remediation is possible.

Despite the fact that these three premises have been shown false, they persist, consciously and unconsciously, on all levels of the educational system. They have never been formally tested; there is not one shred of evidence to indicate their efficacy. The few studies that have been made, in fact, demonstrate their falsity. It has been shown that the child's self image is likely to be damaged by criticism, that his ability to perform can be destroyed by forcing him to perform, and his ability to speak well can only be improved by confronting him with worthy models whom he respects and who offer him ways and means of improvement. Consequently, a new form of training is demanded!

Skill at communication is necessary to success in most occupations. A recent survey of executives and government leaders turned up the interesting fact that ability to talk with others is considered a more vital skill in those seeking advancement than specific technical training. Our society demands oral skills from successful people. The schools cannot assume that the home and the community will provide the necessary training. Neither can they devote their efforts to the training of a skilled few through an extra-curricular program, or rest secure with a program of corrective speech regardless of how effective it might be with the few students partaking of it. These activities can and should go on, but only in a milieu of total communication training for all.

The imperative is to provide a classroom situation which will enable the student to improve his communication without focusing attention on technique and performance. In short, it must take place in the regular curriculum, in *subject matter courses* like language arts and social studies. Oral communication training *should not* be administered as a new course of study! On the contrary, the student should learn to give his reports from the teacher who assigns the report; he should learn discussion when discussion is necessary in his regular classroom. Oral communication should be regarded as a vehicle or *method* necessary to implement the formal part of the curriculum. Thus, all teachers should be trained in the teaching of oral communication so that they can teach the child when he is motivated to learn by normal requirements. Once this has been established, specific attention can be given to the problem of learning to speak to peers, superordinates, parents, teachers, principals, potential employees and the community at large.

The optimum would be a communication-centered classroom in which speaking and writing as well as reading and listening are used as vehicles of instruction rather than as goals of instruction. We do not learn reading and writing because they confer knowledge and wisdom on us. We learn them so that we can acquire knowledge and communicate it. We must learn to speak and listen for the same reason. The child learns to read or to speak to accomplish some goal, to satisfy his curiosity or his urge to express. Fitting communication skills into the norms of life will enable the child to learn to do it without the tension that comes from focusing on it, and he may find, as many do, that reading and listening, speaking and writing, are pleasurable tasks because *they help him achieve his goals.* In short, the child must be assisted to the point where he can fulfill the rhetorical requirements of his life. He will acquire what he knows by reading and listening and he will activate it through speaking and writing, as the occasion and his own needs demand.

Such a program has been put into operation through the Title III program of the Elementary and Secondary Act in the states of Pennsylvania and California. The principles specified above were the foundation for the program. The development of new techniques of teaching centered around two main questions:

1. Can training in oral communication be offered to children without disrupting the on-going curriculum?
2. If so, can teachers be trained to improve the communication climate in their classroom to facilitate learning both of subject matter and communication skills?

Some 500 teachers have participated in various aspects of the program and over 30,000 children have been exposed to the techniques they have learned. The general consensus of evaluators of the program was that it has been highly effective and that it ought to be expanded. The program procedes through summer institutes, in-service training, classroom consultation and demonstration, interchange of successful lesson plans, video tape demonstrations, and personal consultation between teachers and experts in teaching communication skills. While some administrators were taken aback by the kind of active participation that generated because of the program, most became supportive when they discovered the kinds of improvement that can be made in teaching and learning in the "Communication Centered Classroom."

COMPONENTS OF THE COMMUNICATION CENTERED CLASSROOM

To achieve the goals of a communication-centered classroom, four variables must be manipulated:

1. Grading of *Performance* must be eliminated. There is considerable evidence to indicate that objectivity is not possible in evaluating speaking and writing. Most evaluation centers on mechanics anyway, and these are not the main focus of learning. Mechanics are a matter of concern *only* when they interfere with understanding. This is a revolutionary idea, for it means that the diction and "awkward grammar" of the ghetto youngster, for example, are not main points of emphasis in training.

   Punctuation and vocalized pauses do not seem important goals of instruction to the child, though they may become important when he discovers that they can impede his ability to influence others through communication. When teachers attempt to evaluate content of speaking and writing, they find themselves involved in matters of personal taste. Mostly in writing themes and preparing speeches, students learn to please the teacher, and consequently do not have an opportunity to generate communications out of their own needs. They are offered little choice about whether it is more appropriate to speak or to write their communications. The communication-centered classroom offers many alternatives to the child and the emphasis is on his writing and speaking his own ideas for purposes that are important to him.

Most teachers fall into the trap of considering communications amenable to the same kind of grading they administer to examinations. They seem to believe that there is a *relevant* objective mode of grading. Once they discover that there is not, they can use communication to improve cognition. Even if they cannot find a way to do this, they must learn that communication is so intrinsic in personality that to equate it with substantive learning is dangerous. A student who fails chemistry fails a subject, but a person who fails to communicate well *fails as a person.*

Furthermore, it is impossible to learn to communicate by learning about communication, although learning about communication is often interesting and sometimes important. It is only possible to develop real skill in communication in real situations where communication is the instrument by which some other goal is accomplished. Learning to communicate in order to do a satisfactory job on a book report makes sense to a child. Learning discussion so that the child can take a hand in implementing his curriculum results in effective learning of the skill. By using communication this way, the child can learn a more important premise, i.e. what goes on in the classroom has some relevance to his life and ought to be taken outside.

It is difficult to ask a teacher to sacrifice a "weapon" like the grade. However, there are enough things in the curriculum to grade that matters like communication, so close to personality, need not be included. Furthermore, most teachers who have faced an inner-city classroom have already discovered that grades are simply not important to the inner-city child. They do not motivate. They are regarded as penalty, and adherence to a system which demands that they be given only gets in the way of teaching the child something that he might find useful, and more important, interferes with his discovery that school has some meaning for him.

2. *Extreme Care Must be Taken with Criticism.* The two traditional modes of criticism of oral performance feature the omnipotent teacher and the "wolf pack" class. Both represent a serious threat to the student who may have personality problems and do not necessarily do any good for the capable student. In the first place, the appropriate milieu for criticism, even when solicited, is a private conference and this is usually not possible in the public school. In the

second place, criticism is pointless unless there is considerable trust between the person giving it and the person receiving it.

A more effective method of bringing about improvement in communication is to provide an opportunity for the student to analyze his goals and determine how well he has achieved them. If he discovers anything at all, it will motivate him to seek improvement. Under this system, the teacher can provide the student with a set of criteria which would lead her to be pleased with a composition or speech. She can indicate pleasure, displeasure or some intermediate emotional state without putting a grade on the book, and the student can concern himself with what he might do to bring about the response in teacher that he seeks. Experimentation with students shows that students actually prefer a system in which they are not graded for each performance or activity but are graded finally as a Gestalt of their activity for the whole grading period.

By making the teacher a relevant audience, the student may then seek consultation about ways and means of improving. The teacher can provide methodology. Criticism unaccompanied by compensating methodology is totally frightening, and no methodology will make sense unless it seems to be capable of bringing about an improvement that the student wants to effect. It doesn't help to learn you are ineffectual if no one offers you a way to become more influential. Understanding ineffectuality in some specific realm, however, can be helpful, for the student may then seek ways to improve a specific act without putting his entire personality on the line. Teachers would do well to contemplate this point, and to consider how threatened they are by criticism. Presumably, teachers are more mature and better able to control their emotions than their younger students. Consequently, it can be assumed that whatever the teacher feels when she is being criticized by a superior is felt even more strongly by her students when she administers criticism.

The goal of criticism is improvement of performance. Clinical evidence shows that this can only happen when the student identifies the weakness and then receives guidance in a methodology of improvement. The teacher, in this kind of system, becomes a consultant who might also be a trusted friend, rather than a critic and evaluator with the power to penalize. It is easier to trust a person who helps bring change about than it is to place confidence in a person who penalized malfeasance without compensation.

3. *There Must Be An Opportunity for the Student to Reach the Teacher Privately.* Optimum communication takes place in a dyad in a quiet room. Most elementary and secondary schools could not provide the

room even if there were the time. Consequently, the teacher must open channels through which he can be reached *as a person* by the students. Providing means for feedback helps meet this need. This can be done through student diaries commented on by the teacher, private evaluations, setting up "talking tables," letting the students send in anonymous tape recorded or written messages, or merely by sitting face-to-face for brief moments and talking alone to a student as though he mattered, regardless of whatever else is going on in the classroom.

The teacher must perceive himself in rhetorical transaction with the student when he teaches. His job is to motivate or persuade the student to alter his behavior by learning material and putting it to use. Consequently, his strategies must be based on a solid and genuine understanding of the need to have the student put full faith and credit in him. In many ways, the position of teacher is not unlike that of any public persuader. The act of dissemination cannot be equated with the act of acceptance. That means that whatever the teacher offers, it must be done in the light of understanding the goals and motivations of her audience, the students. Open feedback channels can do a great deal to provide this sort of information, and if the teacher responds to it, to improve the trust and confidence between teacher and students. The teacher can, thereby, meet the real needs of the students. In short, the teacher seeks to motivate self-initiated awareness on the part of the student.

4. *Prop Structuring is Important in Generating and Achieving Goals.* Once the teacher has developed sufficient confidence and trust, she can move on to full realization of the power of the communication-centered classroom by establishing a situation in which a student can fail in a sanction free environment, in which the act of failure is not made more threatening by imposition of arbitrary sanctions by a hated authority-figure.

In order to achieve this, the student must be impelled to determine his own goals, and for the most part, the methods by which he wants to achieve them. The student who is receiving help from a speech therapist or psychologist may need outside consultation in determining goals; the others can do it singly, or in groups, in consultation with the teacher. The curriculum remains. Hopefully, it is the result of careful planning by teachers and supervisors and represents materials that can be made meaningful and useful to the student. But even an outmoded and irrelevant curriculum can still come alive, if the student is able to determine his orientation to it.

Goals developed by students are at first likely to be excessively broad or "nitpicking." Students may want more "self confidence," or they may want to develop "poise." Some may want to "learn everything about it," or "how to make my handwriting (or voice) prettier." The teacher must assist the student to put these goals into manageable terms phrased as behavioral outcomes. The speaking and writing that a child does then becomes the method by which he reveals to teacher, and to himself, that he has achieved his goals fully or in part. It is sometimes useful to confront students with a syllabus of subject matter and let them work out singly or in groups the methods they will use to "learn" the subject matter. Experiments with this show that not only do students make more demands on themselves than the teacher is likely to do, but also that they are more effective in meeting them than they are teacher imposed demands.

Support for weaker students in the classroom comes about almost automatically under these circumstances, for a shared problem elicits higher group solidarity. The method of group discussion, so often applied to subject matter learning, thus can also be applied to learning communication. It is a powerful device for encouraging students to look to each other for help and thus to begin to communicate in a situation approximating reality. Result, the bright begin to function as auxiliary teachers and thus expand their own subject matter mastery. The weak find that there are people they can get to and trust who will give them help.

Innovativeness and opportunism are characteristic of teacher behavior in a communication centered classroom. The teacher discovers that by changing environments, i.e., the rules and the problems, she can motivate change by the students much more effectively than if she tried to manipulate students. Since goals are specific for each child, every experience offers a creative challenge to the student, so long as it is perceived relevant to attainment of the goals. Communication is the vehicle, learning is the goal. The classical standards for teaching are no longer pertinent, for the lecture-recitation-drill-test syndrome is defeated. It is astonishing to some teachers when the students come to her and ask that they be tested because they think they are ready. Yet, in a sanction-free communication atmosphere this is not unusual, for the child has learned to communicate about his needs and will, therefore, avail himself of every opportunity to use the teacher's experience and wisdom to help achieve satisfaction of them.

WHAT CAN BE ACCOMPLISHED

The communication-centered classroom often appears disorganized and chaotic to teachers trained in the premise that a quiet class is a busy class. It is hard for most teachers to appreciate a classroom where each child is working on his own, but it is clear that each child can work on his own without sacrificing the integrity of the subject matter. Rigidly locking children into formal procedure and demanding a specific response at a specific time and with specific rules governing the performance makes the school situation unreal to the child. It is only methodologically real to the teacher, for her task is then defined as moving through the steps, not as getting the child to learn.

Tracking becomes unnecessary, for brights and dulls will choose their levels to meet their needs. They will be able to make the commitment they are capable of, without the frustration that comes to a student skilled in language arts when the same skill is expected of him in mathematics. The not so smart student may still find something at which he can show skill, perhaps in making posters, building equipment, or whatever is necessary to complete the kinds of projects the students generate for themselves.

Thus, communication training can be used as a means of implementing curriculum which permits each child to achieve to his maximum without placing him in unfortunate competition with others through a standardization of curriculum. By regarding each student as a unique phenomenon, the teacher may sacrifice the possibility of consistent evaluation against established norms. However, awareness of the individual child permits the teacher to evaluate *progress,* so long as she and the student understand the goals that the student is working toward. The teacher is freed from routinization, and is available to help those who need help without insinuating her presence on those who are perfectly capable of working alone. The teacher remains the authority in the classroom, qualified by age, wisdom, and concern, but the tone is set by student needs.

Active involvement in the communication-centered classroom is based on five action premises.

1. The function of the teacher is to participate with the child in communication transaction, not to control the nature of the transaction and not to control or coerce the student to participate in it on teacher terms. The teacher seeks to achieve her goals by manipulating environments, by confronting the child with problems and challenges and recognizing that whatever output she gets is acceptable and must be evaluated in the light of the student who pro-

duced it. The one certainty about the teacher-centered classroom is that it is not 100% effective. The child who fails in it, however, is penalized and not helped, yet he cannot understand his failure because he cannot understand why he should work toward teacher established goals.

2. The situation as seen by the student determines the extent to which progress toward immediate and future goals can be made. The child must learn to talk about both his assets and limitations. He must understand that what he learns in school has use to him, both in making him more capable at coping with his world and providing for him some personal pleasure that he might not othewise get. The child will tend to set his goals in line with his understanding of these two premises, and should be evaluated neither on the quality of his goals or his conformance with teacher expectation, but rather on the amount of progress he makes. Largely, the students assessment of situation will make up the evaluation. When he is ready to go on and the teacher agrees, he may move, and these critical points determine the amount of progress he has made.

3. The student must play an active role in learning. The teacher must necessarily set the limitations of subject matter in which the students will work, for she must satisfy the requirements of the system that employs her. The student must determine both scope and methodology, and should have the opportunity to choose the way he gets involved with his subjects. To accomplish this, there should be relative freedom to communicate both with classmates and teacher. Such rules as are imposed on the process should be generated out of student needs and concerns, with the teacher acting as arbiter of whether or not the student decision remains within the limits of curriculum.

4. The single most important aspect of the teaching-learning process is interaction between teacher and student. If a satisfactory relationship is established, virtually any pedagogy will be effective. This means that the teacher need not sacrifice her personality style in any way. If she is authoritarian she may implement the student program in that fashion and win respect and perhaps love. If she is permissive, she need not be fettered by rules which may be meaningless to her.

5. Progress should not be controlled by time. Regardless of how long teacher and student are together, some progress can be made. There is nothing sacrosanct about the time divisions made in the school year. It really is not a question of whether the child learns something in the time specified for it, but rather whether the child learns anything at all during the time he is there. The student who learns

it faster should be pushed ahead without penalizing the child for whom it takes a little longer. Thus curriculum becomes a standard rather than a goal and pressing for completion in a given period of weeks becomes irrelevant. Pressure is thus removed from both teacher and student, which usually results in more satisfactory teaching and learning.

Implementation of a communication-centered classroom usually takes some courage at the outset. Administrators are sometimes aggrieved when they see a teacher moving about among the students accompanied by noise and ferment. It is the responsibility of the teacher, however, to interpret the style to the administrator, and be willing to take sanctions if necessary in order to accomplish a higher quality education for the students.

This article is presented without apology as a result of four years of experience in educational innovation. The purpose of Title III of the Elementary and Secondary Education Act is to initiate innovative and exemplary programs in the schools. The communication-centered classroom has passed the innovative stage and is not considered exemplary. In short, that means it works. The substantive theory presented here could be augmented by the usual spate of scholarly footnotes. Those questioning either the premises or the conclusion would submit their hostile questions to the author, who will swamp them with appropriate references and sources. It is precisely this method that is most effective in convincing administrators of the efficacy of a new program.

Criticizing Student Speeches: Philosophy and Principles

DONALD N. DEDMON

In order to make the kinds of oral criticism which improve students' oral communication ability the speech teacher should be guided by a supportable philosophy of the oral communication process and pedagogically sound principles of criticism.

Criticisms of student speeches must be carefully planned and executed if instructors of speech are to modify and improve the speech habits of students rather than to fix more firmly undesirable speech patterns. In speech courses, instructors obviously are not attempting to teach students how to speak. The students have already learned randomly to speak and they have learned their lessons well by the time they reach college. As Donald K. Smith has observed, from "its condition as an action which is learned before it is ever formally taught, we get some important effects on the general methods by which we teach."[1] This paper will deal with two important questions which the speech teacher must answer before he can provide classroom criticisms likely to improve students' oral communicative behavior. What philosophy should guide the instructor in his criticism? On what pedagogical principles should the speech teacher base his criticism?

I

The speech teacher-critic should recognize that (1) each student's oral communication is a unique behavior and (2) meaningful criticisms must be based on a sound view of the oral communication process.[2]

Students vary widely in their oral communication abilities. The instructor who fails to relate his criticisms to the communicative strengths and weaknesses of the *individual student* misses the point of criticizing.

From *The Central States Speech Journal,* November, 1967, pp. 276-84. Reprinted by permission.

Donald N. Dedmon (Ph.D., State University of Iowa, 1961) is Communications Consultant, Smith Kline & French Laboratories, Philadelphia, Pennsylvania.

[1]"What Are The Contemporary Trends in Teaching Speech?" *Speech Teacher,* X (March, 1961), p. 90.

[2]The process of criticizing should not be confused with that of grading. Grades, fortunately or unfortunately, are required by universities. Continuous grading throughout the course may indeed interfere with the teacher's communication with a student about his speechmaking. Because assigning a letter grade may create a psychological barrier to good communication, this writer considers it important to keep criticisms and grades separate; they serve different objectives.

The speech classroom is "a learning situation of the closest personal nature. . . . The teaching transaction is essentially a clinical process, since it is the function of one party to the relationship to alter the behavior of another."[3] The critic should avoid becoming an amateur psychoanalyst while recognizing that criticisms cannot be entirely removed from matters of speaker personality. As Bemis and Phillips, referring to Thomas Szasz and Jordan Scher, have said, "Psychiatric research leads to the conclusion that speech patterns are an intrinsic part of personality and that alteration in speech patterns involves necessary alterations in total personality."[4] Regardless of the teacher's particular psychological and/or communications orientation, criticism must be focused on an individual speaker dealing with a specific communicative event, for as Gregg expressed it, "Behavior is not so much a function of an external event as it is a product of the individual's perception of that event."[5]

Having evaluated and criticized the speech in terms of the individual student, the instructor should next examine the speech as a communicative entity, the total response of a student to a specific situation. To do so the instructor should be able to articulate and support a view of the oral communicative act.[6] An operational classroom philosophy of oral communication, the basis of classroom criticism, should include the following.

Oral communication should be viewed as a process. As a process, oral communication is dynamic, ongoing, and two-way; it involves a speaker and listener, a sender and a receiver. Listening is as important as speaking. The reactions of an audience, feedback, and delivery—vocal and physical—are viewed as unique features of the oral communication event.

Oral communication involves the interaction of several elements. They are a sender-communicator, who thinks, encodes his thoughts in symbols, and transmits this message vocally and physically to a listener who hears, decodes what he hears in symbols, evaluates, and reacts (feedback) to the message. Two other elements are present also. Oral communication does not occur in a vacuum; therefore, we may say

---

[3]James L. Bemis and Gerald M. Phillips, "A Phenomenological Approach to Communication Theory," *The Speech Teacher*, XIII (November, 1964), 262.

[4]*Ibid.*

[5]Richard B. Gregg, "A Phenomenologically Oriented Approach to Rhetorical Oriented Approach to Rhetorical Criticism," *Central States Speech Journal*, XVII (May, 1966), p. 83.

[6]According to Dean C. Barnlund, "A sound philosophy of training is implicit in a sound philosophy of communication." See "Toward a Meaning Centered Philosophy of Communication," *Journal of Communication*, XII (December, 1962), p. 197.

that oral communication is surrounded by occasional factors which may influence the event. Just as the communicative event itself is influenced by the factors surrounding it, the communicator and listener are subject to the influences of many background forces, so much so that they are limited in what they can both say and listen to. To recognize the elements of communication present when one individual attempts to talk with another individual is but the first objective of the teacher and student. A meaningful view of oral communication also holds that the elements of communication affect each other in highly varying ways. Thus, the objective of the critic is to help the student to understand the oral communicative elements, how these elements affect each other, and how the speaker might best adapt to the interrelationships. For this reason, no two communication situations are ever alike. Educating students to meet a specific type of communication situation is inadequate. Weaver and Strausbaugh have properly observed this instructional objective when they say:

> Communicating is much more a process of facing problem after problem, each one different from its predecessor—no matter how much alike they seem—than it is a matter of demonstrating certain skills which someone has decided will do. It seems unlikely that any person can be *trained* to communicate well; rather he must be educated to solve succeeding problems well enough and often enough for achievement of his general goals.[7]

The act of communicating orally is highly transitory. As humans we are confronted with an onrushing series of oral communication situations each different from all that has gone before. We have an opportunity to communicate in a given circumstance only once. The process is as Barnlund has said, "irreversible and unrepeatable."[8] The objective of the teacher of oral communication is to cause his students to view communication situations as *unique opportunities*. This principle of oral communication is at once a great challenge and a source of motivation. Thus, the purpose of the teacher's criticism is no less than to cause the student to see the many needs for efficient oral communication in literally all dimensions of life.

Primary emphasis should be placed on the listener, receiver of the message. Oral communication theory says that meanings reside in the receiver. Barnlund has said in his support of a meaning-centered philosophy of communication that "meaning in the sender, and the words of the messages are important, but . . . most critical [are] the state of

---

[7]Carl H. Weaver and Warren L. Strausbaugh, *Fundamentals of Speech Communication* (New York, 1964), p. 15.

[8]*Op. Cit.*, p. 203.

mind, the assumptive world and the needs of the listener or observer."[9] The objective of the teacher becomes one of helping the student speaker to think about his intended message from the point of view of the intended receiver. Listening should be approached in the classroom as an important, inseparable part of the oral communication act.

Oral communications should be viewed in the classroom as purposeful activities. Stress should be placed in the classroom on the specific behavioral purpose sought by the oral communicator in his communication. The commonly used general speech objectives of informing, persuading, or entertaining, while helpful during preliminary preparation of the speech, are too vague as catalogs of behavioral responses sought from an audience.[10] If we are to succeed in teaching a functional art as opposed to sophistic, students must be required to formulate highly specific behavioral objectives for their oral communications. But we must stress the importance of purpose without becoming preoccupied with effects. The wise classroom teacher will insist that the student speaker articulate his objective in communicating but he will not become so absorbed in assessing whether the speakers actually achieved the objective sought as to become blinded to the many other aspects of oral communication which merit careful criticism.

A meaningful philosophy of oral communication for the classroom must include respect for the process of language. The sender or speaker arbitrarily selects word-symbols to signify his thoughts. The *meanings* attached by the *listener* to words perceived is then the pivotal point in the communication process. The classroom speech teacher must cause students to become aware of language as words, not meanings. Words are but the tools of communication by which meanings in a listener are created. A view of communication which does not include a basic concern for the elementary principles of semantics is in my judgment incomplete.[11]

In summary, the speech teacher should adhere to a philosophy of oral communication which recognizes the elements existent in a given communication situation, the interrelationships which result from the existing communicative elements, and the principles of meaningful adjustment to communicative elements and relationships present. The various theories of oral communication indicate that the individual does not necessarily communicate what he intends to communicate, what he wants to communicate, or what he thinks he has communicated. We may

---

[9]*Ibid.*, p. 201.
[10]See David K. Berlo, *The Process of Communication* (New York, 1960), pp. 7-22.
[11]See, for example, Barnlund, pp. 197-211.

further conclude that two elements, delivery and feedback, are unique in *oral* communication.

II

The speech instructor's pedagogical guidelines for criticism should include the following: (1) adequate time should be allowed for the criticism; (2) the critic should follow principles of effective speech-making in his criticism; (3) a criticism should focus on a very few topics; (4) the critic probably should raise questions in his criticism rather than state dicta; (5) the critic should be constructive in his remarks; (6) the criticism should deal with speech content as well as speech delivery; (7) the instructor should not abdicate his primary responsibility for criticism by turning this important task over to the student audience; (8) if rating scales are used, they should be employed as aids to criticism, not replacements of oral remarks; and (9) one method of criticism probably should be reinforced with another method, i.e., oral comment followed by a written criticism.

If oral criticisms are important in changing student oral communication behavior, then it is imperative that adequate time be allowed for them. Including speaking assignments at the expense of oral criticism is of questionable pedagogical merit. Wofford G. Gardner experimented with course plans calling for varying numbers of speeches of varying lengths in a study entitled, "The Relative Significance of the Length and Frequency of College Classroom Speeches in Developing Skill in Public Speaking." He found "no significant differences in speaking skill of students."[12] The utilization of a heavy percentage of laboratory time for criticism of students' speeches therefore seems justifiable.

When the instructor begins his comments he becomes a communicator, a rhetor. If he is to avoid being guilty of making a less effective speech than the one he has just heard, he will do well to observe the same principles of communication he has admonished his students to follow. As Raymond G. Smith has expressed it:

> The instructor should be capable of offering criticisms by example.
> . . . He should be capable of demonstrating both correct and incorrect
> patterns of communicative behavior.[13]

A communication likely to produce a behavioral change in the student speaker should not be left to chance. As Smith observed, poorly phrased

---

[12]Unpublished Ph.D. diss., Northwestern University. Abstract in *Speech Monographs*, XX (June, 1953), 153-154. Cited in Samuel L. Becker, "Research on Speech Pedagogy," in *Dimensions of Rhetorical Scholarship*, ed. Roger E. Nebergall (Department of Speech, University of Oklahoma, 1963), p. 37.

[13]"The Criticism of Speeches: A Dialectical Approach," *The Speech Teacher*, X (January, 1961), p. 62.

questions such as "How about the introduction? Comments? Questions, class? What are we going to ask the speaker now? How about his conclusion? Criticisms? Would anyone care to react to this speech? Discussion, class?"[14] are not likely to achieve anything but consumption of the little time remaining of the hour. Worse still, such questions are negative suggestions; they create the impression that the instructor has abdicated his role as expert critic judge.

Paul Holtzman has phrased properly the question which should guide the teacher-critic: "What can I say (or write or do) that will result in this student's improving his communicative ability?"[15] Every spoken criticism must be viewed as a separate, different speech prepared in relation to a specific individual and his speech-making. While it may be possible early in the course to discover certain problems of speech-making common to all the student speakers of the day or class, yet for most of the course the basis of the criticism should be one speech by one student.

The teacher-critic should view each assignment as part of the cumulative process of acquiring all the skills included in the course. He should not attempt to review all the principles of oral communication involved in any particular assignment. While the critic cannot afford to let exceptionally good or bad demonstrations of rhetorical principles go unnoticed in any assignment, he should, nevertheless, attempt to limit his observations or questions about the student's oral communication to a few specific principles of effective oral communication. The critic should not only limit the topics to be criticized; he should be very specific in his oral comments on the topics chosen. As Kelley noted in a paper on "Objectivity in the Grading and Evaluation of Speeches," general comments fail to

> . . . pinpoint principles and techniques for the students to follow; . . .
> [The critic should] specify the various weights to be given to the
> various points of the evaluation, and . . . satisfy the students regarding
> their weaknesses and means to their correction.[16]

Further, the specific rhetorical principles to be emphasized in criticism should be clearly indicated when the assignment is made. In the words of Byers, "Pupils learn most effectively when they understand what it is they are expected to learn."[17] Fuzzy assignments seem to this writer to produce fuzzy criticisms.

---

[14]*Ibid.*, p. 59.
[15]"Speech Criticism and Evaluation as Communication," in "A Symposium on Evaluation, Criticism, and Grading," *The Speech Teacher*, IX (January, 1960), p. 1.
[16]Win Kelly, *The Speech Teacher*, XIV (January, 1961), p. 54.
[17]Burton H. Byers, "Speech and The Principles of Learning," *The Speech Teacher*, XII (March, 1963), p. 137.

In the criticism of a student's speech the instructor probably should ask questions rather than state dicta. Psychologists have explained that the individual under guidance must alter his own behavior; no one can alter his behavior for him. Therefore, the student *speaker* himself must be deeply involved in modifying his *speech* behavior. Questions are best suited for achieving this task since they cause the student speaker to think, to probe into his speech habtis. On the other hand, authoritative pronouncements are more likely to produce resistance, argumentativeness on the part of the speaker. As Raymond G. Smith has said, "The dialectical approach involving the use of directed, leading questions seems to present an admirable avenue for achieving the desired objectives."[18] Smith says further:

> Questions . . . serve three functions. They serve first to focus attention upon the desired rhetorical principle or point. Second, they force the respondent to commit himself, thus setting the stage for the follow-up questions. Third, if they should evoke incorrect responses, they enable the instructor to change respondents. . . .[19]

The questioning approach is preferable also because research conducted by rhetorical and communication theorists has suggested strongly that some popularly held views about speechmaking are open to suspicion if, indeed, they are not invalid altogether.[20] In the absence of firm evidence the speech instructor should avoid being overly general or dogmatic in his observations about a particular student's speech.

The writer doubts the validity of relying extensively on negative criticisms at the expense of positive criticisms. Bostrom, in an attempt to check the hypothesis "that rewarding a student's speech with positive criticism should produce positive speech attitudes, and *vice versa*," concludes:

> We can say that the type of criticism caused a change in the students' general attitude. The type of speech made did not have an effect on this variable. The means show that rewarded students experienced a positive change, while punished students experienced a negative change.[21]

---

[18]"The Criticism of Speeches," p. 60.

[19]*Ibid.*, p. 61.

[20]One good example of this is the importance we have traditionally placed on the values of outlining. Outlining and speech organization are two different things. The outline is a device for instructing in organization. Research on the influence of organization on speech effectiveness has yielded seemingly contradictory results. A specific manner of organizing a speech may not be as important to effective speechmaking as we once thought. See, for example, Raymond G. Smith, "An Experimental Study of the Effects of Speech Organization Upon Attitudes of College Students, *Speech Monographs*, XVIII (November, 1951), pp. 292-301; Raymond Tucker and Dominic A. LaRusso, "Discussion Outlines and Skill in Reflective Thinking," *The Speech Teacher*, VI (March, 1957) pp. 139-142.

[21]Robert N. Bostrom, "Classroom Criticism and Speech Attitudes," *Central States Speech Journal*, XIV (February, 1963), pp. 27, 29.

In Goldberg's "An Experimental Study of the Effects of Evaluation Upon Group Behavior," in which he examined among other things, "the influence of positive and negative judgments upon group interaction processes," considerable evidence may be found which seriously questions the worth of overly negative criticisms.[22] The questioning, positive approach is particularly useful in evaluating the message.

The aim of the speech instructor also is to contribute to, in the words of Haberman, the "intellectual integrity and methodology of the student."[23] When the speech instructor treats the ideas in a student's speech, he is dealing with what Haberman calls "the crux of the intellectual process."[24] If the instructor is very well informed on the subject of the student's speech, he must guard against using the time by displaying his own knowledge or perhaps his disagreement. The time is not likely to be used profitably in instructor witticisms rather than criticisms.

If the instructor is inadequately informed on the subject of the student's speech, he nevertheless must treat the ideas expressed. As Smith has noted, "Questions concerning the content of the speech certainly . . . [have] a legitimate place within the framework of speech pedagogy, but . . . should be limited to demonstrating rhetorical principles or strengths and weaknesses of preparation."[25] Smith explains the values of questioning:

> Questions about content can quickly establish for instance, whether the speaker is well versed in his subject, or conversely, whether he has exhausted his knowledge within the scope of one short speech. Questions concerning content can quickly bring to light unacknowledged facts and opinions or evidence taken out of context.[26]

But speech instructors should make a greater effort to structure, at least during part of the course, the content of the students' speeches so that ideas and their rhetorical treatment may be explored in greater depth. Various approaches have been suggested, a notable example being the "common materials" plan described by Hildebrandt and Sattler. In this plan students using resource books are given a choice of three broad subjects which become the basis of three speech activities: speeches to inform, group discussion, and speeches to persuade.[27] Still

---

[22]Alvin Goldberg, *Quarterly Journal of Speech,* XLVI (October, 1960), pp. 274-283.

[23]Frederick Haberman, "Toward the Ideal Teacher of Speech," *The Speech Teacher,* X (January, 1961), p. 2.

[24]*Ibid.*

[25]"The Criticism of Speeches," p. 62.

[26]*Ibid.*

[27]Herbert W. Hildebrandt and William M. Sattler, "The Use of Common Materials in the Basic College Speech Course," *The Speech Teacher,* XII (January, 1963), pp. 18-25.

another method is to have the students speak on topics concerning speechmaking. For example, students could elect such subjects as: the speaking in Congress, the rhetoric of the Negro revolt, campaign oratory, etc. Whatever the specific requirements on content, classes in speech should be characterized by more of what Gunderson calls "ideological warfare." Gunderson would have the speech teacher be a "bold intellectual leader, not a hermit."[28] As Ewbank has said, probably one of the most important prerequisites for handling speech content is to be widely informed ourselves.[29]

The responsibility for the criticism of student speeches should rest with the instructor, not with the student's colleagues in the class. To turn this crucial pedagogical task over to students as Wesley Wiksell,[30] for example, has proposed, is in the judgment of this writer a serious abrogation of responsibility. Student criticisms may actually interfere with the learning process. As Smith has said, "It must . . . be remembered that beginning speech students are by definition incapable of conducting good critical discussions in the absence of trained leadership, because they simply do not have the sound rhetorical background and knowledge upon which such discussions must be based."[31] The reactions of a speaker's colleagues should be ascertained, but this is different from asking a student to give an oral criticism of the speech. Possibly students, as a listening exercise, can write reports, or even complete rating scales, but these should be employed only as a way of *helping* the instructor construct a criticism. Further, to require students actively to take notes while another student is making a speech is to make the communication situation in the classroom unnecessarily artificial. Note-taking by the students may seriously distract the speaker.[32] Student criticisms within the first course, as it is presently and popularly taught, seem academically questionable.

Neither is the oral criticism of a speech the oral counterpart or justification of the marks indicated on a rating scale. Rating scales do not constitute in themselves a criticism because they do not say anything. Even if rating scales could be used to their ultimate worth, the marks on the written page must still be interpreted by a student and

---

[28]Robert G. Gunderson, "Teaching Critical Thinking," *The Speech Teacher,* X (March, 1961), pp. 102-103.

[29]H. L. Ewbank, Jr., "On the Ethics of Teaching Speech Content," *Central States Speech Journal,* VIII (Fall, 1956), pp. 23-25.

[30]"New Methods of Evaluating Instruction and Student Achievement in a Speech Class," in "A Symposium on Evaluation, Criticism, and Grading," *The Speech Teacher,* IX (January, 1960), pp. 16-19.

[31]"The Criticism of Speeches," p. 59.

[32]I am not unmindful of the favorable report on the "Blue Book Criticism" at the University of Michigan. See Herbert W. Hildebrandt and Walter W. Stevens, "Blue Book Criticisms at Michigan," in "A Symposium on Evaluation, Criticism, and Grading," *The Speech Teacher,* IX (January, 1960), pp. 20-22.

applied to his own speaking. While rating scales are often used because they are considered to be a clear and objective tool, research indicates that the rating scale is no more objective than oral criticism. For example, Miller pinpoints the problem with rating scales in these words:

> I believe that the reliability and validity of speech ratings often suffer because of ambiguity and uncertainty regarding what we are about. Here, the need for clear and precise specification of behavioral objectives becomes apparent. . . . Such statements as "We wish to improve voice and articulation skills" or "We wish to develop the student's ability to evaluate evidence critically" are so broad as to be of limited value. Specifically, *what* changes in voice patterns do we wish to engender, *what* behaviors must a student master to evaluate evidence critically, and *how* can we measure appropriate changes in these behaviors.[33]

The apparent concreteness of rating scales may lead us to the conclusion that they engender objectivity. But as Miller observes, "Psychological positions such as learning theory and balance theory suggest that objectivity is more a utopian ideal than a practical possibility."[34] The problems of objectivity have been studied also by Bostrom, and his conclusions support Miller's.[35] The present writer's view is that unless rating scales are clearly designed to supplement an oral criticism, and both then are designed for a specific set of criteria of a specific assignment, either *or* both may be useless.

Rating scales may in fact only compound the possible pedagogical felony committed in the oral criticism. They may encourage scant oral criticism and cause the critic to adapt less to the individual speaker. Too much attention to rating scales can obscure the basic arm of criticism and may detract from, if not altogether destroy, the learning situation in the speech classroom.

Some criticisms should be given immediately after the student speaks or just before the class meeting ends. As Byers in his paper on "Speech and the Principles of Training" observes, "Pupils learn best when they have immediate and valid knowledge of success or failure." Byers also reminds us that the teacher in the face of a difficult, quick evaluation often is tempted to take the easiest course, i.e., comment on nonessentials. What the student needs, says Byers, is "a bold evaluation."[36]

---

[33]Gerald R. Miller, "Agreement and the Ground for It: Persistent Problems in Speech Rating," *The Speech Teacher*, XIII (November, 1964), p. 261.

[34]*Ibid.*, p. 260.

[35]Robert N. Bostrom, "Dogmatism, Rigidity, and Rating Behavior," *The Speech Teacher*, XIII (November, 1964), pp. 283-287.

[36]Pp. 139-140.

To follow up an oral criticism presented in the class with written observations which can be studied by the student at greater length and which may be more exhaustive than the oral comments is a way of seeking message reinforcement. The written comments on the day of the speech may in turn be strengthened by written comments prepared later, after the instructor has returned to his office and had a chance to think on the speech, the reactions of the audience, and the reactions of the speaker to the reactions of the audience and critic. Criticisms might profitably be offered at the end of the hour as opposed to commenting only after each speech, a time-consuming and eventually monotonous routine. Criticisms after all students have completed one assignment are helpful. The instructor can see the work of the entire class in perspective, and the student has the opportunity to judge his execution of the assignment against the speechmaking of his colleagues. Further, as Braden has observed, "Obviously, extended discussion of a given performance is impossible in a large class." Also, the teacher may sense that certain aspects of the students' speechmaking can more profitably be discussed in private.[37]

In summary, much research is still needed on the subject of criticism of student speeches. The possible relationships between techniques of criticism and modification of speech behavior need to be explored. Speech instructors need to know what modifications stay with the student in his speechmaking long after he graduates. Long-range research on the oral communication behavior of those who have had a basic speech course, compared with those who have not had such a course, is sorely needed. Until such time as evidence on this point is forthcoming, speech instructors may remind themselves gloomily, as Becker has done, that

> as a matter of fact, experimental studies to date, especially among college students, provide little evidence that students in speech or composition courses improve *much* more at communicating than students receiving college instruction without a speech or writing course.[38]

In the criticism of student speeches is found the pivotal point of potential advancement from theory to practice, the point at which undesirable speech habits are changed or merely reinforced. Karl Wallace, Donald Smith, and Andrew Weaver in their statement recently prepared for the Speech Association of America have said:

---

[37]Waldo W. Braden, "Teaching Through Criticism," in *Speech Methods and Resources,* ed. Waldo W. Braden (New York, 1961), p. 405.
[38]Becker, p. 31.

The field of speech is still committed to the ideal of the citizen-speaker first set up by the Roman schools, the ideal of the good man speaking well.

In the education of such a man, knowledge and skill meld inextricably. Teachers in their instruction and research recognize this fact. Characteristically, beginning courses in school and college involve students both in the study *of* speech behavior and in directed practice *in* speaking, knowledge serving to shape attitudes and judgment, practice serving to develop effectiveness.[39]

---

[39]"The Field of Speech: Its Purposes and Scope in Education (S.A.A. Committee on the Nature of the Field of Speech)," *The Speech Teacher*, XII (November, 1963), p. 333.

Speech Criticism and Evaluation as Communication

PAUL D. HOLTZMAN

"I can understand why we should attend when the senior professor is teaching. But do we *have* to sit and listen to all those speeches?" This was spoken early in his career by an intern-instructor who now says he knows better. It points to two problems for the beginning teacher that "older heads" may have forgotten about:

1. What is the function of speech criticism and how important is it?
2. What does a speech "grade" mean and how important is it?

From someone who has shared these confusions and grown older with them, this paper is addressed to a point of view of the communicative role of the teacher in dealing with these questions in the basic college course in effective speaking.

The behavior of a speech teacher in the basic course is, presumably, communicative behavior. It *must*, therefore, have a specific desired response (purpose) and everything else (at least!) that is required of the student in his speaking. With this in mind it is interesting to consider the specific responses desired by the teacher in two of his several roles: those of critic and evaluator.

THE AIM OF CRITICISM

The critic of a speech has one primary question to answer: "What can I say (or write or do) that will result in this student's improving his communicative ability?"

Note that this is a very different question from, "What did he do poorly?" or, "What did he do well?" If the teacher is not guided by primary consideration of the (expected) response of the student, how can he expect his student to be guided primarily by consideration of the (expected) response of his audience? Note, too, that this does not mean that answers to the question of "goodness" and "poorness" are forbidden—it's a matter of *selection* of materials and their organization and delivery.

Actually, the critic may look for the things that his student did well and comment on them—*for a purpose*: to have him feel some satisfaction with himself and with it a mixture of eagerness and confidence. If the

From *The Speech Teacher*, vol. IX, no. 1 (January, 1960). Reprinted by permission.

comments are "public" they may have the additional purpose of teaching others by example. Likewise the critic may speak (or write) about a "flaw" in organization, selection of materials, etc.—*for a purpose*: to have the student (moved by that eagerness and confidence) focus on improving some particular aspect of his communicative behavior.

THE FOCUS OF CRITICISM

The "desired response," then, is the primary guide for the critic in this (as in all) communication. Another important criterion—from his own field again—is that to be effective, a piece of communication must focus on a "significant, single idea."[1] The student speaker—like anyone learning a new, complex behavior—can concentrate on only one thing at a time. A novice golfer, for instance, is doomed by the amateur-pro who insists: "keep your head down, remember to keep your left arm straight, don't forget to follow through, shift your weight, swing your hips, etc., etc." (This is the best way to avoid becoming a golf-widow— or to force a husband into the role of condemned widower!) Likewise the novice communicative speaker in the basic course may be doomed by the burden of: "gesture meaningfully, maintain eye-contact, support each point, remember to adapt to your audience in the introduction, don't run overtime, don't fidget, have vocal variety, organize clearly, etc., etc." Any human being, confronted with so many demands at once, will do one of two things. He will try to keep all of these things in consciousness, become frustrated, and give up. Or he will (more intelligently!) give up without trying. Criticism, then, besides having a specific desired response, must have a focus on one main idea.

THE PROGRESSION OF CRITICISM

This suggests immediately a third principle: a general *scheme* for criticism through a semester in the basic course. The student-speaker should be required to learn only so much per speaking experience. The critic should begin with a few fundamental "demands" or expectations and add one or two for each successive speaking experience. That is, he may gain from the student an understanding in successive pieces of communication (teaching) of a prescribed method of preparation, of the purpose on the first "formal" talk, of the concept of support. For the next assignment he may add to his expectations more adaptation to the audience, development of a particular kind of support, etc.

[1] Speech Association of the Eastern States, "Code for Contests in Public Speaking," *Today's Speech*, IV, 4, November, 1956, pp. 29-31.

It should be noted that this concept is complicated by the general practice we share of introducing in successive speaking experiences different kinds (*i.e.*, purposes) of talking. This in itself adds to the new concepts that students must make a part of their nervous systems by way of response to criticism and other teaching.

A third principle, then, is that criticism should be progressive. That is, its desired response must be the development by the student speaker of a single, significant concept which is the *next logical step* in his improvement as a communicative speaker.

CRITICISM PROCEDURES

In dealing with specific techniques for putting these three prime principles in practice, there are a number of available, varying procedures. This variation is inevitable because critics are human beings who, presumably, have found (or are seeking) their own more or less unique most effective modes of communication. The *aims*, however, must not vary any more than the published aims of the course! A few comments on varying techniques or procedures may shed some further light on the application of the prime principles.

ORAL CRITICISM

One teacher may offer spoken criticism after each speech. He has a responsibility of speaking with an effectiveness that is beyond the skills of many experts. He must motivate the student (praise?) to respond in his next talk to the criticism. This means it must be concrete, singular (though supported by numerous examples), and the most important next concept of behavior for the individual student to master. The temptation of the new teacher may be to list uncommunicatively "good points" and "weaknesses." Such may be pertinent, but their chances of communicating—of gaining a specific response—are at best next to nil. Often, too, there is a temptation to criticize by enumerating the most *easily* spotted weakness, *i.e.*, distracting behavior in delivery. But one of the best ways to reduce the probability of teaching communicative speaking as a process of obtaining a desired response is to force the student speaker to focus on the minutiae of his bodily behavior. Many youngsters have learned all the techniques for batting a baseball but have failed to hit until a wise teacher said, "Son, just keep your eye on the ball." The student speaker must, through criticism, be reminded to keep his eye on the ball. Like his critic, he will develop his own style. It may be added, to squeeze more from the analogy, that the successful batter plays one pitch at a time!

Another teacher may offer spoken criticism after the several talks scheduled for one occasion. He will adapt his responses to these talks as noted above and may also draw from the total experience—from the several talks—a single, significant idea to which he will seek a response from the whole class. In other words his teaching will be a piece of communication based upon a set of examples still within the memories of his students.

Still another teacher will elicit spoken criticisms from one or more students. What has been said for the teacher-critic is no different for the student-critic. However, he probably has a different concern and hence a different purpose. At the same time a peer-opinion may carry more weight—be more effective—than a similar instructor-opinion. (An instructor justly proud of his rapport with students might successfully deny this!) In any case the "presiding critic" (instructor) must adapt the student comments by way of further example, emphasis and edited summary to the *aims* of the critic cited above. To do less is to deny the importance of any training whatsoever for teachers of speech!

WRITTEN CRITICISM

Another technique is the writing of the critique. This takes varying forms—from a prepublished check-list to a series of comments on a blank sheet of paper. If the check-list is to meet standards cited here, it will "grow" with each speaking assignment. Or responses to *early* talks will not be noted on all items. The comments checked may be carefully developed as the best way to word-for-communication the next step in improvement or praise for concepts well handled. On the other hand they cannot be individual.

Other "structured" critique forms may have spaces for the instructor's comments on specific aspects of speech. One example is: "Substance, Organization, Style, Bodily Expression, Voice and Diction, Personal Qualities," and, "General Comments," with appropriate subheadings under each.[2] Another (for a talk to inform) is: "Introduction, Body, Conclusion," and, "Delivery," with appropriate questions in each category ("Did the opening catch audience attention?" "Was the audience motivated to want to learn?" etc.)[3]

The blank critique sheet offers some advantages of individual treatment and the disadvantage that it may fail to alert the critic to watch for specific behavior.

---

[2]Robert T. Oliver, Ed., *Effective Speech Notebook*, Rev. 1958, Syracuse University Press, p. 7.

[3]Milton Dickens, *Speech: Dynamic Communication,* Harcourt Brace and Company (New York: 1954), pp. 429-30.

More important than the form, however, is the content and use. The written criticism may also tempt the critic to weaken his communication by listing rather than focusing and/or by describing rather than suggesting. But assuming the written criticism to have aim and focus, it has the advantage of ready reference for the student who may not remember the next day what the professor *said* after the talk.

Instructors need not and do not necessarily rely upon only one of these procedures. They are combined in various ways at various times. This instructor, like many others, most frequently relies upon the "blank critique sheet" for individually focused criticism and the spoken-after-all-talks criticism to focus on a concept of importance to the entire class. For instance, one talk to inform may stand out from the others on a given day as the only one that has materials adapted to the audience. This sets up an opportunity to *teach* audience adaptation based upon the actual responses of the listeners. Similarly one talk to reinforce attitudes may be the only one exemplifying appropriate use of "vital appeals;" or there may be a comparison of talks to entertain that did and did not focus on a clear central idea, etc.

Before leaving this concern with criticism to consider evaluation of student speaking, mention should be made of another common practice that aids in *both* criticism and evaluation.

THE QUESTION PERIOD

Presumably the student speaker is sincerely concerned with obtaining a particular specific response from his classmates. And his classmates constitute a very real audience—not a pretended one. That audience, therefore, can be of great assistance in teaching the speaker, by example, his next area of focus if there is a *question period*. Listeners' questions can sometimes best point up critical errors of the speaker: errors of motive, of ambiguity, of organizational confusion, etc. A talk supposedly designed to gain understanding (inform) may stem from a primary motivation to persuade—a motivation of which the student is not aware, of course. This will often elicit revealing questions of value rather than fact. Or an idea may be developed by a student speaker, he thinks, most clearly only to be subjected to questions which reveal anything but clarity in the minds of the listeners.

An alert critic can make use of the responses that show themselves in short discussion periods. He has clear, real, personal examples for the speaker to help him understand better what created those responses. At the same time, the question-discussion period provides the teacher with some clues to the evaluation of the speaker's effectiveness.

EVALUATION

There is some confusion abroad and at the same time some clear-cut battle lines drawn in answer to the question, "What does the instructor evaluate when he assigns a grade or score to the speaker for his efforts?" A case can even be made for not making the grade represent the evaluation at all! One of this writer's futile dreams is of teaching a semester of the basic course in which only "A's" are awarded for each speech effort. Other things being equal—including purposeful, focused criticism —it seems inevitable that students so encouraged would do at least slightly better. The only deterrent, of course, is the lack of an impregnable office or fortress to withstand the onslaughts of hostile violence when the students receive appropriate ("truly" evaluative) course grades at semester's end.

To return to reality, it is clear to those in the Speech profession, at least, that there are varying concepts of a "good" speech and a "bad" speech. If a speech is to be judged solely on its effectiveness (*i.e.*, Did it achieve the speaker's desired result?) we must classify without reservation Adolf Hitler as a "good" speaker and Adlai Stevenson as a "bad" one. Or if a speech is to be judged solely on its merits as an example of the "Art of Speaking," we must classify without reservation Woodrow Wilson in his vain efforts to get U. S. participation in the League of Nations as a "good" speaker and Huey Long in his successful political career as a "bad" speaker.

Assuming speaker sincerity and honesty—which in the long run at least will have an effect on both the effectiveness and the artfulness of the speaker—which criterion shall guide the evaluation of student speeches? Most of our colleagues will answer, "both," with varying emphasis on one or the other. A few insist upon one *or* the other as the only appropriate criterion. Obviously the Hitlers, Stevensons, Wilsons and Longs would have to choose their instructors carefully as a matter of academic life ("A") or death ("F").

But there are two important facts—glaring yet often overlooked— that must be considered in dealing with speech evaluation in the basic course. One is that the two criteria—effectiveness and artfulness—are inseparable in the dynamics of human communication. The other is that like other instructors, surely, this writer has not had among the last 2,000 students in the basic course a single Hitler, Stevenson, Wilson or Long! Further, if there has been one among them, he didn't get that way in the basic course alone. To believe otherwise is to attribute to oneself the powers of angel or imp-of-Satin—depending upon which criterion one evaluates by.

If the teacher is going to narrow to manageable concepts (he teaches that this should be done); IF he is going to achieve from his students a concentration on gaining audience responses rather than on their own behavior as "performances" (he teaches that this should be done); and IF the teacher believes that his "art" generally contributes to the effectiveness of the honest, sincere speaker (he teaches that this is so), then may he not safely concentrate his evaluation on how successfully the student focuses on and achieves desired results?

In short: the *fundamental* concept of communication is, in itself, enough to hope to achieve—with all of the behavior which stems from its adoption—in the *fundamental* course. Sometimes our colleagues seem to save nothing for the advanced courses. They begin again at the next level with "Choose a topic, NARROW the topic . . . etc." At the first level, evaluation may best be *narrowed* to speech effectiveness.

If the point is made—and that may be too much to expect of this particular piece of communication—it is something else again to implement it. And it is far more difficult to use as a criterion than to talk or write about.

EVALUATING SPEECH EFFECTIVENESS

How can one judge effectiveness as a letter grade, a percentage, or on a rating scale of any number? The mere question makes one want to crawl back off the limb and stick to easier measures—measures of what the *student-speaker* did rather than the seeming imponderable (let alone immeasurable) of what the *audience* did. This is obviously no place for the man who is secure only in the exclusive worship of the "tin god of objectivity." There are no finite calibrations on the speech evaluator's scale. And he must number among his God-given rights the freedom to err.

However, it is likewise no place for unstructured intuition, for the denial of objectivity, for the fickleness of chance or of mere "personality."

Somewhere between the computor in touch with every nerve cell of the listeners (which the hucksters seem to be striving for) and the flip of a coin (or five-sided solid) is a practical answer to the problem of judging effectiveness. It is a necessarily complex and many-sided answer. Here are some specifics—certainly not an exhaustive list—in which the evaluator:

1. Watches the audience during the talk generally for overt signs of interest, concern, agreement, etc.

2. Observes various members of the audience at specific times during the speech (introduction, summary of a point, etc.) for overt signs of response.
3. Is alert to clues particularly at the time that the speech ends and again at the time the question-period (if any) is over. (*Spontaneous* applause, cheering, "buzzing," *no* change in behavior, etc.)
4. Listens and watches for clues *during* the question-answer period. (He must know Speech and people well enough to interpret the meaning, for instance, of *no* questions following an informative talk. It could spell "A" or "F.")
5. Through brief quizzes, shift-of-opinion ballots and other such devices, tests knowledge or feelings or beliefs of the audience.
6. Combines criticism with a discussion of what the speech "did to" members of the audience.
7. Notes whether or not a desired action (if any) really results. (He checks to see who donated blood in response to that old perennial. He asks his class to give him carbon copies of any letters to Congressmen written at the behest of a speaker. He takes his roll-book to the performance of a Shakespearean troupe that his class has been urged to attend.
8. Sounds out knowledge, feelings or beliefs of members of the class during regular student conferences.
9. If this concentration is not entirely on the behavior of his student speaker, can rely to a large extent upon his own response to the speaker and his communication. His necessary objectivity will depend upon his awareness of the differences between himself and his student audience in attitudes, values, knowledge, experience, etc. But he should know if he has learned, been moved, or slightly shaken in his own beliefs, according to the speaker's purpose.
10. Over the years, tests some of these means against each other and develops gradually a dynamic, sensitive "gestalt" of empathy with the student audiences.
11. Etc.

Some of these means of developing sensitivity to the effectiveness of student speakers require a delay in announcement of the evaluation (grade). This may be mildly frustrating to the student but at the same time a most potent means of changing the students concept of communication from one of a stream of utterances to an understanding of the goal of achieving a specific audience response.

SUMMARY

In criticism and evaluation, then, the speech teacher as a communicator in the basic course must rely heavily upon his own primary concepts:

1. Effective communication is that which focuses on achieving a desired response.
2. The effective "piece" of communication has a narrowed focus on a single, significant idea.

Criticism must be a "piece" of communication aimed at encouraging the student to take the next important step in his improvement—and no more.

Evaluation must be a measure of the student's *concept* of communication *in practice*.

A Rationale for Grades

EUGENE E. WHITE

In recent months the nation's press has recorded that several college teachers have refused to grade their students. One instructor, dismissed because of his refusal to rank students on a comparative basis, claimed that "to grade students is, in a sense, to treat them like products in a meat market." According to the *New York Times,* he admitted that his grading policy represented "at least in part" a protest against the draft and the Vietnam war. More than one observer has suggested that a revolt against grades may be developing, especially among the younger segment of the faculty. In the speech field, however, the refusal to rank students upon a continuum from "A" to "F" is not a recent phenomenon, nor is it the exclusive proclivity of youthful instructors. During more than two decades of university teaching I have remarked at the number of instructors of mature years who rarely give grades lower than a "B"—not only in the elective beginning courses but also in compulsory courses which provide a cross section of students and even in "special sections" reserved for students psychologically unable to cope with the oral communicative experiences which constituted the normal course work.

In the hope of stimulating thinking, I propose in this essay to examine a limited area of the subject. I do not wish here to consider such matters as the merits or demerits of grades, the morality of employing academic rankings as a basis for deferments by Selective Service, or the charges that speech teachers and rhetoricians lack verifiable and consistent criteria by which to judge speakers. Although such topics may be relevant concerns, because of space limitations this essay is restricted to a consideration of grading the beginning classes in speech. The method of approach is to discuss certain views which I consider to be misconceptions.

Even when the subject has been thus constricted, the securing of meaningful answers is not easy. Furthermore, each answer seems to provoke new questions. Although the allusion is imperfect, the eradication of misconceptions is in a sense analogous to the second labor of Hercules. As the legend goes, each time Hercules cut off one of the heads of the Hydra, two immediately grew back. Hercules was able

From *The Speech Teacher,* vol. XVI, no. 4 (November, 1967). Reprinted by permission.

Eugene E. White (Ph.D., Louisiana State University, 1947) is Professor of Speech at Pennsylvania State University. Professor White is author of two widely used textbooks.

to slay the monster only after he discovered that the application of a burning bough to the wound would prevent the sprouting of new heads. It is perhaps reasonable to say that misconceptions concerning grading in the elementary courses can be lastingly removed only by the individual instructor's recognition of the assets and responsibilities which are intrinsic to the teaching of speech.

The first misconception is that grading is of little concern. Inasmuch as the beginning courses are the *primum mobile* of the speech field, what happens in those courses is a matter of genuine concern to the prestige, well-being, and even the security of the profession itself. To be informed and to be articulately involved in this matter is a responsibility which no speech person can legitimately avoid.

The second misconception is that the academic grader must kowtow before the truism that all men are mortals and, being mortals, lack divine infallibility of judgment. This is not to deny, of course, that man is fallible—particularly on subjective matters. Everyone knows, for instance, that the humanists have never been able to agree on the number of angels that can dance on the head of a pin or, for that matter, how a camel can pass through the eye of a needle. One could go further than this, however, and state as relevant to the point: we can be absolutely sure of very little in this life, including the scientific conclusions offered by those who work with slide rules, computers, rats, test tubes, or 100 per cent oxygen. First let us look fleetingly at one example of scientific operational procedures on which men's lives depended. The cabin of the spacecraft for Apollo mission 204 was approved by NASA scientists, but it was transformed into an oven— according to the findings of the Review Board—because of "faulty spacecraft design and construction." Now let us turn to the ultimate in scientific certitude, the scientific principles which govern man and his pure research. As an undergraduate I learned that DNA is *the* key to the genetic code. Since that time, thousands of scientists have bowed over their test tubes, worshipping this dogma. So, I received a shock several months ago when I came across a newly published book by Barry Commoner, Chairman of the Botany Department of Washington University. In his book, *Science and Survival*, Dr. Commoner directs critical attention to "weaknesses" in the DNA theory. Commoner believes that the scientific community has lacked sound judgment in accepting and teaching so uncritically the DNA theory. His view is substantially reinforced by Nobel prize winner John Kendrew in his *The Thread of Life* and by Lancelot Law Whyte in his *Internal Factors in Evolution*. Two other scientific dogmas that I accepted as gospel are that the virus is the most rudimentary form of life and that nucleic acids are absolutely necessary to life. Recently, however, the *London Sunday Times* reported that English scientists "have accumulated massive and convincing evidence" that "a completely new kind of agent exists," one which is " 'alive' in the sense that it can reproduce itself" and which "is even smaller and more primitive than the tiniest virus." Furthermore, according to the *Times,* experiments by the English scientists "apparently prove" that this new agent "contains no nucleic acids."

If, for the sake of argument, all of this is accepted as being substantially true to fact, what does it mean to the academic grader? Although some scientific principles may be suspect, scientific research and theorizing go on—as indeed they must if we are to survive. Although the Apollo tragedy took the lives of three of our most talented astronauts, the space program continues—albeit more cautiously, with a greater awareness of the fallibility of science, scientists, and the entire concept of quality controls. All three of the astronauts had stated publicly their recognition that because man is mortal his judgment is fallible and that because his judgment is fallible their own lives were in almost constant jeopardy. Such dangers must be accepted as calculated risks, the astronauts had pointed out; inevitable mistakes, even tragic ones, should be accepted as a necessary consequent of getting the job done.

The first fact—that we cannot feel absolutely certain even about some cherished scientific theories and cannot expect complete accuracy in subjective judgments—does not preclude this second fact: life is one value judgment after another. We cannot escape the necessity of making decisions based upon a discrimination among good, better, best, and unsatisfactory. We cannot with impunity ignore academic requirements that for each course each student must be assigned a grade as an indication of his performance. Making value judgments is an unavoidable necessity of life. Grading is a fact of life. We must do the best we can with the means at our disposal. I shall try to demonstrate that the means at our disposal are not inconsequential.

This brings us to the third misconception: in comparison to other courses, grading in speech is much less reliable and much less indicative of student performance. Let us look at grading in the so-called content courses. Inasmuch as a particular content course may have an enrollment of 200 or 2,000 students, the instructor may never learn the names of his students. If the classroom is large, or if TV is employed, he may not even learn to recognize their faces. Of necessity in such courses, the student's grade is based primarily upon his scores on tests, frequently on only two or three objective tests. What are tests and what are they supposed to measure? Tests consist of a series of questions which are thought to represent in microcosm the much larger body of knowledge to which the student has been exposed during the term. The student's answers are supposed to indicate with reasonable accuracy the scope and dimensions of his knowledge. Inasmuch as the test scores of one student can be compared with mathematical reliability to the scores of other students, it is easy to assume that the test itself is similarly reliable in estimating what the student has learned. What does the word "learned" mean? According to neurophysiologist Patrick D. Wall of the Massachusetts Institute of Technology, in regard to the processes by which the brain thinks, perceives, and remembers, "we are beginning at zero. We don't even know how to ask the right questions." Although much research has been accomplished since Wall made this observation in the spring of 1964, there is no reason to question his conclusion: "What goes on between our ears is the biggest gap in man's knowledge today." What does the word "memory" mean? About a decade ago scientists proposed that, similarly as the information of heredity is coded and stored in a cell's DNA, the information of memory may be stored in a neuron's RNA. About three years ago Dr. W. Ross Adey of the brain research institute of the University of California at Los Angeles suggested that the ridge of the brain called the hippocampus may provide the key to memory. According to Dr. Ross, the hippocampus may serve the functions of approving what information is to be stored, determining how and where the information is to be filed in other brain structures, and deciding when it is to be recalled. Although other theories have been propounded and much investigation is now being conducted, science has not explained how thinking occurs or how information is stored or retrieved. Despite this, some persons assume that a sample test will reflect accurately a student's thinking—whatever thinking is—and his memories—whatever memory is.

Now, what kind of thinking and what kind of memories are estimated by a test? Does a single test, or all the tests taken by a student during college, provide a verifiable and consistent set of criteria by which to evaluate the "total" student in terms of the purpose of higher education? (Inasmuch as critics do not agree on the "purpose," perhaps such a disagreement of basic goals may in itself jar off balance any attempt at "reliable" measurements of student performance. Nevertheless, to provide some basis for answering this question, perhaps we can accept as being a reasonable estimate of the aim of higher education the view expressed by Kenneth Eble in his *A Perfect Education*: "I would define its over-all task as helping the student develop a mind, heart, and life of his own.") Does a test estimate what will be remembered by a particular student in two weeks or two years? Does it distinguish between over-learning and cram-learning? Does it esti- mate the associations made by the student? The effect which his new knowledge and understanding has already made, and will make, upon his thinking, his values, his attitudes toward life and toward others? Does the examination procedure fully account for the test-taking ability of the student? The state of his physical and emotional health at the time? Whether he tenses up waiting for the test to begin? Whether he emotionalizes his response to the test situation so that his performance is "minimalized"? Whether previous unfortunate experiences with the instructor or the subject have conditioned him to do poorly?

In order to "maximalize" student individuality in the grading process, a number of well-intended reforms have been introduced in some con- tent courses. Perhaps the following examples are fairly representative of such efforts. In one class of huge enrollment in which the student's grade depends upon his scores on two examinations, the class for test purposes is divided into sections; each section takes an examination which has been prepared by a graduate assistant; each of the graduate assistants attends the lectures in the course and prepares and corrects an all-essay test which is based upon his notes of the lectures and upon the text. In one content course of limited enrollment, the student's grade is based completely upon the answers to three take-home tests, each of which consists of a single question with the answer limited to 1,500 words. With growing frequency content courses employ the "personalization" of term reports or "in-term" essays as important bases for determining grades. The numerous problems involved in establishing the "reliability" of grades ascertained by the methods described above are obvious. Space permits the mention of only one. This spring a student was graduated from a major university and granted admission to one of the most distinguished law schools in the country. During his undergraduate career this young man, like an unknown number of other talented students, subsidized his education by writing reports for others. Although over the years he developed skill in adjusting the quality of his writing to the academic image of his customers, a few months before his graduation he committed an almost fatal blunder. One of his "reports" was so distinctly superior to the intellectual level of his freshman client that the teacher, sensing the imposture, failed the student for the semester's work. If the instructor had gone one step further and turned the matter over to the university honor council, the freshman would have "blown the whistle" on the ghost writer—or so he told his friends.

In contrast to some other courses, the intimate speech course may provide a more realistic opportunity for the professor to judge the performance of the student. Instead of two or three test grades, the speech instructor has a sweeping area of opportunities for judgment. As a basis for estimating the student's communicative ability, the instructor can judge the student's speaking on a potentially wide continuum of speaking assignments. As a basis for estimating the student's grasp of rhetorical principles, the instructor can judge the student's written, or oral, response in a term report, in a final examination, and in outside-class assignments. An important additional basis for estimating the student's speaking ability and his grasp of principles is the unexcelled opportunity to test daily his performance in the class sharing, which can follow each classroom speech.

There is much reason for the speech instructor to approach the task of evaluating student performance with apprehension—for he is less than God. Nevertheless, there is no reason for him to feel that his judgment is necessarily inferior to the judgment rendered by an instructor of a different course.

The fourth misconception is that the process of grading intrudes between the student and his acquisition of speech skills. That this sometimes occurs, I do not doubt. That it must occur, I stoutly deny. Let me state more tersely than I should like certain principles which may facilitate the proper climate for grading.

1. By his own attitude and manner, the instructor should help to place grades in the proper perspective as being a fact of life, but not the end of the course.
2. The instructor should evidence a sympathetic and understanding attitude. He should establish himself as being genuinely interested in, and responsive to, the students.
3. The instructor should be fair. For instance, if one of his assignments is ambiguous or unintentionally stringent, he should be willing to receive and act reasonably upon student protests.
4. The instructor should be consistent. Even if absolute consistency were possible, it would perhaps be undesirable. Nevertheless, the student has a right to know that he is being rated according to a basically consistent policy in grading. He should understand what is expected of him and what standards of measurement will be employed; if standards change during the course, he should be told why and in what manner they have been altered.
5. The instructor should be firm. Anarchy in the classroom does not serve to prepare the student to live constructively in a society which

requires its members to adhere to acceptable norms of behavior. If an instructor's attempts to please and placate go beyond reasonable bonds, he performs a disservice to his students.

The last misconception is that grading is the exclusive prerogative of the individual instructor. The point at which individual freedom stops and license begins is, of course, debatable. I wish merely to suggest here that any unilateral policy of grading by any individual, or individuals, which is at striking variance from the policies of the institution itself—unless the circumstances are exceptional—is not in the best interest of the speech profession.

In order to remove the misconceptions concerning grade, the individual instructor must recognize the assets and responsibilities which are intrinsic to the teaching of speech. To promote this recognition I have attempted to demonstrate that grading in the elementary course is a matter of considerable significance, that the grader should not be intimidated by the fallibility of subjective judgments, that the speech instructor should not consider that his judgments are necessarily less valid than those of an instructor in a different area, that the process of grading need not intrude between the student and his acquisition of speech skills, and that grading in the beginning course is not the exclusive prerogative of the individual instructor.

The Measurement of Speech in the Classroom

JACK DOUGLAS

A few years ago I was asked to give a paper at a convention of the Speech Association of America on "standardized instruments of speech measurement." The chairman of the section wrote to me, "There has been great demand for a talk about speech tests and the whole question of evaluation is one of great concern to the high school people."

The topic puzzled me because I had taught for many years without encountering any "standardized tests of speech measurement." I thereupon began an extensive search through the standard indices of the speech, psychology, and education journals to find what tests were available.

The search turned up only a few published tests of speech abilities which claimed validation upon a sizable group of subjects. These few tests are limited by the authors' own admission in their comprehensiveness and their usefulness in measuring speech ability or achievement. A list of those published will be found at the end of this article.

The measurement of learning is of great concern to any good teacher of speech, but it is fortunate, in an important sense, that standardized tests in speech are, by and large, not available.

The teacher's desire for such tests is understandable. If she had them, grading and testing would be much easier. She could take copies from the shelf, distribute them to students, send the score sheets to the IBM office for tabulating, and then hand the student a "reliable" measurement of his speaking achievement—all with no difficult and uncomfortable decisions for the teacher to make at all. Other teachers do it—why can't we?

Speech teachers are not alone in their wishing for standardized measurements of speech performance. Were one to develop a method of securing such measurements validly, reliably, and practically, he would

From *The Speech Teacher,* vol. VII no. 4 (November, 1958), pp. 309-319. Reprinted by permission.

The author has been very active professionally in trying to solve many of the problems of speech education facing high school and college teachers. The problem of testing and evaluating speech performance has been one of those to which he has devoted considerable time. He presents in this article a practical synthesis of much of his work. As Associate Professor of Speech at the University of Oklahoma, he has been concerned with teaching of the basic course, as well as with secondary school speech programs in the state. During the present year he is on leave and is teaching at the University of Texas. He was awarded the A.B. degree at the University of Oklahoma (1936) and received his M.A. (1941) and Ph.D. (1951) from Northwestern University.

become a renowned scholar and the broadcasting advertisers, among others, would make him wealthy. Congress might make the method top secret, available only to the Voice of America which might use it to shoot holes in the Iron Curtain.

As for the speech teachers, we could demonstrate clearly to ourselves and to administrators, colleagues, and students just what we are accomplishing in our speech instruction. We would be able to test our teaching, content and method, until we could eliminate all but effective, sure-fire teaching. And why not? It was E. L. Thorndike who said, "Everything that exists, exists in some quantity, and can be measured."

It is a beautiful dream. The vision of the rewards that would come to one who developed highly valid and reliable measures of speech performance should be enough to lure a great many more bright young graduate students than we now have into the pursuit of this vision.

Instead, the vision tempts us into short cuts. We feel envious of the mathematics or science teacher who so confidently grades his students by numbers and percentages and the bell-shaped normal curve. Such methods save much time and make the teacher feel more secure in his judgments.

And so it is these days that we come to worship blindly the practice of quantitative measurement. Many are they who will listen respectfully, if vacuously, to anyone who recites numbers or statistics. Such a speaker bears the shibboleth of an "expert." The unfamiliarity of large proportions of our society with mathematical concepts, together with the false respect that accompanies such unfamiliarity, makes a happy hunting ground for him who discourses learnedly about statistical processes and mathematical laws.

Persons trained only or primarily in the arts are peculiarly susceptible to such blind respect. Being ignorant of quantitative processes, they are easily misled. Before we worship the quantitative, we had better examine it more closely (even though embodied, possibly, in that rising new cultural image, the mathematician or physical scientist).

Closer examination may reveal a specious "accuracy" often (not always) contained in the quantitative expression. The appearance of accuracy in statistics and figures often traps us into dogmatic or absolute judgments. It was Albert Einstein who authored the statement, "Insofar as mathematics is certain, it does not represent reality; and insofar as mathematics represents reality, it is not certain." Now if Einstein felt that his mathematics did not represent reality in an absolute sense, what should be our attitude toward our quantitative measurements of student performance?

Even in the physical sciences, the location of absolute zero and the equivalence among the units of measurement are sometimes uncertain;

while in our measurements of human behavior we seldom indeed know where zero is or the degree of fluctuation in our units of measurement.

This is not to deprecate the importance of measurement—quite the contrary. The problems in speech testing are not insurmountable, and the quest must never be abandoned. Significant progress has been made, even greater progress will be made, and the alert teacher will keep himself abreast of the flow.

Sound measurement is the means to a firmer grasp of truth, to a clearer perception of the reality in speech behavior. Careful measurement is the means of knowing what we are doing and thereby achieving better results in teaching.

Thorndike's dictum may be true for the long run, but for today it is clear that there are many important aspects of speech which we cannot now measure quantitatively except for experimental purposes.

May I call another witness?

> Many teachers think that measurement in education can be accomplished only through the use of tests, and they think that tests are exclusively paper-and-pencil instruments. Within such a frame of reference, a serious question arises as to whether or not changes in behavior which are the ultimate goal of speech instruction can be measured at all. Certainly, no paper-and-pencil test of information, attitude, skill in applying data, and so on, can be regarded as a very exact measure of the speaking proficiency of any individual. . . . Some such tests have been developed which will predict reasonably well the speaking proficiency of groups of students. Perhaps the *Knower Speech Attitude Scale and Experience Inventory* is the best known of such instruments.[1]

. . . .

> There is no paper-and-pencil test, or laboratory instrument, known today which will measure, either directly or indirectly, the effectiveness of the total act of speech, or the sum of an individual's skills in speaking.[2]

Let us suppose for a moment that there were indeed such a "laboratory instrument" as Weaver, Borchers, and Smith refer to. Imagine, if you will, a gleaming, complicated, impressive machine mounted in your classroom—a combination of a sound movie camera, a speech and gesture analyzer, and an electronic computer, all in one. Let us suppose that it focuses its glaring camera eye upon John B. as he delivers his assigned speech for the day.

As John finishes his speech, the camera shuts itself off, the analyser kicks in, lights flash, gears whir, and triumphantly the machine gurgitates an IBM card with John's score notched neatly in the margin.

---

[1]Weaver, Borchers, and Smith, *The Teaching of Speech* (New York: Prentice-Hall, 1952), p. 524.
[2]*Ibid.,* p. 529.

Further, the machine has stored the score in its memory where it will be available for averaging all the student's grades at the end of the semester. So, throw away your roll book, and after delivering your lecture and making your assignment, you the teacher won't be needed either—just someone to keep order and a man to keep the machine running.

Without such a machine, however, we must fall back on the sometimes poor and pitiful, sometimes penetrating and profound, judgment of the speech teacher, e.g., the following actual record from a teacher's notebook:

> John, as usual, had some ideas of his own about an uncommon subject. His conclusions appeared carefully drawn from an extensive amount of documented data. The structure of the speech was firm and clear and inherent in the subject although yielding little to the audiences's unfamiliarity. The language was cogent and even, in spots, vivid with fresh imagery. The trouble seems to lie in the delivery, but perhaps more likely in attitudes. John seems inordinately shy, inhibited, hesitant. He never quite lets go. He watches the audience warily as if fearful they are not listening to him. In a talk with him yesterday John told me that he couldn't talk plainly when he started to school. He had lived a rather isolated childhood as the oldest child with a mother who was apparently a very quiet and undemonstrative woman. A first grade teacher worked with him after school till his speech became understandable to the other children. John is very grade-conscious; also, very firm in his convictions and devoted to his loyalties, but he never raises his voice. He doesn't take part much in social activities. Grade: B.

Until the miraculous machine is put on the market, the teacher, the parent, the prospective employer, and John himself will have to depend upon such frail human judgment as this. Even P. M. (post machine) we shall have to depend upon human judgment since machines solve problems by equations fed into it by human beings.

Our best hope, then, lies in the teacher's understanding of the nature of measurement and out of that understanding improving her frail human judgment. The remainder of this article is devoted, therefore, to a summary reminder of some basic principles of measurement and some suggestions for its improvement in evaluating speeches.

NATURE OF MEASUREMENT

It must be recalled, first, that all measurement is a kind of observation. All the scientists' instruments, from the ruler to the electronic microscope, are simply means of extending, making more exact and precise, the evidence of his senses. Even the beloved paper-and-pencil test is only a means of pulling from the student certain data we wish to observe and getting it on record for mathematical treatment or for more extended observation.

Every observation, as Carmichael said, is the product of the observed and the observer (including the observer's methods). Every observation, and therefore every measurement, has error in it. It is more important to know what kind of error the measurement has and its probable extent than it is to try to eliminate the error because the first is possible, the second is not. We cannot eliminate error, but we must know where it lies.

Every score, or observation, is based on a sample. We never observe all of a student's speech behavior nor do we observe it under all conditions. Every paper test, of course, selects from all the items that might be asked. We *assume* that the student's response to all the other questions which *might* have been asked, or the student's speech behavior under all the other conditions which he *might* experience, is similar to the responses or behavior we *did* observe. This assumption is always partly true and partly false, true in one degree or another, depending on the representativeness or randomness of the sampling. Even with the soundly drawn sample there is error. The advantage of such a sample, however, is that it permits us to eliminate much error and to estimate the size of the remainder.

We do not, for example, expect a student's performance in an acting situation to tell us all we need to know about his performance in a public speaking situation. All scores, observations, judgments, grades, are, then, approximations—part of the score is due to the thing we are trying to measure and part of it is due to the observation or testing process itself. We should eliminate any effects of the measuring instrument we can, but since such effects cannot be eliminated entirely it is most important that we know what they are and allow for them in our interpretation.

This brings us to those old familiars, validity and reliability. Reliability, of course, refers to the consistency or dependability of a test score—with the amount of variation among repeated measurements. What is not ordinarily understood is that it is possible to achieve very high reliability with little or no validity. Such a measurement is worse than useless; it is misleading.

Josh Billings put it in the vernacular, "It's better to believe nothin' than to believe so much that ain't so." Reliability without validity is reminiscent of the old vaudeville story about the wife who was the most consistent woman her husband ever knew—she was mean all the time. It may take a little effort, but it is possible to be consistently, dependably, reliably wrong.

The most important question in measurement is that of validity: what are we actually measuring—just what is determining the scores, judgments, or observations we are getting; are we measuring what we suppose we are? If so, how exactly or fully are we measuring it? In the case of speech behavior we know, for example, that writing performance tells us something but not nearly enough about speech performance. Further, it must be remembered that a test may be quite valid for measuring one thing and worthless for measuring another, therefore, a test is never just valid, it must be valid *for some particular thing*. A teacher who cannot define clearly what it is she is teaching cannot be expected to devise an accurate measurement of it.

Another essential requirement for good testing, which is seldom mentioned, is that of practicality. The test must be worth the time, effort, and expense in terms of the data it provides. We must be sure that valuable class time is not taken for measurements which are not eminently useful.

FUNCTIONS OF MEASUREMENT

It is next required that we consider the uses to which test results are to be put for otherwise a test cannot be properly devised or selected. The purposes which measurements may serve in education seem to be these: (1) diagnosis, (2) estimating achievement or progress, (3) guiding and motivating learning, and (4) research. It is not impossible for a test to serve all four purposes, but unlikely that it will serve any two equally well. This paper is not directly concerned with measurement in research which presents special problems and requires more stringent controls. There are many similarities, however, and knowledge of measurement contributes to both teaching and research. Such knowledge can lead the classroom teacher into interesting and profitable research projects which will contribute to effective teaching.

The third purpose, guiding and motivating learning, is seldom acknowledged for some strange reason, but every teacher knows it operates. Considerable research now indicates that the student's awareness of his achievement and progress, his strengths and weaknesses, contributes greatly to the efficiency of his learning. Knowledge of the results of his performance can clarify and intensify the student's goals, show where he is in relation to those goals, and often reveal the means of achieving them.

Diagnosis is possibly the most neglected of these uses and yet the most fruitful in its possibilities for improving teaching. Every speech performance by the student should provide a diagnosis of his needs and the abilities he can learn to capitalize upon. Each performance should also provide an evaluation of his present stage of development in specific factors and an estimate of how far he has progressed since the last performance.

OBJECTS OF MEASUREMENT

If those just listed be the functions of measurement, what now are the things to be measured? This is the central question of validity in another form. And this question, will ye, nill ye, takes us straight to the heart of the great debate in speech education which began with Socrates and the Sophists, if not earlier. The basis of our judgment of a speech performance depends inevitably on our values, our experience, what we have been taught or have yet failed to learn, our knowledge of the nature of speech behavior itself, our concept of the functions which speech serves among men.

The teacher's judgments will be affected by whichever of the four great historical criteria of rhetorical theory she subscribes to or the relative weight of each in her philosophical make-up: the truth, the results, the ethical, and the artistic (or methods) standards. Probably no speech scholar will deny some validity for each of these. The layman will put his money on results and so will many debate coaches. Most modern rhetoricians follow Aristotle in the primacy of the artistic standard. Many scientists and intellectuals would put truth first, and those who are concerned with the individual tend toward the ethical. Modern theory seems consistent in including each of these in some degree in the standards of speech criticism.[3]

There is a strong tendency among the untrained in speech to judge on the basis of the most obvious and easiest observed, and many teachers find it easier to comment on delivery, sometimes to the exclusion of more fundamental factors which, if set right, would eliminate many delivery faults. I have often heard Franklin Roosevelt's power described to his voice: yet specific analysis of the voice alone reveals little that was remarkable. The trained speech teacher develops the insight to see beneath the superficial to the fundamental factors below, and even to grasp the particular pattern of approach to communication which

---

[3]See, for example, McBurney and Wrage, *The Art of Good Speech* (New York: Prentice-Hall, 1953), pp. 21-52; also, Thonssen and Baird, *Speech Criticism* (New York: Ronald Press, 1948), pp. 331-464.

is unique with each individual and which probably explains most about
the effect he achieves.

Certainly, speech measurement must respond primarily to the total
performance or total effect as a unit. Nowhere is the Gestalt principle
more demonstrable than in speech behavior: the whole does not equal
the sum of the parts. Adding up scores on individual items to arrive
at a sum is a meaningless procedure, especially since we are not able to
weigh the individual items with any sound knowledge of the amount
they contribute to the whole.

The testing procedure must also provide for each of the major variable components which influence the total performance. Modern theory
and textbooks are fairly well agreed on these basic components; they
haven't changed greatly since Aristotle. They may be listed as speech
attitudes and adjustment, ideas, supporting materials, organization, style,
delivery; not everyone will agree on the exact listing and, what is
more important, the definition of these. The list will vary, somewhat,
and the emphasis will certainly change from one type of speech activity
to another. How far these may be further broken down depends on the
purposes of the testing and the clarity with which the measurement
process can keep them discrete and pure.

It is generally assumed that the object of measurement in a speech
class is a speech. If we are teaching speech behavior, however, not
simply pubilc speaking, we will want to measure the whole range of
the student's oral communication as it alternates between speaking and
listening, in formal and in informal situations. So we must also measure
his listening ability and development, including his critical and appreciative powers, and his skills in the various speech activities, provided,
of course, that we seek to teach these.

In summary, *we must measure, actually, whatever we seek to teach.*
The individual best equipped to prepare a test for a speech class is
the teacher of that class, the one who knows what the course is designed to do, what its objectives are, and just what the instruction has
covered.

TYPES OF MEASUREMENT

If the teacher is to prepare the speech test, then, from what types
may she select? Monroe lists these: (1) simple judgment, (2) controlled judgment, (3) audience response, (4) instrumental, (5) subjective report, and (6) subject matter.[4] Knower employs the following

---

[4]Alan H. Monroe, "Testing Speech Performance," *The Bulletin of the National
Association of Secondary School Principals,* XXIX, No. 133 (November, 1945),
pp. 159-163.

division: (1) observational, including intuitive, analytically systematic, and instrumental; (2) objective; (3) pragmatic, including listener comprehension, retention, attitude change, changes in listener activity, group balloting, audience meters, photography, and observations and ratings of audience.[5] Thompson uses a listing based on types of observer ratings: (1) paired comparison, (2) rank order, (3) linear scale, (4) letter grades, (5) descriptive letter scale, (6) speaker attitude scales, and (7) rating scales.[6] Weaver, Borchers, and Smith suggest the following paper-and-pencil tests for the speech class: tests of (1) information, (2) understanding, (3) attitudes, (4) student criticism, (5) listening comprehension, and (6) standardized tests of critical thinking, personal adjustment, personality, listening comprehension reading skill, or other products of speech training.[7] They also list these observational measures: (1) accumulation of anecdotal reports on speaking performances, (2) accumulation of analytical rating scales, (3) accumulation of ratings on general effectiveness in a series of speaking activities, (4) anecdotal notations on changes in the amount and content of criticism, and (5) comparative ratings of paired recordings.[8]

With this plethora of types, which is the teacher to select? Again, the answer lies in what she desires to measure. The problem may be simplified by recalling that the objectives of the speech class may be usefully divided into knowledge and understanding, attitudes, and skills.

Factual knowledge is probably best measured by the traditional "objective" test, better named by Robert Seashore as the "limited-response" test. Understanding and insight, however, are better measured by the so-called essay test, or more exactly the problem-type test in which the student must recall, organize, and apply his knowledge. A good example of this type of test is one in which the student writes a critical evaluation of a stimulus speaker or speech based on a list of principles and techniques which the class has been studying. This type of question measures not only the student's knowledge and his ability to apply it but also his attitudes and his listening and critical abilities, which are important objectives of the speech class.

The wide substitution of the "objective" test for the "essay" test is a notable instance of the cart-before-the-horse method of achieving reliability (sometimes) at the expense of validity. This has, besides, produced an unfortunate side effect. Many of my college students in

---

[5]Franklin H. Knower, "What Is a Speech Test?" *Quarterly Journal of Speech,* XXX (December, 1944), pp. 489-492.

[6]Wayne N. Thompson, "An Experimental Study of the Accuracy of Typical Speech Rating Techniques," *Speech Monographs,* XI (1944), pp. 67-79.

[7]*Op. cit.,* p. 530.

[8]*Ibid.*

their freshman year do not know how to take an essay test and cannot do themselves justice because they have never taken one before.

The reader will remember that the "essay" test has been frequently criticized for its subjectivity and lack of reliability in scoring, but there are ways, as Simon has pointed out, of objectifying the scoring of such tests and making them more reliable.[9] These include (1) writing out an answer before grading to serve as a standard, (2) grading one question at a time through a set of papers, (3) reversing the order of the papers in grading the next question in order to compensate for alterations in the standard, and (4) folding back the title page of the quiz books before beginning the grading in order not to be influenced by knowing whose paper is being graded. The teacher should have definitely in mind what she is looking for in grading and may of course award quantitative values for each item. Perhaps the best written examination is a combination of limited-response and problem-type questions.

No one suggests, however, that the written test is adequate for the measurement of speech skills. This consideration makes speech measurement a special educational problem. All writers on the subject seem to agree that the *trained observer* is the only practical means to satisfactory testing of speech skill, and that the *training* of the observer is the single most important factor. The most highly trained observer, and the only one available ordinarily, is the speech teacher.

Weaver, Borchers, and Smith maintain that:

> The most accurate measurement of the most significant outcome of the speech instruction must be based upon the observation and evaluative judgment of an auditor, or group of auditors. After all, a speech teacher's grades on the general effectiveness of a series of speech performances may constitute the most direct and significant measurement of the outcomes of instruction.[10]

Knower, the author of the best known standardized test in speech, says: "The evaluation of the student's achievement becomes a matter for expert interpretation and a critical judgment. . . ."[11] Speech teachers are understandably reluctant to pass judgment on an activity so complex and personal as speech, but there appears no acceptable alternative.

If the teacher must do the job, what rating system or scale shall she use? Thompson and Knower both found in experimental investigations that it makes very little difference.[12] Knower comments:

---

[9]Clarence T. Simon, lectures in the psychology of speech, Northwestern University, summer, 1944.
[10]*Op. cit.,* 529.
[11]*Op. cit.,* p. 492.
[12]*Op. cit.*

> There is no evidence that experienced observers improve their evaluation by use of such scales. They serve such purposes as a guide for the training of inexperienced observers, a convenient form for recording judgments, and a record of the observational evaluation rendered.[13]

The reader is urged to consult the excellent discussions provided by Knower and Robinson.[14] A number of good rating scales are reproduced in Robinson's text. The teacher would do well to study a variety of these and then to make her own, adapted specifically to the purpose, a different one for each assignment or for each type of speech performance. These may be handed to the student as guides for his preparation and criticism. Every type of speech performance, in truth, every speech situation, calls for a distinctive set of criteria inherent in that situation. Validity and reliability are both increased, we have considerable evidence to show, by the careful defining of the criteria of judging, and learning is heightened by defining these for the student. This is the consideration that makes the devising of one's own rating scale or criticism blank of some significance and denies validity to the enjoyment of standardized scales.

FACTORS AFFECTING JUDGMENT

Far more important than the method of judging is the judge himself. The most effective method of improving the judge is through his understanding of what is involved in judging. The difficulties incident to measurement of speech performance have been summarized by Robinson as

> (1) the complexity of the speech performance; (2) the scope of the test or what should be tested; (3) variations and lack of consistency in the behavior of the speaker, either within a given performance or from day to day; (4) the effect of the testing situation upon the speaker; (5) its effect upon the listener-tester; (6) variable affecting the tester in his relationship to the speech performance; (7) the rating or testing technique used.[15]

Thompson found the following factors to be significant influences upon the judge of speech performance: lighting, acoustics, attention span, irregular waning of attention, shifting of certain stimuli, combination of individual items of the rating scale, the observer's criteria of good speaking, his expectations, his habituation regarding the individual speaker, and errors in the rating device.[16] Knower listed these factors:

---

[13]*Op. cit.*, p. 490.
[14]Knower, *op. cit.*, pp. 485-493; Karl F. Robinson, *Teaching Speech in the Secondary School* (New York: Longmans, Green, 1954), pp. 114-131.
[15]*Op. cit.*, p. 115.
[16]*Op. cit.*, pp. 67-79.

sensory capacities of the rater, alertness, concentration, knowing what
to look for, lack of bias, freedom from fatigue, ability to interpret, and
ability to record observations quickly.[17] Simon has pointed out significant factors within the observer which affect his decisions: attention (how much and to what); knowledge of speech acquired from
training and experience (amount and kind); emotional state or mood;
response to what has preceded the speech; expectancies; desires (what
the observer wishes to see and hear); beliefs and convictions (whether
the speaker agrees with the observer); personal likes and dislikes; and
perceptual habits.[18]

There is not space or need to discuss each of these here, or to con-
solidate them into a single list: the reader is referred to the original
sources cited. As a group, however, what may be done about these
factors? A few of them may be reduced or standardized in their effect,
but few if any can be eliminated. The teacher can, instead, become
aware of these factors and *understand* how they influence her judgment so that she can allow for them and not be left at their mercy
because unrecognized. There are two large factors within the judge
which are most telling in their effects: (1) his knowledge of speech
behavior, which is determined by the amount and kind of training
and experience he has had; (2) his mental or emotional health—freedom
from emotional compulsion and irrational impulses, awareness and control of his mental predilections and biases, his objectivity and consistency, his awareness of the grounds upon which his decisions rest.

PROCEDURES FOR IMPROVING MEASUREMENT

From the foreging consideration of the nature of measurement and
what it involves, it is possible now to offer definite suggestions which
can be expected to improve measurement and, thereby, our feelings
of security about it.

1. Begin with the thing to be measured. Tests, like assignments, must be
   directly related to objectives. Goal, activity, and evaluation must be a
   closely knit unity.[19]
2. Use tests to generate learning. Keep grading secondary.
3. Do not be concerned with reliability until you have first checked validity.
   What does the test actually measure?
4. Make your own tests and rating scales. No one else can possibly know
   as well what you wish to measure.
5. Use a variety of types of tests, selecting them to fit the thing to be
   measured. Use good published tests when they do fit the purpose. The

---

[17]*Op. cit.*, p. 489.
[18]*Op. cit.*
[19]See the excellent discussion provided in Weaver, Borchers, and Smith, *op. cit.*,
pp. 90-103.

most thorough type of measurement, to be used in special cases, is the case study with the results of many tests and observations, expertly evaluated.

6. When you have no adequate data, refuse to judge. Avoid jumping to conclusions about students; refrain from characterizing and labeling them. Every student is unique and no one will ever know all there is to know about any of them.

7. Review fundamental statistics, know these basic concepts: central tendency, dispersion, distribution, normal curve, sampling, validity, and reliability.

8. Check periodically on your standards and your philosophy of speech education. Review the four historical theories of rhetorical criticism.[20]

9. Learn to accept, emotionally, the necessity for using your own judgment, and to rely on it humbly. Expect to make mistakes occasionally.

10. Depend on your trained and experienced observation as the primary tool of measurement. Continually improve it by: (a) learning to listen closely, to concentrate, keep mentally alert, extend the attention span—this is done only through practice; (b) keep your mind open; (c) checking your judgment against others now and then: other teachers, contest judges, student judges (let the students judge each other occasionally); (d) formulating the criteria for each assignment clearly, both for yourself and the students—what is crucial varies from speech to speech; (e) not letting grading interfere with criticism; (f) beware of concentrating on the easily observed and the easily quantified at the expense of more significant and fundamental matters; (g) remember that the whole need not equal the sum of the parts—the whole exceeds the sum.

In summary, the good observer is one whose feelings about himself, his students, and his work permit him to see through the prism of his own personality to reality and whose mind is sharpened through the discipline of training and experience to alert and perceptive comprehension.

SOURCES TO READ

There are several good discussions of measurement in the speech literature with which every teacher of speech should be familiar. Here is a minimum list:

1. Franklin H. Knower, "What Is a Speech Test?" *Quarterly Journal of Speech*, XXX (December, 1944), 492-93.
2. Alan Monroe, "Testing Speech Performance," *The Bulletin of the National Association of Secondary School Principals*, XXIX, No. 32, 156-64.
3. Karl F. Robinson, "Diagnosis, Evaluation, Testing, and Criticism" and "Judges and Judging" in *Teaching Speech in the Secondary School* (New York: Longmans, Green, 1954), 114-49 and 352-87.
4. A. T. Weaver, G. L. Borchers, and D. K. Smith, "The Criticism of Classroom Speaking" and "Measuring the Results of Instruction" in *The Teaching of Speech* (New York: Prentice-Hall, 1952), pp. 491-540.

---

[20]For condensed modern treatments, see McBurney and Wrage, *op. cit.*, pp. 21-52 and Thonssen and Baird, *op. cit.*, especially pp. 331-464.

BIBLIOGRAPHY OF PUBLISHED SPEECH TESTS

The speech teacher will find no standardized or published tests of most of the speech skills and types as such. Many so-called speech tests are no more than check sheets for voice and articulation.[21] Voice and articulation tests are too numerous to include here and are available in standard texts in speech correction. The other available tests divide themselves into three headings:

I. Tests of Speech Attitudes, Adjustment, Personality

1. *Guidance Questionnaire for Students of Speech*, F. H. Knower and H. Gilkinson. C. H. Stoelting Co. Grades 13-16; 1940; Form C; $2.20 per 25; 30 (35) minutes. References: F. H. Knower, "A Study of Speech Attitudes and Adjustments," *Speech Monographs*, V, 130-203; H. Gilkinson and F. H. Knower, "Individual Differences Among Students of Speech as Revealed by Psychological Tests," *Quarterly Journal of Speech*, XXVI, 243-255.
2. *Speech Attitude Scale*, F. H. Knower. C. H. Stoelting Co. Grades 9-16; Form F; $2.20 per 25; 30 (35) minutes. References: (See #1 above.)
3. *Speech Experience Inventory*, F. H. Knower. C. H. Stoelting Co. Grades 9-16: 1937; Form C; $1.60 per 25; 15 (20) minutes. References: (see #1 above).
4. *The Speech Inventory, S. A. Fessenden.* New York: Psychological Corporation, 1943. College students and adults. Reference: G. H. Hildreth, *A Bibliography of Mental Tests and Rating Scales*: 1945 Supplement, Psychological Corporation.

II. Tests of Problem-Solving and Critical Thinking

1. *Steps in Problem Solving,* The Evaluation Staff in the Eight Year Study of the Progressive Education Association. Grades 10-18. Lansing, Michigan: Cooperative Bureau of Educational Research, 1937.
2. *Watson-Glaser Tests of Critical Thinking*, G. Watson and E. M. Glaser. Yonkers, N. Y.: World Book Co., 1942. Grades 10-16. Reference: E. M. Glaser, "An Experiment in the Development of Critical Thinking," *Teachers College Contributions to Education*, No. 843, 1941.

III. Rating Scales

1. Several rating scales are reproduced in Karl F. Robinson, *Teaching Speech in the Secondary School* (New York: Longmans, Green, 1954), pp. 123-128.
2. *Speech Criticism and Speech Rating* in A. T. Weaver, G. L. Borchers, and D. K. Smith, *The Teaching of Speech* (New York: Prentice-Hall, 1952), p. 516.
3. *Speech Performance Scale* in A. C. Baird and F. H. Knower, *General Speech: An Introduction* (New York: McGraw-Hill, 1957), p. 19.

---

[21]See Hannah P. Mathews, "Voice and Speech Examinations in American Educational Institutions," *Quarterly Journal of Speech*, XXVIII (December, 1942), pp. 456-461 and Elbert Moses, "A Survey of Speech Tests in Thirty American Universities and Colleges," *ibid.* (April, 1942), pp. 206-211.

The Message of the Speech Classroom

WILLIAM I. GORDEN*

School supposedly is preparation for life, but school is not life itself. Similarly, the speech course is training for communication with others rather than communication with real people. The classroom theoretically is the practice field, but it is not the stadium. Fortunately, we have voices questioning these assumptions—they ask: 1) what should the teacher say qua teacher? 2) what should the instructor say in dealing with the messages of his students? and 3) what role should both teacher and student assume as communicators in the outside classroom?

I

What should the speech teacher say in the classroom? The quick answer is: The speech teacher should teach speech, just as the biology teacher should teach biology and the math instructor, math.

Even this simple response implies more than sophistry and elocution. The speech profession, or, if you prefer, the science and fine arts of oral communication, ranges over expansive territory. Conventionally, speech has included rhetorical theory and criticism, forensics, and public address; oral interpretation of literature, voice and diction, linguistics; stagecraft and design, technical theater, dance, music, directing, and acting; dramatic literature and playwriting; speech pathology, correction and voice science; and mass media, radio, and television. In addition to these several specialties, many of which have become separate departments, disciplines new to and interrelated with speech include psycholinguistics, interpersonal relations, social psychology, anthropology, kinesics, general semantics, general systems, and cybernetic theory.

This is content abundant. This is content enough. Yet, in comparison to most disciplines, the typical speech course seems to find no subject matter not suited to class speeches or discussions; it even accepts subjects traditionally taboo in polite conversation.

Such wide latitude for the speech professor may cause students to jest, "Bring a clipping to him on anything. He will love it because he thinks his field is directly related to everything." Moreover, his colleagues may justly wonder why the speech teacher coaches the debate team when the propositions usually fall into the province of the social sciences as did the 1966-67 intercollegiate proposition: "Resolved that the United

*Mr. Gorden is Associate Professor of Speech at Kent State University.
From *Western Speech,* Spring, 1969 pp. 75-81.

States should substantially reduce its foreign policy commitments." In a case such as this, should the debate instructor teach only analysis and refutation or should he also talk about the "arrogance of power"? Should he remain aloof and noncommittal or should he be an advocate, be he hawk, dove, or rose-breasted grosbeak? The basic issue is: should the speech teacher, within the sacred confines of the classroom, express his opinion or become an advocate in an area other than his discipline? In our specialized, departmentalized, modern educational establishment, does not this encyclopedic tresspassing by the speech discipline beg the question of territorial rights, and, like Socrates, corrupt our youth?

Obviously, the most defensible position for the speech teacher, or any teacher for that matter, is that he confine his remarks within his classroom to his discipline, and that when he speaks or acts as a private citizen, he is careful to avoid the impression that he speaks or acts for his school or university. The American Association of University Professors has not found this seemingly clear-cut position always so clear-cut. The professor who is both a responsible citizen and a vital teacher is not easily rent in twain—consider the Texas sociology professor who was dismissed after he protested, outside the classroom, against the film, "Operation Abolition"; or the Illinois biology professor who was dismissed after he expressed, outside the classroom, his opinion favoring extramarital sex relations; or the Arkansas speech instructor who was fired after he initiated, outside the classroom, a petition against the beatings of prisoners; or a California high-school teacher who was thoroughly investigated and intimidated for writing a play which seemed objectionable to self-appointed vigilantes of community morality. In no case were these persons dismissed for neglecting their classrooms, for passing students without appropriate instruction. They were dismissed because it is difficult, if not impossible, to be two people in one community—in spite of "the games people play."

We who believe in the preservation of our freedoms must not dismiss lightly the "speech teacher should teach speech" argument. The speech teacher who, under the banner of freedom of speech, argues anything goes in his classroom is the same person who is grateful that our police are not allowed to politick and that the June 1962 and 1963 Supreme Court decisions grant him legal recourse should his child in a public school be led in prayer during Lent or any other day. So, are there things which ought not be said in the speech classroom too? Obviously, any teacher who uses the classroom as a place of worship or uses grades as reward of punishment for certain political behavior of students has to some degree adopted pages from a theocratic or totalitarian state. Perhaps equally malodorous classroom behavior, though not quite so dangerous, occurs when the teacher uses himself as the norm to demand certain dress, cut of hair, or absence of taboo words from students. As far-fetched as all this may seem, these events do happen.

But there is yet a more subtly insidious language which some speech teachers use. The speech teacher's coloring book says, "I am a speech instructor, color me true obscure blue. I am permissive with my students. I want them to be authentic persons, color them red and green and golden. However, I am only a critic who reacts to how it is said: invention, disposition, style, *logos*, pathos, *ethos*, and delivery. Outline me in black. Better make that anonymous grey because I do not react to the message itself. In the speech classroom I am a blur with no visible political, religious, or personal beliefs."

The AAUP statement on professional ethics speaks to the hypercautious speech teacher as it describes the role of the professor:

> His primary responsibility to his subject is to seek and state the truth as he sees it. . . . As a teacher, the professor encourages the free pursuit of learning in his students. . . . He respects and defends the free inquiry of his associates. In the exchange of criticism and ideas, he shows due respect for the opinions of others. . . . As citizen engaged in a profession that depends upon freedom for its health and integrity, the professor has a particular obligation to promote conditions of free inquiry and to further public understanding of academic freedom.[1]

How can a speech student get involved if he speaks of subjects far from where the action is, far from the forces battling for men's minds, and far from life and glands? Obviously, he can not. I would argue that to teach effective oral communication is to join all others who are involved in the quest for meaning. If education is to be personalized, professors must care, and risk having students, departmental chairmen, or even Boards of Regents accuse them of teaching pacifism, atheism, nudity, or communism.

Now does this view mean that the speech teacher must be a radical, play the fool, or the devil's advocate? No. Admittedly, role playing at times stimulates thought; however, for the speech teacher to evade taking a stand by playing a role is just another escape clause.

Should the speech professor talk about his philosophy or life at the expense of his talking about how to communicate effectively? No. His views about Vietnam or God or how to "make love" ought to provide examples of how to deal with ideas that matter or how to see the "territory and not just the map." And his response to a student who says "faith is enough" ought to be violent enough to cause that student to seek definitions and to rethink his platitudes, and yet the speech teacher's re-

---

[1] *AAUP Bulletin* (Autumn 1966), pp. 290-291.

sponse must also be gentle enough that he conveys respect for that student's personal choice. References to content outside the speech teacher's discipline usually ought to be integral to the teaching of his course, but occasional references to a civic concern or a personal opinion should serve only to make the professor more human.

Should the speech teacher stand as an authority or norm for what is to be considered right or true in the classroom? No. The ground rules prescribed by the educational establishment range from requiring the teacher to get to work on time to telling him to keep order. But the rules should not make the teacher the standard for rightness, although we must admit the teacher does pretty much set the norms. The secondary schools, Paul Goodman asserts, are essentially an arm of the law. Obedience to authority is their message. The teacher's word is law. Only when the teacher relinquishes his superior position will the students learn the message of democracy. Where is there a better place than the speech classroom for the teacher to limit the sacredness of his word?

II

What, then, should the instructor say in dealing with the messages of his students? Does this limitation implicitly suggest that one should have no concern for technique? Emphasis upon the message need not overlook an appraisal of the transmission. Even golden dreams and ideas must be symbolized to be transmitted clearly and persuasively. What is to be said must be effectively related to the external circumstances which permit or provoke the speech. Communicator, time, space, and receiver-reactor affirm each other. For the teacher to stress technique means he ignores the affirmations of existence, the person crying out to *be* and to be heard. Marshall McLuhan argues that the TV generation has "an unconscious demand for depth involvement in all situations of home and society" and that "the need for dialogue is a mounting one."

One of the most serious pedagogical errors found in the speech classroom, I believe, is for the teacher to permit the typical series of speeches on different topics and to save little or no time for reactions from the listeners. Speaking in monologue is both unrealistic and contrary to the democratic tradition. Meaningful dialogue can exist only if listeners' reactions to speeches are given as much or more time and value as the speeches themselves are given, and only if assignments for a round or series of speeches are centered upon a limited number of subjects, preferably those selected by the student.

Feedback and continuing dialogue in response to the message may teach the student more about how to get through to someone and how to be someone than the best stock designs and voice drills. "Relating to," then, becomes superior to the winning of arguments. Listeners are persons with responses and, in my view, they are not objects to be manipulated by the superior mind; I believe that freedom to buy should always be at the option of the customer and not at that of the disarming salesman.

Should the speech teacher, then, avoid critical comment? Words of speech criticism may often threaten and sometimes crush the student. These criticisms might best be expressed only after the listeners have responded to the student's message—and then only if solicited by the student—and this criticism must be expressed with sensitive honesty. Occasionally, candid statements seem very necessary for egocentric students who feel little motivation to produce a worthy product. If a teacher doesn't "level" with his class when he is displeased, he once again is "playing it safely anonymous." One would hope that the growth of the student's personality toward independence (with all its corollary attributes of interdependence, venturesomeness, resourcefulness, persistence, and reflectiveness) will be positively influenced by what the speech instructor says and is.

III

What role should the teacher and the student assume outside the classroom? Should the speech teacher limit student speaking to the classroom? No. No. No! The vigor of my answer indicates that this question is not hypothetical and that the battle for academic freedom for the student is hot. The public school or university administrator usually believes in freedom of speech *in general,* but naturally he feels that decorum must be preserved during his tenure. After all, he must plead for next year's budget; his chief argument is that nothing ought to blemish his record. If his argument is carried to the extreme, no word in opposition to the status quo should appear in print or on the radio or tube. The student must be kept within the four walls of the classroom. It is safer that way. Whatever the motivation for such pressures, whether it be an over-reaction to the "dirty speech" movement or simply the good intentions of respected citizens, the most damaging blow to free speech comes with a superior's command or weighted suggestion: "Limit your student panels and symposiums to the classroom, speech teacher."

The classroom is more than four walls. The window, slate, plaster, and hardwood are a medium which transmits a forceful message, more forceful than the curriculum itself. The message, all too often, is one of authoritarianism: carefulness, adjustment, restriction, limitation. The message is surely taught: "This is not the real world. The classroom is not life. Beyond these walls we must speak differently. We want to hear what you have to say inside, but we don't want you to voice your honest opinion outside. Your voice is irrelevant. Involvement is for others properly conditioned." But the classroom does speak, and the speech classroom does have a positive message to proclaim.

No one in this free society is free so long as the speech instructor is discouraged from scheduling controversial dialogue for the wider classroom, for the student union, for the school assembly, for the market place, or for the mass media. No one is free so long as what the student says must conform to the standards of decency prescribed by the teacher, the dean, or the regents. The word is not the thing, and it will never be relegated to its proper place as a symbol until ordinary students can level with the outside. When the community hears what students really say rather than what it would like them to say, a new dawn will be upon us. Probably, traditional educators would say, "All hell will break loose." The rumblings of an authentic society will bother, bewilder, and bless us because ordinary people broke the silence, and these sound waves disintegrated the classroom walls.

There is a tendency for many to think of students "as less than citizens of the United States," although constitutional rights are not subject to age, except in case of election to office. An aura of careful subservience to authority in the schoolroom is certainly transferred to a society. How can speech education, or any education for that matter, be a truly rich experience under the "chattel-to-lord relationship"? Alienation, dropouts, vandalism, and nonconformist youth can not be blamed upon permissive schools because I believe we have never really had permissive schools.

The school building, whitewashed with benevolent authoritarian ideals, leaves little room for self-discovery or civil liberties. The freedom of expression is the most precious message any person can speak or learn in the classroom. However, such freedom will not be realized unless it is both the basic assumption of the instructor and is a carefully formulated policy of the institution.

August Gold recently spelled out such specifics for secondary-school students. He declared all student rights should be "subject only to limitations on the place and timing of the exercise of rights, to avoid interference with the process of teaching and learning."[2]

Rights referring to freedom of speech head his list:
(1) freedom of speech in the classroom, at student meetings and in general assembly

---

[2]*American Civil Liberties Union Bimonthly* (March 1967).

(2) access to any or all materials in print, in speech, on film or in recording

(3) freedom to publish and broadcast their own ideas and to circulate the ideas of others, without censorship, without political test and without fear that the ideas expressed will be recorded for future use against them

(4) the right to assemble and to organize for discussion or for advocacy, without limitation on purpose or program, and without prejudice because of participation

(5) freedom to petition, to demonstrate, to picket, to "sit down," to propagandize via printed matter, spoken word, buttons.

I would like to predict that the speech instructor who hears these words and does these things will live a happy life. He is likely, however personable, to be misunderstood and disliked by those in authority at his institution at one time or another. Forthright discussion with superiors may help, a sense of humor may help, getting a policy in writing may help, and keeping a careful chronological account of a situation where freedom of speech is seriously challenged may help. If he works through existing channels for grievance and solicits the aid of organizations such as the American Civil Liberties Union, he may strengthen the cause. Even if he wins a victory for free speech, he will experience great emotional upheaval during the struggle, indigestion and constant fatigue perhaps, community uproar sometimes, and loss of friends and job sometimes.

The struggle will not be labeled a case of academic freedom or free speech but more likely subversive instruction by a dirty-minded administrator or teacher. The opponents to complete freedom on students' speaking outside the classroom will resist putting in writing any specifics; they will prefer, rather, that instructors simply understand what should not be said. Good taste and responsibility are reasonable expectations, they believe, and the speech teacher with similar values will probably fare well in such a school system.

In summary, the speech teacher ought to take a new look at both his obligation to the freedom of speech and to the student's need for dialogue. If the speech instructor can acquire with his students those human relationships which contain less anxiety, less defensiveness, and less unpleasantness left over from inappropriate past interractions; and those which are more honest, more friendly, more spontaneous, more warm, and more respectful; and if the speech instructor can get his students committed to relevant issues—with all these developments at least—then, the instructor will achieve personality growth, and the odds are that the students will, also. The message of the speech classroom should be the "free play of the spirit" in "sensitive areas."[3]

EXERCISES

1. What grading policy is most effective in an introductory speech course? Justify your position.
2. What relationship exists between performance ability, motivation, confounding variables, and the grading of oral performance?
3. What is "reliability and validity"? Why are these terms important to the critic-evaluator?
4. How can an instructor be consistent in his evaluation of student speeches?
5. How are student conferences relevant to establishing a favorable learning climate? How often should the student meet with his instructor? What should be the nature of these conferences?
6. Should improvement in performance be a factor in grading? What implications has this for the "natural-born speaker"?
7. Should the distribution of grades in an introductory speech course be similar to the distribution found in the introductory courses of other disciplines?
8. What is the purpose of criticism? How can the teacher become more alert and sensitive to the problems and needs facing the student speaker?
9. What steps must the critic undertake in planning and making preparations for effective criticism? Outline ten essential criteria necessary in offering criticism.
10. What is the relationship between written and oral criticism? Do each of these pedagogical devices serve separate or equivalent ends? Which of these techniques is more effective.
11. How and when should oral criticism be conducted? What effect does oral criticism have upon the motivation and personality of the learner?
12. Should an instructor employ critique or rating scales? To what extent are these instruments reliable, valid, and effective indicators of student achievement?
13. What is meant by a standardized measurement? What advantages would such a measure afford the teacher of speech?
14. What accounts for discrepancies in critic judgments? Why is it difficult to expect ten judges (evaluators) to rate five speakers identically?

---

[3]See *The United States Supreme Court Reports,* Keyishan v. Board of Regents, 385 US 589, 1967, and Adler v. Board of Education, 342 US 485, 1952.

15. Does a student's awareness of his natural propensity for speaking influence his willingness to improve his communicative ability? How is this seen as a motivational problem?

PROJECTS

1. Develop a rating and critique form for each of the following speech activities: public speaking, group discussion, debate, oral interpretation and parliamentary procedure. Take care to insure for maximum reliability and validity in your instrument.
2. Deliver an impromtu speech before your class. Following the conclusion of your presentation allow your classmates to severely criticize your speech. Describe your feelings and reactions to such criticism. What implications for criticism has this experience demonstrated? How would you have preferred criticism to have been conducted?
3. Arrange with an instructor of an introductory speech course an opportunity to evaluate the oral performance of his students. After each round of speaking compare your ratings with those of the instructor. Discuss each speakers performance thoroughly. If any serious discrepancies appear, try to account for them. Describe to your classmates how this experience affected your perception of evaluation.

Chapter 4

The Reticent,
the Fearful, and
Defective Speech
and Hearing Student

A common misconception held by the general public is that the goal of speech education is to mold learners into model orators. In actuality, however, quite the opposite is true. An effective speech education program whether it is found on the elementary, secondary, or collegiate level is both an academic and performance discipline. The Speech Association of America in defending its academic legitimacy has attempted for many years to make clear to both professional and lay audiences the cognitive structure of its discipline. The association has not always been successful. Even teachers of speech misjudge or misevaluate the goals of the discipline. For some teachers personal goals or aspirations take precedence over those of the discipline. At the high school level the number of winning debate teams (and perhaps the shine of their trophies) is often equated with one's teaching prowess. Thus, some teachers take great pride in pointing to students who speak like the second coming of Patrick Henry or William Jennings Bryan. It is unfortunate these teachers of speech think to measure their success by the "winners" they have tutored. The "failures," apparently, are forgotten easily enough. While the teacher of speech may justifiably take pride in students demonstrating superior achievement as advocates, he must not write off those having failed to achieve mastery as public speakers.

If ever a challenge lay open to teachers of speech calling for their resolve and action it is this: They must assess the problem of the "under-communicator" and assist him in developing the necessary skills, attitudes, and materials essential for becoming an effective communicator. We clearly must face reality. No student need ever become an orator. The day and the need for "hell and damnation" speakers is past. Rather, speech training must place a priority upon interpersonal as well as intrapersonal communication. Obviously, each individual (reticent or proficient in speaking) must learn to communicate *with* rather than speak *at* his fellow man to live effectively in our complex society.

Replete in any school system are learners who are ineffective oral communicators. These students do not exhibit "normal speaking behaviors." The communication problems of these students may take a number of different forms symptomatically related to physical and/or psychological causes. This chapter attempts to focus upon three critical areas representing diagnostically different symptoms. The first article is an interpretation and analysis of reticent students; the second and third are concerned with stage fright and speech and hearing defects, respectively. Each of the personality and speech behavior types discussed may be found in a speech classroom.

Gerald M. Phillips, "The Problem of Reticence," investigates the relationship of personality disorders to speech disorders. He indicates that any disorder in the personality of an individual will be reflected in his verbal behavior. Speech behavior, then, is inseparable from the personality of the speaker. Thus, one is incapable of effecting behavior change in one area without accounting for the other.

Reticence is defined by Barnett, "*American College Encyclopedic Dictionary* (1950) as the "avoidance of social, verbal interaction: unwillingness to communicate unless prodded; disposed to be silent: not inclined to speak freely: reserved." Phillips suggests that reticent characteristics may be pathological in nature. On a continuum, suggests Phillips, we might expect to find reticence somewhere between stuttering and stagefright.

Many teachers of speech labor under a misconception that all students are capable of becoming polished public speakers. Unfortunately, there are many individuals to whom this proposition is not generalizable. Any teacher of speech having taught courses required of all students has undoubtedly encountered students who seemed to make little if any real progress as oral communicators. Teachers often mistake reticent students for students suffering from stage fright, thus concluding erroneously that such students are capable of overcoming their "fright" through repeated exposure to public speaking situations. As a result, the teacher of speech may be inflicting psychological damage upon the reticent student by his demands for perfection in communication skills. Phillips suggests that this may be particularly evident "in the potential induction of iatrogenic disturbances triggered by stimulating awareness of performance criteria (voice, gesture, etc.) over which the subject has no apparent control."

There is no question that the reticent individual must be identified and reached. It would be easy enough to allow this small percentage of individuals to remain in their isolated world, but the con-
science of any dedicated teacher of speech cannot allow this. Each
individual must provide for and contribute to his society. It would
be a devastating blow to the nature of preventive mental health if we
were to avoid reticent individuals by pretending not to recognize their
particular problem, thereby allowing them to take refuge as best they
can from the world about them.

How may the teacher of speech reach reticent individuals and assist
them in restructuring their speech behaviors? Initially, the teacher of
speech must provide a socio-emotional classroom climate which provides maximum opportunity for self-exposure under conditions of minimum threat. There are, however, a number of threat variables built
into the typical public speaking course. Grades, for example, which
reflect how well and, obviously, how poorly one speaks may intimidate
a reticent speaker. Likewise, student criticism offered in the classroom
will serve no other purpose to a reticent speaker than to demonstrate
in his mind his inabilities, thus reinforcing his own negative self-image.
Rating scales are also performance oriented. Somehow someone concluded (i.e., the canons of speech) that a speech was little more than
a grouping of parts whose proper integration would lead to effective
speaking. A reticent speaker should expect to be evaluated as a person
rather than as a performer. To Phillips the speech classroom is "only
a clinic in which real problems can be worked out with a minimum of
threat." This suggests that reticent students should be thought of as
clients and the teacher as a non-directive clinician. Although there is
a clear need for this type of application the clinical approach is yet
to be worked out.

The second area under examination in this chapter is stage fright.
Theodore Clevenger, Jr.'s monograph "A Synthesis of Experimental Research in Stage fright," attempts to make consistent statements about
the nature of stage fright. One of the major problems which has faced
the researcher in stage fright is to determine the reliability and validity
of their measuring instruments. Much of the inconsistency in research
findings may be attributed to researchers justifying their own measurement tools as capable of measuring stage fright. Consequently, we have
conflicting reports. In addition, many studies of stage fright fail to
take into account essential differences operant in the communication
act, such as introspective, physiological and observational factors affecting the outcome of communication.

Stage fright, such a fear arousing word that even the mention of it
brings shudders to the hearts of most speakers, must be comprehended

and its instructional implications understood by the teacher of speech. The antiquated and inane business of requiring students to speak before a mirror has too long characterized the level of thinking of many teachers of speech. There is a reason for stage fright. No amount of wishful thinking will make it disappear. But the purpose of Clevenger's article is not to provide teachers with clever little aids or bromides by which to distort, disguise, or otherwise dismiss stage fright, but rather to demonstrate the interrelationships of variables leading to reportable hypotheses about the nature of stage fright.

Clevenger reports his analysis of several studies, many as yet unpublished, in an objective manner avoiding obtrusive value judgements about pedagogical corrective methodologies. Instead he reports eleven hypotheses which in light of present research may be generalizable to the nature of stage fright. The hypotheses are clear and valid conclusions drawn from the research reported. The reader upon completing his reading ought to make reference to the work of Phillips on reticence, in order to establish that continuum, as Phillips suggests, existing between stage fright, reticence and stuttering.

C. Cordelia Brong indicates in "Helping Speech and Hearing-Defective Students" the necessity of every teacher of speech, including non-corrective teachers, to be able to recognize speech and hearing defects in students. It is of utmost importance that every teacher of speech seek and detect such students and assist them either in adjusting their behavior or in reaching appropriate clinical aid. Because of the "attuned" ear of the trained teacher of speech he should be capable of recognizing in the first few weeks of a term speech and hearing defective students. In certain cases where the size of the classroom makes nearly impossible a casual observation of speech and hearing defectives, a screening test ought to be employed.

Brong offers many sound suggestions to aid the teacher in detecting the hearing-defective student. Ultimately, however, a school system ought to conduct hearing surveys which may reflect scientifically and medically the extent of hearing loss and the conditions contributing to such loss. Students ought to be tested by a trained professional audiologist each year. If for one reason or another such services are not provided by the public school, it is imperative the teacher of speech be cognizant of visual cues exhibited by individuals possessing diminishing hearing. The teacher, by recognizing this loss, may refer the student for hearing tests offered either by the school audiologist or local otologist. The teacher may save a student one of his most valuable possessions—his sense of hearing.

Speech defective students are present in nearly all classes. It is unwise to employ "corrective" measures if you are untrained for such assistance. Brong suggests, however, that the teacher must "(1) treat the defect in a casual objective manner, (2) avoid penalizing the speech defective for any aspect of his handicap, (3) require him to participate in activities in range of his abilities, (4) expect the defective, in skill courses, to make gains within the boundaries of his limitations."

In addition, the essay clarifies the function of a teacher of speech in a school with and without a therapy program for speech and hearing defects. A discussion of private conferences in schools with and without remedial programs is also presented as is an examination and description of suggestions for helping students with mild articulatory problems. Brong concludes her article with an analysis of voice disorders and suggestions for assisting students in overcoming this handicap.

The Problem of Reticence

GERALD M. PHILLIPS

SPEECH AND PERSONALITY

The field of speech pathology has recently come of age. Articles have proliferated on the etiology, diagnosis and treatment of organic and functional speech disorders. There is an implied inference that the dialogue between the speech pathologist and the public speaking teacher is ended. This is far from so! Much early research conducted by the speech therapists centered on the pathological aspects of speech disorders. However, recent investigations have increasingly been focused on the psychological and psychiatric involvement in pathologies of speech.[1] Travis states:

> Speech pathologists have manifested in both practice and research an ever-quickening interest in psychotherapy. To them have come those suffering from troubles in communication without organic impairment of either the sensory or motor speech equipment. Voice and speech drills have not always been too effective with these cases. The recognition of emotional disturbances as etiological factors in these disorders have forced speech therapists to seek the promising help of psychotherapy as developed by psychiatrists and psychologists.[2]

In dealing with abnormalities of speech behavior, some definition of "normal" appears to be necessary. To provide one appears impossible in the context of the ever-increasing association made between speech and personality. Recognition of the connection between psychology and speech disorders led to a search for possible relationships between personality patterns and disorders of speech and communication. Speech disorders and personality disorders are now widely acknowledged to be related malfunctions. This attitude is implicit in such definitions as, "a speech disorder is a disorder of the person as well as a disorder in the reception and transmission of spoken language,"[3] or ". . . speech is a peculiarly *human* function and its disorders reflect all the complex troubles of humanity."[4] Confirmation from psychiatrists can be found in Becker's[5] statement that speech is the most significant projection of human personality, so intrinsic that it cannot be studied or treated without a holistic involvement of personality. The implications here are obvious. If there is any disorder at all in a speaker's personality, it will, in some way, be reflected in his verbal patterns.

From the *Pennsylvania Speech Annual,* September, 1965, pp. 22-38. Reprinted by permission.

Scher[6] refers to "verbal dysrhythmia" as a main symptom of personality disorder. Thus speech therapist and psychotherapist alike agree on the relationship between speech and personality. Berry and Eisenson sum up:

> Speech may be considered defective if the speaker is excessively self-conscious or apprehensive about objectively small deviations in his manner of speaking. In a broad sense, any speech deviation, however small, becomes a significant defect if it interferes with the speaker's social adjustment.[7]

The awareness expressed by Johnson of the semantogenic involvement in etiology of speech pathologies is confirmed again by psychologists and psychiatrists.[8] It appears that a social definition is made of a 'deviation' and a human becomes involved as a total personality. It is this very admission of the psychological and social context of speech problems that re-opens the dialogue between speech pathology and public speaking. Examining the real potential of the psychological etiology means that a relationship can be hypothesized between stuttering, the domain of the speech pathologist, stage fright, the province of the speech teacher, and reticence, which no one works with at all.

All of these can be connected by a concept which designates normality as the set of 'neurotic behaviors' accorded positive value by society, as opposed to equally neurotic, but not necessarily more serious behaviors denigrated by society. Thus, the fluent, smooth, quick-witted speaker given high value in both the speech classroom *and* the social situation may be suffering from anxieties equivalent to those of the shy, withdrawn person who is often ignored. Speech behavior as a facet of total personality would be one of many responses to threat-inducing situations. Some would be motivated to take control; others to withdraw. Some would be positively evaluated in their behavior and thus reinforced, others would be negatively evaluated and induced to withdraw.[9]

A variety of social and psychological connections have been proposed for deviation in speech communication patterns. Brady[10] notes that a primary symptom of schizophrenia is reduced or modified verbal output. Freedman, Ebing and Wilson[11] add that quantity and quality of verbalization and vocalization must be considered in any diagnosis of schizophrenia. Schachter, Meyer and Loomis[12] generalize that any failure to use speech for conventional purposes of communication may be considered a sign of mental illness to a greater or lesser degree. Rowley and Keller[13] refer to social approval as the influential factor in verbal effectiveness or failure, while Rogler and Hollingshead[14] demonstrate a relationship between movement in social classes and disturbances in speech. Speech, as a projection of personality, is evaluated by society against implied standards. Individuals assume a role based largely on the reflection of their personality back from society.[15] That means that abnormal speech must be considered a function of normal speech in any deviation where a physiopathological diagnosis cannot be made.

Speech behavior is neither separable from personality nor trainable apart from personality as a whole. Any approach to speech training with alteration of behavior as the goal means a revision of total personality is necessary. Any alteration in treatment level or motivation will alter speech behavior. The precise nature of the personality change will not be so obvious. Masserman[16] demonstrated that conflict in motivations may induce coping behavior but heighten anxieties in subsequent experiences. For example, the needs motivated by the grading system may induce a student to manage his fears and survive in the speech classroom, but impair his ability to function in future experiences. Attention to compensatory paralinguistic and kinesic behaviors has been noted by Szasz[17] and Sebeok and Hayes[18] as they demonstrated that the emotional state of the personality demands one sort of communication or another: if not verbal, then through some sort of bodily action not excluding hysterical or psychosomatic manifestations. A human may be able to mask a personality disturbance by controlling overt speech behavior, but the necessity to communicate the phenomenal self will produce a variety of other types of communication more indicative of the 'true' personality state. Quantitative and qualitative withdrawal from oral communication, therefore, may be considered as a sign of personality problems, requiring total treatment rather than symptomatic treatment in the form of speech training. The student who displays 'enthusiastic' gesture patterns and who receives an 'A' therefore may also require total treatment rather than reward in a speech class for manifesting neurotic symptoms.

Reticence is defined as, "avoidance of social, verbal interaction. Unwillingness to communicate unless prodded; disposed to be silent; not inclined to speak freely; reserved."[19] Teachers of speech and academic advisers are familiar with people who fit the definition. They are a small, but noticeable, proportion of the total student body. It would require a rather gross stretch of psychiatric nosology to classify these people as 'schizophrenic.' They do not show the symptoms of blocking and tension usually associated with stuttering. However, their behavior assists them to achieve the same ends as the schizophrenic or the stutterer, i.e. avoidance of the communication act. For this reason, their behavior can be considered pathological in terms of Van Riper's definition, "speech is defective when it deviates too far from the speech of people that it calls attention to itself, interferes with communication, or causes its possessor to be maladjusted."[20] The fact that we have a definition of reticence generally applied to 'non-verbal' persons would indicate that our society negatively evaluates individuals who withdraw from communication. Ruesch and Bateson underscore this point as they state, "disturbances in communicative behavior of the speaker when he acts contrary to general expectations, when he says too much or too little, or when his expressions are unintelligible."[21] Where effective verbal behavior is demanded, inability to perform according to society's expectations would signal a deviation. In this dimension, reticence could be construed as existing on a continuum with stuttering and stage fright. As mental disturbance permeates all individuals, each of these 'verbal problems' would be complicated by whatever 'mental disturbance' overtones existed. At any event, the problem of failure to perform up to the expectations of society appears more complicated than simply revealing a resistance to the directed learning of the classroom.

It would be simple to declare a manifesto of 'civil rights' for quiet people: to declare that no one need speak in our society unless he wants to. The demands of our modern society preclude this easy way out. Full utilization of the talents of human material, the integration of personalities into connection with "useful work" demands that each man contribute his share to his society.[22] Allowing an individual to take refuge from the challenges of life by refusing to participate in the communication level of the game would be to deny the whole concept of preventive mental health. Speech teacher and speech clinician alike assume the role of quasi-psychotherapist as they attempt to alter the behavior of the people who come to them, many of whom are inadequate in communication behavior *and* inadequate in total personality.

It is generally assumed by teachers of public speaking that everyone is trainable to some degree in communication skills. However, over the years it becomes evident that a noticeably large number of students do not seem to profit from the training, and a few, in fact, seem to regress. While few speech teachers fail to recognize the existence of these 'failures,' the phenomenon has not been studied in an organized way. Muir, in a series of interviews with reticent persons, demonstrated the possibility between regression of speaking skill and the training given in the conventional speech class.[23] Several of her 'reticent' subjects traced their inability to cope with speech situations back to an unpleasant or intimidating verbal performance, sometimes in a speech class, often in classes where 'speech' was being taught by an untrained teacher.

In general, the therapy of the speech class is based on the classical Greek model which holds that 'strength of will' is sufficient to remedy any human defect.[24] This approach may be reasonably effective in training the speech of those who suffer from no disturbance of personality. For those who are moderately disturbed to begin with, however, public speaking classes may do considerable psychological damage, particularly in the potential induction of iatrogenic disturbances triggered by stimulating awareness of performance criteria (voice, gestures, etc.) over which the subject has no apparent control. The apprehensions thus induced may act in somewhat the same fashion as the etiological factors in stuttering, i.e. setting of hypertonic, apprehensive reactions about the malfeasance in question. Most studies of apprehension use objective evaluations as a validity criterion.[25] There is no available data using the subjective testimony of students about their own apprehension levels. It has already been noted that the drive to succeed in the broad academic game may temporarily permit masking of anxiety symptoms, but there is no reasonable guarantee that the result of the whole experience has not been a heightening of the desire to avoid communication. Muir's study poses this as a possibility.

Syllabic repetitions do not seem to become problems until a name, "stuttering," together with a pejorative connotation has been given to them, and anxieties triggered.[26] Denigrating comments about 'eye contact,' 'gesture patterns,' 'voice quality,' etc., may evoke similar apprehensions in some students, which would heighten the general anxiety when facing a public speaking situation. If the pattern were carried to its logical end, a whole complex of avoidance-type symptoms could be set off.

If we were to assume a continuum of personality, we would also assume that a reasonably high number of students would be 'threatened' by a directive mode of speech criticism.[27] Direct criticism and the attendant directive therapy has not seemed to work so well in the psychological clinic.[28] Today the pattern appears to follow a non-directive mode in order to allay rather than heighten anxiety.[29] If the speech teacher could identify in advance which of his students would profit from a directive approach, there would be little problem. Since the tendency of the human, however, is to mask personality disruptions, the teacher can really never know that his directive approach is not causing hidden psychological damage. An analysis of diary reports of 300 subjects with 10 different instructors shows an incidence of physiological and emotional symptoms in response to criticism in about 15% of the cases. The anxiety level expressed here may represent a burgeoning core of personality-disturbed individuals whose potential is for regression unless given a very special sort of treatment.

Masserman reports that subjects confronted with conflicting goals may use their desire to achieve a greater goal to help them overcome anxieties about a lesser goal.[30] In the speech classroom this could mean that desire for 'survival' in the grading system would enable the student to surmount anxieties in the speech classroom. The question is, of course, what happens to anxiety levels in subsequent speech situations. If Masserman's evidence can be believed, we must assume that anxieties would be substantially increased.

As a first step in determining the potential for existence of 'problem-speakers' or 'reticents' the relationship between the various types of identified speech disorders and normal speech needs to be investigated. There is virtually no material dealing, with the problem of reticence *per se,* nor, indeed is it recognized as a problem. Lillywhite, however, points out that generally, inability to communicate is a disease; for example, the person who is *psychologically* incapable of listening is suffering from just as much of a defect as the person who sustains an organic hearing loss.[31] More relevant:

> Our very limited concepts of what we call 'speech defect' and disorders of communication have prevented us from seeing the relationship between clinical communicative disorders and disorders of communication in 'normal' speakers. It would be helpful if we could think of disordered communication as a continuum with difficulties arising from many different causes; some pathological, some psychological, and some social—all contributing to the failure to be understood or to understand. Such a point of view would enable us to make use of the techniques employed in the clinics and the laboratories of speech pathologists and audiologists for help in evaluation, diagnosis and treatment of the problems in communication outside as well as inside the clinic.[32]

Lillywhite may have an extended role for the speech pathologist in mind. His statement also takes cognizance that the wide nosological range of identified speech problems requires the combined diagnostic talents of speech pathologists, psychologists, psychiatrists, and teachers of 'normal speech!' If we accept the premise that many speech disorders result from societal evaluation, there would be no lacuna between normal and abnormal. Any 'normal' speaker enrolled in a public speaking class may be considered a potential 'defective.' That is, any identified pattern may develop to the point where it interferes with his communication and requires special treatment. The public speaking teacher thus finds himself in a new role, that of clinical diagnostician. He may be called upon to do therapy also, in a given case. If so, his whole classroom necessarily takes on the aura of a clinic. Each student would have to be treated as a unique personality with equally unique communication patterns. Diagnosis would reveal those who would benefit from directive training in the form of performance criticism as well as those whose anxiety state would permit only non-directive approaches. Also, such restructuring of the classroom would enable the speech teacher to coordinate his efforts with those of the speech clinician or psychologist to assist rehabilitation of released subjects. If properly trained, the teacher of normal speech could play a significant role in reinforcing clinical gain, in addition to his own clinical role of improving the speech patterns of 'normals.'

Training would involve attempting to derive insights into the factors contributing to 'disordered communication' requiring involvement in a number of fields. Psychological problems and speech problems can be temporary or permanent, chronic or acute. Insights that apply to both temporary deviations in normal speakers and chronic patterns in diagnosed communication defectives must be sought. Above all, an understanding of verbal behavior in general and its relation to personality in general is necessary.

Several authorities believe that communication behavior is so direct a function of personality that any maladjustment, temporary or permanent, would be projected in some way through deviant communication. Johnson speaks of a "language of personality maladjustment,"[33] and Barbara refers to a "neurosis in speaking."[34] Under the general heading of "Language of Maladjustment," Johnson discusses two kinds of individual, classified according to verbal output. Admitting the difficulty of arriving at an accurate estimate of what might constitute a normal amount of talking, Johnson says:

> Among the definitely maladjusted there would appear to be a disproportionate number of these over-verbalized and under-verbalized individuals. Both appear to have great difficulty in expressing themselves with any considerable degree of satisfaction either to themselves or to their listeners.[35]

He goes on to classify verbose individuals into three categories: (1) "those who talk mainly to avoid silence," (2) "others who use language chiefly to conceal truth," and (3) "those whose incessant talking appears to serve the function of a great nervously twitching proboscis with which they explore unceasingly in search of certainty. Of people who talk very little, Johnson says, "as a broad generalization it can be said that they have progressed more deeply in stages of demoralization."[36] Apparently he feels that the person who is still speaking offers some hope for therapy. He considers the person who withdraws from speech a more severe case. He says, for example, of the stutterer:

> A person's speaking time is a fundamental indicator of the degree to which he is handicapped by the communicative difficulty . . . the importance of a particular individual's speech problem is felt by him in a peculiarly basic way in the extent to which he restricts or inhibits his communication with other people.[37]

We are concerned with stuttering not only because it is a verbal deviation accorded low status by society, but more important, because of
its effect on the individual stutterer. We are not distressed by 'syllabic
repetitions.' In most cases, a simple directive, corrective remark remedies
the 'defect.' In a few cases, the context of the directive reinforces tension and a stuttering syndrome is induced. Stuttering inhibits communication with others. It is one of many ways in which persons whose
personality needs impel them to withdraw or avoid the communication
meet this need in their communication behavior. The vector is not
certain. Sometimes communication disorders result from personality problems. Sometimes the disorder is conditioned or present and a personality disorder results. Once the personality disorder has been rooted,
however, treatment solely directed to speech phenomena is generally
useless.

Szasz sets up a "games theory" model for understanding such personality disorders which offers a wide range of explanations also for
avoidance of communication each of which involves personality problems.[38] A human being who seeks to mask his emotions or hide his
values and/or suffers threat from the existence of potential responses
to his communication may elect to withdraw through stuttering, through
manifest stage fright, through monosyllabic responses, through maintenance of a phatic level of communication, through compulsive iteration,
etc. Regardless of the specific method elected, it serves as an explanation to the individual for failure to cope with the role-demands of
society. Reticence may thus mean more than low quantity in verbal
output, but rather denote a nosologic category for any communicative
disorder which results in reducing the effectiveness of the individual
in the normative verbal intercourse demanded by his culture. The psychiatrist may conveniently classify these deviations as 'mild schizophrenia' or 'manic-depressiveness.' However, few persons with mild personality disorders will ever see a psychiatrist. Their problem must be
treated in the normal routine of their daily existence if it is treated
at all. The fortunate ones may perhaps learn to stutter and be referred to a speech clinic for help. Those who deviate in an unclassi-
fiable format will be labelled "weird" and rendered permanently unable
to contribute their verbal share to society. Even worse, they will be
prevented the privilege of self-actualization simply because they are
unable to integrate their own personality with society.

Barbara also discusses in great detail the relationship between personality traits of 'neurotic' persons and the characteristics of their
speech.[39] One classification is "the man of few words," the resigned
speaker, of whom he says:

> Unable to face himself most times in a realistic sense, one of the resigned person's active neurotic solutions is to remove himself from the conflicting situation by assuming the attitude of being the on-looker or non-participating spectator. He represses or denies many of his real feelings and desires by placing inhibitions and checks in the path of their expression.[40]

Society often reinforces such withdrawn behavior with the classification, "good listener." The premium on "good listeners" as sounding boards for the excessively fluent might also be examined in terms of the development of an authoritarian hierarchy in which verbal quantity alone determines the acceptance of ideas. Muir, for example, detected a trend among classified 'reticent' persons toward variance or clash in their basic value structure with those of the modal group of which they were ostensibly members.[41] That means that a prevailing style of values exists in national cultures, an assumption definitively documented by Charles Morris.[42] Examination of micro-cultures or sub-cultures within the American culture might also indicate that sub-styles emerge and those individuals who are members of a sub-culture by propinquity or ascription may avoid threat to his value structure by electing a reticence pattern. Thus the total culture is denied the contribution of their ideas, and they are denied the opportunity to release the tensions they feel.

While 'normals' may be reticent on occasion, the chronically reticent may have adopted a permanent game behavior because of inability to cope with felt or projected values in the group around him. Riesman refers to the ability of the genuinely other-directed individual to detect the basic operant value pattern in his social group with the metaphor of "internal radar."[43] If the individual is suitably other-directed, he will also have no trouble altering his behavior and values to suit those of the mode. On the other hand, the individual who still clings to an inner-directed set may feel values and behaviors hostile to his own and find it necessary to adopt a reticence mechanism to prevent discovery and threat to his value deviation. Stuttering, stage fright, verbal withdrawal and various types of compulsive speaking may be variously elected. Riesman's hypothetical constructs were experimentally confirmed by Williams.[44]

Barbara also discusses two qualities of deviant speech behavior. The self-effacing speaker, he says:

> . . . is in constant dread of failing in the speaking situation. He is in a perpetual state of self-consciousness, tension apprehension and in fear of suffering stage fright or freezing at some particular stage of speaking.

His nervous mannerisms call attention to themselves, his voice often lacks control, his speech is full of vocalized or unvocalized pauses. He has a fear of using words which may have connotations of violence, aggressiveness, presumption or arrogance. He avoids direct assertion and carefully selects his vocabulary.[45] The average speech teacher is familiar with this type. His behavior generally leads to the classification of "lazy" or "unwilling" and earns him a 'C' or less in the course.

The expansive speaker, Barbara continues, is one who has a compulsive need to talk and whose speech is egocentric, aggressive, one-sided and two-valued:

> In the speaking situation, the expansive speaker feels he should be and is the *last word*. In any discussion he fears mutual exchange of ideas, is usually stubborn, resistant, and highly reluctant to face issues squarely and honestly.[46]

Frequently this type of speaker is rewarded with high grades because of fluency alone! Highly developed performance criteria succeed in masking the personality disturbance that enabled him to develop as a "capable" speaker.

There are apparently two levels of disturbed speech behavior with which the classroom speech teacher might be confronted. These may be classified as (1) restricted verbal output, and (2) excessive verbal output. In either case, the disturbed speech pattern would be indicative of a disturbed personality pattern requiring special treatment. The frequency with which such cases are encountered may imply the non-applicability of a uniform pedagogy and the adoption of a clinical format for the teaching of 'normal' speakers.

CLINICAL IMPLICATIONS FOR THE TEACHER OF SPEECH

If we accept the twin premises that (1) speech problems are related to personality problems, and (2) the bulk of such cases exist in the 'normal' population rather than in the clinic, some drastic revisions must be made in the assumption underlying speech pedagogy. Currently the speech teacher functions as a diagnostician, but does so in the framework of the classical view of speech as a separable human behavior capable of pedagogical manipulation in isolation through a variety of directive methods. The "canons" are interpreted to mean that it is possible to train speech in 'parts' or 'units' in which emphasis may be variably placed on sources of ideas, organization, language, delivery patterns or use of notes. That is, if we make the diagnosis "faulty organization," "poor research," "soft voice," "poor eye contact," "sloppy gestures," and the like, specific directions for improvement are warranted as though each were equally capable of improvement separately. The assumption is made that there is a correct standard, which the student must measure up to.

Improvement, however, is judged by the teacher, not by an objective observer nor by subjective report from the student. Observed improvement is attributed to the success of the method; non-improvement is the fault of the student. The relationship between training methods and improvement has not been measured—only hypothesized from the hopes of the instructor! An equally tenable hypothesis would be that the mere opportunity to speak has a salubrious effect and motivates improved performance by desensitizing the speaker to the audience situation in the absence of threat.

Becker notes that society imposes on man the necessity to speak clearly and fluently.[47] Offering a student a chance to speak in a classroom also provides a mechanism for catharsis. This is the one place in the college environment where the student will receive a little undivided attention, not only from peers but also from an authority figure whose approval is being sought. This opportunity makes his personality more vulnerable to threat, because the rules of the academic game as he understands it do not seem to prevail. His improvement may be analyzed in terms of Szasz's games definition.[48] The student understands what is expected of him generally in the academic game, and is ready to comply, since compliance also serves to fit the rules of his own 'game' of socially motivated self-expression. Society rewards the fluent, coherent speaker for his behavior and so reinforces his desire and ability to play the game. Reticent behavior is not rewarded. The reticent (substitute 'C') speaker is penalized by both criticism *and* a poor grade. This is a shock to a vulnerable personality that may have exposed itself. Negative reinforcement results, particularly when peers are permitted to join in the criticism. Their insensitivity to threat-cues often leads them to overcriticize, particularly projections of intrinsic personality mechanisms, heightening the threat to the phenomenal self of the speaker that was exposed, ostensibly to meet the new rules of the speech class game. The unthreatened students can learn something of the nature of social response by listening to their peers criticize. For the reticent speaker, peer criticism only reinforces negative self image and a further penalty is exacted for a failure he has already admitted and expected would not figure in the game. Up until the time the speech teacher asked him to express himself he had devised a method of working around the threat he felt from speaking, but now the classroom situation demands reversal of his internalized behavior in order to succeed. He may try, or he may withdraw, but his internal tension is heightened, whatever he elects to do.

When the threatened speaker exposes his personality and his values, he expects to be reacted to as 'person' rather than 'performer.' But standard criticisms are performance oriented. One response is to withdraw into dullness, to play the game as best he can and preserve a little self-esteem. The threat of the criticism, however, will affect his personality and his communication ability for a long time to come. Muir has traced back several adult speech problems to criticisms offered by teachers (sometimes not speech teachers), parents, significant others in the subject's ontogenesis.[49] In the light of this, an even more satisfactory framework for evaluations would be to examine the student's manifest and covert apprehension levels to determine whether transferable training has come about. Emphasis should be on problems in communication felt external to the speech class. The speech class is only a clinic in which real problems can be worked out with a minimum of threat.

Becker contends that a child develops his verbal patterns in the framework of a total social setting. The child must learn the arbitrary nature of symbolization and its effect on his world.[50] He learns that he can manipulate the world to greater or lesser degrees through the use of his symbolic capacity. He may learn that he is capable of mature control, or he may learn futility, or something in between. In any case, the response of his world of peers and superiors will alter his total personality and this will be reflected in his verbal behavior. The speech teacher can do little short of using clinical methods to altar verbal patterns so inculcated. The speech teacher is not a psychoanalyst, but he cannot be permitted to be an authoritarian director of performances. For the student who 'succeeds' the class as traditionally operated may represent a successful directive therapy. For those who do not succeed, another therapeutic pattern is indicated. There is too little evidence that traditional directive methods succeed in altering human communication behavior to warrant continuation with present methods without solid testing.

The 'normal' approach to the problem of reticence is through the designation "stage fright." The approach to the compulsive over-talker is often "get off my back" or "go out for debate." In either case, the assumption is that conditioning through training under criticism will improve whatever criteria are diagnosed as deficient. The literature on "stagefright" is insightful, but it has not as yet been generally translated into an approach to pedagogy in the typical classroom.

Douglas noted that feelings of personal security are related to effectiveness in public speaking.[51] Those individuals who were rated as 'better speakers' tended to possess the characteristics of mature personal security, self assurance, group identification, and optimism. Poorer speakers gave evidence more typical of chronic insecurity. Penalizing the poorer speaker with a low grade heightens the feeling of insecurity, while the 'A' speaker has his feelings of acceptance heightened. The rift between the two widens and the potentiality for authoritarian domination of the 'better speaker' over the 'poorer' becomes apparent. The poor speaker tends to withdraw even further from participation and plays the game with a little less elan than before. He may rationalize his discouragement by verbalizing a need to study for other courses, or complain about the unfairness of the speech requirement. His limited preparation time is spent mostly in generating anxieties and thus his performance potential is even further reduced.

Ainsworth tended to confirm the connection between stage fright and personality problems by noting tendencies toward shyness, seclusiveness, withdrawal, depression, guilt feelings, and inhibited disposition in stage fright subjects.[52] Several other authorities agree with the findings: Jones,[53] Gilkinson,[54] Wilkinson,[55] and Greenleaf[56] offer similar conclusions that frightened speakers are threatened people. The logical inference is that maximization of threat will heighten anxiety and reduce the potential for effective speaking.

Apprehension or nervousness does not necessarily mean failure on the platform. In the greater number of cases, anxiety is generalized toward the unfamiliar context. Once the teacher and the class become 'knowns' automatic desensitization has had its effect and performance improves in a familiar situation. This leads to success in the class and *possible* carryover. In the minority, perhaps a large minority, of cases, however, anxiety deepens. We assume that mastery of tension in the classroom will carry over, but this assumption is not fully tenable. Those students who master the situation because of the greater fear of failure in the total college context will not necessarily have their anxieties quelled in relation to an unrelated speech performance. Management of anxieties, not necessarily elimination of anxieties is the apparent key to platform success. Mastery imposed by authoritarian threat is temporary, and it has already been noted how, in such circumstances, they may return in a specific situation and interfere even more with performance potential. Thorough measurement of both the long and short term effects of speech training must be made to determine what proportion and what type of student does succeed in making a carryover of performance skill from classroom to more typical public situations. There is enough new evidence about the association of speech problems and personality problems to invalidate the blanket assumption that success in class equals success out of class.

If we accept the idea that there is some connection between reticence, verbal withdrawal, and dysrhythmia with personality disturbances, the need for special treatment is sharply delineated. Gold[57] reports his view that current thinking in psychiatry classifies any verbal withdrawal as a form of schizophrenia. Goldfarb shows that schizophrenics are general disjointed in conceptual responses, particularly space-time orientations.[58] Guertin offers evidence that schizophrenic verbal patterns range over a wide field of difficulty, varying by social conditioning.[59] Seth and Beloff generalize the verbal problem of schizophrenics by showing their inability to handle abstract ideas spontaneously.[60] Fenichel, Freedman, and Klapper construct a theory of therapy which has as its base the removal of the schizophrenic from the offending environments.[61] Recent studies by the Chapmans underscore this point by showing the differentiation in verbal responses by schizophrenics and normals.[62] Connect all these things together and the weight of the evidence supports the contention that the only rational approach to the treatment of personality associated verbal disorders is through special treatment in a constructed environment preliminary to release into a normal environment. The speech pathologists have recognized this for a long time. Severe cases usually require institutionalization. These cases, however, would probably not appear in a typical speech classroom. The mild personality associated speech disorders commonly seen by the speech teacher demand little more than an alteration of pedagogical approach designed to minimize threat and allow personality to come more in harmony with the social context.

Morse, among others, attacks the overuse of the schizophrenic diagnosis by psychiatrists but does so without minimizing the importance of a verbal disturbance for the person who suffers from it.[63] Certainly specialists in the field of speech are not sufficiently sophisticated in psychiatric nosology to diagnose or treat 'schizophrenia.' However, the field has already assumed the burden of special clinical treatment for one type of verbal disorder, stuttering. It has been demonstrated that stage fright, verbal withdrawal, and excessive compulsiveness in speech, regardless of psychiatric diagnosis, exist on a continuum with stuttering and fit the same dimension of aiding the subject to avoid the normal communicative context. These, therefore, should be considered worthy of special treatment as well.

Research findings for stuttering show a pattern similar to those for verbal problems in general. Goodstein[64] and Johnson[65] both demonstrate an association between stuttering and desire for social withdrawal. In this sense, the typical speech problems encountered by the public speaking teacher may be regarded as related to stuttering. Those individuals most intimidated by the classroom situation deserve an essentially similar approach. It cannot be inferred that conditioning a speaker by forcing him to speak will work any better than forcing an acrophobic to go up in an airplane, or locking a claustrophobic in a broom closet, particularly in the light of Heilbrun's findings that authoritarian environments heighten personality disintegration and communication disturbance.[66] The broadness of the agreement about stuttering is significant, despite surface disagreements among experts. Barbara notes that regardless of the approach to *therapy*, there appears to be general agreement that stuttering has an emotional base; Blanton, Fletcher, Gifford, Robbins, and Solomon are offered in evidence.[67]

It is clear that not all fearful people stutter or show manifest stage fright symptoms, nor even display patterns of reticence. Some attempt must be made to connect situation with speech disturbance. Perhaps disturbed oral communication is a function of a specific anxiety in a pre-determined social setting. Berry and Eisenson note that the variation in stuttering pattern depends on social context:

> Students of stuttering have long known that stutterers have varying difficulty according to the nature and size of their audience. Almost all stutterers are completely fluent when talking aloud to themselves in the privacy of their own rooms. They can talk with normal or almost normal fluency when addressing animal pets. Adult stutterers usually have little difficulty talking to small children. When we analyze the relatively easy situations for most stutterers, we find that a 'common denominator' of the speaking situations is a relative absence of communicative responsibility.[68]

Johnson says almost the same thing about stage fright:

> Relative particularly to fluency problems are anxiety-tension manifestations commonly termed 'stage fright.' That is, of course, not confined to the stage, and involves a more or less serious disturbance of speech. This is very common and in severe cases, the effects on speech are both disintegrative and restrictive.[69]

Social context appears critical, and this is the peg on which therapy can be hung, for by altering social context as in a clinical environment, it is possible to bring about some adjustment to the difficulty, though not necessarily elimination of it. West refers to context when he says:

> Some persons classify themselves as stutterers and consider their problem serious who have few or no obvious breaks in the fluency pattern. Judged by over symptoms alone, the latter would frequently not be classified as stutterers at all. . . .[70]

In short, the internal feelings of the individual, conditioned by social cues, result in the self-evaluation of difficulty. Many times the depth of feeling-involvement cannot be inferred from overt symptoms. Once an individual has given a name to his feelings, they can become tokens in the game that the individual has elected to play. Blanton notes:

> Stuttering is a blocking of the person's ability to adjust to other people. It is a personality defect due to anxiety in meeting various social situations, rather than a speech defect.[71]

The words "stage fright," "reticence," or "disturbed verbal behavior" could be neatly substituted for "stuttering." Further, it is clear that therapies offered for stuttering could not be carried on in the normal speech classroom.[72]

There seems to be sufficient indication that stuttering and stage fright are, in some way related, and further, that they are related to a general category of personality disturbances characterized by inability to function well in situations where oral interaction is necessary. Recent preliminary investigations of subjects classified into the categories of "stutterer," "stage fright victim," and "reticent" serve to confirm this connection. Interviews with some forty subjects, including written projectives, tend to indicate a uniform fear of social context, a uniform expression of capability when confronted with inferiors, and most important, a generalized deviation from the value structures of the norm. If these findings are confirmed in a more rigid experimental context, then the significance for the teacher of speech cannot be overestimated. He would cease to be a teacher in the classical sense, imparting knowledge and directing behavior, but would become a nondirective clinician. Each student would have to be approached as an individual clinical subject. Backus has already stated vigorously that there is no real separation between 'normal' and 'abnormal' behaviors, let alone a separation between the various categories of abnormality. She states:

> Speech is viewed in psychological terms for all persons, not just for those judged to have 'maladjustments,' or not just for those who have 'speech disorders.' The concept of a dichotomy between normal and disordered speech may have a convenience administratively in speech departments, but it is not considered relevant in discovering causal relations in a client's behavior. For instance, available evidence appears to indicate that the same laws . . . govern phenomena classed 'stage fright' in the classroom and . . . 'anxiety' in the clinic.[73]

A similar view is expressed by Nelson:

> It may be possible now to discern that these people (reticents) have actual communication disorders or 'speech defects,' and certainly they experience a concern similar to that of a person with a clinically diagnosed speech or language disorder. These individuals may reasonably require diagnosis and clinical type treatment before they can expect to function successfully before an audience.[74]

The precise nature of the clinical approach necessary in the typical public speaking class has not yet been worked out. There is no question but what it is necessary. Imposition of arbitrary threats like grades on speeches, peer criticisms, and the variety of personality-attacks that result from instructor criticism honestly and sincerely given may have some success in improving overt verbal quantity and quality for the majority of students. The incidence of physiological symptoms, emotional fantasies, verbalized threats, etc. in a typical population of speech students, however, is large enough to warrant a broad re-evaluation of pedagogical assumptions and methods, leading to the development of a new set of goals and methods for the teaching of speech. One thing is sure. The traditional motif of teaching speech on a recitation-criticism basis now has the burden of proof, and must show it is not harmful or be revised!

FOOTNOTES

[1]Leonard Goodstein, "Functional Speech Disorders and Personality; A Survey of the Literature," *Journal of Speech and Hearing Research* (December, 1958). Cf. also
Franklin Knower, *Table of Contents of The Quarterly Journal of Speech, 1915-1960, Speech Monographs, 1934-1960, and The Speech Teacher, 1952-1960* with a revised index complete through 1960. Bloomington, Indiana: The Speech Association of America, 1961.

[2]Lee Edward Travis (ed.), *Handbook of Speech Pathology,* New York: Appleton-Century-Crofts, 1957.

[3]*Ibid.*

[4]Charles Van Riper, *Speech Correction: Principles and Methods,* 4th Ed., Englewood Cliffs, New Jersey: Prentice-Hall, Inc., 1963.

[5]Ernest Becker, *The Birth and Death of Meaning,* New York: The Free Press, 1962.

[6]Jordan Scher, "Ontoanalysis, the New Psychiatry," Unpublished paper written for delivery at the Speech Association of America Convention, Denver, 1962.

[7]Mildred F. Berry and Jon Eisenson, *Speech Disorders: Principles and Practices of Therapy.* New York: Appleton-Century-Crofts, Inc., 1956.

[8]Wendell Johnson, *People in Quandaries.* New York: Harper and Brothers, 1946.

[9]Jules Masserman, "Ethology, Comparative Biodynamics, and Psychoanalytic Research," in Jordan Scher (Ed.) *Theories of The Mind.* New York: The Free Press, 1962.

[10]John Paul Brady, "Language in Schizophrenia," *American Journal of Psychiatry,* XII, 1958.

[11]Alfred M. Freedman, Eva V. Ebing and Ethel W. Wilson, "Autistic Schizophrenic Children," *Archives of General Psychiatry,* VI, 3 (1962).

[12]Francis Schachter, Lucie Mayer and Earl Loomis, "Childhood Schizophrenia and Mental Retardation: Differential Diagnosis Before and After One Year of Psychotherapy," *American Journal of Orthopsychiatry,* XXXII, 4 (1962).

[13]Victor Rowley and Dwayne Keller, "Changes in Children's Verbal Behavior as a Function of Social Approval and Manifest Anxiety," *Journal of Abnormal and Social Psychology,* vol. 65 (July, 1962).

[14]Lloyd Rogler and ugust Hollingshead, "Class and Disordered Speech in the Mentally Ill," *Journal of Health and Human Behavior.* II (Fall, 1961).

[15]Arthur W. Combs and Donald Syngg, *Individual Behavior.* New York: Harper and Bros., 1959.

[16]Masserman, *Op. Cit.*

[17]Thomas Szasz, *The Myth of Mental Illness.* New York: Harper-Hoeber, 1962.

[18]Thomas A. Sebeok, Alfred S. Hayes and Mary Catherine Bates, *Approaches to Semiotics.* The Hague: Mouton & Co., 1964.

[19]Clarence L. Barnhart (Ed.) *American College Encyclopedic Dictionary.* Chicago: The Spencer Press, 1950.

[20]Van Riper, *Op. Cit.*

[21]Jurgen Ruesch and Gregory Bateson, *Disturbed Communication.* New York: Norton & Co., 1957.

[22]Paul Goodman, *Growing Up Absurd.* New York: Random House, 1960.

[23]Laura Muir, *Case Studies of Selected Examples of Reticence and Fluency.* Unpublished M.A. Thesis. Washington State University, Pullman, Washington, 1964.

[24]Jurgen Ruesch, *Therapeutic Communication.* New York: Norton & Co., 1961.

[25]Paul D. Holtzman, *An Experimental Study of Some Relationships Among Several Indices of Stage Fright and Personality.* Unpublished Ph.D. dissertation. University of Southern California, 1950.

[26]Johnson, *Op. Cit.*

[27]Masserman, *Op. Cit.*

[28]W. Stein, *Contemporary Psychotherapies.* New York: The Free Press, 1960.

[29]Carl Rogers, *Client Centered Therapy.* New York: Harper & Bros.

[30]Masserman, *Op. Cit.*

[31]Harold Lillywhite, "Symposium on 'A Broader Concept of Communication Disorders,' An Introduction," *The Journal of Communication.* XIV.I (1964).

[32]*Ibid.*

[33]Johnson, *Op. Cit.*

[34]Dominick Barbara (Ed.) *Psychological and Psychiatric Aspects of Speech and Hearing,* Springfield, Illinois: Charles Thomas, 1960.

[35]Johnson, *Op. Cit.*

[36]*Ibid.*

[37]*Ibid.*

[38]Szasz, *Op. Cit.*

[39]Barbara, *Op. Cit.*

[40]*Ibid.*

[41]Muir, *Op. Cit.*

[42]Charles Morris, *Varieties of Human Value.* Chicago: University of Chicago Press.

[43]David Riesman, *The Lonely Crowd.* Garden City: Doubleday, Anchor Books, 1953.

[44]Walter Williams, "Inner-Directedness and Other-Directedness in New Perspective," *The Sociological Quarterly,* V, 3 (Summer, 1964).

[45]Barbara, *Op. Cit.*

[46]*Ibid.*

[47]Becker, *Op. Cit.*

[48]Szasz, *Op. Cit.*

[49]Muir, *Op. Cit.*

[50]Becker, *Op. Cit.*

[51]Robert L. Douglass, "The Relation of Feelings of Personal Security to Effective Public Speaking," *Speech Monographs,* 1948.

[52]Stanley H. Ainsworth, "A Study of Fear, Nervousness, and Anxiety in the Public Speaking Situation," *Speech Monographs,* XVIII, 3 (1949).

[53]Marnetta Jones, "The Relationship of Certain Personality Traits to Stage Fright," *Speech Monographs,* IX (1943).

[54]Howard Gilkinson, "Social Fears as Reported by Students in College," *Speech Monographs,* IX (1943).

[55]Esther Jensen Wilkinson, "A Study of Disintegrating Background Factors in the Development of Effective Speech Personality," *Speech Monographs,* XI (1944).

[56]Floyd I. Greenleaf, "An Exploratory Study of Social Speech Fright," *Speech Monographs,* XII (1948).

[57]Frank Gold, M.D., Interview conducted in Cleveland, Ohio, August, 1964.

[58]William Goldfarb, "Self-Awareness in Schizophrenic Children," *Archives of General Psychiatry.* VIII, 1 (1963).

[59]Wilson H. Guertin, "Are Differences in Schizophrenic Symptoms Related to the Mother's Avowed Attitude Toward Child-Rearing?" *Journal of Abnormal and Social Psychology.* Vol. 63, (1961).

[60]George Seth and Halla Beloff, "Language Impairments in a Group of Schizophrenics," *British Journal of Medical Psychology.* vol. 32, (1959).

[61]Carl Fenichel, Alfred Freedman, and Zelda Klapper, "A Day School for Schizophrenic Children," *American Journal of Orthopsychiatry.* vol. 30, (Jan., 1960).

[62]Loren J. Chapman and Jean P. Chapman, "Interpretations of Words in Schizophrenia," *Journal of Abnormal and Social Psychology.* 1, 2 (Feb., 1965).

[63]Hilde L. Morse, "The Misuse of the Diagnosis 'Childhood Schizophrenia,'" *American Journal of Psychiatry.* vol. 114 (1958).

[64]Leonard Goodstein, "Functional Speech Disorders and Personality: A Survey of the Research," *Journal of Speech and Hearing Research.* (December, 1958).

[65]Wendell Johnson, "Problems of Impaired Speech," *Journal of the American Medical Association,* CLXX, 17 (1959).

[66]Alfred B. Heibrum, Jr., "Perception of Maternal Child-Rearing Attitudes in Schizophrenics," *Journal of Consulting Psychology.* 24 (April, 1960).

[67]Dominick Barbara, *Stuttering.* New York: The Julian Press, 1954.

[68]Berry and Eisenson, *Op. Cit.*

[69]Johnson, *Op. Cit.*, 1946.

[70]Robert West, Marle Ansberry and Anna Carr, *The Rehabilitation of Speech.* 3rd Ed., New York: Harper and Bros., 1957.

[71]Smiley Blanton, "Stuttering," *Journal of The American Medical Association.* CLX, 17 (1956).

[72]Robert W. Rieber, "Suttering and Self-Concept," *Journal of Psychology.* 55, (1963).

[73]Ollie Backus, "Group Structures in Speech Therapy," in Lee Travis, *Op. Cit.*

[74]C. Donald Nelson, "Student Speaking Disorders—Beyond the Symptoms," *The Journal of Communication,* XIV, 1 (1964).

A Synthesis of Experimental
Research in Stage Fright

THEODORE CLEVENGER, JR.

Experimental research into rhetoric and public address is growing rapidly in scope and volume, and a few areas of study have been so extensively exploited by experimental and quasi-experimental methods that the time has arrived for synthesis of the findings.[1]

Nowhere are experimental findings readier for synthesis than in stage fright. Many investigators, following independent lines of research, have accumulated an impressive backlog of findings. Viewed as a whole, this body of research first appears contradictory and confusing, but a thorough-going analysis of it reveals a remarkable consistency. Analysis also suggests hypotheses which emerge only when experiments are compared.

The key to fruitful comparison of experiments lies in an understanding of the problems of definition and measurement as they apply to research in stage fright, where these two problems become inextricably intertwined.

A typical approach to the problem of definition for experimental purposes was that of Floyd I. Greenleaf, who defined "social speech fright" as: ". . . an evaluative disability, occurring in social speech situations, and characterized by anticipatory negative reactions of fear, avoidance, and various internal and overt manifestations of tension and behavioral maladjustment."[2] Validation of this definition proceeded as follows.

Students in a basic speech course rated themselves on a four-point self-rating scale of social speech fright. Those who placed themselves in the "severe" category were interviewed, and on the basis of these interviews and some external materials, a "Situational Speech Inventory" was prepared and administered, along with the original four-point self-rating scale of social speech fright, to 786 public speaking students. The inventory consisted largely of a list of symptoms. Those symptoms

---

From *The Quarterly Journal of Speech*, vol. XLV, no. 2 (April, 1959), pp. 134-145. Reprinted by permission.

Mr. Clevenger is Instructor in Speech at the University of Illinois. Portions of this article first appeared in the author's doctoral dissertation, "An Analysis of Variance of the Relationship of Experienced Stage Fright to Selected Psychometric Inventories," submitted at The Florida State University in 1958, under the direction of Dr. Clarence W. Edney.

[1]The writer and a colleague plan syntheses of other experimental areas in addition to that offered here.

[2]Floyd I. Greenleaf, "An Experimental Study of Social Speech Fright," Unpublished M.A. thesis, State University of Iowa, 1947.

which distinguished well between persons indicating much and persons indicating little stage fright on the scale were said to be typical of stage fright.

It is important to note that the method of determining who had and who had not stage fright had nothing to do with the verbal definition offered. In the Greenleaf study, the subjects chosen for analysis were persons who rated themselves high on a self-rating scale of social speech fright. Presumably, if these persons had responded in the interviews in a way that was incompatible with the verbal definition, then the definition would have been discarded. The real definition, then, was not the verbalization, but the scale used to detect the presence of stage fright.

In a similar case, Chenoweth was concerned with "adjustment to the speaking situation," which he defined as follows: "The Process of Adjustment to the Speaking Situation . . . is the process by which the speaker, in executing the speech act, adjusts, organizes and controls the functioning of his bodily mechanism in accordance with, and in spite of, conditions within the immediate speaking situation."[3] This definition, however, did not play a crucial role in the experiment, since the criterion of speech adjustment was a seven-point judges' rating scale.

Gordon Low defined stage fright as: ". . . the emotional disturbance of the physical and mental behavior of the public speaker as it is manifest by the observable characteristics: poor eye-contact, nervous hand movements, restless shifting of feet, awkward posture, body quiver, timid voice, embarrassment and other physical and vocal cues empathically perceived."[4] In the experiment, however, Low designated as possessing high degrees of stage fright only those persons who received high self-ratings on a scale similar to those of Chenoweth and Greenleaf.

The joint study performed by Gibson and Prall ostensibly makes no effort to define stage fright, but says nevertheless: "It has been assumed that the term stage fright may be used conventionally to indicate the complex, and usually unpleasant, emotional states which frequently accompany the experience of performers."[5] But in the experiment, the measure of stage fright was a five-point judges' rating scale. It had nothing to do with the definition.

No case may be found in which a categorical verbal definition played a controlling role in a stage fright experiment, though there are few

---

[3]Eugene Chenoweth, "The Adjustment of College Freshmen to the Speaking Situation," *QJS*, XXVI (1940), 585.

[4]Gordon Low, "The Relation of Psychometric Factors to Stage Fright," Unpublished M.S. thesis, University of Utah, 1950.

[5]Milton Dickens, Francis Gibson, and Caleb Prall, "An Experimental Study of the Overt Manifestations of Stage Fright," *SM*, XVII (1950), 37.

experiments which do not offer one. In each case, the ultimate definition of stage fright—and the only one which makes sense experimentally—is the operational definition which describes the instrument used to measure it. In other words, the measuring instrument in a stage fright experiment is not only the measurement of stage fright, it is the definition as well.

Stage fright measures fall into three rough categories: observer rating scales, introspective measures, and devices for measuring physiological changes during speaking. Under appropriate conditions, any of the three may be highly reliable, but reliabilities of various rating scales for observers have received the most intensive study.

Dickens, Gibson, and Prall report a study of a five-point rating scale of stage fright. When sixty-one speech teachers and graduate students rated forty student speakers, the split-half reliability of the scale was .98. When groups of five were correlated against the whole judging group, the coefficients ran between .92 and .98. Since the correlation of a sub-group with a larger group including it will usually produce spuriously high coefficients, we may assume that the true reliability of groups of five judges who are college speech teachers and graduate students in speech falls somewhat below this figure—say, between .85 and .95. Since differences between individual judges' ratings were pronounced, the true reliability of individual judges' ratings on a five-point scale of degree of stage fright is probably quite low. These findings, taken with Eckert and Keys' finding that groups of three and four judges produced correlation coefficients of .68 on a similar scale,[6] suggest the hypothesis that *groups of judges are able to make judgments of stage fright of an order of reliability varying as a negatively-accelerated monotonic growth function of the number of judges.*[7]

In addition to number of judges, the reliability of rating scales of this type seems to be affected by characteristics of the speakers and the judges. Dickens, Gibson, and Prall report that sex, experience, and area of interest did not affect reliabilities of the rating scales used in their experiments. However, they were working with a rather select group of speech instructors and graduate students. Parker found reliabilities on the identical scale, when used by groups of sixteen and more undergraduate students, to be substantially below the reliabilities found in the Gibson and Prall experiments.[8] This suggests that *either*

---

[6]Ralph G. Eckert and Noel Keys, "Public Speaking as a Cue to Personality Adjustment," *Jour. of Applied Psych.*, XXIV (1940) 153.

[7]The same is true of other psychological phenomena. See J. P. Guilford, *Psychometric Methods* (New York, 1936), Chapter 14.

[8]Milton Dickens and Williams R. Parker, "An Experimental Study of Certain Physiological, Introspective and Rating Scale Teachniques for the Measurement of Stage Fright," *SM*, XVIII (1951), 251-259.

age or training in speech or experience in speaking or some combination of these bears some relation to reliability of judgments of stage fright, but that reliability is not a linear function of these factors.

The data of the Gibson and Prall experiments suggest that judges are less reliable in judging fearful speakers than in judging confident ones. *Teachers of speech are evidently in stronger agreement concerning what constitutes the absence of stage fright than what constitutes its presence.*

Reliabilities of introspective measuring devices have rarely been established. In the case of introspective rating scales, like that used in the Hendrickson study,[9] it is impossible to establish reliability, because the two usual methods for testing it cannot be employed. Since the scales are one-item scores, it is impossible to perform a split-half correlation, and since the precise speech experience is unrepeatable, it is not fruitful to perform a test-retest correlation.

In addition to rating scales, introspective measures of stage fright include subjective reports, like the Lomas questionnaire,[10] and inventory tests. Extensive reliability study of quantified subjective reports is not available at the time of this writing. On the other hand, the reliability of one inventory test is well established. An extensive study of the reliability of the "Personal Report of Confidence as a Speaker" (PRCS), involving over 400 students, produced a split-half reliability coefficient of .93. As a measure of reaction to a specific speaking experience, split-half and odd-even coefficients are the best means of establishing reliability. The test-retest correlation of .60 reported by Gilkinson is of little value in assessing the reliability of the instrument, since a speech experience cannot be repeated.[11]

Obviousy, the reliability of instruments for measuring physiological reactions to the speech situation is the most highly reliable of the three classes of stage fright measures. Though test-retest and split-half coefficients cannot be performed on pulse-rate, psychogalvanometer, and sphygmomanometer readings, one may assume high reliabilities for such instruments.

To summarize the results of research into the reliabilities of various measures of stage fright: Under proper conditions a measurement of very high reliability can be made using either observer ratings, subjective responses, or measures of physiological change, although the

---

[9]Ernest Hendrickson, "A Study of Stage Fright and the Judgment of Speaking Time," *Jour. of Apllied Psych.*, XXXII (1948), 521-535.

[10]Charles W. Lomas, "A Study of Stage Fright as Measured by Student Reactions to the Speech Situation," Unpublished M.A. thesis, Northwestern University, 1934.

[11]Howard Gilkinson, "Social Fears as Reported by students in College Speech Classes," *SM*, IX (1942), 141-160.

reliability of observer ratings is apparently influenced by the number, age, and experience of the raters, and by the specific range of stage fright represented by the subjects of the experiment.

Surprisingly, instruments which are so reliable display comparatively poor intercorrelations. Results of comparisons of various indices of stage fright suggest that the emotional disturbance which is recorded on physiological measuring devices is different from both the emotional disturbance which the speaker reports having experienced, and the emotional disturbance which a group of judges report having observed, and that the latter are different from each other.

Dickens reported that for his group of forty male speakers, selected to form a normal distribution of stage fright, averaged judges' ratings of a group of college speech instructors produced a correlation co-efficient of .59 with the PRCS. The reliabilities of both instruments used in this study were above .90.

Using identical measurements, but a less sophisticated group of judges, Parker found that for 100 students similar to those in the prior study, the correlation between PRCS and averaged ratings was a mere .20.

Williams, using similar but not identical instruments, found that ob-server judgments ran below subjective reports in the majority of the cases.[12] Gibson and Prall obtained the same result.

These findings suggest two hypotheses. First, considering the high reliability of the instruments and low correlations between them in separate experiments involving different subjects and judges, the Dickens-Gibson-Prall experiments and the Parker experiment taken together suggest that *introspective measures of stage fright measure a variable that is somehow different from that which is measured by averaged judges' ratings.* Second, the consistency with which judges' ratings ran below introspective accounts of stage fright suggests that *a group of observers tends to notice less disruption in the speaker than the speaker reports having experienced.* In connection with the second hypothesis, it is interesting to note that Wrenchley's group of prominent speakers defined stage fright largely in cognitive terms. The kinds of experience which they reported suggested that they viewed stage fright as a largely covert experience with only occasional overt concomitant behavior.[13]

Measures of various physiological changes during speaking coincided no better with either introspective or judges' ratings than did these with each other. When Redding compared introspective accounts with

---

[12]Norma G. Williams, "An Investigation of Maladjustment to a Speaking Situation Shown by Seventh, Eighth, Ninth and Tenth Grade Students in a Secondary School," Unpublished M.A. thesis, State University of Iowa, 1950.

[13]Elma Dean Orr Wrenchley, "A Study of Stage Fright Attacks in a Selected Group of Speakers," Unpublished M.A. thesis, University of Denver, 1948.

measures of galvanic skin response he found no consistent relation.[14] Comparing circulatory fluctuations with both judges' ratings and the PRCS scores. Parker found that the amount of circulatory disruption correlated rather poorly with the other variables.

These findings concerning the intercorrelations of various measures of stage fright suggest strongly that they are not measures of the same variable. Although they may be associated with each other in some way, the hypothesis is advanced that *audience-perceived stage fright, cognitively-explained stage fright, and physiological disruption are three variables which operate with only moderate interdependence during the course of a public speech.*

It therefore seems that referring to a measure of any one of these as a measure of stage fright is not justified, since any one measurement will not bear a direct relation to any categorical verbal definition of stage fright nor will it be likely to correlate well with any other dimension of measurement. Instruments like the Lomas questionnaire and the PRCS are devices for measuring *cognitively-experienced stage fright;* instruments like the judges' rating scale are devices for measuring *audience-perceived stage fright;* and instruments like the sphygmomanometer and the psychogalvanometer are devices for measuring *physiological reactions to speaking.* These may be thought of as the amount of fright a speaker says he has, the amount his audience says he has, and the amount a meter says he has. At least for the present, it appears wise to think of these as three separate variables.

All studies reported to date have made the implicit assumption that one or another of these instruments was a more or less valid and reliable "measure of stage fright." This has led to apparently conflicting findings. If one adopts the position that these are three different variables, and maintains the distinctions among them, conflicts between studies disappear and the entire body of research assumes an orderly structure.

Studies of stage fright symptoms have been complicated by failure to grasp the essential differences between introspective, physiological, and observational variables at work in the speech situation. This may account for the apparent conflict between Henning's findings and those of Gilkinson. Henning correlated quantified Lomas questionnaire scores with judges' observations of specific speech behavioral patterns, and found no regular "symptoms of stage fright."[15] On the other hand,

---

[14]Charles W. Redding, "The Psychogalvanometer as a Laboratory Instrument in the Basic Course in Speech," Unpublished M.A. thesis, University of Denver, 1936.

[15]James H. Henning, "A Study of Stage Fright Through the Comparison of Student Reactions and Instructor Observations During the Speech Situation," Unpublished M.A. thesis, Northwestern University, 1935.

Gilkinson compared similar observations with PRCS scores, and found significantly more listlessness, lack of eye contact, lack of projection, and lack of expression in badly frightened students than in those displaying virtually no stage fright.

Despite an apparent conflict, these studies complement rather than contradict one another. It must first be noted that both Henning and Gilkinson were comparing measurements in the cognitive dimension with measurements in the observational dimension. King's independent evidence leads us to expect that any such relationship will be relatively weak.[16] Furthermore, each was comparing partial measures of audience-observed stage fright with an over-all measure of experienced stage fright. Thus, the relationship between experienced stage fright and specific observable behaviors should be, on the average, quite weak indeed. Gilkinson's method involved comparing mean scores on the behavioral measures between the top fifty and the low fifty PRCS scores selected from a group of some 400 students—a procedure which has no predictive value with respect to persons between these extremes but is certain to reveal as significant virtually any trace relationship. On the other hand, Henning's test of significance for the correlation coefficient used the whole range of confidence rather than the extremes, a procedure which will yield significance only if there is a strong linear relationship between the variables. Both studies, then, produced results which are reasonable in view of the hypothesis that experienced stage fright and observed stage fright operate with only moderate interdependence in the speaking situation. Both studies suggest that *between overall measures of experienced stage fright and observational indices of specific speech behaviors, a positive but weak relationship prevails.*

Because of the failure to distinguish sharply enough among types of measurement, studies like those of Jones and Lerea, if taken as analyses of stage fright symptoms, are subject to serious limitations. Jones found that fifty students who were rated high in stage fright by two instructors in speech reported that they experienced significantly more forgetting, confusion, weakness, pounding of the heart, fear of audience disapproval, fear of failure, and insecurity about their speech materials than did a group of fifty students rated low in stage fright by the instructors.[17] It is interesting to note that the Jones study is a precise mirror image of the Gilkinson study. Where the Gilkinson experiment

---

[16]Thomas R. King, "An Experiment to Determine the Relationship Between Individual Visible Manifestations of Stage Fright and the Degree of Stage Fright Reported by the Individual," Unpublished M.A. thesis, The Florida State University, 1958.

[17]Marnetta M. Jones, "The Relationships of Certain Personality Traits to Stage Fright," Unpublished M.A. thesis, Stanford University, 1947.

compared over-all measures of experienced stage fright with partial measures of observed stage fright, the Jones study compares over-all measures of observed stage fright with partial measures of experienced stage fright. Both studies contrasted groups drawn from the extremes of fear and confidence. However, on the basis of neither study can we draw firm conclusions concerning symptoms of stage fright. To claim that Gilkinson showed that listlessness, lack of eye contact, and other behaviors are symptoms of stage fright, is to claim that specific overt behaviors are symptoms of cognitive states. In the Jones study, to say that fear of failure, confusion, and the other states are symptoms of stage fright, is to claim that cognitive states are symptoms of overt behavior classes. Both positions are of doubtful defensibility.

Likewise misleading are Lerea's conclusions, if interpreted to mean that low verbal output, low vocabulary, stammering, and errors are symptoms of stage fright. The most one can say from this study is that students who rate themselves high in stage fright at the beginning and low in stage fright at the end of a course in speech tend to display lower output, smaller vocabulary, and more stammering and errors at the beginning than at the end of the course. We would expect this kind of improvement in a first course in speech whether students improved in confidence or not; hence the findings here are by no means clear concerning the experimental variable. Even if they were, it would be difficult on this basis to assert that the verbal behaviors are symptoms of stage fright, since the "symptoms" were measured in one dimension, while the "stage fright" was measured in another.[18]

Without suggesting in any way that experimentation into the relationships among experienced stage fright, observed stage fright, and physiological change is worthless, the above studies do imply a principle which might guide research into stage fright symptoms in the immediate future: those experiments may be expected to produce the most fruitful results which measure both stage fright and its symptoms in the same measurement dimension. That is, if stage fright is measured by an instrument such as the PRCS, then those symptoms should be measured which are cognitive in nature. If stage fright is measured by an observer rating scale, then the appropriate symptoms are classes of behavior.

Such studies have not been altogether neglected. For example, Hendrickson found that students who report having experienced severe stage fright are able to make much better judgments of elapsed speak-

---

[18]Louis Lerea, "A Preliminary Study of the Verbal Behavior of Speech Fright," *SM,* XXIII (1956), 229-233.

ing time than are other students.[19] Greenleaf reported that students indicating high experienced stage fright reported having experienced inability to finish speaking, weakness of voice, inability to look at the audience, tremors of bodily extremities, feelings of audience disapproval, and stammering. Both of these studies help to define symptoms of one dimension of stage fright, the cognitive experience.

Studies of the relation of stage fright to other factors also fall into a more coherent pattern when the distinction between types of measures is preserved. Gilkinson reported that college women experienced more fear as indicated by PRCS scores than did college men, and Williams found that girls in the seventh, eighth, ninth, and tenth grades reported more fear and less confidence than did boys on a "Student Reaction Sheet."[20] At the same time, Gilkinson and Knower reported that college men displayed more random behavior and fidgetiness according to judges' observations than did women, and Williams found that boys scored lower in confidence on an "Observer Check Sheet." Parker reported that men made more confident scores on the PRCS than did women, while classmates tended to rate women higher in confidence on a rating scale. Clevenger found a consistently higher mean PRCS score for women than for men, in groups matched for other variables.[21] Ainsworth and King found no significant difference in degree of stage fright between groups of college men and women.[22]

Clearly, most studies show a sex difference for degree of stage fright. In every case where a significant difference was observed, men indicated less experienced stage fright while women were judged to display less stage fright by audience observers. These studies suggest that *judges observe stage fright more in men than in women, while women experience more stage fright than men, but the differences in both cases are small.*

Observed stage fright clearly bears some relation to judgments of speaking ability. Gilkinson and Knower reported that poor speakers are more often rated by judges as fidgety and nervous than are good speakers. Eckert and Keys reported that the correlation of "poise" and ratings of general speaking effectiveness was .77, higher than that for any of the other factors of speaking.

---

[19]Ernest Hendrickson, "A Study of Stage Fright and The Judgment of Speaking Time."

[20]Howard Gilkinson and Franklin Knower, "Individual Differences Among Students of Speech as Revealed by Psychological Tests," *QJS*, XXVI (1940), 243-255.

[21]Theodore Clevenger, Jr., "An Analysis of Variance of the Relationship of Experienced Stage Fright to Selected Psychometric Inventories," Unpublished Ph.D. dissertation, The Florida State University, 1958.

[22]Stanley H. Ainsworth, "A Study of Fear, Nervousness, and Anxiety in the Public Speaking Situation," Unpublished Ph.D. dissertation, Northwestern University, 1949. Also King.

On the other hand, experienced stage fright may not bear a close relation to judgments of speaking ability. Gilkinson found that the PRCS for 420 college students correlated only .39 with judges' ratings of speech skill. This raises the hypothesis that *observed stage fright bears a strong negative relationship to judgments of speaking ability, while experienced stage fright bears a weak negative relationship to judgments of speaking ability.*

Apparently conflicting studies concerning the relation of experienced stage fright to speech experience may be reconciled if a careful distinction is preserved between experimental samples. Kinsley interviewed sixty prominent speakers, quantified the results, and found no correlation between amount of stage fright regularly experienced by these speakers and either extent of speech training or amount of speech experience.[23] On the other hand, Chenoweth interviewed fifty speakers who obtained high confidence ratings on the Barnes Scale and fifty who had obtained low ratings, and found that the more confident speakers had undergone more training and experience in speech.[24] Low, using a similar technique, found that students with high stage fright tended to have little speech experience.[25]

Of course, it is possible to explain these differences in terms of computational procedure. Quartile and octile comparisons in general yield significance more often than tests of significance for the correlation coefficient. However, it is not necessary to resort to a comparison of statistical methods in this case, since the differences between the samples suggest a more fundamental explanation. It may be noted that Kinsley's group of prominent speakers represented a rather narrow range of variation in both speech experience and degree of stage fright—all displayed very high experience and very low stage fright. On the other hand, Chenoweth and Low drew samples from beginning speech classes, doubtless representing a very wide range of variation in both variables, though unquestionably well below Kinsley's sample in speech experience. It is a fact that a correlation coefficient performed upon data from a narrow range of variation in both the x and the y variables, will generally run much lower than a coefficient performed upon a sample including a wide range of those variables. Thus, for experienced speakers, where virtually all of the sample had low stage fright and high experience, the correlation would run low; but in a basic speech class, where wide ranges of both prevail, a higher co-

[23]Wade Allen Kinsley, "An Investigation of the Phenomenon of Stage Fright in Certain Prominent Speakers," Unpublished Ph.D. dissertation, Northwestern University, 1950.
[24]Chenoweth, "The Adjustment of College Freshmen to the Speaking Situation."
[25]Gordon Low, "The Relation of Psychometric Factors to Stage Fright."

efficient would be expected. It is also a fact that the bottom end of a negatively-accelerated monotonic growth function conforms more nearly to the assumption of rectilinearity implicit in the Pearson *r* than does the top end of the same function. Violation of this assumption will generally produce a spuriously low coefficient. The hypothesis is suggested that *speaker confidence is a negatively-accelerated monotonic growth function of experience in speaking.* This conjecture draws some support from Kinsley's report that all of the speakers he interviewed reported great reductions in stage fright since their early speaking careers, and that their stage fright diminished most within the first year of speaking.

Emery found that eleventh grade students received generally higher confidence scores on the PRCS than did eighth grade students.[26] Williams found that, for both observed stage fright and experienced stage fright, tenth grade students received higher confidence scores than did students in the lower grades. Ainsworth found that age was not significantly related to introspective or observational measures of stage fright for a large sample of college students. These findings are not in conflict if we hypothesize a relationship between stage fright and age that is other than a simple rectilinear one. Taken together, these studies suggest that *experienced stage fright is a curvilinear decay function of age, the asymptote of the function being approached before age twenty.*

The relation of stage fright to intelligence has received collateral attention in several studies. Gilkinson found correlations of PRCS and ACE-T scores of .05 for men and .12 for women. Eckert and Keys found a correlation of .34 for a mixed gorup of men and women between ACE scores and ratings of poise. Low found significantly lower ACE-L scores for a group of students with both high experienced stage fright and high observed stage fright, than for a group of students with low experienced and observed stage fright; but he found that Q and T scores were not significantly different for the groups. Clevenger discovered no significant difference in mean PRCS scores for high, median, and low scoring groups on the ACE-T score. These combined findings suggest that observed stage fright may correlate better with intelligence test scores than does experienced stage fright, and that linguistic aptitude may correlate more strongly with certain measures of stage fright than does over-all intelligence.

Certainly, the Low study hints at some relationship between stage fright and verbal skill. Although Ainsworth found that students with

---

[26]Richard M. Emery, "An Evaluation of Attitudes of Fear and Confidence in Speaking Situations at the Eighth and Eleventh Grades," Unpublished M.A. thesis, Boston University, 1950.

high experienced and observed stage fright did not differ significantly in reading ability from students with low experienced and observed stage fright, he found that the confident students read more.
Low found differences between similar groups in vocabulary, reading
ability, reading speed, and English achievement. He found that students in the high stage fright categories disliked English Composition
more than any other course. Since there is no clearly-defined single
variable running through all of these findings, their meaning must
remain a question for the moment. Further, because of the method
of selection of groups in these two studies, it is not clear whether the
relation, if one exists, is with experienced stage fright, observed stage
fright, both of these, or some complex function of them.

More often than any other variable, personality has been studied
in its relation to stage fright. The personality factor expected to correlate best with stage fright is social adjustment. Gilkinson found that
for a large group of college students, Social Adjustment scores on the
Minnesota Personality Test correlated .46 with PRCS scores. However,
Eckert and Keys found practically no correlation between judges' ratings of poise during speaking and either unsociability or social adjustment as measured by the Bernreuter and the Bell respectively.

Preserving a distinction between measures, it is possible to reconcile
these two studies. It is possible that introspective measures of stage
fright correlate moderately well with inventory measures of social adjustment, but that the latter might not correlate well with judges' ratings of stage fright. There are no studies in conflict with this hypothesis. Greenleaf found that students leading social lives which they
considered limited, also reported high stage fright. Ainsworth's sample
of students with both high experienced and high observed stage fright
reported having fewer friends. They also displayed more shyness, seclusiveness, withdrawal, and inhibition on various psychological tests.
This might well be a function of the self-ratings.

It may be said in general that where introspective accounts of
stage fright have been compared with introspective or inventory accounts of social behavior or adjustment, the two have tended to show
a relationship. In the one case where inventory measures of social adjustment were compared with observers' judgments of stage fright, the
relationship was practically non-existent.

With regard to introversion and emotional adjustment is found the
only direct conflict in the findings of these studies. Eckert and Keys,
rating college students for degree of poise on a seven-point scale, found
no significant correlation between their introversion and averaged
judges' ratings of stage fright, or between emotional adjustment and
averaged ratings of stage fright. Jones, comparing fifty high and fifty

low stage fright students as determined by a seven-point scale of stage fright, found that high stage fright was characterized by more introversion, neuroticism, submissiveness, and low-self-confidence. The difference can hardly be an artifact of the statistical models, since Eckert and Keys' correlations were so low that even quartile comparisons would probably not have yielded significance. It cannot be an artifact of the tests used, since both studies employed the Bernreuter. This conflict leaves in doubt the question whether observed stage fright is related to specific personality traits, such as introversion or submissiveness.

On the other hand, experienced stage fright may well be related to certain specific personality traits. Between above-median and below-median subjects on Taylor's Manifest Anxiety Scale, Clevenger found a large and significant difference in mean PRCS scores.

Others have reported findings in a similar vein which might appear to confirm the Jones finding and negate the Eckert and Keys findings. However, a careful distinction between dimensions of stage fright makes it clear that the findings in these studies are collateral to both the Jones and the Eckert and Keys experiments. The Jones and Eckert and Keys investigations both used judges' ratings of stage fright, while the Low, Gilkinson, and Ainsworth experiments all involved either introspective accounts or mixed measuring devices including introspective accounts.

Gilkinson found that PRCS scores correlated .30 with emotionality on the Minnesota test. Ainsworth found that students rating themselves high in stage fright tended to choose an undesirable emotion to characterize their feelings. When students with high stage fright were compared with students having little stage fright, Low could find no differences in the MMPI categories at the 1% confidence level, but he did find differences in depression and psychaesthenia at the 5% level. Holtzman found that MMPI profiles were significantly related to PRCS scores, but were not significantly related to judges' ratings.[27] Taken together, these findings suggest the hypothesis that *introspective adjustment inventories bear a moderate inverse relation to experienced stage fright, but not to observed stage fright.*

A possible complicating factor in research into the relationship between experienced stage fright and personality tests is the likelihood that sex differences interact with the relationship. Gilkinson, for example, found that women's scores on the PRCS tend to correlate more

---

[27]Paul D. Holtzman, "An Experimental Study of Some Relationships Among Several Indices of Stage Fright and Personality Structure," Unpublished Ph.D. dissertation, University of Southern California, 1950.

closely with most psychological test scores than did men's. Holtzman found that the relationship between PRCS scores and MMPI profiles was somewhat stronger for women than for men. Low's findings, while not quite so clearcut as these, indicate that on the average men's scores correlated more poorly with psychological tests than did women's. The hypothesis is raised that *the relationship between experienced stage fright and personality test scores is similar in nature for both sexes, but is stronger for women than for men.*

Two studies indicate that introspective accounts of stage fright are not related to projective tests of personality. When Shepherd selected high and low stage fright groups by means of PRCS and judges' ratings, he found no significant difference between groups in scores within any of the Rorschach scoring categories.[28] When Iverson compared upper and lower quartiles on the PRCS for differences in TAT scores, he found no differnce in general and over-all personality problems. However, both the Shepherd and the Iverson studies suggest that experiments with projective tests might prove fruitful. Iverson's finding that high and low stage fright groups differed in "methods of handling conflicts" seems related to Holtzman's finding that differences in stage fright are characterized by "type rather than amount" of adjustment problem.[29]

Considering only the relationship of stage fright to other factors, probably the least exploited field of research at present is the relationship of various audience variables to the three dimensions of stage fright. Kinsley's report that most experienced speakers say that different audiences have varying effects on them is provocative, but it tells us little about the variables at work which produce such differences. One possible source of variation is simply the familiarity of the audience. Lomas found that changing audiences tended to raise stage fright. Paulson, on the other hand, found that introducing a new audience had no effect on PRCS scores.[30] Of course, until the adaptation curve of the PRCS is known, the real meaning of Paulson's finding remains in doubt. If the rise in PRCS from one speech to another were sufficiently sharp, a constant PRCS from one speech to another might

[28]John R. Shepherd, "An Experimental Study of the Response of Stage Frightened Students to Certain Scoring Categories of the Group Rorschach Test," Unpublished Ph.D. dissertation, University of Southern California, 1952.

[29]Norman E. Iverson, "A Descriptive Study of Some Personality Relationships Underlying a Range of Speaker Confidence as Determined by the Thematic Apperception Test," Unpublished Ph.D. dissertation, University of Denver, 1952.

[30]Stanley F. Paulson, "Changes in Confidence During a Period of Speech Training: Transfer of Training and Comparison of Improved and Non-Improved Groups on the Bell Adjustment Inventory," Unpublished M.A. thesis, University of Minnesota, 1949.

signify a substantial net increase in stage fright. At present, however, an insufficient backlog of evidence exists to allow even tentative hypotheses concerning the relation of stage fright to audience variation.

One of the more provocative experiments concerning the relation of stage fright to other variables was reported by Simon a number of years ago, and was apparently never followed up. Simon reported the finding that stage fright was related to "ability to integrate under stress," as measured by number of errors in a high-speed card sorting task, and that stage-frightened students fell in the middle of a continuum of such ability, between non-frightened students on the one hand and stutterers on the other.[31] The experiment stands alone, and the hypothesis must be subjected to a greater variety of experimental conditions before conclusions can be drawn from it.

Synthesis of stage fright research performed to this time has yielded the following hypotheses:

1. Audience-perceived stage fright, cognitively-experienced stage fright, and physiological disruption are three variables which operate with only moderate interdependence during the course of a public speech.
2. As with other psychological phenomena, groups of judges are able to make judgments of stage fright of an order of reliability varying as a negatively-accelerated monotonic growth function of the number of judges.
3. Either age or training in speech or experience in speaking or some combination of these bears some relation to reliability of judgments of stage fright, but reliability is not a linear function of these factors.
4. Teachers of speech are evidently in stronger agreement concerning what constitutes the absence of stage fright than what constitutes its presence.
5. Between over-all measures of experienced stage fright and observational indices of certain specific behaviors, a positive but very weak relationship prevails.
6. Judges observe stage fright more in men than in women, while women experience more stage fright than men, but the differences in both cases are small.
7. Observed stage fright bears a strong negative relationship to judgments of speaking ability, while experienced stage fright bears a weak negative relationship to judgments of speaking ability.

---

[31]Clarence T. Simon, "Complexity and breakdown in Speech Situations," *JSHD,* X (1941), 199-203.

8. Speaker confidence is a negatively-accelerated monotonic growth function of experience in speaking.
9. Experienced stage fright is a curvilinear decay function of age, the asymptote of the function being approached before age twenty.
10. Introspective adjustment inventories bear a moderate inverse relation to experienced stage fright, but not to observed stage fright.
11. The relationship between experienced stage fright and personality test scores is similar in nature for both sexes, but is stronger for women than for men.

Helping Speech-and-Hearing-Defective Students

C. CORDELIA BRONG

FINDING THE DEFECTIVES

Every teacher can recite the basic principle that stresses the consideration of individual differences in the educational process. Such a philosophy becomes a mere platitude "as sounding brass or a tinkling cymbal" if the speech and hearing defectives are allowed to *just sit* in the classroom. If we are going to "educate the whole person" we must study the background of each individual with a problem and deal with him in the light of pertinent findings. This does not mean mere acceptance with kindness; it means also the adoption of an important premise that may be stated as follows: the person who is "different" needs a different kind of education in addition to his regular course of study. Hence, an important objective of the teacher of speech is to recognize and sort out those students who require specialized attention.

Suggestions for Finding Speech-Defective Students

In some high schools and colleges an annual speech survey is made by speech and hearing therapists to discover the students who need rehabilitation. Fortunate indeed is the school system with this service! Because of the scarcity of specialized personnel, however, the procedure often does not extend into the upper educational levels. Here the referral system is commonly used, which means that the classroom teacher finds and refers the defectives to the therapy program. The teacher of speech, with his trained ear for speaking irregularities, should have no difficulty in performing this task.

Usually, as a result of the oral opportunities offered as a function of the course, the teacher is familiar with the speech of his students within the first few weeks of the term. If, however, the class is unusually large, or if referrals are to be made to the therapy program before a scheduled deadline, the teacher can find the speech defectives in a short time by means of a *screening test*. For older children and adults this usually consists of two parts: a reading phase and a speaking phase. The reading portion consists of a few sentences or a paragraph containing all the vowels, consonants, and major consonant blends in the English lan-

From *Speech Methods and Resources*, Waldo W. Braden, ed., pp. 443-465. Copyright 1961 by Waldo W. Braden. Reprinted by permission of Harper & Row, Publishers.

guage. The material is read by each student in the class and the teacher records pertinent information as defects are recognized. Both articulatory and voice deviations may thus be detected. An opportunity for a minute or two of spontaneous speaking serves the purpose of getting a sample of the student's communication intelligibility and for finding stutterers who may exhibit no symptoms when reading.

With a modicum of ingenuity, the teacher of speech can prepare the reading test himself. The sounds most likely to be found defective should be used freely in the composition. In surveying the speech of 1998 pupils in grades seven through twelve, Saylor found consonants and consonant blends to be missed in the following order: [w, z, o, v, t , n, st, sk, f, g, s, 0, 1, b, t, str, k, r, p, d, d3, fl, dr, w, .][1] Useful screening tests are provided in various standard texts. The student is referred especially to tests suggested by Anderson, Irwin, and Van Riper.[2]

Suggestions for Finding Hearing-Defective Students

Many public school systems conduct hearing conservation programs annually. Through systematic planning (with certain grades included each year), total student populations are testing periodically by professional audiologists or by speech and hearing therapists. In this way, hearing deviations are determined in an organized way and rehabilitation programs are recommended.

Where no hearing surveys are made, the classroom teacher can make a contribution by finding students with hearing defects. The task is not an easy one; nor is it possible through observation alone to suspect other than gross losses. In a study reported by Watson and Tolan, teachers were capable of detecting only about 22 percent of the pupils who were subsequently found through audiometric testing to have significant hearing impairments.[3] Most adults with major hearing losses are aware of the disorder. Some may wear hearing aids as a result of previous testing. But a surprisingly large number of persons are not conscious of the problem, especially in its milder forms. While anything the teacher can do is a poor substitute for the professional survey, if he is alert to the signs of hearing deficiency he may be instrumental in helping a student by making appropriate referral for examination.

---

[1]Helen K. Saylor, "The Effect of Maturation upon Defective Articulation in Grades Seven through Twelve," *Journal of Speech and Hearing Disorders,* September, 1949, 14:206.

[2]Virgil A. Anderson, *Improving the Child's Speech,* Oxford University Press, 1953, p. 51; Ruth Beckey Irwin, *Speech and Hearing Therapy,* Prentice-Hall, 1953, pp. 31-34; Charles Van Riper, *Speech Correction: Principles and Methods,* Prentice-Hall, 1954, pp. 178-181.

[3]Leland A. Watson and Thomas Tolan, *Hearing Tests and Hearing Instruments,* Williams and Wilkins, 1949, pp. 236-238.

To organize his suspicions of hearing loss into a "clinical hunch," a teacher may use the following procedure:

1. Observe the student in class.
   a. Does he seem to watch your face very carefully as though he is trying to read your lips?
   b. Does he sometimes turn his head as though he is turning his better ear toward the speaker?
   c. Does he frequently ask the speaker to repeat what he has said?
   d. Does he often make mistakes in following your directions?
   e. Does he frequently not pay attention?
   f. Does he seem unusually restless?
   g. Does he seem excessively shy or overly aggressive?
2. Listen to his speech.
   a. Are certain phonemic elements in his speech omitted or distorted? Does he have special difficulty with the high-frequency sounds such as sibilants?
   b. Is his voice abnormally weak or loud? Does it have a strange quality or unusual intonation pattern?
3. Discuss the matter with him.
   a. Has he had frequent earaches, running ears, or colds?
   b. Has he had infectious diseases, as scarlet fever, measles, or influenza?
   c. Has he had a brain disease, such as meningitis, or sleeping sickness?
   d. Has he had a head injury including a skull fracture?
   e. Has he been exposed to unusually loud noises over a period of time?
   f. Does he complain of strange head noises or ringing in the ears?

Affirmative replies to any of these questions point toward diminished hearing. This is not to say that the clue implied in each item can conclusively be traced to a hearing loss; other factors may be operating. Nor, in most instances, is one affirmative response sufficient to make a judgment. However, if the information gained from these questions adds only slightly to the teacher's original suspicion, he should refer the student for hearing tests. If audiological services are not offered in the school, the student can be referred directly to a local otologist.

HELPING SPEECH DEFECTIVE STUDENTS IN THE CLASSROOM

In Any Classroom Situation

"How shall I treat the speech defectives in my classes?" is a common question asked by teachers. To present a rule-of-thumb reply is impossible. Every situation is surrounded by its own special circumstances which must be examined with the help of all the information that can be accumulated. There are, however, a few general principles that may offer assistance to the beginning teacher of speech.

1. Treat the defect in a casual and objective manner. Some teachers, embarrassed by the presence of a handicapped student in the class, go to extremes in exhibiting sympathy; others ignore the disorder completely. Most disabled persons abhor sympathy; they want to be accepted, not pitied. And to treat the problem as though it did not exist is just as unwholesome. When it is necessary to speak of the abnormality, do so with as little emotionality as one might use in referring to Mary's broken arm or Ben's new glasses. Talk about it frankly but always with a sensitive, empathic understanding and a motive of helpfulness.

2. Do not penalize the speech defective for any aspect of his handicap that he cannot change as a function of the course. Just as a cripple who walks with crutches is not expected in a physical education course to play tennis or run a race, so the speech or hearing cripple should not be required to carry out the assignments that are impossible for him. If the teacher understands the student's problem, he can often make adjustments that will place his assignments within both the capabilities of the student and the requirements of the course. If such adjustments are not possible, the student should probably find another course.

3. On the other hand, require him to participate in the activities that are within his range of abilities. The articulatory case in an acting course would not be expected to try out for a role in a public performance, but he should be required to participate in class productions. Many adult defectives report that through their public school years they learned to depend on the "generosity" of well-meaning teachers who released them from all oral responsibility. Most of them admit that these teachers performed for them a distinct disservice.

4. In skill courses, expect him to make gains within the boundaries of his limitations. Often a teacher does little more than carry the speech defective on the roster, requiring participation in course projects but having no concern about improvement. True, at times it is difficult to find areas in which the defective can work for improvement without specialized assistance; if no such area exists, he does not belong in the course. Often, however, with some extra consideration of his speech needs on the part of the teacher, the focus of attention can be delineated and the student's gains in specified particulars pointed out. For example, a cleft palate case in

a public speaking class should not be expected to work toward articulatory normalcy. But gains in other phases of speaking—such as organization of material, English usage, and audience contact should be expected.

In a School With a Speech and Hearing Therapy Program

If the teacher of speech works in an institution that maintains a remedial program, his role is uncomplicated yet important. In the first place, the teacher may well investigate certain factors when a speech defective joins a speech class. He should ask the question, "Is this the appropriate time for the student to take this course?" Let us say that a severe stutterer enters a public speaking class. He cannot talk without long pauses, excessive bodily tension, and distracting facial contortions. Perhaps he should not be taking the course at this particular time. If a concentrated therapy program can be provided for him now, he may in another semester or two be ready to profit from the public speaking activities. The course may then serve a terminal therapeutic purpose, in addition to providing him with an elective. By cooperative planning with the therapist and arranging for schedule changes, a situation that could have been a nightmare for both pupil and teacher becomes at a later time a satisfying experience.

Or the coordination of a therapy program and a speech offering during the same term may be desirable. A functional voice case, for example, may be significantly benefited from a course in interpretation while taking remedial work in the clinic.

The speech teacher can offer the defective student valuable assistance in the carry-over phase of the remedial program. Schooled as he is in the science of phonetics, he should have little difficulty, for example, in helping the articulatory case to stabilize the new speech sounds that are being established in his therapy sessions. Usually the therapist periodically informs the teacher which sounds are in need of strengthening and offers suggestions for "holding" the student for the correct production; on the adult level the case himself reports his needs to the teacher.

In a School Without a Speech and Hearing Therapy Program

The role of the speech teacher in the classroom in a school without a remedial program does not differ significantly from that already discussed. Since he has no specialist with whom to coordinate his efforts in behalf of the speech or hearing defectives, he is in complete charge of all the communication irregularities of his pupils. His role out of the classroom is quite different and is discussed later in this chapter.

HELPING SPEECH AND HEARING DEFECTIVE STUDENTS
IN PRIVATE CONFERENCE

"Come to my office and we will talk about the problem." This invitation is the first step toward assisting a speech- or hearing-defective student found in a speech class. The point here is so obvious that it could be overlooked: All conversations touching even remotely on the confidential should be carried on in private. Such a conference, if conducted with warmth and perception, serves several purposes. It assures the student that the teacher is taking a sincere interest in him as an individual. It not only provides an opportunity for a frank discussion of the difficulty in private; it also establishes the necessary rapport between teacher and pupil for future handling of the subject in class. The teacher can thus lay the groundwork for the special program he will recommend.

In a School With a Speech and Hearing Therapy Program
Make the Student Aware of His Defect

Most speech defectives are aware of their abnormalities, but not all are. Persons with serious as well as moderate impairments sometimes find their way into high school—or even college—without realizing that they have atypical speech. Junior high school students in particular are often unaware of their substandard utterance until it is brought to their attention. Probably few adults have major speech deficiencies without knowing that they exist, but there are exceptions. Not long ago a student with a history of brain injury entered college and registered in a speech curriculum. When the matter of her own speech problem was mentioned in conference, she was so shocked that she withdrew from college the following week. She knew that the muscles in one arm and one leg were affected, but no one had ever told her that her speech was impaired also.

Usually accepting the fact of a speech deviation is not so traumatic as the above illustration may suggest. It does, however, point up the possibility of such a reaction and the need for extreme care in making a student aware of his defect. In most instances, the person responds with gratitude for the information, especially if specific plans for rehabilitation are immediately offered. He must, of course, be convinced that he has a deviation that will require remedial help. The teacher can use a mirror to assist the pupil in observing the visual aspects of the defect, and he can use a tape recorder to point out its deviate auditory characteristics.

Motivate Him to Want Help

In some instances, the student is not ready to be referred to the speech and hearing therapist. He may need a planned program to motivate him to want therapy. Because of immaturity he may be unwilling to tie himself down to an extra series of "lessons"; he may object because the scheduled sessions conflict with his football or baseball practice. Sometimes he may resist for more basic reasons. One college student with a juvenile voice required several months of counseling in a clinical setting before actual therapy could begin because of his fear of what he would sound like with a "man's voice."

The teacher should attempt motivation, however, only against a background of understanding of the total problem. Perhaps the disorder is such that little can be done for him. For example, consider a cerebral palsy student with unintelligible speech. The possibility of improvement, given the best rehabilitation program available, may, at his age, be slight. His particular handicap sets up physiological limits that no educational process can transcend. For the teacher to serve as a high-pressure salesman and to convince such a student of the miracles to be expected in a speech therapy program is not only unwise but harmful. On the other hand, speech disabilities with good prospect for improvement may require ingenious devices to create the necessary willingness for tackling the job of changing speech behavior.

In difficult cases, motivation becomes a joint enterprise to be shared by the teacher and therapist. Whenever he is in doubt the teacher should consult the specialist.

Make the Referral to the Therapy Program

The teacher of spech should work closely with the speech and hearing therapist. He should know the schedule for making referrals. Usually in the public schools the rehabilitation programs are started within the first few weeks of the fall term. In order that students from speech classes may receive maximal benefit, they should be referred as early in the term as possible.

In a School Without a Speech and Hearing Therapy Program

The teacher of speech who finds himself in a school without a remedial program faces a dilemma. How far should he go in taking the place of a speech and hearing therapist? This problem is intensified if (as is often the case) the administrator makes the declaration that he expects the speech teacher to carry on corrective work with the speech defectives in the school. Such a pronouncement is usuallly the result of lack of understanding of the professional requirements for dealing with speech and hearing impairments. But knowing this fact does not alleviate the teacher's predicament. He is caught between what he believes is his assigned duty and what he knows he is not qualified to do. There are two main courses of action he may take: He may accept the assignment in toto, knowing full well that most of his effort will be wasted and that in some instances his therapy may prove actually harmful. Or he may (with outside professional help if possible) examine the defectives, sorting out for his remedial class only those students he is relatively certain he can help without risk, and then make plans to find therapy programs elsewhere for the severe cases. If he chooses the second alternative, the teacher should be able to explain the reasons for his stand.

General Suggestions for Helping Speech and Hearing Defectives in Schools without Remedial Programs

1. Refer the severe cases to an established evaluation center for examination. If funds are needed to finance the project, perhaps the assistance of a local civic organization may be enlisted.
2. Try to find therapy services for those who require the help of specialists. Try university clinics, nearby public school programs, hospital clinics, and rehabilitation centers.
3. Search for private therapists. If no therapy center can be found, it may be possible to locate qualified therapists in the vicinity who will take private cases. It should be made clear, however, that many private practitioners (as do some centers) charge high prices for their services. Of even greater concern should be the possibility of employing unqualified persons who pose as speech and hearing specialists. Because of the great demand for correctionists, the private practice is wide open to the charlatan. One way to determine the qualifications of a speech and/or hearing therapist is to refer to the most recent issue of the *A. S. H. A. Annual Directory, a Supplement of the Journal of Speech and Hearing Disorders.*[4]
4. If none of these attempts brings results, recommend a change of schools. The parents of a high school student with a severe problem may be willing to send him to a private school that offers a re-

---

[4]*Journal of Speech and Hearing Disorders* is the official publication of the American Speech and Hearing Association. For subscription or for single copies, address: Business Manager, *Journal of Speech and Hearing Disorders,* American Speech and Hearing Association, 1001 Connecticut Avenue N. W., Washington 6, D. C.

medial program. Certainly in choosing a college the speech or hearing defective should consider the clinical services offered.

5. Use your influence to bring to the school the services of a speech and hearing therapist. Often a school lacks these programs because no one has ever presented the need to administrators. It may be advisable to make a survey to determine the number of speech defectives who require therapy. If financial considerations provide substance for objection, look around for help. In many states the state department of education provides funds for employing speech correctionists in the public schools. Some state departments of health sponsor hearing programs. Also, the state or local chapter of the National Society for Crippled Children and Adults and the state Office of Vocational Rehabilitation may offer assistance.

Suggestions for Helping Students with Mild Articulatory Problems

A mild articulatory problem may be defined as a defect known to be functional[5] and to include only several deviate sounds. If organic or personality problems are causally related, if the speech pattern reveals errors in more than several different speech sounds, or if the few errors are strongly habituated, the case may be one for the specialist.

Let us say that you teach in a school system with no therapist. In your speech class you find a student who lisps. You make the necessary investigation and rule out organic and emotional factors. Here is a student for whom you can plan a remedial program.

TESTING PROCEDURES. The first step is to find out as much as possible about the articulatory errors as they exist in the student's speech pattern. Judging from your impression in casual conversation, you assume that only the [s] and [z] sounds are affected. But you want to be sure. Before starting to teach a new sound you should know: (1) what sounds are defective; (2) what type of error is made in each instance, and (3) in what position in the word each error is made.[6]

1. Let the student read sentences or paragraphs loaded with all the sibilants to determine whether others are defective. Let us say that you found no additional deviations. The error sounds may now be recorded as [s] and [z].

2. Analyze these sounds as the student speaks to determine whether they are represented by omissions, substitutions, or distortions. Ask him to read the sentence: "I went to the store to buy celery, lettuce, bananas, and roses for Elizabeth." Suppose he says the nouns as follows: "thtore" [0t r], "thelery" [0 l ri], "lettuth" [l t 0], "ba-

[5]See discussion on pp. 422-423.
[6]Van Riper, *op. cit.*, p. 166.

nanath" [b næn o], "rotheth" [rooɪo], and "Elithabeth" [ilɪo b 0].
Note that in each instance the substitution error is used.

3. Now determine in what position within each word the error is made.
Phonetic flaws may occur in the initial (I), medial (M), or final (F)
positions in words. All three positions are here represented. To use
Van Riper's system of recording,[7] the articulatory errors in these
words may be indicated as follows:

store	[0t/st] (I)	bananas	[o/z] (F)
celery	[0/s] (I)	roses	[o/z] (M, F)
lettuce	[0/s] (F)	Elizabeth	[o/z] (M)

Examine closely the student's production of the error sounds.
Does the tongue tip protrude between the teeth for the [0] and
[o], or does it touch the inner surface of the upper incisors? Usually it is well for the teacher to learn to imitate the student's production of the error sound so that he will be better able to offer
specific assistance in changing tongue movement.

The question of consistency should also be explored. To what
extent are these two sound errors ingrained in the student's speech
pattern? Does he always use the same substitution, or does he
sometimes substitute other consonants and at other times omit the
sound altogether? Are his errors different as the [s] or [z] enters
different phonetic environments? Is there one particular word, or
one position in words (initial, medial, or final), or one consonant
combination (as [st], [sk], or [sn]) in which the sound is said
correctly? To elicit this information, the student should read material
loaded with [s] and [z] sounds in as many different phonetic contexts as possible.

Let us say that this student uses the lingual-protrusion production
exclusively for the [s] and [z]. No words were found in which these
sounds were said correctly.

THE CORRECTION PROGRAM. Only one sound is taught at a time. For
the purpose of demonstrating the steps to be employed we shall use the
[s].

1. *Teaching the student to differentiate between the* [0] *and the* [s]
sounds. Most persons hear words as "lumps" of sound. As a result
of the change from the "phonic" to the "whole" method of teaching
reading in the elementary grades, many students complete public
school and even college without an opportunity to analyze words
into their component sounds. Fortunately the pendulum of reading
pedagogy is beginning to swing back to the phonic approach. Thera-

---

[7]Van Riper, *op. cit.,* pp. 164-172.

pists report that where phonics is taught, their work is favorably affected because the students have learned to listen to the phonetic ingredients of words. For the student who has had no phonetic training of any kind, a planned listening program is often a first step.

Before a speech defective can start the chore of changing the production of a speech element, he must be able to hear and to recognize the difference in the correct and the incorrect sounds. In this instance he must hear the difference between [0] and [s]. To him a *pencil* is a "penthil." Ask him to pronounce the name of the writing tool as "pencil" and he will probably respond, "Thatth what I thaid—penthil!" He has not developed the ability to listen to his own speech and to match the phonemic components with those of the model pattern presented by another speaker. Before the new sound can be established, "penthil" and all other error words must sound *wrong* to him.

In such ear training procedure some kind of label is usually employed to assist the person in detecting the correct and the incorrect elements. On the adult level perhaps the most effective means of identification is the phonetic symbol. After representing the error sound as [0] and the correct one as [s], the teacher can provide the following experiences:

a. *"Spotting" the* [s] *sound.* Present orally a random series of consonant sounds, including [s] at irregular intervals. The student writes the phonetic symbol [s] each time he hears you say the [s] sound. Example: [p, t, m, s, f, s,] etc. Present in like manner a series of nonsense words. In some words use no [s] and in others include it. The student writes [s] each time he hears the [s] in a nonsense word. Example: [ritu;soso; f m; ætsu] etc. The same procedure may be used with words and short sentences.

b. *Discriminating the* [0] *and* [s] *sounds.* Present an irregular sequence of [s] and [0] sounds. The student writes the appropriate symbol each time he hears a sound. A sequence might be: [s, s, 0, s, 0, 0], etc.

Present these sounds in nonsense syllables, asking the student to write the appropriate symbol each time he hears a nonsense word containing that sound. For example:

Teacher says, [0 0]; pupil writes [0];

Teach says, [sisi]; pupil writes [s], etc.

Present a series of [s] words, sometimes saying the [s] correctly and at other times using the [0] error. For example:

Teacher says "sock"; pupil writes [s];

Teacher says "thoap" (for soap); pupil writes [0].

Another experience may be carried on as follows: The teacher writes on the chalkboard in large symbols [s] and [0]. He then reads aloud a paragraph containing many [s] words. In the reading he sometimes substitutes [0] for [s]. The student listens carefully and points to the [s] when an [s] word is said correctly, and to the [0] when it is said with the [0] substitution.[8]

2. *Establishing the* [s] *sound in isolation.* The term *establish* emphasizes a procedure of implanting in a person's speech a sound that has heretofore not existed there. He has probably not, even by accident, arranged his tongue, teeth, and soft palate in the proper relationships to produce a standard [s] sound. To build such coordination is his present task. The therapist has at his command many techniques for helping an articulatory case to say the new sound for the first time. If one fails, another and another are tried until success is achieved. This case has been described as having a "minor" defect, which by implication should respond to treatment without difficulty. Hence, only one method is discussed here. If additional procedures are needed, the student should be sent to a specialist.

LISTEN-TRY PROCEDURE. Stimulus-response is the natural process of learning to talk. During the early stages of language development the infant repeats, parrotlike, the sounds that are said to him. As mother shows the baby the ball she says "ball," and the little one responds with a fair approximation of the word. The child listens, integrates the heard pattern with the necessary lip and tongue movements, and then produces the word.

Of course the process is really not that simple. And certainly when a sound that has never before existed in the phonetic repertoire of an adult is to be learned, the stimulus-response event must be fractionated in order to build a sequence of steps to be used in the learning process. Actually, when the stages are analyzed they represent not a simple "listen-try" activity, but rather a "listen-search-try-compare" series of steps.

First the learner must *listen* to the model presented by the teacher. Then he must *search* for just the right shape of the tongue, for its proper proximity to the teeth, for the appropriate distance between the upper and lower incisors, and for the necessary position of the soft palate to produce a sound like the stimulus. He will probably use a mirror and a view of the teacher's mouth to help him determine pos-

---

[8]For further information see Van Riper, *op. cit.,* pp. 221-234.

sible postures for exploration.[9] With the search terminated and a position located that may bring results, he *tries* the sound. At first the
heard product of his attempt is probably far from that of the stimulus.
Now he must *compare*. He must hold on to the self-produced sound
in his "mind's ear," compare its characteristics with those of the [s]
made by the teacher, and decide what articulatory adjustments he can
make to bring the product of his next try closer to the model. Only
then is he ready to try the entire cycle again. Not until he has said a [s]
that is a recognizable facsimile of the standard sound has he "established" the sound in isolation.[10]

3. *Strengthening the* [s] *sound.*

   a. *In isolation.* The new consonant is weak and unstable. Sometimes
      careful positioning results in the desired sound; at other times
      it does not. Thus, much practice is necessary. As soon as the
      student has memorized the auditory pattern of the teacher's [s]
      he can practice alone. By this time the "search" stage can prob-
      ably be eliminated, and drill takes the form of "listen (to the
      model [s] in his mind's ear), try, compare." Every try needs an
      evaluative phase for the purpose of matching the produced [s]
      against the model [s] and determining the degree of success.

   b. *In nonsense material.* Clinical research and experience have
      shown that the use of nonsense material assists significantly in
      strengthening the newly learned sound. Through assimilation in
      running speech, a sound is changed slightly by the other sounds
      that comes next to it. The muscular coordination required to say
      [s] in *see, soup, step,* and *desk,* for example, varies from word
      to word, and more difficulty may be encountered in certain sound
      combinations than in others. Then, too, the old phonetic asso-
      ciations with familiar word configurations may stand in the way
      of correct production of the new sound in words without this
      intermediate stage. To the student, for example, that writing in-
      strument may still be a "penthil." By using nonsense material the
      [s] can be combined with various vowels and consonants, and
      it can be practiced in the initial, medial, and final positions in

---

[9]The teacher must necessarily know the "standard" positions for the speech
sounds he will teach. For discussions of the production of consonants see: Johnnye
Akin, *And So We Speak: Voice and Articulation*, Prentice-Hall, 1958, pp. 83-136;
Jon Eisenson, *The Improvement of Voice and Diction*, Macmillan, 1958, pp. 180-
298; Elise Hahn, Donald E. Hargis, Charles W. Lomas, Daniel Vandraegen, *Basic
Voice Training for Speech*, McGraw-Hill, 1957, pp. 163-202.

[10]For further information see Charles Van Riper and John V. Irwin, *Voice and
Articulation*, Prentice-Hall, 1958, Chapter 6.

words without meaning. Example: The teacher provides the stimulus; the pupil responds to each nonsense word.

(I) [s , si, so, su; st , spi, sko, slu], etc.
(M) [s , isi, oso, usu; st , ispi, osko, uslu], etc.
(F) [s, is, os, us; ts, ips, oks, uls], etc.

4. *Establishing the sound in words.* The sound [s] is now ready to be learned in words. The student collects lists of words containing [s] in the initial, medial, and final positions. In practice sessions he listens carefully and evaluates the heard product of each try.

5. *Carrying over the newly learned sound into everyday speech.* The new sound is not yet ready to be relied on in free speech. It must first be practiced in planned communication situations. By starting with structured phrases and sentences in a natural conversational setting, the sound is blended into normal speaking patterns. Because of the reduced thought content in these small language fragments, the student can concentrate on the mechanics of producing the [s] correctly. As the new sound becomes habituated, less and less structure is used in the practice material.

Sequences ranging from highly structured questions and answers with only one response, to loosely structured conversation samples, are used according to the needs of the learner.

Example: Highly structured sequence
(Almost no thought content)

Teacher: Will our team win tonight?
Student: Yes, I think so.
Teacher: Are you going to the game?
Student: Yes, I think so.
Teacher: Is Mary going too?
Student: Yes, I think so.

Example: Moderately structured sequence
(Some thought content is introduced.)

Teacher: Will you meet me at the First National Bank?
Student: I'd rather meet you at Smith's Grocery Store.
Teacher: Will you meet me at the corner of Fourth and Fifth Streets?
Student: I'd rather meet you at the corner of Sixth and Seventh Streets.

Example: Loosely-structured situation
(More thought content is introduced.)

The teacher and student carry on a conversation on a chosen topic.

The student will be "held" for the correct production of [s] in certain predetermined words. These words may be written on the chalkboard or on paper so that they will be before the student as the conversation ensues.

The topic: Building a new house

Practice words: cost, first floor, basement, ceiling, sunporch, fireplace, color scheme.

Before the new [s] can be said to be completely stabilized in free speech, one more step is frequently necessary. This last approach aims to make the student aware of slips into error with the newly learned sound during everyday speech. The student may ask friends to help him catch his phonetic lapses at certain designated times. He may schedule for himself nucleus situations in which he is specifically aware of his faulty [s] sounds and corrects them immediately during conversation. The use of a tape recorder of high fidelity may help him to detect his errors. Any plan that brings to his attention his inaccurate [s] sounds for correction during communication will be helpful in this final stage of therapy.

The [z] sound may be taught in the same way as that outlined for the [s]. The student will probably have little difficulty in mastering this sound, however, since the necessary muscular coordinations have been established while learning the [s].

Suggestions for Helping Students with Voice Disorders

In the discussion of voice disorders in Chapter 15 it was indicated that nonspecialists should handle only functional voice disturbances not casually linked to emotional problems. What is the role of the teacher of speech in a school where there is no therapist? Here are a few suggestions.

1. Determine which voice disorders can be treated by nonspecialists. Perhaps the most common vocal deficiency in any school population is excessive nasality. Sometimes known as "our American blight,"[11] it is a voice problem which, like the poor, is always with us. Unless it is caused by some structural deformity, such as cleft palate, the speech teacher with training in voice science should have no difficulty in planning an improvement program.

    Though denasality is considered by some authorities to be an articulatory rather than a voice problem, it often demands attention.

---

[11]Adaline Bullen, "Nasality, Cause and Cure of Our American Blight," *Quarterly Journal of Speech, February,* 1942, 28:83-84.

Frequently it results from posterior nasal obstruction, such as enlarged adenoids. The teacher of speech can adequately handle an improvement program *after the cause has been removed.* The main goal in such treatment is to teach vibrant production of [m], [n], and [n].

2. Learn to recognize those vocal qualities that are frequent symptoms of pathology. Actual harm may result from inappropriate handling of certain types of vocal disorders. The qualities deserving special consideration are hoarseness, breathiness, and harshness. The speech teacher should learn to identify each of these.

   Of the three disorders, hoarseness is most likely to prove serious. Listen closely to the sound of a voice during an attack of laryngitis. Carry that quality always in your "mind's ear" as a potential danger signal when hoarseness persists.

   Breathiness, also a possible symptom of organic or personality abnormality, can be recognized as a whisperlike tone, usually weak in volume.

   A harsh voice may or may not indicate organic origin; perhaps it more frequently reflects improper vocal usage. Recall the too-loud, tense, rasping voice of the politician for an example of high harshness. To recognize low harshness, listen for a "gravelly" low-pitched tone and not signs of hypertension. To simulate a low-harsh voice, try the following and listen to the resulting quality. Start to swallow, then say a low-pitched [a] just before the swallow is completed. Listen to the tense, noisy tone. Using a hard glottal plosive attack, say words beginning with vowels, like "apple," "eat," and "onion." Or vocalize on an inhalation.

3. Refer to a laryngologist any student whose vocal quality may be a symptom of pathology. A safe rule to follow is to recommend for laryngeal examination *by a throat specialist* any student who has had a hoarse or breathy voice for a period of time. Since hoarseness is frequently confused with harshness, the teacher is on the safe side to make the same suggestion to students with harsh voices.

   An incident that allegedly occurred some time ago in a junior high school points up the importance of the precautionary measures just described. An uninformed teacher of speech, noting the hoarseness of one of his pupils, searched for exercises to correct the condition. Realizing that the girl's voice was weak, he chose drills designed to strengthen the voice. Under his direction she read poems demanding excessive loudness to large imaginary audiences. A year later the girl died of cancer of the larynx. Whether the inappropriate procedures contributed to the malady will never be known. This much is certain: if the teacher had recognized the danger potential of a chronically hoarse voice and had sent the girl to a laryngologist for examination, he might have been instrumental in saving her life.

The point that cancer is only one of many possible vocal pathologies cannot be empasized too strongly. The student is not asked to have an examination for the detection of a dread disease; rather he is asked to seek medical diagnosis to *rule out* the possibility of organic irregularity of any kind. If the teacher makes such procedure a routine matter, there should be no reason for trauma. The student can be advised that in either event he is the winner. If the results are negative, the good news is worth the price of the examination; if a pathology is revealed, the information is invaluable for planning a course of action.

4. Refer for professional help any student whose voice disorder seems to be a symptom of an emotional problem. Since speech and personality are closely interrelated, a deviation in one probably affects the other in some degree. Voice seems to be an especially sensitive index of attitudes and feelings. Voice irregularities may be related to emotional factors extending on a continuum all the way from minor deviations in outlook to severe emotional disturbances. The point at which psychological or psychiatric assistance should be sought is not easily established, and the classroom teacher may somtimes need professional help in making such determination. Perhaps the school psychologist or a local psychological clinic is available for consultation. Psychogenic voice problems should never be treated by the teacher of speech.

5. Teach improved vocal production to students with uninvolved functional deficiencies. Most voice irregularities result from improper usage—even in the areas of hoarseness, breathiness and harshness. But only after organic and serious psychological factors are ruled out can an educational program be planned.

This chapter is not designed to provide specific techniques for working with functional voice defects. Excellent voice improvement texts are available. The teacher of speech should be familiar with the ones by Akin, Anderson, Eisenson, Fairbanks, Hahn et al., and Van Dusen.[12]

---

[12]Johnnye Akin, *And So We Speak: Voice and Articulation,* Prentice-Hall, 1958.

Virgil A. Anderson, *Training the Speaking Voice,* 2nd ed., Oxford University Press, 1961.

Jon Eisenson, *The Improvement of Voice and Diction,* Macmillan, 1958.

Grant Fairbanks, *Voice and Articulation Drillbook,* 2nd ed., Harper, 1960.

Elise Hahn, Charles W. Lomas, Donald E. Hargis, Daniel Vandraegen, *Basic Voice Training for Speech,* McGraw-Hill, 1957.

C. Raymond Van Dusen, *Training the Voice for Speech, A Guide to Voice and Articulation Improvement,* McGraw-Hill, 1953.

Suggestions for Helping Stutterers

In order to cope with stutterers the teacher should know as much as possible about stuttering. This abnormality was discussed in the previous chapter and reading references provided. We are now ready to consider specific suggestions for helping stuttering students in the classroom and in private conferences.

HELPING THE STUTTERER IN CLASS

1. *Accept him, stuttering and all, as a worthwhile member of the class.* He is probably a normal person except for his speech difficulty. At the upper high school and college levels, chances are more than even that he is average or above in intelligence. He has probably been considered "different" ever since childhood. The teacher's attitude toward him as a person may be important to him.

2. *Encourage him to talk.* For many stutterers the speaking experience is one of struggle and anguish. Often they give up and withdraw from social situations entirely. In class they usually prefer not to participate in discussion. Anything the teacher can do to encourage a stutterer to carry on as a noraml social being is helpful from a mental hygiene point of view. His speech may also profit from more talking. In a therapy program the silent person has little chance for improvement, since he has nothing to work with. Willingness to talk will lay the groundwork for rehabilitation.

3. *Be a patient listener.* Look at the stutterer when he is talking just as you would look at any person who is speaking to you. It is not easy to maintain natural eye contact when he is caught in a block, especially if he manifests secondary symptoms of facial contortion. But to look away may add to his embarrassment.

4. *When a stutterer is caught in a block, do not try to help him.* Normal speakers talking to a stutterer often supply words for him or pick up the conversation, thus cutting short his contribution. Most conversationalists resent having their sought-for words given them, and the stutterer is no exception.

5. *Do not make homespun suggestions for getting the words out.* He has probably listened to such "helpful hints" ever since childhood; he may have tried some of them and found them to increase the complexity of his problem. In studying parental attitudes toward stuttering children, Darley found that in forty-eight cases out of fifty, one parent or both had made suggestions to their children for overcoming the stuttering. The most frequent were: "talk more slowly," "stop and start over," "think of what you are going to say," "take it easy," "relax," "take a deep breath," and "repeat." Such

helps were given at least daily to thirty-five of the children, according to at least one of the parents.[13]

6. *Do not tell him to try not to stutter.* If it were possible for him to
turn on and off the blockages at will, he would not be a stutterer.
According to Johnson the very crux of his problem lies in his trying
too hard not to stutter: "stuttering is what a speaker does trying not
to stutter again."[14]

7. *Do not praise his moments of fluent speech.* Fluency is his most
coveted goal, yet his efforts for gaining it only strengthen the power
of the nonfluencies. Consciously or subconsciously he devises schemes
to circumvent or to postpone his suttering blocks. He learns to use
"starters" and other tricks to win his freedom from the plague of
blocking. When therapy is begun, these devices must be eliminated.
Do not make the task more difficult for him than it now is.

HELPING THE STUTTERER IN PRIVATE CONFERENCE. The rehabilitation of
stutters is an assignment for specialists only. Where they are not available, the next best is hands-off policy. Too many stutterers have tried
nonprofessional "schools," neighbors' recipes, and their own techniques
gleaned from suggested readings. Each unsuccessful trial adds to fru-
tration. The best assistance the teacher of speech can provide includes
the following steps: (1) determining whether this particular student is
a good prospect for therapy; (2) if he is, motivating him to undertake
treatment; and (3) helping him find a program. Not all stutterers are
good clinical risks; some may need help from a psychiatrist rather than
a speech pathologist, and others may be lacking in basic intelligence.
But in high school and in college many of them have a high potential
for improvement. Make a study of the stutterer as a person. Is he an
above-average student? Does he seem to have a wholesome outlook on
life? Can he tackle a difficult task and carry it through to completion?
(Success in therapy requires strong initiative and hard work.) Does he
accept as his responsibility the task of changing his behavior—given the
necessary guidance? If these questions can be answered affirmatively,
motivate him to search for professional assistance and help him find it.

EXERCISES

1. Ask a friend of yours who speaks a foreign language to teach you
to say a consonant sound from that language that you have never

---

[13]Frederic L. Darley, "The Relationship of Parental Attitudes and Adjustments
to the Development of Stuttering" in Wendell Johnson (ed.), assisted by Ralph R.
Leutenegger, *Stuttering in Children and Adults,* University of Minnesota Press, 1955,
p. 140.

[14]Wendell Johnson, Spencer J. Brown, James F. Curtis, Clarence W. Edney,
Jacqueline Keaster, *Speech Handicapped School Children,* rev. ed., Harper, 1956,
p. 216.

heard before. Try to describe the learning process as you attempt to master the new sound. Make a list of the questions you ask as you are attempting to produce it acceptably. From this experience, make a list of steps that you might use to teach a new English sound to a student with an articulatory defect. Compare this sequence of steps with those given in this chapter.

2. An articulatory case was giving the following information to his friend: "Yesterday Charles and I drove to school in his new Rambler. Just as we were approaching Sixth Street a tire blew out and we found ourselves climbing a tree."

    Following is a transcription of his speech as he said it. Indicate in phonetics each error sound and designate the type of error in this way: [0/s] = a substitution of the [0] for [s]; − [s] = an omission of the [s]; + [s] = an addition of the [s] sound. Write each word containing an articulatory fault and follow it with a designation of the error or errors found in that word.

    [j 0t de t rlo nd aɪ dwov tʊ kul m hɪ3 nu wæmbl . d3ʌt æ3 wi w pwot m 0ɪk0 twit, taɪr bju aut n wi faund aur0 lvo klaɪmɪnk twi.]

3. Prepare a screening test for discovering the speech-defective students in your class, using the sounds listed on page 363.

4. From the text discussion of speech and hearing defectives, make an outline specifying the following: (a) which deviations must be handled only by specialists; (b) which may be attempted by the teacher in situations where specialists are not available; and (c) which speech irregularities the competent teacher of speech should be prepared to handle whether or not a rehabilitation program is available.

5. What would you do if, after accepting a position to teach speech in junior or senior high school, your principal indicated that you were expected also to conduct a therapy program for the speech defectives in the school?

EXERCISES

1. What is reticent behavior? How do reticent students differ from speakers exhibiting stage fright?

2. Should every student be required to meet a minimally acceptable level of oral communication? What implications has this for the required introductory speech course?

3. How should the teacher offer oral and written criticism to reticent students?

4. To what extent is speech behavior a function of personality. Does a teacher have the obligation or right to alter or effect change in the personality structure of his students?
5. How is a feeling of personal security and confidence related to the ability to express oneself?
6. Estimate the number of students in a "typical" speech course who exhibit communication problems. How can a teacher spot speech or hearing defectives? Under what circumstances should the teacher of speech screen students to discover hearing or speaking defects?
7. Which "psychology" do you accept as capable of meeting the problems of individuals exhibiting reticent or stage fright behaviors? Why?
8. How can we detect stage fright in students? What procedures should the teacher take to aid such students?
9. How can the non-clinically trained teacher of speech aid speech and/or hearing defective students in the classroom?
10. To what extent is mental health determined or related to the verbal capability of an individual?
11. Describe verbal characteristics attributable to the "normal" speaker. What standard of "normal speech" did you employ? Justify your standard.

PROJECTS

1. On a specified day avoid speaking to anyone from the moment you awake until your day ends. Record your experiences. Discuss what effects your reticent behavior had upon your friends and acquaintances. What personal, inner feelings toward yourself and others did you develop? Discuss how your action impeded your behavior as a social animal.
2. Participate in the following experiment only if you possess the courage to meet strangers in an unfamiliar role. While on campus or shopping downtown exhibit to strangers a severe case of stuttering. Record the reactions of individuals to your speech. Discuss how and why individuals reacted to you as they did. Explore the implications of stuttering this experiment demonstrated.

List of Contributors